BIG ISLAND OF HAWAI'I

BREE KESSLER

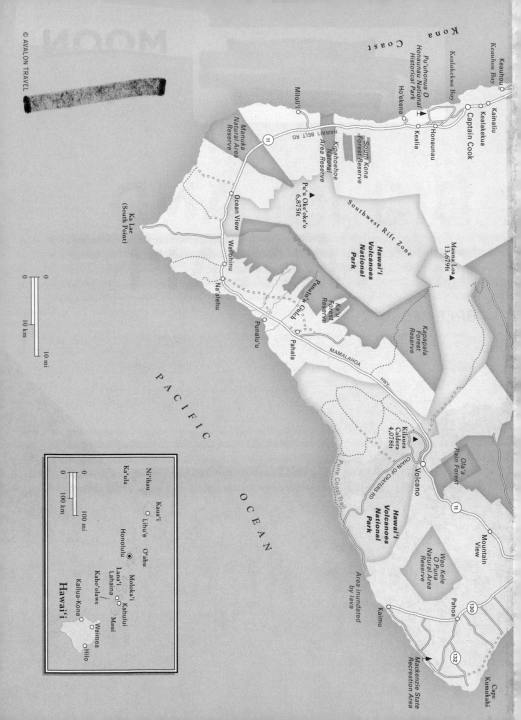

MOON

Kona Coast

Keauhou
Keauhou Bay
Kainaliu
Kealakekua
Captain Cook
Kealakekua Bay
Pu'uhonua O
Honaunau National
Historical Park
Ho'okena
Honaunau
Kealia
Miloli'i

HAWAI'I BELT RD
11
South Kona
Forest Reserve
Kipahoehoe
Natural
Area Reserve

Manuka
Natural Area
Reserve

Ocean View

Pu'u Oke'oke'o
6,875ft

Southwest Rift Zone

Mauna Loa
13,679ft

Hawai'i
Volcanoes
National
Park

Ka Lae
(South Point)

Wai'ohinu

Na'alehu

Punalu'u

Pahala

Puna'lu'u Gulch

Ka'u
Forest
Reserve

Kapapala
Forest
Reserve

MAMALAHOA

HWY

Kilauea
Caldera
4,078ft

Volcano

Ola'a
Rain Forest

11

Mountain
View

Pahoa

130

132

Cape
Kumukahi

Mackenzie State
Recreation Area

Kaimu

Area inundated
by lava

Wao Kele
O Puna
Natural Area
Reserve

Hawai'i
Volcanoes
National
Park

CHAIN OF CRATERS RD

Puna Coast Trail

PACIFIC

OCEAN

0   10 mi
0   10 km

Hawai'i

Ni'ihau
Ka'ula
Kaua'i
Lihu'e
O'ahu
Honolulu
Moloka'i
Lana'i   Kahului
Lahaina   Maui
Kaho'olawe
Waimea
Kailua-Kona
Hilo

0   100 mi
0   100 km

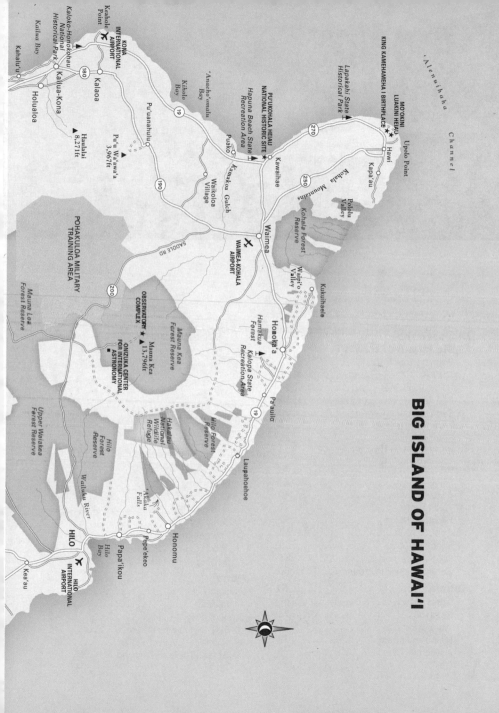

Contents

DISCOVER

the Big Island of Hawai'i

Everyone knows the Big Island of Hawai'i has beaches and sunshine. But the island is so much more than its unbelievably good weather. It's not hard to get off the beaten path here: the majority of the Big Island offers seclusion and adventure with easy access.

The Big Island of Hawai'i is the newest island, geologically speaking, in the chain of islands that make up the state of Hawaii. While lava formed the island's physical structure, it is the sugar plantation industry, established in the mid-1800s, that is credited for creating the Big Island's culture, through bringing numerous immigrants to work the island's land. Much of the island's modern-day customs, from language (Hawaiian pidgin, or *da' kine*) to food (like the *loco moco* or Spam *musubi*) to clothing (the classic aloha shirt), reflect this merging of Chinese, Filipino, Japanese, Polynesian, Portuguese, and Mainland American cultures.

It's sometimes hard to tell locals from visitors—the only real way to confirm a true local is by checking for the Locals brand *slippahs* (flip-flops) on someone's feet. These preferred shoes, which anyone can pick up for $3.99 at nearly every grocery or drugstore, embody the Hawaiian notion of *aloha*, the laid-back way of

Clockwise from top left: Waipi'o Valley; sunset; Hawai'i Volcanoes National Park; large green sea turtle; Rainbow Falls; hibiscus flower.

life in Hawai'i that attracts new residents and visitors every year. (Your first order of business when arriving to the island should be picking up a pair yourself.)

Many visitors are beckoned by the Big Island's warm weather and well-known spectacular landscape—including pristine Hapuna Beach, picture-perfect Waipi'o Valley, and the lava flow jumping out of the crater at Hawai'i Volcanoes National Park. Of course the island provides an array of activities for outdoor lovers, from horseback riding through *paniolo* (cowboy) country to surfing the popular Honoli'i Beach Park; from night snorkeling with the manta rays in Keauhou Bay to stargazing at the Mauna Kea Observatory. And you're never more than 10-20 minutes from a gorgeous beach.

The Big Island offers more than just one kind of experience: When the weather gets too hot seaside, drive upcountry to Waimea, the cool interior part of the island, where a fireside meal will be waiting for you. Or spend an early Sunday morning at one of the island's numerous farmers markets adorned with tropical fruits, *malasadas* (Portuguese doughnuts), and food carts with mouthwatering *huli huli* chicken and kalua pork.

When your visit is over, say *"a hui hou"* (until we meet again). You'll want to come back.

Clockwise from top left: wooden statues of idols; view from inside a lava tube in Hawai'i Volcanoes National Park; swimming with dolphins; Punalu'u Black Sand Beach.

Planning Your Trip

What makes the Big Island so great is also what makes it so difficult for trip planning. Every nook and cranny of the island is unique, and it's hard to not want to experience it all. The Big Island isn't the kind of place where you can say, "Well, the beaches on the east side are probably the same as here." They aren't. And the interior part of the island is worlds away from the coast, while actually only being 15 minutes away. Don't worry, though. Just take a deep breath—you can see it all.

Where to Go

Kona

Kona is dry, sunny, and brilliant—most visitors' introduction to the island. When watered, the rich soil blossoms, as in the small artists' enclave of Holualoa and South Kona, renowned for its diminutive **coffee plantations.** As the center of this region, **Kailua-Kona** boasts an array of art and designer shops, economical accommodations, great restaurants, and plenty of historical and cultural sites like **Moku'aikaua Church,** a legacy of the very first packet of missionaries to arrive in the islands, and **Hulihe'e Palace,** vacation home of the Hawaiian royalty. **Kealakekua Bay,** one of the first points of contact with foreigners, is also one of the best snorkel sites that Hawai'i has to offer. Nearby is **Pu'uhonua O Honaunau National Historical Park,** the location of a traditional Hawaiian safe refuge.

Kohala

North of Kailua-Kona, otherworldly black lava bleeds north into Kohala. Up the coast is **Hapuna Beach,** one of the best on the island. In 1965,

The sun sets along Ali'i Drive in the beach town of Kailua-Kona.

Laurance Rockefeller opened the Mauna Kea Beach Hotel near there. Since then, other expansive resorts have been added, making this the island's luxury resort area, barren lava turned into oases of green. Peppered among these resorts are **petroglyph fields** left by ancient Hawaiians. As you travel north on Highway 19 it becomes Highway 270 and you'll find yourself in the hilly peninsular thumb at the northern extremity of the island. The **Kohala Mountains** sweep down to the west to a warm and largely uninhabited coast, and to the east tumble into deep valleys cut by wind and rain. Several isolated beach parks dot the coast, and here and there are cultural sites, including a modern-day ruin at **Mahukona Beach Park.** The main town up this way is sleepy **Hawi,** holding on after sugar left. At road's end is the overlook of stunning **Pololu Valley.**

Ka'u

One of the best scenic drives on the island, the "underdeveloped" southernmost region of the island is primarily an arid coastal region with a few towns at the base of Mauna Loa and the recognizable **Ka Lae,** also known as **South Point,** the southernmost piece of real estate in the United States. Below the ranches, macadamia nut farms, and coffee fields are lovely beaches, some of which can only be reached by harsh four-wheel-drive roads like the **Road to the Sea.** Or skip the four-wheel driving and take an hour-long stroll to the **Green Sand Beach,** which truly has green-tinted sand (caused by olivine), or an easy paved drive to the **Punalu'u Black Sand Beach,** where you're almost guaranteed to see turtles lounging in the sand.

Hawai'i Volcanoes National Park

The great lava fields that have spewed from **Kilauea** dominate the heart of Hawai'i Volcanoes National Park. While miles of **hiking trails** crisscross the park, most visitors see it by car (but some by bike or by foot) along the rim drive that brings you up close to sights like the impressive **Halema'uma'u Crater,** the mythical home of Madame Pele, the fire goddess. **Chain of Craters Road** spills off the *pali* through a forbidding yet vibrant wasteland of old and new lava to where this living volcano fumes and throbs. Nights in Volcano Village can be cold, but you'll be so distracted by watching the lava glow from the **Thomas A. Jaggar Museum** and then singing karaoke alongside park employees at **Kilauea Military Camp** that you'll hardly notice the drop in temperature at all.

Puna

Puna lies south of Hilo and makes up the majority of the southeast coast. It is one of the last bastions of tropical old Hawaii, a place of independent-minded people willing to live on the edge and off the grid. While it once grew sugarcane, it's now best known for anthuriums, orchids, and papayas. Recent **lava flows** cover this region. One embraced a forest in its fiery grasp, entombing trees that stand like sentinels today in **Lava Tree State Monument.** Another formed **Cape Kumukahi** in 1868, becoming the easternmost point in Hawaii. The **Kapoho tide pools** anchor the eastern end of this coast, and from there a string of ebony-black beaches dot the shoreline, including **Kehena Beach,** where on Sundays locals come to beat drums and sun their naked bodies. The coastal road dead-ends where it's been covered by lava at the small village of **Kaimu,** and the more recent work of **Pele** can be seen behind the **Pahoa** transfer station where the lava flow of 2015 amazingly stopped just short of entering the town.

Hilo

Hilo is the oldest port of entry and the only major city on the island's windward (east) coast. This is where it feels like old Hawaii. The city is one tremendous greenhouse where exotic flowers and tropical plants are a normal part of the landscape. The town boasts Japanese gardens, **Honoli'i Beach** (the best place to watch surfing), the **Lyman Museum and Mission House,** the **Pacific Tsunami Museum,** and a profusion of natural phenomena, including **Rainbow Falls** and **Boiling Pots** as well as black-sand beaches

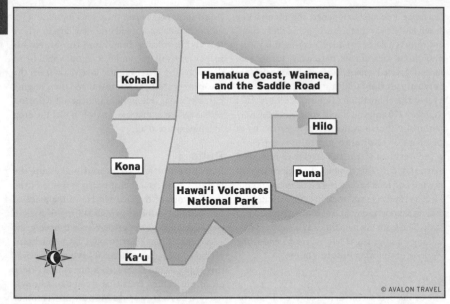

Kohala

Hamakua Coast, Waimea, and the Saddle Road

Hilo

Kona

Puna

Hawai'i Volcanoes National Park

Ka'u

© AVALON TRAVEL

on the east side of town. Drive 20 minutes west of town to the mesmerizing **'Akaka Falls.** As the focus of tourism has shifted to the Kona side, Hilo has become a place where there are deals to be had.

Hamakua Coast, Waimea, and the Saddle Road

Hamakua refers to the northeast coast above Hilo, where streams, wind, and pounding surf have chiseled the lava into cliffs and precipitous valleys. The road north from one-street Honoka'a dead-ends at the lookout at **Waipi'o Valley,** the most spectacular and enchanted valley on the island. Upcountry is **Waimea,** the heart of Hawaiian cowboy country and home to the **Hawaii Regional Cuisine** movement. From Waimea one can traverse the island via the **Saddle Road** separating the mountains of Mauna Loa and Mauna Kea. Along the Saddle Road are long stretches of native forest, barren lava flow, and rangeland, plus a number of worthy spots for a stretch. From the Saddle Road, a spur road heads up to the top of **Mauna Kea,** where, at 13,796 feet, **observatories** peer into the heavens through the clearest air on earth. Heading south, another road zigzags up the slope to an atmospheric observatory, from where a hiking trail for the hale and hearty heads to the top of **Mauna Loa.**

When to Go

As with all of the Hawaiian Islands, the **prime tourist season** for the Big Island starts two weeks before **Christmas** and lasts until **Easter.** It picks up again with **summer vacation** in early June and ends once more in late August. Everything is more heavily booked and prices are higher. Hotel, airline, and car reservations are a must at this time of year. You can generally save substantially and avoid a lot of hassle if you travel in the **off-season—September** to **early December** and **mid-April** (after Easter) until **late May.** Recently, the drop in numbers of tourists during the off-season has not been nearly as substantial as in years past, indicating the increasing popularity of the island at all times of the year, but you'll still find the prices better and the beaches, trails, activities, and even restaurants less crowded.

The **weather** in Hawaii is moderate all year round, and any time can be pleasant. Rains come and go—more so in winter—and are seldom sustained, so usually you can move a few miles down the coast to a sunny spot or wait for the warm breezes to blow away the clouds and dry things up.

While nearly all activities are available throughout the year, there are some exceptions. For instance, if you intend to see **humpback whales,** you must visit from late winter through spring, as these lovable giants of the sea are in Hawaiian waters only from December through April. Plenty of **coffee** is grown on the Big Island, and if you intend to view its **harvesting** and **processing,** it's best to go from September through January when the bulk of that job is done.

Green Sand Beach

The Best of the Big Island

The Big Island is big—at least in relation to the other Hawaiian Islands. While it's possible to "do" the island in a few days, it is preferable to go at a more leisurely pace. The average visitor from the Mainland spends nine days on a vacation in Hawaii, and this time frame is a good choice for an all-encompassing Best of the Big Island tour. If you like to take it slow or build some beach time into each day, you can easily expand this itinerary to 10 or even 14 days.

Day 1

Fly into **Kona,** knowing that the bleak, black lavascape that you come in over will not be how the entire island looks (though it does appear as if you've landed on the moon). Pick up your rental car and, if you are staying in Kailua or Keauhou, head into town and take the shoreline route down **Ali'i Drive** to your hotel. Settle in, have a look around the property, and take a leisurely stroll along the beach or on Ali'i Drive after dinner in Kailua.

Day 2

Prebook a morning kayak tour of **Kealakekua Bay** and spend a few hours cruising around watching the dolphins or viewing (via snorkel or diving) a spectacular underwater world. Dry off and head to **Pu'uhonua O Honaunau National Historical Park** and try to catch an extremely informative tour with a ranger. If you want to get back in the water, snorkel **Two Step,** located next to the national historical park, or the quieter **Manini Beach.** In the later afternoon travel uphill to the quaint town of **Holualoa** to peruse the galleries and eat dinner. Serious water lovers will want to book themselves on a night **manta ray** snorkel tour in **Keauhou Bay.** Those who want to remain dry can watch the manta rays (and the snorkelers) from happy hour at the **Sheraton Kona Resort and Spa.**

Day 3

Head to **Ka'u,** where you'll take a quick morning tour of the private lava tubes at **Kula Kai**

If you're lucky, Pele will be putting on a show while you're at Hawai'i Volcanoes National Park.

Caverns. Then drive to the southernmost point in the United States of America, **Ka Lae,** also called **South Point,** where you can try out your amateur cliff-diving skills (it's quite the drop to the ocean) or just GoPro others jumping into the ocean. From South Point, walk to **Green Sand Beach**—because where else are you going to see a beach with a green tint? Then drive to the **Punalu'u Bake Shop,** the southernmost bakery (you'll also pass the southernmost restaurant and southernmost bar), to fill your belly with multiple *malasadas.* Leave a little room and time for your visit to the **Ka'u Coffee Mill** to sample coffee and macadamia nuts. Then get to **Punalu'u Black Sand Beach** for a sunset you'll share with a bunch of turtles hanging around the beach. Consider spending the night at one of several unique lodgings in Ka'u (like a Buddhist temple or a vacation rental in **Wood Valley**) or drive back to your hotel in Kona.

Day 4

Wake up early! This is the day for **Hawai'i Volcanoes National Park.** From Ka'u it's a 30-minute drive, from Hilo it's an hour's drive,

from Kona it's perhaps twice that. Make your first stop at the **Kilauea Visitor Center** for a quick introduction to the wonders of the park. For the best overall tour, travel the open sections of the **Crater Rim Drive,** stopping at all the marked sites. Be sure to spend time at the **Thomas A. Jaggar Museum** to learn more about the geology of the park. Pay your respects at **Halema'uma'u Crater,** the home of the Hawaiian goddess Pele, before heading down the **Chain of Craters Road** to experience the ever-changing landscape at the shore. Spend the night in Volcano Village so that you can come back at night for stargazing and to watch the lava glow (you'll never forget it).

Day 5

Finally, a day at the beach. Travel to the southern part of **Puna** (about an hour from Volcano Village or Hilo) and leave your worries (and cell phone reception) behind. Follow the **Red Road** as it curves around the southeast part of the island, stopping for top-notch snorkeling at the **Kapoho tide pools.** Then warm up at the **Ahalanui Beach Park** warm ponds or the semisecret warm

Lili'uokalani Gardens in Hilo

While the entire island was inhabited by the Hawaiians, most of the readily accessible precontact and early postcontact historic remains are found on the Big Island's dry side. The island is also home to unofficial modern archaeological sites—discarded machinery and buildings from the plantation days, mainly located on the Hamakua Coast.

KEALAKEKUA BAY STATE HISTORICAL PARK AND CAPTAIN COOK MONUMENT

Kealakekua Bay was the site of the first significant and sustained contact between Hawaiians and Europeans. While it started off well, the relationship deteriorated, ending in the death of many Hawaiians, Captain James Cook, and several of his crewmembers. Across the bay is a **white obelisk memorial** to Cook, marking the spot where he fell (page 45).

KALOKO-HONOKOHAU NATIONAL HISTORICAL PARK

Just north of Kailua, this park contains many relics of an old Hawaiian community and is one of the largest concentrations of such relics in the state. Points of interest include a **heiau, home sites, petroglyphs,** and **fishponds** (page 34).

HISTORICAL KAILUA

King Kamehameha lived his last years at Kamakahonu Beach, using **Ahu'ena Heiau** for governing purposes. Later rulers built **Hulihe'e Palace,** an escape from the affairs of state in Honolulu. Land was given to the first missionaries to put up **Moku'aikaua Church** across the street from the palace (page 34).

PU'UHONUA O HONAUNAU NATIONAL HISTORICAL PARK (PLACE OF REFUGE)

South of Kealakekua Bay is the state's best-known

Kaloko-Honokohau National Historical Park

temple of refuge, a safe haven for wrongdoers, *kapu*-breakers, and defeated warriors in ancient times. Outside its walls is a reconstructed **royal village** site (page 38).

PU'UKOHOLA HEIAU NATIONAL HISTORIC SITE

In a prophecy regarding his domination of the islands, Kamehameha I was told to build a **temple to the war god Ku.** Sitting high on the hill overlooking Kawaihae Harbor, this commanding **stone structure** was the last large *heiau* built before the dissolution of the Hawaiian religious system (page 69).

HAKALAU BAY

This untouched modern-day archaeology site is filled with the plantation-era ruins of **Hakalau Mill,** destroyed in the tsunami of 1946 (page 186).

pond secluded in the trees of **Isaac Hale Beach Park.** If it's a Saturday visit the **SPACE market** to catch an authentic glimpse of lower Puna's culture while munching on raw vegan treats. If it's a Sunday you'll hear the drumming (and see the cars lined up) down the road from **Kehena Beach.** You'll know you've reached the end of the road because it's covered with lava (and your cell phone reception has magically returned). Take a leisurely walk out to **Kaimu Beach** to get a sense of what the area was once and to see how locals are replanting it to transform it back to its original glory. If it's a Wednesday, end your day at **Uncle Robert's Awa Bar,** home to a pop-up market and live music. Drive back to Volcano Village to sleep.

Day 6

Spend the morning on a walking tour of downtown **Hilo.** Visit the **Lyman Museum and Mission House** and don't miss the **Pacific Tsunami Museum,** which tells the story of the two deadly tsunamis that wreaked havoc on this city in the mid-20th century. Stroll along **Banyan Drive,** walk through the bayside **Lili'uokalani Gardens,** and then watch the surfers do their thing at **Honoli'i Beach Park** or snorkel and people-watch at **Richardson's Beach Park.** Natural sites only a few minutes from the center of town are **Rainbow Falls** and **Boiling Pots.** Hilo is a foodie town, so make plenty of time (and space) to eat at least several meals there (even if you just have one day). Excellent options include **Paul's Place Cafe, Ken's House of Pancakes, Puka Puka Kitchen,** and **Sombat's Fresh Thai Cuisine.** Stay in Volcano Village or book a room in Hilo (they're a great deal).

Day 7

The Hamakua Coast is deeply cut by "gulches," and many waterfalls and scenic points abound along the shoreline. As you leave Hilo, turn off the main highway and take the **Onomea Scenic Route,** stopping at the **Hawaii Tropical Botanical Garden** or hiking down to **Onomea Bay.** Soon after, back on the highway, you'll pass the turnoff for **'Akaka Falls,** which is really two falls, and a must-see sight for even non-nature lovers (it might convert you). Continue on Highway 19 toward Honoka'a enjoying the top

petroglyphs

Mauna Kea

scenic drive on the island, but you might have to hurry to ensure that you get to **Waipiʻo Valley** in time for your afternoon horseback riding or ATV or carriage tour of the valley. If you'd rather do it yourself without the tour, take the nearly vertical hike down to the beach. Bring plenty of water and a good spirit. If you make it back up, travel 20 minutes to the "upcountry" of **Waimea** for dinner. The hardest part of your day will be deciding at which excellent restaurant to dine. If you still have energy, take yourself (and your loved one) dancing at the open-air **Blue Dragon Coastal Cuisine & Musiquarium.** It's one of few places on the island where people get dressed up for a night out. Spend the night in Waimea or on the Kohala Coast.

Day 8

You probably need some rest by now so pick any one of the stunning beaches on the **Kohala Coast** and enjoy the morning basking in the sun. If you need a little adventure with your beachgoing, walk the **Ala Kahakai National Historic Trail,** sections of which are part of the historical **King's Trail** linking together several beaches (some hidden because they don't have easy access). Make a quick trip to the **Hamakua Macadamia Nut Company** on your way to the artist towns of **Hawi** and **Kapaʻau.** Make sure to eat at least a lunch or dinner (or both) in Hawi. This small town is a culinary mecca. **Sweet Potato Kitchen** is a real treat for the health-conscious eater. Where Highway 270 ends you'll find yourself at **Pololu Valley** (the other side of Waipiʻo Valley). Hike down to the beach at the bottom if you have time (the hike down isn't so bad, but the hike up is another story). In the later afternoon, take a self-guided or prearranged guided tour to the top of **Mauna Kea** for a sunset spectacle and for stargazing after sundown. Spend the night in Waimea or on the Kohala Coast.

Day 9

This will be your last day on the Big Island and your last chance for another dip in the ocean or to pick up gifts before heading to the airport for your trip home.

Best Beaches

This is why you came to the Big Island: the fabulous beaches. Some of these beaches do take a little work to get to (either by a short walk or rough four-wheel-drive road), but to find such sheer beauty, sometimes you have to do a little work.

MAKALAWENA BEACH (PAGE 43)

It's a bit of walk over a desolate lava field to the Makalawena Beach part of **Kekaha Kai State Park,** but the payoff is worth it: a **nearly uninhabited** white silky-sand beach, with truly nothing around you but sun and ocean.

MANINI'OWALI BEACH (PAGE 43)

If a sweltering walk isn't your idea of a vacation, no worries—Makalawena has a sister beach, Manini'owali Beach, in the **Kua Bay** section of Kekaha Kai State Park. Remember, though, when you've got it this good (beautiful **white-sand beach, great snorkeling** and **bodyboarding,** close parking, bathrooms), it can get very crowded.

HAPUNA BEACH STATE RECREATION AREA (PAGE 75)

Locals swear that Hapuna Beach is ranked one of the **top 20 beaches** in the world. A smooth and wide white-sand beach that's welcoming to **swimmers, bodyboarders,** and **snorkelers,** Hapuna draws huge weekend crowds—a good indication of just how nice this beach really is.

MANUKA BAY (PAGE 98)

The **rough drive** on the unmarked road to Manuka Bay will take you almost 45 minutes, but when you finally arrive, you'll think that you've transported yourself to a desolate beach in Mexico. You've got a **small beach shack** behind you, crabs strolling around, and blue water **all to yourself.**

Halape beach

Turtles are almost a guarantee at Punalu'u Black Sand Beach.

PUNALU'U BLACK SAND BEACH (PAGE 101)
Easy to access, this **black sand beach** is popular with both tourists and animals—you're almost certain to see **turtles** lolling in the sun here. Remember just to look and not touch.

HALAPE (PAGE 124)
Although the park borders the ocean, there isn't very good access to it now, thanks to the lava flow that has essentially covered this area. One exception is Halape, an **unspoiled beach** with swaying coconut trees on the southern coast of the park. The bad news: The **hike** there is grueling. The good news: The park limits the number of visitors (you have to get a permit to camp there), guaranteeing that the beach will retain an **untouched** feel.

SECRET BLACK-SAND BEACH (PAGE 143)
If **basking in the sun** on a towel perched on the sand is your delight, then head to this small **black-sand beach** with hidden **tide pools** set behind a coastal forest. (It's only a few minutes' walk from the road, so this beach likely won't remain a secret for long.)

RICHARDSON'S BEACH PARK (PAGE 165)
There are **drive-up beaches** galore on Kalaniana'ole Avenue, all with something different to offer the beachgoer. This is one of the favorites for its shade, full facilities, and clear blue water perfect for **swimming** and **snorkeling.**

WAIPI'O BEACH (PAGE 198)
You have to hike down a nearly vertical road before you arrive at the beach at **Waipi'o Valley,** but with **black sand** and a **waterfall** (far) behind you, you can't really argue with its appeal. Stay the whole day and explore the valley.

Best Outdoor Adventures

Surfing
KAHALU'U BEACH PARK (PAGE 44)
Just a couple miles south of **Kailua** in Kona, this beach park is the ideal setting for the vacationing **beginning surfer.** Kids and adults practice their moves side by side without pressure to show off.

PINE TREES (PAGE 43)
Pine Trees is a classic surf spot that is a favorite among locals. Inexperienced surfers need not apply, but feel free to come watch. You'll need **four-wheel drive** to get to this spot located behind the **Natural Energy Laboratory of Hawaii Authority.**

HAPUNA BEACH STATE RECREATION AREA (PAGE 75)
With an **exposed beach break,** which offers both lefts and rights, Hapuna Beach State Recreation Area is a reliable surf spot (though it can get crowded on weekends). The winter season offers the best time to surf here. Watch out for the riptide.

ISAAC HALE BEACH PARK (PAGE 143)
There is no sand at this rocky beach on **Pohoiki Bay.** The **long rides** and consistent wave size make this surf spot perfect for moving into and out of the break.

HONOLI'I BEACH PARK (PAGE 166)
Even if you're not planning on riding the waves, this is one of the **best places to watch** classic surfing. This is a hangout spot for locals, but they are friendly to non-locals, especially if you are a mindful paddler (watch out for others). Grab your **shortboard** and look out for the sharp rocks.

Hiking
CAPTAIN COOK MONUMENT (PAGE 52)
While it's only a round-trip four-mile hike, this

dirt trail is not an easy jaunt: It's a **steep, rocky** moderate hike. A great **trail run** or **sprint hike,** you'll know you've arrived at your destination when you see the **white obelisk** standing in front of **Kealakekua Bay.** Fun fact: The land surrounding the monument is technically British sovereign soil.

POLOLU VALLEY (PAGE 72)

This **switchback trail** is about three miles round-trip, but those miles are fairly **vertical.** The hike isn't technically difficult and plenty of kids and those with bad (or new) knees have happily completed this journey. You'll want to have your camera handy; the views of the valley are jaw-dropping and keep you inspired the entire way down (and back up again).

KAHUKU SECTION OF HAWAI'I VOLCANOES NATIONAL PARK (PAGE 102)

Filled with large old trees, native forest birds, and **rare yellow-flowering ohia lehua trees,** this section of the **national park** looks completely different from the park's main section. Hike on

your own or sign up for one of the free semi-monthly guided hikes.

KUMUKAHI LIGHTHOUSE (PAGE 139)

Kumukahi in Hawaiian means **"new beginnings"** or **"the source"**—it's the easternmost point of the Hawaiian Island chain and the first place that air hits after it has traveled thousands of miles across the ocean, making for some of the **purest air** in the world. Walk east from the lighthouse over uneven lava to the ocean to find a **tide pool with a lava roof.**

WAIMANU VALLEY (PAGE 199)

The hike down to **Waipi'o** and over the pali to Waimanu Valley is considered by many **one of the top three treks in Hawaii.** Come fully prepared for camping and in excellent condition to attempt this two- (or more likely three-) day hike.

LAKE WAIAU ON MAUNA KEA (PAGE 200)

Although this hike is short (less than 2 miles), make sure to acclimate to the altitude before embarking on this trek. At close to **13,000 feet**

Pololu Valley Lookout

Underwater Exploration

The Big Island offers a range of snorkeling and diving experiences, from those that begin inches from your car door to those that require a hired boat to take you a little farther offshore. No matter how you arrive to your snorkel or dive spot, you won't be disappointed by what is on display below.

MANINI BEACH

This is paradise: a **grassy park,** picnic tables, some shade, and views of the **Captain Cook Monument** in the distance—but that's not even the highlight of a visit to Manini. This beach is a neighborhood favorite for its wide underwater spaces teeming with **colorful fish**. It's the kind of spot that you'll want to visit more than once (page 45).

TWO STEP

It's called Two Step because of the lava shelf that requires you to take two steps down into the ocean, which is filled with brightly speckled marine life. A great pick for the **first-time snorkeler,** the access to this spot is located right next to **Pu'uhonua O Honaunau National Historical Park**. Bring your own snorkel equipment and lose your sense of personal space, as it can get crowded here underwater (with both people and fish) (page 39).

PUAKO TIDE POOLS

One of the most developed **fringing reefs** on the island, this **underwater nirvana** offers some of the best snorkeling and diving on the island and it's a bit **off the beaten path**. Bring your own equipment and look for **submerged lava tubes** and **garden eels** (page 75).

KAPOHO TIDE POOLS

It's like swimming in your own **personal aquar-**

Manini Beach is a prime snorkeling and kayaking location.

ium. This is **the ultimate spot for beginners** because the water is shallow here, but the more experienced swimmer/snorkeler can swim out to greater depths for more viewing opportunities. Wear water shoes and bring Band-Aids: the **coral** and **lava rocks** will cut your feet if you don't pay attention (page 142).

CHAMPAGNE POND

This **crystal-clear, naturally occurring warm pond, heated by the volcano underneath,** offers one-of-a-kind views of sealife. It doesn't get too crowded here—it most likely will just be you lounging around with some **sea turtles** (page 141).

above sea level, this sacred site is one of the **highest lakes in the United States.** If you time it just right, head back to the **summit** to watch the sunset **above the clouds.**

MAUNA LOA (PAGE 202)

One of the most extreme hikes on the island (if not *the* most, due to altitude and weather) is the hike to the **summit of Mauna Loa.** This hike has two access points (the other is in Volcano near the park); however, it's a shorter hike if you begin from near the Mauna Loa observatory on the Saddle Road.

Best for Families

You thought of leaving them behind on the Mainland, but in the end you were nice and brought the keiki (children) with you. Many resorts have keiki programs that occupy children throughout the day, but if you want to keep your kin close the Big Island offers numerous family-friendly adventures that will delight everyone involved (but no guarantees for that snarky teenager).

adults there is often an **open bar** and for the kids, craft-making activities, hula lessons, and that crowd favorite, temporary tattoos. The **buffet dinner** offers an opportunity to try local foods like **lau lau** (usually pork wrapped in taro leaves), but the menu also offers foods like french fries and chicken nuggets to satisfy even the pickiest of eaters. There is also a separate **dessert** buffet.

Lu'au

It's like a Lady Gaga **concert** meets a Broadway show. Yes, they are for tourists and are kitschy, but that doesn't mean they aren't fun. For the

Waterslides

Nope, there are no height limitations. Anyone can go on a waterslide—even if you're six foot two. Not all the hotels have them, but the ones that do

lu'au dance

SUNRISES AND SUNSETS

Wake up before dawn and drive to the Green Sand Beach (page 100) for sunrise—there is nothing more spectacular than watching the pink hues of sunrise spread across the greenish sand. Stop at Ka Lae (South Point) (page 96) and make the literal big leap off the cliff together.

Watch the sun set at the Black-Sand Beach (page 143).

Pack a picnic, blankets, and lots of warm clothes and drive the Saddle Road to Mauna Kea (page 182)—sunset on top of the summit is mystical.

ON THE WATER

Take a sunset cruise, complete with a champagne toast, with Ocean Sports (page 78).

IN THE WATER

Book a manta ray night dive/snorkel trip (page 47) and hold hands underwater as you (and 30 other people) try to stay afloat in order not to accidentally kick a manta ray (much harder than you'd think).

Book a room at The Mauna Kea (page 223), a midcentury modern paradise. Or play house (really upscale house) at Puakea Ranch (page 226) and relax in the antique copper tub or your private pool.

Visit Kehena Beach (page 144), where clothing is optional, or the secluded, jungle-like warm ponds in Isaac Hale Beach Park (page 143), where you should definitely keep your clothes on (there are kids around!).

manta ray night dive

ROMANTIC CUISINE

For dinner and swing dancing, put something nice on and head to the Blue Dragon Coastal Cuisine & Musiquarium (page 85).

Share a slice of macadamia nut pie at Hana Hou (page 104).

Stop at the Volcano Winery (page 110) for a tasting or private tour, and purchase a bottle of wine or mead.

Make a reservation at the Volcano House (page 131) for a table near the window. Watch as the sun sets, the stars come out, and the night sky is set ablaze with the glow from the volcano.

---

are in an informal competition with one another. The **Sheraton Kona Resort and Spa** boasts one of the best slides, and even better, it's claustrophobe friendly. The same can't be said for the slide at the **Hilton Waikoloa Village**—that one is enclosed.

Lapakahi State Historical Park

For an educational interlude, this site contains numerous **stone remains** that have been partially restored to better give a sense of this **ancient coastal settlement.** The self-guided tour is set up for families, and during the winter migrating humpback whales can be viewed from the park.

Ziplining

Swing through a tree canopy and then swim in a waterfall with Kohala Zipline. Tours range from three hours to a full day depending on how long you think you want to be strapped into a harness.

Eating *Malasadas*

Nothing brings a family closer together than sugar and, more specifically, **doughnuts** or malasadas as these Portuguese delights are called in Hawaii. Visit the Punalu'u Bake Shop, the **southernmost bakery in the United States,** to satisfy your craving or become addicted to one of their many **sweet breads.**

Jumping Off a Cliff

Families that jump together, stay together. Travel to **Ka Lae (South Point)** and get your adrenaline going when you GoPro yourself leaping off the point 50 feet into the ocean. The jump and subsequent climb back up will surely be cause for some high fives, hugs, and possibly even kisses.

Kilauea Iki Hike

Start the day by getting your little one deputized as a **junior ranger** at the national park visitors center and then drive or bike to Kilauea Iki where you can walk across a **once-molten lake of lava.** It feels like you're on the moon or the set of Game of Thrones. This four-mile route is rated moderate but well maintained and can by done by both keiki and grandma alike.

Thurston Lava Tubes

Continuing on the path from the Kilauea Iki Trail, you'll arrive at these well-maintained open lava tubes. At twilight the tubes have a **creepy, almost spooky** feel to them. It's a great place to tell a ghost story.

Maku'u Market

From **live music** to **food trucks** to **local food vendors,** the atmosphere at the Maku'u Market is always joyous. If you ever wanted to try a **mangosteen** or **rambutan** or buy old Nintendo games while listening to **Hawaiian bluegrass,** this **Sunday** market will become your happy place.

Plant a Tree

Ever since it was safe to return to this area after the **Kalapana lava flow,** locals have planted **coconut trees** into the earth in an effort to regenerate the landscape. Purchase a tree on your way to **Kaimu Beach** and leave the right kind of trace behind.

Pana'ewa Rainforest Zoo

You can pretend that the **petting zoo** is only for kids, but really, adults love it too. The **only tropical rain forest zoo in the United States,** the **spider monkeys** are a crowd favorite.

Waipi'o Valley Tour

The hike down an incredibly steep road isn't for everyone—but getting in a van and riding down the very same **vertical road** is not only thrilling, but also suitable for everyone regardless of ability. The **Waipi'o** Valley Shuttle tours the back of the valley, an area that most tourists don't get to see, while the driver shares stories of **Hawaiian folklore** and life in the valley.

Horseback Riding

Sometimes family activities can happen at the same place, but separately. At the **Dehana Ranch,** you can drop the little ones off for **Kids Camp** at the ranch, while better-trained (in horseback riding) family members can pick from various rides through the ranch with photo-worthy **views of Mauna Kea and the ocean** below.

Kona

Kona can feel like the hottest place on the island—and not just because of its warm temperatures.

There is always something going on in Kona, from frequent festivals celebrating everything from coffee and chocolate to beer and fishing, as well as serious nightlife, which locals will tell you means anything open later than 9pm. It's no wonder that most visitors spend the majority of their time on the Kona side. Although Kona is talked about as if it were a city, it is actually a large district. From national historic sites to some of the best white-sand beaches on the island to nearly every ocean activity possible, Kona is a microcosm of what the larger island has to offer.

ORIENTATION
North of the Airport: North Kona

This is what you were imagining when you booked your trip to Hawaii: turquoise waters beside long stretches of white-sand beaches. Amazingly, there are several of these types of beaches within 20 minutes of Kona International Airport—and they are all open to the public! What might surprise you the most is that parts of this area look like a desolate moonscape. The landscape is made up of lava fields, and in recent years, the black rocks have become dotted with white stones that spell out names of favorite teams and loved ones. Don't be thrown off by the lack of infrastructure in the area: The ocean and beaches lurking behind the lava fields are some of the most magical the island has to offer for those looking for white sands and astonishing underwater life.

South of the Airport

The small area south of the international airport looks a lot like anywhere else in suburban America. When giving directions locations in this area are referred to as near or around Costco, which is a beacon of light up above Hina Lani Street, or Target in the Kona Commons shopping center. You'll likely use this area to get from one place to another and for its resource-laden shops, but don't miss out on Pine Trees, one of the best surfing spots on the island.

Ali'i Drive: Kailua and Keauhou

The heart of Kona, Ali'i Drive is the

Look for ★ to find recommended
sights, activities, dining, and lodging.

Highlights

★ **Pu'uhonua O Honaunau National Historical Park (Place of Refuge):** Get a glimpse of ancient Hawaii at this safe haven for defeated chiefs and *kapu*-breakers. It's especially magical at sunrise (page 38).

★ **Kiholo Bay:** Get off the beaten path at Kiholo Bay where a short 30-minute walk will take you to this pristine, rarely busy beach, a guaranteed turtle viewing spot, with great access to swimming and snorkeling (page 40).

★ **Kikaua Point Park Beach:** Bring a picnic to this uncrowded beach—the water remains calm here, making it a perfect spot for kids (page 42).

★ **Makalawena Beach:** a favorite beach of many locals, this unspoiled beach is picture perfect with its white sand and turquoise water. There's not much shade here, so bring your sunscreen and get ready for a day cooling off in the water (page 43).

★ **Diving and Snorkeling:** Because its reef is so close to the shoreline, nearly the entire coast presents ideal snorkeling conditions. The best spots are **Kealakekua Bay** and **Pawai Bay** during the day and **Keauhou Bay** at night for the manta ray sightings (page 47).

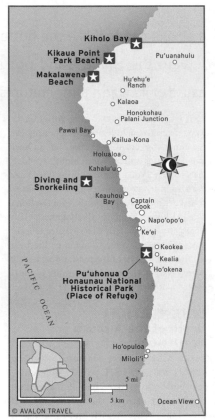

Kona

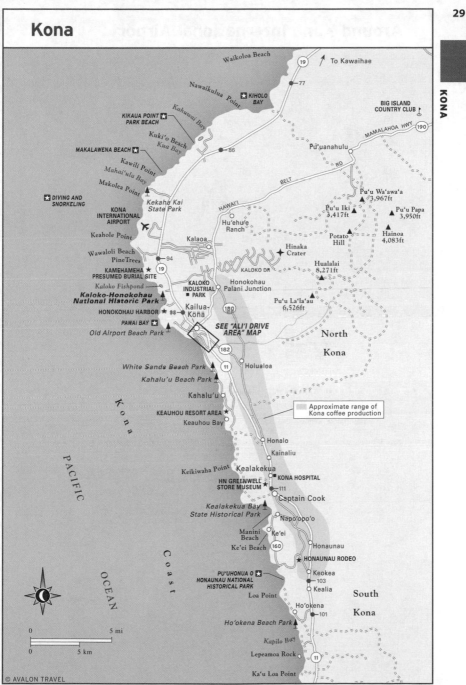

Waikoloa Beach

To Kawaihae

19

77

Nawaikulua Point

KIHOLO BAY

Kahuwai Bay

BIG ISLAND COUNTRY CLUB

KIKAUA POINT PARK BEACH

Kuki'o Beach
Kua Bay

MAKALAWENA BEACH

Kawili Point

Mahai'ula Bay

Makolea Point

DIVING AND SNORKELING

KONA INTERNATIONAL AIRPORT

Keahole Point

Wawaloli Beach

PineTrees

KAMEHAMEHA PRESUMED BURIAL SITE

Kaloko Fishpond

Kaloko-Honokohau National Historic Park

HONOKOHAU HARBOR

PAWAI BAY

Old Airport Beach Park

86

MAMALAHOA HWY

190

Pu'uanahulu

RD

BELT

HAWAI'I

Kekaha Kai State Park

Hu'ehu'e Ranch

Kalaoa

KALOKO DR

KALOKO INDUSTRIAL PARK

Honokohau Palani Junction

Kailua-Kona

98

94

19

180

SEE "ALI'I DRIVE AREA" MAP

182

Pu'u Wa'awa'a 3,967ft

Pu'u Iki 3,417ft

Pu'u Papa 3,950ft

Potato Hill

Hainoa 4,083ft

Hinaka Crater

Hualalai 8,271ft

Pu'u La'la'au 6,526ft

North Kona

White Sands Beach Park

Kahalu'u Beach Park

11

Holualoa

Kahalu'u

KEAUHOU RESORT AREA

Keauhou Bay

Approximate range of Kona coffee production

Honalo

Kainaliu

Keikiwaha Point

Kealakekua

KONA HOSPITAL

HN GREENWELL STORE MUSEUM

111

Captain Cook

Kealakekua Bay State Historical Park

Napo'opo'o

Manini Beach

Ke'ei

Ke'ei Beach

160

Honaunau

HONAUNAU RODEO

PU'UHONUA O HONAUNAU NATIONAL HISTORICAL PARK

Keokea

103

Kealia

Loa Point

South Kona

Ho'okena

101

Ho'okena Beach Park

Kapilo Bay

Lepeamoa Rock

11

Ka'u Loa Point

Kona Coast

PACIFIC OCEAN

0   5 mi

0   5 km

© AVALON TRAVEL

Around Kona International Airport

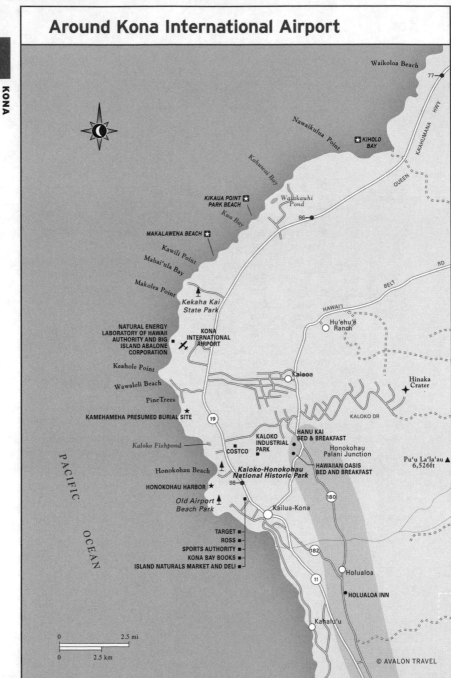

KONA

Waikoloa Beach

77

Nawaikulua Point

KIHOLO BAY

Kahawai Bay

QUEEN KAAHUMANA HWY

KIKAUA POINT PARK BEACH

Walakauhi Pond

Kua Bay

86

MAKALAWENA BEACH

Kawili Point

Mahai'ula Bay

Makolea Point

BELT

RD

Kekaha Kai State Park

HAWAI'I

Hu'ehu'e Ranch

NATURAL ENERGY LABORATORY OF HAWAII AUTHORITY AND BIG ISLAND ABALONE CORPORATION

KONA INTERNATIONAL AIRPORT

Kaloaa

Hinaka Crater

Keahole Point

Wawaloli Beach

Pine Trees

KAMEHAMEHA PRESUMED BURIAL SITE

KALOKO DR

19

PACIFIC

Kaloko Fishpond

KALOKO INDUSTRIAL PARK

COSTCO

HANU KAI BED & BREAKFAST

Honokohau Palani Junction

Pu'u La'la'au 6,526ft

Honokohau Beach

HONOKOHAU HARBOR

Kaloko-Honokohau National Historic Park

HAWAIIAN OASIS BED AND BREAKFAST

98

Old Airport Beach Park

Kailua-Kona

OCEAN

180

TARGET
ROSS
SPORTS AUTHORITY
KONA BAY BOOKS
ISLAND NATURALS MARKET AND DELI

182

Holualoa

11

HOLUALOA INN

Kahalu'u

0   2.5 mi

0   2.5 km

© AVALON TRAVEL

north-south thoroughfare stretching from the Keauhou resort area (the south end) through downtown Kailua and ending in the north near where Highway 11 becomes Highway 19 (and the counting of the mile markers starts all over again—actually, it starts backward). Starting at the south end of Ali'i Drive are a few larger resorts, like the Sheraton Keauhou Bay Resort and Spa and Outrigger Keauhou Beach Resort. Keauhou is one of only two big resort areas on the Big Island (the other is the Kohala Gold Coast). Since Keauhou is designed as a resort area, it is constructed so that a visitor never really has to leave its environs. The beach access here from the hotels and Keauhou Bay is rocky and the water can get rough. Most visitors use their hotel's or condo's pools and save a dip in the water for an evening excursion to view the manta rays that hang out in the bay.

As you drive north you'll pass by vacation rentals and crowded urban beaches. The downtown area, which is Kailua, is a combination of New Orleans and Key West. This is the area where the cruise ships dock (usually on Wednesdays), and you'll see passengers running ashore to shop. At night there is street life on Ali'i, so if you're looking to go out on the town, this is where you go. Especially on the weekends there is music blasting from the bars overhead, local kids cruising and parking in their rigged-up trucks, and tourists strolling from shop to shop. There are many stores in the downtown Ali'i section—but it's a lot of the same T-shirt shops, jewelry stores, and tour agents hawking luau and kayak adventures.

Captain Cook Area: South Kona

Captain Cook is an actual town, named for the explorer James Cook, who in 1778 was the first European to have contact with the Hawaiian Islands. An obelisk dedicated to Cook adorns Kealakekua Bay at the spot where he was killed. There are several other little towns in the area, like Kainaliu and Kealakekua (all off Highway 11), but the area generally is referred to as Captain Cook or South Kona.

A visit to Kona would not be complete without spending as much time as possible in this area, where kayak trips and snorkeling adventures are plentiful and the beaches are easily accessible. If you are waterlogged and looking for some drive time, head to the main road for antiquing or to try one of the area's several excellent restaurants.

PLANNING YOUR TIME

There is probably more to do in the Kona district than any other place on the Big Island, and the good news is nothing is actually that far from anything else. If there is no traffic, you can make it from the airport to the town of Captain Cook in about 40 minutes.

It's best to treat the Kona region like a mini road trip starting in either the north or the south. **Kealakekua Bay** to the south should not be missed. The water here is perfection for nearly every aquatic activity, and there are abundant tours to choose from that will assist you in exploring the underwater grandeur. If you feel like staying dry for a bit, there are several nearby historic sites well worth exploring.

The bulk of your day's activities will occur before lunchtime; early morning is great for kayaking, snorkeling, dolphin-swimming, and deep-sea fishing tours. The warm afternoons are a perfect time to relax on a nearby beach, such as **Kikaua Point Park Beach** or **Manini'owali Beach** in north Kona. If it's too hot out, head north up the hill to **Holualoa,** where the weather is cooler and the street is lined with art galleries. The late afternoon is the best time to hike to one of the beaches, like **Makalawena,** which requires some walking—usually over an open lava field.

Kona is one of few places on the island with nightlife. Many first-time visitors arrange to see a luau at one of the hotels or take a stroll on **Ali'i Drive** to people-watch and enjoy live music.

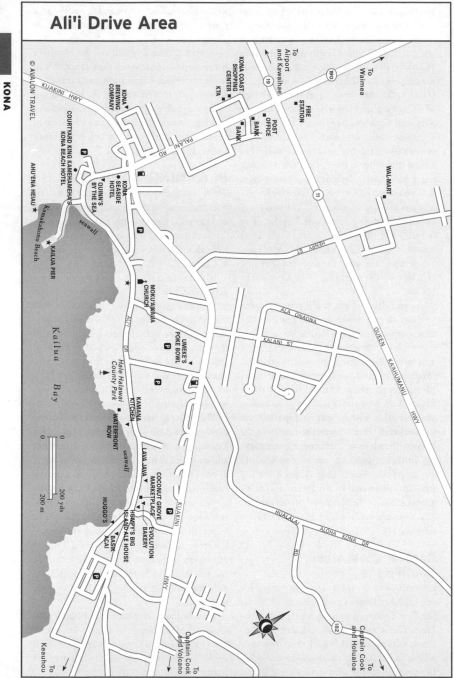

Ali'i Drive Area

Captain Cook and South Kona

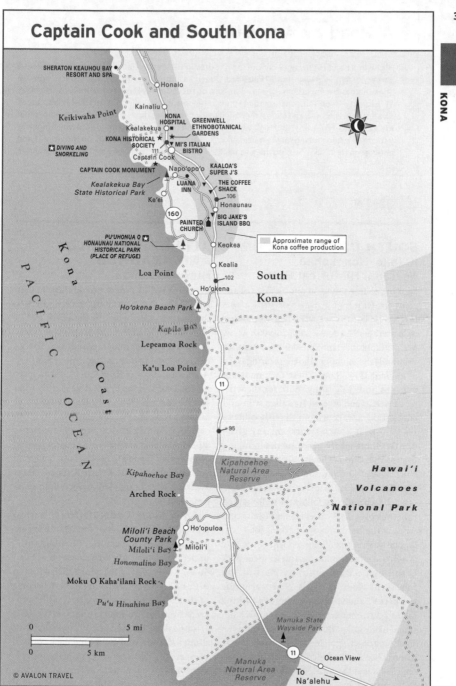

SHERATON KEAUHOU BAY
RESORT AND SPA

Honalo

Kainaliu

Keikiwaha Point

KONA
HOSPITAL

GREENWELL
ETHNOBOTANICAL
GARDENS

Kealakekua

KONA HISTORICAL
SOCIETY

MI'S ITALIAN
BISTRO

DIVING AND
SNORKELING

111

Captain Cook

KAALOA'S
SUPER J'S

CAPTAIN COOK MONUMENT

Napo'opo'o

THE COFFEE
SHACK

LUANA
INN

Kealakekua Bay
State Historical Park

106

Ke'ei

Honaunau

160

PAINTED
CHURCH

BIG JAKE'S
ISLAND BBQ

Approximate range of
Kona coffee production

PU'UHONUA O
HONAUNAU NATIONAL
HISTORICAL PARK
(PLACE OF REFUGE)

Keokea

Kealia

Loa Point

102

South

Ho'okena

Kona

Ho'okena Beach Park

Kapilo Bay

Lepeamoa Rock

Ka'u Loa Point

11

95

Kipahoehoe
Natural Area
Reserve

Hawai'i

Kipahoehoe Bay

Volcanoes

Arched Rock

National Park

Miloli'i Beach
County Park

Ho'opuloa

Miloli'i Bay

Miloli'i

Honomalino Bay

Moku O Kaha'ilani Rock

Pu'u Hinahina Bay

Manuka State
Wayside Park

0   5 mi

0   5 km

© AVALON TRAVEL

Manuka
Natural Area
Reserve

11

Ocean View

To
Na'alehu

PACIFIC OCEAN

Kona Coast

A Road by Any Other Name

Highway 11 and Highway 19 are the main routes in the Kona region. Highway 11 has several names: Kuakini Highway, Hawai'i Belt Road, Queen Ka'ahumanu Highway, Mamalahoa Highway. These names are sometimes used in addresses, but occasionally businesses simply use Highway 11. Highway 19 on some maps and in some addresses is also called Hawai'i Belt Road, Queen Ka'ahumanu Highway, and Mamalahoa Highway when it runs through Waimea. Remember that in Kailua town, Highway 11 and Highway 19 merge, and thus it is important to note which highway you are on when looking for the mile marker (i.e., there is a mile marker 100 on Highway 11 and another on Highway 19). Using the mile markers is a great way to gauge how far you must travel.

Sights

SOUTH OF THE AIRPORT
Kaloko-Honokohau National Historical Park

Looking to learn more about the lives of ancient Hawaiians? **Kaloko-Honokohau National Historical Park** (Hwy. 19 between mile markers 97 and 98, 808/326-9057, www.nps.gov/kaho, 8:30am-4pm daily, free) houses fishponds that highlight the engineering skills of ancient Hawaiians. These fishponds are home to birds migrating south for the winter as well as endangered Hawaiian stilts and coots. Take a walk around the fishponds to **Honokohau Beach,** where on any given day you'll see plenty of sea turtles lounging in the sand. If you're lucky you might also see a monk seal. Continue on the sand and visit the *heiau* (temple) that sits on the south end of the beach and then follow the well-marked trail back over the lava field to the visitors center near the restrooms and parking lot.

The park is serious about locking the gate at 4pm. Another option for accessing the park is through the **Honokohau Harbor** (on Kealakehe Pkwy. off Hwy. 19 between mile markers 97 and 98), where there is a parking lot and restroom area. Although this is a national historical park, quite a few people use it solely as a beach spot. It's a nice enough beach, usually not that crowded and with calm waters, but it is at the small boat harbor and next to the airport, making the water a bit murky.

ALI'I DRIVE: KAILUA AND KEAUHOU
Historic Kailua

In reality, Kailua proper extends farther than Ali'i Drive, but commonly Kailua refers to the historic area, which is the north end of Ali'i Drive with the shops. For instance, Ali'i Drive is the location for the Hulihe'e Palace—the last royal palace in the United States of America and where King Kamehameha spent his final days. If historic Kailua is truly what you are seeking, contact the **Kona Historical Society** (808/323-3222, www.konahistorical.org, khs@konahistorical.org). The society's 90-minute tours are given only to groups of 10 or more, but if you are not part of a big group you can order online their Kailua Village Walking Map book ($10), which then must be picked up in person.

Body Glove Cruises offers historical lunch (800/551-8911, www.bodyglovehawaii.com, 1pm Wed., $98 adults, $78 children 6-17, under 5 free) and dinner cruises (4pm Sun., Tues., Thurs., Sat., $118 adults, $88 children 6-17, under 5 free) that will take you to some of the coastal historic sites; part of the proceeds from the two-hour cruise go to the Kona Historical Society. The price includes lunch or dinner, dessert, and complimentary cocktail (dinner only). It's sort of a luau on the water—combining food, entertainment, and education with the promise of seeing dolphins and/

or whales, depending on the season—and a good way to check lots of must-do activities off your list at once. Booking online through their website can save you 15 percent.

AHU'ENA HEIAU

Directly seaward of Courtyard King Kamehameha's Kona Beach Hotel (75-5660 Palani Rd.), at the north end of "downtown" Kailua, is the restored **Ahu'ena Heiau.** Built on an artificial island in Kamakahonu (Eye of the Turtle) Beach, it's in an important historical area. Kamehameha I, the great conqueror, came here to spend the last years of his life, settling down to a peaceful existence after many years of war and strife. The king, like all Hawaiians, reaffirmed his love of the *'aina* and tended his own royal taro patch on the slopes of Mount Hualalai. After he died, his bones were prepared according to ancient ritual on a stone platform within the temple and then taken to a secret burial place, which is believed to be just north of town somewhere near Wawahiwa'a Point—but no one knows for sure. It was Kamehameha who initiated the first rebuilding of Ahu'ena Heiau, a temple of peace and prosperity dedicated to Lono, god of fertility.

The tallest structure on the temple grounds is the *'anu'u* (oracle tower), where the chief priest received messages from the gods while in deep trance. Throughout the grounds are superb *kia akua* (temple image posts) carved in the distinctive Kona style, considered some of the finest of all Polynesian art forms. The spiritual focus of the *heiau* was humanity's higher nature, and the tallest figure, crowned with an image of the golden plover, was that of Koleamoku, a god of healing. Another interesting structure is a small thatched hut of sugarcane leaves, Hale Nana Mahina, which means "house from which to watch the farmland." Kamehameha would come here to meditate while a guard kept watch from a nearby shelter. The commanding view from the doorway affords a sweeping panorama from the sea to the king's plantations on the slopes of Mount Hualalai. Though the temple grounds, reconstructed under the auspices of the Bishop Museum, are impressive, they are only one-third their original size. The *heiau* itself is closed to visitors, but you can get a good look at it from the shore.

KAILUA PIER

While in the heart of downtown, make sure to visit **Kailua Pier,** which is directly in front of Ahu'ena Heiau. Tour boats and the occasional

Honokohau Beach

Your Best Day in Kona

- Visit **Pu'uhonua O Honaunau National Historical Park** in the early morning when you'll have the place to yourself.

- Join a guided **kayaking** tour of **Kealakekua Bay,** where you'll be side by side with the dolphins and experience some of the best **snorkeling** on the island.

- After a busy morning, relax at the white-sand **Manini'owali Beach/Kua Bay** in Kekaha Kai State Park (or any number of gorgeous white-sand beaches north of the Kona airport).

- In the late afternoon, cool off by heading up the mountain to gallery-filled **Holualoa,** also home of the fabulous **Holuakoa Gardens and Café,** where a dinner reservation is a must.

- Finish this long day with some bar-hopping or dancing on **Ali'i Drive.**

RAINY-DAY ALTERNATIVE

It doesn't often happen in Kona, but every once in a while you'll catch yourself in less-than-perfect weather. If so, visit the **Natural Energy Laboratory of Hawaii Authority (NELHA)** for an indoor talk on natural energy technology and the efforts to generate such energy in Hawaii. A visit here includes a tour and tasting at an abalone farm.

fishing boat use this facility, so there is some activity on and off all day. Shuttle boats also use this pier to ferry cruise ship passengers to town for land excursions. More of these large ships make Kailua a port of call during the late spring and fall months than during the rest of the year, while interisland cruise ships make regular stops here throughout the week. When periodic canoe races and the swimming portion of the Ironman Triathlon competition are held in the bay, the pier is crowded with onlookers.

MOKU'AIKAUA CHURCH

Kailua is one of those towns that would love to contemplate its own navel if it could only find it. It doesn't really have a center, but if you had to pick one, it would be the 112-foot-high steeple of **Moku'aikaua Church** (75-5713 Ali'i Dr., www.mokuaikaua.org, dawn-dusk daily). The highest structure in town has been a landmark for travelers and seafarers ever since the church was completed in January 1837. The church claims to be the oldest house of Christian worship in Hawaii: The site was given by King Liholiho to the first Congregationalist missionaries, who arrived

on the brig *Thaddeus* in the spring of 1820. Much thought was given to the orientation of the structure, designed so the prevailing winds blow through the entire length of the church to keep it cool and comfortable. The walls of the church are fashioned from massive, rough-hewn lava stone, mortared with plaster made from crushed and burned coral that was bound with *kukui* nut oil. The huge cornerstones are believed to have been salvaged from a *heiau* built in the 15th century by King Umi that had occupied this spot. The masonry is crude but effective—still sound after more than 170 years.

Inside, the church is extremely soothing, expressing a feeling of strength and simplicity. The pews, railings, pulpit, and trim are all fashioned from koa, a lustrous, rich-brown wood that begs to be stroked. Although the church is still used as a house of worship, it also has the air of a museum, housing paintings of historical personages instrumental in Hawaii's Christian past. The crowning touch is an excellent model of the brig *Thaddeus,* painstakingly built by the men of the Pacific Fleet Command in 1934 and presented to the church in 1975.

HULIHE'E PALACE

Go from the spiritual to the temporal by walking across the street from Moku'aikaua Church and entering **Hulihe'e Palace** (75-5718 Ali'i Dr., 808/329-1877, www.huliheepalace.com, Mon.-Sat. 9am-4pm, except major holidays). You can look around on your own or ask the staff for a tour, which usually lasts 45 minutes. Admission is $8 adults, $6 seniors, $1 students under 18. This two-story Victorian structure commissioned by Hawaii's second royal governor, John Kuakini, dates from 1838. A favorite summer getaway for all the Hawaiian monarchs who followed, especially King Kalakaua, it was used as such until 1914. At first glance, the outside is unimpressive, but the more you look the more you realize how simple and grand it is. The architectural lines are those of an English country manor, and indeed Great Britain was held in high esteem by the Hawaiian royalty. Inside, the palace is bright and airy. Most of the massive furniture is made from koa. Many pieces were constructed by foreigners, including Wilhelm Fisher, a German. The most magnificent pieces include a huge formal dining table, 70 inches in diameter, fashioned from one solid koa log. Upstairs is a tremendous four-poster bed that belonged to Queen Kapi'olani, and two magnificent cabinets built by a Chinese convict serving a life sentence for smuggling opium. King Kalakaua heard of the man's talents and commissioned him to build the cabinets. They proved to be so wonderfully crafted that after they were completed the king pardoned the craftsman.

Prince Kuhio, who inherited the palace from his uncle, King Kalakaua, was the first Hawaiian delegate to Congress. He decided to auction off all the furniture and artifacts to raise money, supposedly for the benefit of the Hawaiian people. Providentially, the night before the auction each piece was painstakingly numbered by the royal ladies of the palace, and the name of the person bidding for the piece was dutifully recorded. In the years that followed, the **Daughters of Hawai'i,** who now operate the palace as a museum, tracked down the owners and convinced many to return the items for display. Most of the pieces are privately owned, and because each is unique, the owners wish no duplicates to be made. It is for this reason, coupled with the fact that flashbulbs can fade the wood, that a strict *no photography* policy is enforced. The palace was opened as a museum in 1928. In 1973, Hulihe'e Palace was

Hulihe'e Palace, dating back to 1838, is full of period furniture and artifacts from the early 1900s.

Cooling Off in Holualoa

Want to get away from the beach for a few hours? The village of Holualoa (www.holualoahawaii.com), on the mountainside above Kailua-Kona, is quaint, and the panoramic view of Kona below is unbelievable. Plan to visit Holualoa, where the weather is cooler, for a couple of hours—or overnight in one of the choice bed-and-breakfasts here—to stroll the upscale galleries (not too upscale) and to have a meal at Holuakoa Gardens and Café. Holualoa is on Highway 180, which breaks off from Highway 11 to the south and connects to Highway 190 to the north.

Holuakoa Gardens and Café (76-5901 Mamalahoa Hwy., 808/322-2233, www.holuakoacafe.com, brunch Mon.-Fri. 10am-2:30pm Sat.-Sun. 9am-2:30pm; dinner Mon.-Sat. 5:30pm-8:30pm; café Mon.-Fri. 6:30am-6pm, Sat. 8am-6pm, Sun. 8am-2:30pm) is a restaurant where people actually do dress up (but you don't have to). The seating is all outdoors (but covered) in a lovely garden, and the waitstaff is attentive. The menu changes daily, the meat and greens are local when available, and the choices aren't the same old dishes seen on most menus in Hawaii. There are vegetarian and gluten-free options (including a very tasty flourless chocolate cake) and the wine list is extensive.

If you're in Holualoa during the day, be sure to check out **Holualoa Ukulele Gallery** (Hwy. 180, 808/324-4100, www.konaweb.com/ukegallery, Tues.-Sat. 11am-4:30pm). The building was the original town post office, and the current store owner refurbished the building's exterior with original postal boxes (not from the Holualoa post office, just from the same era). If you're thinking about buying a ukulele, but not sure what to get or how one would learn to play, Sam Rosen, the shop's owner, will patiently answer all your questions. Contact Mr. Rosen to learn more about his private workshops (from a few days to a week), where you can make your own ukulele.

Also in town is the **Donkey Mill Art Center** (78-6670 Hwy. 180, 808/322-3362, www.donkeymillartcenter.org, Tues.-Sat. 10am-4pm); check the website to see what one-day or weekend workshops the center is offering. The selections range from painting to woodcarving to silk-screening.

added to the National Register of Historic Places.

Historic artifacts are displayed in a downstairs room. Delicate and priceless heirlooms on display include a tiger-claw necklace that belonged to Kapi'olani. You'll also see a portrait gallery of Hawaiian monarchs. Personal and mundane items are on exhibit as well—there's an old report card showing a 68 in philosophy for King Kalakaua—and lining the stairs is a collection of spears reputedly belonging to the great Kamehameha himself.

CAPTAIN COOK AREA: SOUTH KONA

H. N. Greenwell Store Museum

It's *Little House on the Prairie* meets Hawaii. Constructed in the 1870s to make supplies available to the Euro-American immigrant community, the **H. N. Greenwell Store Museum** (Hwy. 11 between mile markers 111 and 112, 808/323-3222, www.konahistorical.org, Mon. and Thurs. 10am-2pm, $7 adults, $3 children 5-12) is the oldest surviving store in Kona and one of the oldest buildings in the area. A great experience for kids or history buffs, the volunteer-led tour of the building filled with historical pictures and relics of the area takes about a half hour and occurs on demand. Foodies will want to visit around 10am on Thursdays, when you can assist in baking Portuguese bread in the stone oven located behind the building. If you're just passing by on a Thursday, stop and pick up a loaf—but know that they are usually sold out by 2pm.

★ Pu'uhonua O Honaunau National Historical Park (Place of Refuge)

If you are going to do one historical activity while on the Big Island, do **Pu'uhonua O Honaunau National Historical Park** (off

Hwy. 11 on Hwy. 160, 808/328-2326, www. nps.gov/puho). The gate is open daily 7am-7pm, while visitors center hours are daily 8:45am-5:30pm. Admission is $5 per car, $3 to walk in, free with a national park pass, or included in the $25 pass for three national parks on the Big Island. To get there from Highway 11, between mile markers 103 and 104 turn onto Highway 160 and travel down the hill a few miles to the entrance on the *makai* side.

This is where you see the true old Hawaii, circa the 1600s. A park ranger explains that there is a calming feeling here because it is a religious site dedicated to the god Lono. No killing or wars occurred at Pu'uhonua O Honaunau; it was, as it is sometimes called, a place of refuge. During times of war, women and children would seek safety on the grounds, and if defeated chiefs or those accused of sins could make it to the shore by swimming across the bay, they would be absolved of their sins and given a second chance. There were 30 such places like Pu'uhonua O Honaunau across the islands, but this site is the only one that remains.

Some of the structures at the park are original, but many are replicas. Kids tend to be particularly impressed by the imposing structures and sculptures of ancient times. The best time to visit the park is early morning—even before the gate opens. There is a wonderful sense of peace just after sunrise. Tours with the knowledgeable staff are free and offered daily at 10:30am and 2:30pm, and are highly recommended. Pamphlets are also provided for self-guided tours, which would take a half hour if you just walked straight through, or you can do a self-guided audio cell phone tour by calling 808/217-9279.

The majority of tourists head straight to **Two Step** (turn *makai* off Hwy. 160 where you see the Pu'uhonua O Honaunau park sign, and instead of driving straight into the gate turn right onto the road directly before the gate), called such because of the lava shelf that requires you to take two steps down into the water. The area offers great snorkeling and is shallow, making it popular with non-experts and kids. There are no facilities, so it is recommended that you park in Pu'uhonua O Honaunau's lot, where there are bathrooms, and from where it's a two-minute walk to Two Step.

Pu'uhonua O Honaunau National Historical Park features original structures.

Coffee Farm Tours

The upland Kona district is a splendid area for raising coffee, and Kona coffee has long been accepted as gourmet quality and is sold in the better restaurants throughout Hawaii and in fine coffee shops around the world. It's a dark, full-bodied coffee with a rich aroma.

There are a lot of options for tours of working coffee farms, and many include quick coffee tastings followed by a brief nudge for you to buy their product. One of the better, non-pushy tours is at **Greenwell Farms** (81-6581 Mamalahoa Hwy./Hwy. 11, Kealakekua, between mile markers 111 and 112, 808/323-2275, www.greenwellfarms.com, daily 8:30am-4pm, last tour at 4pm). They offer a free 30-minute walking tour through their coffee farm, discussing the roasting and processing of coffee and ending with some coffee sampling. If you're going to take just one coffee tour, this one is a good option because the tour experience is not only quirky and fun, but also very laid-back.

Beaches

Many of the best Kona beaches require some work to get to them. Keep in mind that it's often the destination, not the journey. The majority of routes to the beaches can be accomplished in a good pair of sandals, but the walk, which is usually over uneven lava, can be difficult for some. There are an equal number of beaches that don't require any walking beyond from the parking lot to the sand, so don't fret if you opt out of the beaches that require more effort to reach.

NORTH OF THE AIRPORT: NORTH KONA
★ Kiholo Bay

If you stop at the scenic viewpoint near mile marker 82 you get a great panorama of **Kiholo Bay** (Hwy. 19 near mile marker 81 and also between mile markers 82 and 83, gate open 7am-7pm), and chances are you'll want to get closer to it to see what looks like completely untouched paradise: a deserted beach with turquoise water and what appears to be an island off in the bay. If you start your journey at the south end of the beach, you'll find a cold freshwater lava tube bath called the **Queen's Bath** (Keanalele Waterhole). It is a sacred site, so please be respectful. A sign there asks people to refrain from using the site for bathing—but you can get in the water and peek

around. As you continue along the shoreline you'll see fancy homes with Private Property signs. If you continue walking north on the beach, you'll see turtles nesting nearby. Feel free to jump in and take a dip with them, but be careful not to touch them. This also is a good place for snorkeling when the water is clear. The beach ends and then you need to walk over the lava rock around the bend to a wonderful little shaded cove. From here you can swim out to that "island," which is actually attached to the landmass on its north side.

To drive to the south end of the bay, look for the stick with the yellow reflector on it on the *makai* side of the road between mile markers 82 and 83. If you're driving north on Highway 19 and you pass the blue Scenic Point sign, you have gone too far. The road you turn onto is gravel, but a rental car can make it to the end, where there are portable bathrooms. If you decide to walk all the way from Highway 19 to the beach, the makeshift parking lot is right before mile marker 81. Usually there are other cars parked on the side of the road. The trail, which will take you about 20 sweaty minutes to walk, starts to the left of the parking lot and veers left as you walk. The benefit in walking and not driving down is that the walk will get you much closer to the bay. If you drive, you end up on the south side of the bay and need to

Scenic Drive

This scenic drive is definitely a full, fun-packed day. Begin at the junction of Highway 11 and Highway 160 by turning onto Ke Ala O Keawe Road (Hwy. 160) toward Honaunau. Your first stop will be at **Pu'uhonua O Honaunau National Historical Park** as early as you can manage to get up (hopefully before the crowds get there). Either snorkel at **Two Step** or leave the park and turn left back onto Highway 160 and travel about 10 minutes (enjoying the ocean views) to **Manini Beach** for snorkeling.

Your next stop should be **Kealakekua Bay** for kayaking to the **Captain Cook Monument.** Afterward, backtrack to the intersection (right before the Dead End sign) and head left (or *mauka*) on Highway 160, which is also called Napo'opo'o Road. Travel up the hill until you see the **Kona Pacific Farmers Cooperative** (82-5810 Napo'opo'o Rd., 808/328-8985, www.kpfc.com, Mon.-Fri. 10am-4:30pm). Stop in for a treat and a self-guided coffee tour and tour of their fruit orchard. Save enough room in your belly (there are lots of free samples to be had here) and continue around the corner to **Big Island Bees** (82-5780 Napo'opo'o Rd. #100, 808/328-1315, www.bigislandbees.com, Mon.-Fri. 10am-4pm) for a honey tasting and beekeeping tour. You'll see their products in nearly every store around the Big Island—but taste them and purchase them at the source for a bit of a discount.

When you leave, continue up the hill (north) and make a right turn onto Middle Ke'ei Road (it's where the road forks). From Middle Ke'ei Road make the next right onto Painted Church Road. Look for **Paleaku Gardens Peace Sanctuary** (83-5401 Painted Church Rd., 808/328-8084, www.paleaku.com, Tues.-Sat. 9am-4pm, self-guided tours $10 adults, $7 seniors, $3 children 6-12). One local innkeeper described these gardens as a "mishmash of shrines dedicated to different traditions." It's actually seven acres of manicured gardens with the highlight being the Galaxy Garden, the world's first walk-through model of the Milky Way formed by flowering plants. It truly is peaceful there, with a grand view of Kealakekua Bay—an ideal place to sit and eat lunch or meditate or practice yoga (which is offered Tues. and Fri. 9:30am-11am for $14).

Farther along Painted Church Road you'll arrive at the **Painted Church** (84-5140 Painted Church Rd., *mauka* side, 808/328-2227, www.thepaintedchurch.org, daylight hours) itself. The church, erected in 1899 by Father John Velghe, offers beautiful, detailed paintings of scenes from the Bible painted onto wood (there are some bits of Hawaiian words intermixed). It's not a must-see, but it's worth spending a few minutes investigating the photos and the small church. From the Painted Church you are less than a mile from Highway 160 where you started; when you get to the intersection of Painted Church and Highway 160, turn left to get back to Highway 11.

walk around it for about 15 minutes. I recommend wearing hiking shoes—not because the walk is challenging, but because the rocky terrain makes it a bit difficult to do in flip-flops.

Kuki'o Beach (Four Seasons Resort Beach)

The wonderful thing about Hawaii is that the entire shoreline is public—so even when the beach is at a five-star hotel, as it is in the case of **Kuki'o Beach** (Hwy. 19 between mile markers 86 and 87), the public must have access to it. Kuki'o usually offers calm water for swimming and has a pleasant, unshaded, narrow white-sand area off a paved path that extends into an excellent oceanfront jogging trail—an ideal place to get your steps in. The path is part of the historic *ala loa* (long path) route that islanders would use for a nightly procession. The beach is maintained by the Four Seasons Resort, and since they don't want "the public" sneaking off into the hotel to use facilities, they have provided bathrooms, showers, and drinking water for the public here, and those facilities are nice (I mean, it is the Four Seasons). There is no lifeguard on duty. This bay is a fisheries management area, which means that you can fish here but

a board alerts you to how many fish you can catch of each type.

To get to Kuki'o Beach, you are required to stop at the Four Seasons Resort gate and notify the guard that you are going to the public-access beach. Note: The resort itself is open to the public, so you can also say you are visiting it and go take a peek if you want. Follow the signs that read Public Access and park in the lot where the road ends.

★ Kikaua Point Park Beach

Kikaua Point Park Beach (Kuki'o Nui Dr., off Hwy. 19 between mile markers 87 and 88) is perfect in so many ways. Entry is limited (passes are handed out at the security gate), so it's never as crowded as you'd expect it to be. The water is glorious. Even when there are waves at other places on the same shoreline it remains calm here, making it a perfect spot for kids (although there is not a lifeguard on duty). Pack a picnic—locals tend to bring pizza from Costco—and head to the grassy area shaded by coconut trees. Bathrooms, showers, and drinking water are available, and these privately maintained facilities are lovely.

To get to Kikaua Point Park Beach, turn *makai* onto Kuki'o Nui Drive and proceed to the security booth. The guards only hand out

Turtles are frequent visitors to Kiholo Bay.

28 passes per day, but the turnover is pretty high, so if you wait around long enough, and people do, you'll likely end up with a pass (however, the earlier you arrive the better your chances are at getting a pass quickly). Another option is to park at the Kuki'o Beach parking lot near the Four Seasons Resort and walk south to Kikaua—it's only a 10-minute walk. Don't get tricked in the parking lot with the Beach Access sign pointing to the left—this is only the tide pool area. Take the paved path straight back, about a five-minute walk, to the sandy portion. When you're done with the best beach day ever, don't forget to return your access card to the security guard so that someone else can enjoy the beach.

Manini'owali Beach (Kua Bay)

Until about 15 years ago there wasn't a road to get to **Manini'owali Beach** (Hwy. 19 between mile markers 88 and 89, daily 9am-7pm) in the Kua Bay section of Kekaha Kai State Park. One had to really want to get there by hiking or finding a four-wheel-drive route. And even with all those barriers, people still went—so you know it has to be good. It's a smallish white-sand beach with turquoise water that is excellent for bodyboarding and snorkeling. There is not much shade, but if you're aching for sun this is a perfect place to spend the day absorbing some rays. Nowadays, the state has made it easier to get here. A lovely paved road reaches a parking lot and full facilities. It's getting so crowded that now there is sometimes a security guard at the entrance to the beach itself (he doesn't seem to do much besides protect the beauty of the place). To get there from Highway 19, look for the Kehaha Kai Park sign and turn *makai* across from West Hawaii Veterans Cemetery.

★ Makalawena Beach

In the state beach section of Kekaha Kai State Park, **Makalawena** (Hwy. 19 between mile markers 90 and 91, daily 9am-7pm) is a favorite beach of many locals, probably because it's an authentic Big Island experience given that it requires a little bit of hiking to

get there. If you make the 30-minute trek to the beach, you'll be rewarded with isolated white sand and turquoise water. Given the walk, Makalawena is often fairly deserted (it has no facilities). The beach itself is made up of three crescent-shaped white-sand areas that are backed by trees (although there isn't much shade). Bodyboarding and snorkeling are possible.

Before you get excited about coming here, you should know that while you can do it in a standard rental car, it's a slow-going 20-minute drive and then there is a 30(ish)-minute walk over a lava field. From Highway 19, look for the Kekaha Kai Park sign and turn *makai*. The initial road starts off as paved but then quickly becomes uneven lava.

To get to Makalawena, walk from the parking lot through the first beach, **Mahai'ula,** where the bathrooms are located, and then through the lava field. When you reach sand again, you're close. You might want to wear good shoes on the walk, as the lava field can be tricky to navigate.

SOUTH OF THE AIRPORT
Pine Trees

Although famous among surfers and the site of many competitions, **Pine Trees** (Hwy. 19 between mile marker 94 and 95, access road gate open daily 7am-7pm) is not a good swimming beach, nor are there any pine trees. There are a few one-towel coves along the rocky shoreline where you can gain access to the water, but mostly it's a place from which to observe the action. To get to Pine Trees, turn *makai* where you see the sign for the Natural Energy Laboratory of Hawaii Authority (NELHA). Follow the road toward the NELHA facility a short way to **Wawaloli Beach,** a small public beach of sand and crushed coral that is used mostly by locals for relaxing and barbecuing. There are a few restrooms and some picnic tables. To continue to Pine Trees from here you'll need a four-wheel-drive vehicle. When you reach the T-intersection, turn makai on to a dirt road (the paved part continues to the right) and continue for about a mile. There is no real parking lot here—just park near the trees where other cars likely are parked.

Old Airport Beach Park and Pawai Bay

We should thank whatever politician decided to take this old abandoned airport and turn it into **Old Airport Beach Park** (Hwy. 19 between mile markers 99 and 100). To reach it, turn makai on Makala Boulevard. Go to the end of the road, and then turn right on Kuakini to the dead end. There are nicely kept picnic areas that get busy, and the facilities are placed between the parking lot and sandy area, which doesn't make for an ideal beach. The former runway is now a jogging area, but if you're looking for some beach jogging, head north on the sand toward Pawai Bay. Since you are near a reef here, the little bay with sand is the best place to get in the water for some excellent snorkeling. Locals will tell you that you can camp here, but I don't recommend it.

ALI'I DRIVE: KAILUA AND KEAUHOU
Kahalu'u Beach Park

With a large covered picnic pavilion, barbecue pits, a guy sitting around playing ukulele on a bench, and locals drinking from the backs of their trucks in the parking lot, **Kahalu'u Beach Park** (Ali'i Dr. between mile markers 4.5 and 5, daily 6am-11pm) has all the makings of a quintessential urban beach park. Although there is a small, rocky beach area and a lifeguard on duty, it's not so much a place to lie out. But it is a great spot for snorkeling and ideal for kids since the water is shallow and calm. Bathroom and shower facilities are available as well as a food truck that has small storage lockers for rent; it hangs out next to the big parking area. Kahalu'u Bay Education Center, a nonprofit organization, rents gear at fair prices and uses the profits to support the local ecosystem. The beach area is smoke-free.

White Sands Beach (La'aloa Beach Park)

Even though **White Sands Beach** (Ali'i Dr. between mile markers 3.5 and 4, daily 7am-11pm, gate closes at 8pm) is also right off the road, it still retains a peaceful feel to it. Officially known as La'aloa (Very Sacred) Beach Park and nicknamed Disappearing Sands Beach, it is popular for bodyboarding, surfing, and sunning (there is little shade here). Grab your towel and head out early

White Sands Beach

because this beach gets crowded on weekends. Bathroom and shower facilities are available and there is a lifeguard on duty.

Parking can be tricky. Locals park on the *makai* side of the road or in a small lot across the street.

CAPTAIN COOK AREA: SOUTH KONA
Kealakekua Bay State Historical Park

Tourists flock to **Kealakekua Bay State Historical Park** (Beach Rd. off Hwy. 160, daylight hours) to kayak, go on ithkayak tours to the Captain Cook Monument, or to simply snorkel. The park is at the intersection of Beach Road and Napo'opo'o Road. There is a parking lot with a boat launch right at the intersection, and a few yards away is the historical park with bathrooms, showers, picnic areas, drinking water, and an ample parking area.

Given the proximity to the reef, the snorkeling here is excellent, and depending on the season, it's common to see dolphins swimming next to you. The kayaking here is some of the easiest ocean kayaking, so it's suitable for novices.

It is required that you obtain a permit to land at the monument across the bay. Visitors do not need to acquire their own permits when renting a kayak, but must confirm with the vessel owner that the vessel they rent possesses a valid permit for transiting the bay. There are only three companies that have valid permits (**Adventures in Paradise, Aloha Kayak,** and **Kona Boys**), so make sure you are renting kayaks from one of those companies or joining one of their tours.

You don't need a permit if you're just going to paddle around rather than land on the beach.

Manini Beach

Manini Beach (off Hwy. 160) is a prime snorkeling and kayaking area with great views of the Captain Cook Monument in the distance. Greatly affected by the tsunami in March 2011, which forced two beachfront homes into the ocean, the beach is now restored and even nicer than it was before, with a large, partly shaded grassy area and several picnic tables. There are very few places to park here so it may be hard to find a spot, but the good news is that the water never gets too crowded. From Highway 160, also called Pu'uhonua Road, turn *makai* onto Kahauloa Road and then right onto Manini Beach Road—follow it around for 0.2 mile until you see parked cars and a bay.

Ke'ei Bay Beach

A real locals' place, **Ke'ei Bay Beach** (off Hwy. 160) has a lovely strand, and it can get surprisingly busy given how you have to be in the know to get here. There is white sand and the water is calm for swimming or snorkeling. Since you're staring at prime real estate you'll likely be surprised by the small, somewhat underdeveloped homes surrounding the area: The land is owned by the Kamehameha Schools trust, and long-term leases are given for less than market value to native Hawaiians.

From Highway 160, also called Pu'uhonua Road, turn onto an unmarked dirt road on the *makai* side between Ke'ei transfer station and Keawaiki Road, which it is gated. Four-wheel drives are best for this road to the beach, but you can reach it in a standard car with some careful, slow driving. Drive toward the ocean (or you can walk about 15 minutes) until you can't drive anymore. Park in the semi-designated lot in front of the houses.

Ho'okena Beach Park

The road down to **Ho'okena Beach Park** (Hwy. 11 near mile marker 101) is worth the trip: It has excellent views of the coastline and the surrounding area, and if you are an advanced biker you might want to try this route for a challenge. There is an actual sandy beach here, and it makes for a nice place to bring a towel and laze the day away. There is even some shade.

The water here is not too rough, so it's a nice place to swim, snorkel, or kayak (rentals are available at the beach or by calling 808/328-8430, $20 for a single kayak for two hours or $25 for a tandem). If you get here early you might see a spinner dolphin, as this area is one of their habitats. Facilities such as showers, bathrooms, barbecues, and a large covered picnic area are available. Camping is allowed in designated areas, and permits can be obtained online (http://hookena.org/camping.html) a recommended 72 hours in advance, or at the beach from the attendant beginning at 5pm daily. It is advised that you consult the park website, as there are extensive instructions about how to obtain a permit and there is different pricing for residents and nonresidents. There is a separate area to park if you're camping here, to the left of the main parking lot. The area is popular with locals and can get crowded and rowdy at night, so it might not be the best place if you're camping with kids or looking for a peaceful evening.

From Highway 11 a two-mile paved windy road leads to the entrance. Where the road splits when you are almost at the ocean, fork to the left—don't go straight—where there is usually a sign for kayak rentals, and head on the one-lane road into the parking lot. You will see the sign for Ho'okena on the ocean side of the road.

Ho'okena Beach Park

Water Sports

CANOEING AND KAYAKING

Kealakekua Bay is the perfect place to canoe or kayak given the calm water, the abundance of dolphins, and the lure of boating toward the Captain Cook Monument; however, there are a lot of rules surrounding this activity. If you are a DIY kayaker and want to rent or have your own kayak to use, you are required to obtain a permit (go to www.hawaiistateparks.org/parks/hawaii and click on Kealakekua Bay State Historical Park). Please note, according to the state's website, "Transiting the bay by individuals is allowed so long as the vessel has a valid permit (both private and commercial rental vessels). Permitted vessels are prohibited from landing at Ka'awaloa flat, or launching from Napo'opo'o wharf. Visitors do NOT need to acquire their own permits when renting a kayak, but must confirm from the vessel owner that the vessel they rent possesses a valid permit for transiting the bay." There are only three kayak tour companies (listed below) that have been issued permits by the Division of State Parks.

The larger companies all offer the same tour of the bay, which includes four-hour morning or afternoon combination trips of kayaking, snorkeling, looking for dolphins, and paddling to the Captain Cook Monument. The differences between the tours are the quality of the boats and expertise of the tour guides.

The preferred company for the Kealakekua kayak tour, because of the quality of its tours and equipment, is **Kona Boys** (79-7539 Mamalahoa Hwy./Hwy. 11, 808/328-1234, www.konaboys.com, $119-169 adults, $99-149 children), who offer both morning and afternoon tours of the bay. They also offer a trip in an old-style canoe, which leaves from the Kailua dock (1 hour, $50); someone boats you around the bay while giving you the history of the coastline.

Other choices for kayak tours include the capable **Aloha Kayak Company** (79-7248 Mamaloahoa Hwy. 11 between mile markers 113 and 114, 808/322-2868, www.alohakayak.com, $99-130 adults, $55-70 children). This company offers 3.5-hour and 5-hour tours—although both tours are not offered daily. Visit their website to receive $20 off per person on their 5-hour tour. If you are into sea spelunking (cave exploration), Aloha offers a 3.5-hour sea cave-with-snorkel tour that they tout as the best option for cruise ship passengers with limited time.

Adventures in Paradise (75-560 Kopiko Street C7-430, 808/447-0080, www.bigislandkayak.com, $90-$100) touts itself as the kayak company with the lowest prices for the bay trip, although their stated prices don't include taxes or the $5 state park fee or a more robust lunch like the other companies. Nonetheless, their guides are personable and knowledgeable and their small group sizes are a plus.

For a different kind of kayak adventure (and one that might be a little less crowded and a little later in the morning), try **Ocean Safaris** (on Keauhou Bay, 808/326-4699, www.oceansafariskayaks.com, Mon.-Sat., 3.5-hour morning tour, $85 adults, $45 children). This tour starts in Keauhou Bay and journeys to a sea cave in Kuamoo Bay. You'll snorkel on the way in an effort to view dolphins and turtles.

★ DIVING AND SNORKELING

Nearly every kayak trip or boating trip includes snorkeling, but if you're simply looking to rent gear on your own, there are several long-standing shops in the area, and good deals on snorkel sets can be had at both Costco and Target. Nearly the entire coast presents ideal snorkeling conditions given how close the reef is to the shoreline; however, some areas are harder to access due to the rocky geography. Beginners can easily start at Two Step or Pu'uhonua O Honaunau National Historical Park. The best spots are Kealakekua Bay and Pawai Bay during the day and Keauhou Bay at night for the manta ray sightings.

Big Island Divers (74-5467 Kaiwi St., 808/329-6068, www.bigislanddivers.com) offers competitive deals relative to other providers in the area. A two-tank guided tour ($130 per person includes snacks) is offered daily (8am-1:30pm), and most nights they offer manta ray night dives and snorkeling trips ($120 per person diving or $100 snorkeling) with several different combinations of options, from one tank to two tanks and depending on the length of trip. This is one of the few manta ray trips with a dive and snorkel option on the same boat. The best thing about this company is that it offers discounts the more you dive—so if you think you'll go out at least twice, Big Island Divers is a good deal for you.

Body Glove Cruises (75-5629 Kuakini Hwy., check in at Kailua Pier, 800/551-8911, www.bodyglovehawaii.com) is one of the larger companies that is now outsourcing some of its tours to smaller outfits (which might be a good thing). The 4.5-hour deluxe snorkel and dolphin-viewing tour ($128 adults, $88 children 6-17) is a full-service excursion with breakfast, lunch, snacks, cash bar, snorkel gear, and instruction. If you want to learn how to scuba or snuba, instruction is available on board for an additional $88/$69 plus tax. Note: given the immense amount of time that you're eating and drinking, the in-water time only accounts for approximately half the time that you're on the boat.

Captain Zodiac (Honokohau Harbor, 808/329-3199, www.captainzodiac.com) offers a four-hour snorkel and dolphin-watching tour, but does it from a Zodiac boat and leaves from the harbor near Kailua, although the tour travels to Kealakekua Bay ($95 per adult, $79 per child with online discount). This is an extremely professional and dedicated company that truly values customer service.

Also, Zodiacs are a good option if you don't want to paddle around yourself but still want to be close to the dolphin and snorkeling action.

Fair Wind (78-7130 Kaleiopapa St., Keauhou Bay, 808/322-2788, www.fairwind.com, snorkel and dive tour $129 plus tax adults, $79 plus tax children, $29 plus tax toddlers under 3, manta ray diving $109 per person, discount if booked online) is your first-class deluxe option for snorkeling and diving tours. Fair Wind offers a five-hour morning snorkel and dive that includes breakfast and lunch. The boat, the *Hula Kai,* is comfortable, and staff is there to meet your every need. The manta ray night snorkel (6:30pm-8:30pm) includes all gear and a snack. Other places offer manta ray night tours, but Fair Wind's service sets them apart. A manta ray expert on board films the entire experience for purchase after the trip.

A longtime favorite of locals, **Jack's Diving Locker** (75-5813 Ali'i Dr., 808/329-7585, www.jacksdivinglocker.com) offers two-tank morning dives (8:30am, $135 per person plus gear rental for certified divers, $195 for intro divers, $65 for snorkeling; all prices include a light meal) and manta ray night trips that are really two dives, with one at sunset and a second dive to view the manta rays ($155 per person plus gear rental and $125 per person for snorkeling, not offered Tues. or Sat.). Serious divers might want to consider the Pelagic Magic dive (Tues. and Thurs., $175 for certified divers), which won the Best Night Dive category in Scuba Diving magazine's 2014 readers' choice awards. This "extreme dive" is a one-tank dive to view an underwater light display, compliments of some spectacular jellies.

Kona Honu Divers (74-5583 Luhia St., 808/324-4668, http://konahonudivers.com) is another outfitter with a good reputation for service and luxury, and this one really specializes in diving (not just snorkeling). They offer a few different types of tours, from a manta ray night dive ($105 for one tank and $135 for two tanks) to manta ray night snorkeling

Watching Manta Rays

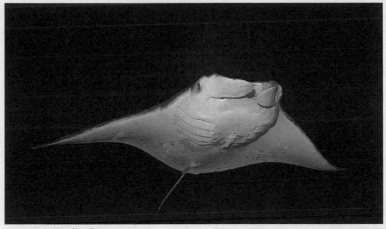

manta ray in Keauhou Bay

Many say that Kona is the number one place in the world to see manta rays, partly because they have become conditioned over time to feed at night in Keauhou Bay, eating the plankton attracted to the light at the Sheraton hotel. Snorkeling companies offer nighttime excursions into the bay so that you can snorkel with the manta rays.

Manta rays are completely harmless. Although their wingspan averages 5-8 feet, they have no teeth or stinger—but given their large size, seeing a manta ray up close can be both terrifying and exhilarating. If you are apt to get seasick, this might not be the best trip for you. Even though the tour boats don't travel far, the water can be rough at night. Once one person gets sick, it seems like several more people follow.

While you won't be up close and personal with the manta rays, an alternative is simply to watch them from the Sheraton Keauhou Resort and Spa. The aptly named **Rays on the Bay** restaurant and bar (dinner served 5:30pm-9:30pm and the bar stays open until 11pm) has a viewing area where you can spot the mantas from dry land.

($100 per person) to two-tank daytime dives for beginning to advanced divers ($125 for divers and $65 for snorkelers). On Fridays they have a black-water night dive that takes place after the manta ray dive for those who really want to experience the ocean by night ($146). Their more specialty tours are not offered daily and they require a minimum number of passengers to run their charters, so availability may dictate whether or not you decide to dive with Kona Honu. Discounts are available for multiple bookings such as a charter plus manta night dive or by adding the black-water dive to any package.

Kona Boys (79-7539 Mamalahoa Hwy./ Hwy. 11, 808/328-1234, www.konaboys.com) rents snorkeling gear and offers discounts if you rent for several days.

Sandwich Isle Divers (75-5729 Ali'i Dr., 808/329-9188, www.sandwichisledivers. com, daily 8am-6pm) is a reputable company that offers a slew of services, from rentals to charters (two tanks, two locations runs $120-165 per person depending on level of instruction and equipment needed). In addition to their daily dives, they also offer a four-day open-water PADI certification course ($550).

SURFING AND STAND-UP PADDLEBOARDING

Surfing is not as significant a sport on the Big Island as on the other islands. Proportionally for the size of the island, there are fewer good surfing spots here, and many of the traditional surfing sites are just not easy to access. Whether this is due to the lack of the underwater environment necessary to create the right kind of waves or for some other reason, conditions seem to be lacking for great surf that the other islands have in abundance. However, a few local sites on the Kona side do draw the faithful. Perhaps the most popular is the break along the reef at **Kahalu'u Bay** in front of the beach park. Two alternative spots are **Banyans** near White Sands Beach (aka Disappearing Sands Beach) and **Pine Trees,** north of town near the airport. Any of the shops that sell or rent boards can give you current information about surfing conditions and sites.

On the other hand, stand-up paddleboarding is sweeping the island. In many cases, paddleboarders can be found where the surfers are. However, you'll also see paddleboarders out with boogie boarders since smaller waves are much more practical for the stand-up paddleboard and essential for novices. If you are just beginning, try a lesson or rent a board and test it out on some flat, still water. Most places that rent surfboards also rent stand-up paddleboards.

If you need a rental, oftentimes there will be beachfront peddlers hawking boards at hourly rates (you can bargain). Many of the tour outfitters, such as the ones located near the Kailua Pier, rent boards out by the day or week. **Kona Boys** (79-7539 Mamalahoa Hwy./Hwy. 11, 808/328-1234, www.konaboys. com) is one of few providers in Kona that offers stand-up paddleboard instruction ($99 per person for 1.5-hour group class, minimum two people, or $149 for private instruction). They also rent stand-up paddleboards ($29 per hour or $74 per day) and offer daily 1.5-hour tours ($99 group tour, $149 private tour). If you're looking for surf instruction,

contact **Ocean Eco Tours** (Honokohau Harbor off Hwy. 19, 808/324-7873, www. oceanecotours.com, 8:30am or 11:30am check-in, $95 group lessons, $150 for 2-hour private lesson), which also offers stand-up paddleboard lessons for the same price as surf lessons.

DOLPHIN SWIMS AND WHALE-WATCHING

Many of the kayaking and snorkeling trips offer dolphin options (both viewing and swimming with dolphins), since Kealakekua Bay has it all. The majority of boat trips will state that whale-viewing is available during the winter season. Listed here are outfitters and excursions that are fully dedicated to dolphin and/or whale swims and watches. If you want to swim with the dolphins it's best to join an organized trip so that you have some instruction and assistance with this undertaking.

Dan McSweeney loves whales and wants you to love them too. At **Dan McSweeney's Whale Watching Learning Adventures** (Honokohau Harbor off Hwy. 19, 888/942-5376, http://ilovewhales.com, Dec.-Mar. only, $110 adults, $99 children), he personally conducts each tour and guarantees that you will see whales. If you're interested in learning about whales, this tour is for you. There is no open bar on the boat. Morning and afternoon departures are available and the tour lasts three hours.

Sunlight on Water (Honokohau Harbor off Hwy. 19, 808/896-2480, sunlightonwater. com) offers whale-watching tours (afternoons daily during winter, $80 adults, $60 children), a four-hour tour to swim with spinner dolphins (mornings daily, $120 adults, $80 children if booked online, includes snorkel gear) and manta ray swims (nightly, $87 adults, $75 children if booked online). The good deal here is that they will offer you a discount if you book more than one trip with them. They are highly recommended for the dolphin swim since that is their real passion, but other companies might be better for whale-watching and manta ray trips.

SPORTFISHING

The fishing around the Big Island's Kona Coast ranges from excellent to outstanding. The area is legendary for its marlin fishing, but there are other fish in the sea. The best time of year for big blues is July-September; August is the optimal month. Rough seas can keep boats in for a few days during December and early January, but by February the waters have calmed. A large fleet of charter boats with skilled captains and tested crews stands ready to take you out on the water. Most of the island's 80 charter boats are berthed at Honokohau Harbor off Highway 19, about midway between downtown Kailua and Kona airport. (Honokohau Harbor has eclipsed Kailua pier as the area's fishing epicenter, as the latter is now tamed and primarily used by swimmers, triathletes, and bodyboarders.) When the big fish are brought in, they're weighed in at the fuel dock, usually around 11:30am and 3:30pm.

There is some correlation between the amount you pay for your charter or tour and the experience you have. When booking a tour, check if there is if there is a minimum number of passengers required if you are signing up for a shared boat. Not all boats have the shared option, instead requiring you to charter the entire boat. Also, for larger companies that have multiple boats and captains, you might want to check what boat/captain you'll be joining and what their success rate is out at sea. If you visit **Honokohau Harbor** (on Kealakehe Pkwy. off Hwy. 19 between mile markers 97 and 98) and walk around the dock, you'll surely find someone eager to get you onto their boat early the next morning. Here are some places to get started for booking your fishing excursion.

Several charters now offer online bookings, among them *The Silky* (808/938-0706, www.silkysportfishing.com) and *Sea Wife II* (808/329-1806, seawifecharters.com, shared charter $109 per person for 4 hours). **Bite Me** (808/936-3442, www.bitemesportfishing.com) is a well-known corporate option with many boats and captains, and the family-run *The Camelot* (www.camelotsportfishing.com) is an excellent option. The latter offers shared-boat options only if others call for the same day (it rarely happens), but their charters are reasonably priced, their boat is in good shape, and the family that operates the boat is experienced and boasts a good track record.

Boat tours are the best way to watch the sunset.

BOAT TOURS

Boat tours are more popular during the winter season when whale-watching is at its prime; nevertheless, during off-season an evening (or day) on the water can still be a fun experience, and don't fret—the dolphins are present year-round.

Kailua Bay Charter (Kailua Harbor in front of Courtyard King Kamehameha's Kona Beach Hotel, 808/324-1749, www.konaglassbottomboat.com, daily 11:30am or 12:30pm, $40 adults, $20 children under 12) offers the unique experience of an hour-long glass-bottom boat cruise. It's sort of like snorkeling but on a boat—you get to see wonderful marine life without getting wet. It's a nice way to see coral and tropical fish—and an especially easy way to show young children what lies beneath the ocean—but for the hour-long excursion your money and time might be better used elsewhere, since at times it can be difficult to actually see anything from above the glass.

What is most notable about **Body Glove Cruises** (75-5629 Kuakini Hwy., check in at Kailua Pier, 800/551-8911, www.bodyglove-hawaii.com) is that they can accommodate wheelchairs on their boat. Body Glove will also accommodate gluten-free and vegan dietary restrictions with 48 hours' notice. Their historical dinner cruise ($118 adults, $88 children) includes a full dinner, one complimentary cocktail, live entertainment, and a narrated tour of historical sites on the coast. A lunchtime cruise option also is available.

Hiking and Biking

HIKING

If serious hiking is what you're looking for, you'll want to visit other regions of the island. Instead, the Kona area offers a lot of moderate trails that are almost always the means to getting to some awesome beach.

For instance, you can hike to **Captain Cook Monument** via the inland Ka'awaloa Trail. It's not the most exciting hike ever, but the destination is the goal. The trail starts on Napo'opo'o Road just 500 feet below where it drops off Highway 11 (between mile markers 110 and 111). Look for a group of three coconut trees right near a telephone pole. The trailhead will be obvious, as it is worn there. The round-trip hike is nearly four miles. The descent will take you 60-90 minutes, with a much longer return to the top. While on the trail, if you see any side paths, remember to always keep to the left. Please note that this is a not an easy hike (look for a sign near the trailhead that explains the risks of this particular trek). Wear proper footwear and bring lots of water.

If you are looking for something more organized, try **Hawaii Forest and Trails** (74-5035B Queen Ka'ahumanu Hwy./Hwy. 19, 808/331-8505, www.hawaii-forest.com). Although their headquarters is in the heart of Kona, their tours are outside this region, mainly to Kohala and Volcano for activities such as bird-watching.

BIKING

Home to the famous Ironman World Championship, Kona takes biking seriously. Highway 19 is an ideal ride: smooth and flat and uninterrupted for many miles. On any given day you'll see many serious bikers riding along the highway, sometimes faster than the cars. Some areas have semi-designated bike lanes (the lane will be marked for part of the road, but not the entire way; many bike riders end up on the gravel road next to the paved road). Check out PATH (www.pathhawaii.org) to learn more about efforts in Hawaii to develop bike lanes.

Since Kona is a bike town, there are many shops that build custom bikes for elite athletes. If you're just looking for a rental, visit **Cycle Station** (73-5619 Kauhola St.,

808/327-0087, www.cyclestationhawaii.com or www.konabikerentals.com, Mon.-Fri. 10am-6pm, Sat. 10am-5pm, $30-75/day). The website has an extensive list of what bikes are available, ranging from hybrid to luxury bikes; however, bikes cannot be reserved online (you need to call or email the shop). Another shop with online booking options is **Bike Works** (74-5583 Luhia St., 808/326-2453, http://bikeworkskona.com, Mon.-Sat. 9am-6pm, Sun. 10am-4pm, $40-60). Discounts are offered for longer rentals, making this company a good option for a multiday bike trip around the island.

Golf

Sometimes it seems that half the available land on the Big Island is dedicated to golf courses (that's not a real statistic, it just seems that way). With perfect weather for the sport, the Kona side has done a good job of creating enough courses to meet demand. The majority of resorts have their own courses (or courses that they partner with to offer discounts). However, some truly public courses do exist and usually offer lower prices than those of the resorts. If the greens fees seem a little much for you, wait until midafternoon when the fees tend to drop substantially.

The **Kona Country Club** (78-7000 Ali'i Dr., 808/322-3431, www.konagolf.com) has a lovely property near the end of Ali'i Drive in Keauhou, with two 18-hole courses offering grand views over this eminently rocky coast. Greens fees run $150 for the Mountain Course and $165 for the Ocean Course, with senior and twilight (after 12pm) discounts available. The pro shop is open daily.

A little farther afield but still close enough to Kailua to make a good play date are Big Island Country Club and Makalei Hawaii Country Club, both of which are along Mamalahoa Highway heading toward Waimea. The **Big Island Country Club** (Hwy. 190 at mile marker 20, 808/325-5044, www.bigislandcountryclub.com) is a rolling, challenging course with wonderful vistas over the Kohala Coast. Greens fees run $95 for morning play and $79 in the afternoon (*kama'aina* discount available). Carved from ranchland on the steep hillside closer to Kailua is the equally challenging **Makalei Hawaii Country Club** (72-3890 Hawai'i Belt Rd., 808/325-6625, www.makalei.com), where play costs $99 before noon, $79 after that. A nice *kama'aina* discount is available.

Shopping

ALI'I DRIVE: KAILUA AND KEAUHOU
Ali'i Drive
The shops that line Ali'i Drive are tchotchke central. There are many gift shops—the kinds with the "My grandmother went to Hawaii and all I got was..." T-shirts and assorted items needed for a day at the beach, such as snorkel equipment and sunscreen. There are also local, independent jewelry stores selling the island specialty of black pearls. The quality of goods at these shops tends to be low, so buyer beware.

Keauhou
If you need to escape the heat during the day, there is the **Keauhou Shopping Center** (78-6831 Ali'i Dr.). It contains a good independent bookstore, **Kona Stories** (808/324-0350, www.konastories.com, Mon.-Fri. 10am-6pm, Sat. 10am-5pm, Sun. 11am-5pm), that has a

Is It Worth Going to a Lu'au?

Answer: How much do you like watching musicals or theater? A lu'au might not be what you think it is. Gone are the days of roasting a pig as onlookers watch in awe. Attending a luau is like going to dinner theater. It's a good opportunity to try a lot of local foods at once, but nearly all the buffets are only mediocre. If the food is what you're most interested in, it would be better to go to a restaurant (like Jackie Rey's in Kona) instead of spending $100 (the average price for most luau). Drinkers may get their money's worth—nearly all the luau include an open bar.

If you really enjoy a good Broadway show, then you might enjoy a luau, and kids seem to love them. The productions vary, but **Island Breeze** (http://ibphawaii.com/luaus), the company that puts on luau at the Courtyard King Kamehameha's Kona Beach Hotel (in Kailua-Kona), the Sheraton Keauhou Bay Resort and Spa (in Keauhou), and The Fairmont Orchid (in Kohala) offers the best show. For a traditional luau with lots of hula, try the King Kamehameha version. For a more Cirque de Soleil-type experience (with more modern dance and less hula), head to The Fairmont Orchid, which offers a more pricey experience—but the food and service is better here than at other luau. Lastly, all luau offer preferred-seating options, meaning that you pay about $20 per person extra to sit closer but you are still eating the same food as everyone else (although you get to visit the buffet line first). Unless you have extra money to spend, preferred seating isn't really worth the splurge.

significant stock of new books, some of which are discounted.

CAPTAIN COOK AREA: SOUTH KONA
Kainaliu

It's only about a city block in length, but Kainaliu (Mamalahoa Hwy./Hwy. 11 between mile markers 113 and 114) makes for a pleasant stroll. There are also several good restaurants if you get hungry while you're shopping.

Yoganics (79-7401 Mamalahoa Hwy. Ste. C, 808/322-0714, www.yoganicshawaii.com, Mon.-Fri. 10am-5pm) is an eco-boutique to go to if you forgot your organic or hemp yoga pants at home. Aside from the somewhat pricey exercise and yoga wear, there is jewelry and locally made bath products. Check the website or call for the schedule of yoga classes, which are offered in-store nearly every day.

Next door to Yoganics is **Kiernan Music** (808/322-4939, www.kiernanmusic.com, Mon.-Fri. 10am-6pm, Sat. 10am-5pm), the best place to buy that ukulele you promise you'll learn to play. The instruments are beautifully crafted, some are vintage, and they also do custom-made pieces. If you don't have enough room to put one in your suitcase, no worries: They'll ship your uke home for you for a reasonable price.

Antique Row

In Kealakekua (South Kona) between mile markers 111 and 112, you'll come upon a slew of antiques shops that are definitely worth browsing. They tend to be a mix of Hawaiiana, old bottles, and beautiful furniture made of koa wood. All the shops are within walking distance of one another, so park your car and take a stroll.

Food

ALI'I DRIVE: KAILUA AND KEAUHOU

While there are many restaurants on Ali'i Drive, most of them cater to tourists and offer poor service. So beware: While a crowded restaurant is a usually a sign of high quality, that's not necessarily the case on Ali'i Drive. Huge and inexpensive portions make **Quinn's Almost By The Sea** (75-5655A Palani Rd., Kailua, 808/329-3822, www.quinnsalmostbythesea.com, daily 11am-11pm, $13-24) notable. Whereas many other restaurants in the area cater to tourists, Quinn's keeps it local and casual. As the restaurant's name indicates, there aren't any views here, just a covered outdoor area bordering a parking lot and an inside bar scene with several beers on tap and reasonably priced cocktails. The fish-and-chips are fresh and one of the more popular dishes, but you should also try the short ribs. Touting itself as the only Indian food on the island, **Kamana Kitchen** (75-5770 Ali'i Dr., Kailua, 808/326-7888, daily 11am-9:30pm, $12-22) is American-style Indian food. There is more outdoor seating than indoor seating at this establishment—but that's a good thing, as the patio area provides an ideal place to watch the sunset. The usual dishes you'd spot at your favorite Indian restaurant on the Mainland also are here: tandoori chicken, lamb curry, naan—with only a few choices of fish dishes. If you're looking for something a bit different than kalua pork or ahi tuna to eat, Kamana Kitchen isn't a bad choice. They serve beer and wine, with happy hour prices in effect from 3pm to 5pm.

With a great oceanfront view (the majority of seating is outside), **Lava Java** (75-5799 Ali'i Dr. next to the Coconut Grove shopping area, Kailua, 808/327-2161, www.islandlavajava.com, daily breakfast 6:30am-9:30am, lunch 9:30am-5pm, dinner 5pm-9pm, coffee anytime, $12-30) keeps busy. In fact, sometimes it's hard to get a table at 7am for breakfast;

luckily, they offer reservations through Open Table. If you can plan ahead, I highly recommend making that reservation (you'll make a lot of those waiting in line very jealous). The service can be slow at times, but the food is consistently good and the portions are large. If you're in a rush for breakfast you can grab a pastry to go. The non-breakfast cuisine is mostly pizzas, salads, and burgers, but vegetarian and gluten-free options are available and the sandwiches are highly recommended.

Humpy's Big Island Alehouse (75-5815 Ali'i Dr., Kailua, 808/324-2337, www.humpyskona.com, Mon.-Fri. 11am-2am, Sat. 8am-2am., Sun. 9am-2am., happy hour daily 3pm-6pm, $13-20) is the second location of an Anchorage mainstay. Humpy's is where to go to watch sports, to drink, and to eat breakfast. At night this place gets packed upstairs, where sometimes there is a live band. Downstairs is a bit calmer and cooler, and you can enjoy drinks on the patio facing the ocean. Lunch and dinner are good enough, with a menu featuring the usual bar food. The real winner here is weekend breakfast, perfectly paired with football watching. The blackened halibut Benedict is fantastic. Those with smaller appetites can order a side, which also comes with potatoes.

Most people on the Kona side brag about their access to Costco bagels, but **Evolution Bakery and Cafe** (75-5813 Ali'i Dr., Kailua, 808/331-1122, www.upcountrybakerycafe.com, daily 7am-3pm, $4-12) has really upped the ante by not only baking their New York-style bagels from scratch, but also baking their own gluten-free bagels. In addition to bagel sandwiches (with vegan cream cheese as an option), there are pancakes, pastries, juices, smoothies, and large cups of coffee. It's an excellent grab-and-go option especially for those New Yorkers craving a bit of home (Hawaiian-style).

Right on the oceanfront, **Huggo's**

(75-5828 Kahakai Rd., entrance off of Ali'i Dr., Kailua, 808/329-1493, www.huggos. com, dinner Sun.-Thurs. 5:30pm-9pm, Fri.-Sat. 5:30pm-10pm, brunch Sun. 10am-1pm, $15-37) is a great spot if you're looking for a romantic dinner or just cocktails (try getting there for the sunset). Huggo's has one of the best and most innovative mixologists on the island. They haven't changed the menu in quite a while, with simple dishes plated to look elegant. But perhaps sticking with what they know has allowed Huggo's to survive in the same location for the last 40 years (while other restaurants on the strip have come and gone). The fish, especially the fresh catch of the day ($36) cooked in different ways, is recommended given the restaurant's close relationship with local fishers. Note: Huggo's has parking in a small lot right in front of the restaurant.

Essentially right in front of Huggos, **Basik Café** (75-5831 Kahakai Rd., entrance off of Ali'i Dr., Kailua, 808/238-0184, www.basikacai.com, Mon.-Fri. 7am-4pm, Sat.-Sun. 8am-4pm, $6-13) looks like a beach shack reminiscent of Ipanema Beach in Brazil, with only a few stools at the second-story bar overlooking the ocean. The hardest part of breakfast is picking just one antioxidant-packed bowl to try. The small (not even the large!) acai bowls and smoothies are large enough to fill two like-minded eaters.

With at least a dozen variations of fish, seasonings, sauces, and the make-your-own option, **Da Poke Shack** (76-6246 Ali'i Dr., Kailua, 808/333-7380, http://dapokeshack. com, daily 10am-6pm) is a *poke* dream come true. If you're not sure what to get, the friendly staff will let you sample as many kinds as you need to convince you that *poke* is for you. There isn't really anywhere to sit here, but it's not that kind of place. Grab a to-go container and bring it with you to the beach.

In the Keauhou Shopping Center, **Bianelli's Gourmet Pizza and Pasta** (808/322-0377, http://bianellis.com, Mon.-Sat. 3pm-9pm, $20 for large pizza) is notable for its signature pink sauce, a white wine mushroom sauce mixed with marinara pasta sauce. If you happen to be in the area and hungry weekdays 5pm-6:30pm, try **Kenichi Pacific** (808/322-6400, www.kenichihawaii. com) for an excellent happy hour of half-price sushi and drink specials. On Saturdays stop by the **Keauhou Farmers Market** (8am-noon) near the movie theater and Longs Drugs.

Keep an eye on the action on Ali'i Drive from Humpy's Big Island Alehouse.

Parking on Ali'i Drive

Parking is no fun on Ali'i Drive. But luckily, it's probably the only place on Hawai'i where you can't find parking. There are very few spaces on the actual street itself and only a handful of free public lots, as well the option to pay for parking. If you are spending a night on the town, try the Coconut Grove parking lot via Kuakini Highway (it's the one with Outback Steakhouse). Usually parking is plentiful there and you can avoid the slow nighttime traffic of Ali'i Drive.

Near Ali'i Drive

If you just landed at the Kona airport or are about to take a stroll around Kaloko-Honokohau National Historical Park, **Pine Tree Café** (70-4040 Hulikoa St., Kailua, 808/327-1234, daily 6am-8pm, $4-14) is the restaurant for you: It's quick, it's cheap, it's local food (remember that "local" on the island doesn't mean locally sourced). Breakfast includes ten different kinds of omelets and classics like *loco moco* and Spam *musabi*. Plate lunches ($10.95) such as chicken katsu and kalbi ribs come with rice or fries and mac salad or green salad. The indoor seating area is a bit reminiscent of dorm life, but you'll be in and out of here within a half hour, so the ambience doesn't matter much.

In an unassuming strip mall in the old industrial area near Target, **Broke da Mouth Grindz** (74-5565 Luhia St., Kailua, 808/327-1113, http://brokedamouthgrindzkailuakona.com, Mon.-Sat. 8:30am-8pm, Sun. 9am-5pm $3-15) is for the hungry—and definitely those on a paleo diet. This is "local" food, but there is something a bit more foodie about it than the usual joint. Moving beyond the usual Spam *musabi*, the short rib "footlong" musabi roll ($4.99) is a nice addition to the musabi family and surprisingly huge. Fried rice (which is a side with most dishes) can be ordered in a garlic kimchee variety. In the beverage cooler you'll find "chili peppa watah" ($7.99), a spicy, watered-down juice made from chilies. If you're afraid to commit to the entire mason jar full of juice, you can grab yourself a small taste of it near the condiments.

A craft beer lover's fantasy, **Kona Brewing Company** (75-5629 Kuakini Hwy., 808/334-2739, http://konabrewingco.com, Sun.-Thurs. 11am-9pm, Fri.-Sat. 11am-10pm, happy hour Mon.-Fri. 3pm-6pm, $5 brewery tours daily at 10:30am and 3pm, $9-18) offers not only supreme beer on tap, but also pretty good food. The "brew your own" pizza allows you to pick your toppings and sauces, and there are fish and salad options (although the salads sound much better on the menu than they appear in person). The restaurant can get crowded on the weekends, so call ahead or expect to wait for a bit. If you're going to be in town a while, pick up a growler (full growler $22, refill $13.50, 20 percent off daily 5pm-7pm) and save some money on beer.

A must-try spot for *poke* lovers, the owner of ★ **Umeke's Poke Bowls** (75-143 Hualalai Rd. #105., 808/329-3050, www.umekespoke808.com, Mon.-Sat. 10am-8pm, $10-25) won the Sam Choy Poke Contest two years in a row. You could order teriyaki beef or kalua pork—but why would you? Instead, order a container (or six) filled with the various kinds of *poke* ($16.99 per pound), from spicy ahi to avocado seasoned, grab a fresh Kona-grown mamaki leaf iced tea (the ginger or cinnamon flavors), and head outside to the picnic tables to enjoy the best *poke* around. If you're interested in more of a sit-down experience, try their location in the industrial area near Target.

This is old-school Kona at its finest: A great family restaurant, **Jackie Rey's Ohana Grill** (75-5995 Kuakini Hwy., Kailua, 808/327-0209, www.jackiereys.com, lunch Mon.-Fri. 11am-2pm, appetizers Mon.-Fri. 2pm-5pm, happy hour Mon.-Fri. 3pm-5pm, dinner daily 5pm-9pm, lunch $12-16, dinner $16-32) has a well-deserved reputation for excellence. The restaurant itself has a casual atmosphere with butcher paper lining the tables (and crayons for coloring), but the food is consistently good and the service usually attentive. Most dishes are either fish or meat served in a way that makes them local style—either by including fruit salsas or macadamia nuts or local sweet potatoes. A favorite of mine is the *mochiko*-crusted fish (*mochiko* is sweet rice flour). There is a children's menu available as well as a full wine list. If you like cocktails try the off-menu Ling Mui martini (*li hing mui*, a salted dried plum, is a specialty flavoring in Hawaii).

Markets

Kailua has one of the larger locations of **Island Naturals Market and Deli** (74-5487 Kaiwi St., Kailua, 808/326-1122, www.islandnaturals.com, Mon.-Sat. 7:30am-8pm, Sun. 9am-7pm), a local chain of natural foods stores. It has a coffee and smoothie bar as well as an excellent hot bar. Beer and wine (nonorganic and organic varieties) are available and on sale for 20 percent off every Friday.

Although the hours are posted, it always seems that the **Kailua Village Market—Kona Farmers Market** (in the parking lot next to the Kona Public Library, at Hualalai Rd. and Ali'i Dr., across from Waterfront Row, Kailua, www.konafarmersmarket.com, Wed.-Sat. 7am-4pm) stays open later and that the crafts vendors are there at all times. Beware: Not all the produce and food items sold at the market are in fact locally grown.

CAPTAIN COOK AREA: SOUTH KONA

The best barbecue on the island, **Big Jake's Island BBQ** (Hwy. 11 near mile marker 106, *mauka* side, Honaunau, 808/328-1227, Mon.-Sat. 11am-6pm, $7-12) will make you feel like you're in Memphis. The portions are huge, mouthwatering, and slow-cooked on local keawe wood. The plates all come with rice, coleslaw, and beans. For Hawaiian fusion, try their barbecue bowls of pulled chicken or pork over rice. There is only outdoor picnic-style seating, so it's not the best place if it's raining. BYOB is encouraged and you can grab a beer

from the store next door while you wait. Call ahead because hours vary due to the business's catering schedule.

You might not know what lau lau is, but ★ **Kaaloa's Super J's** (Hwy. 11 near mile marker 107, *makai* side, Captain Cook, 808/328-9566, daily 10am-6:30pm, $10, cash only) will teach you what it is and how it's done right. Yes, it's like you're eating lunch in your auntie's house and that might feel a bit weird for some people, but Super J's true Hawaiian home cooking offers the best lau lau on the island (way way better than what's served at the luau). So what is it? Lau lau traditionally is slow-cooked pork (or chicken) mixed with butterfish and steamed in taro leaves (which are nutrient packed). The meal comes with rice, mac salad, and lomi lomi salad (tomato and salmon salad—like a salsa). Food Network's Guy Fieri has stopped by here—meaning Super J's is now on the foodie tour—but don't let that stop you from getting some of the best (and cheapest) local food you'll have on the Big Island.

The killer view of Kealakekua Bay from the balcony of **The Coffee Shack** (Hwy. 11 between mile markers 108 and 109, *makai* side, Captain Cook, 808/328-9555, www.coffeeshack.com, daily 7:30am-3pm, breakfast mains $12, lunch $10-13) sends tourists flocking here. It can get quite crowded, especially on the weekend. The food is good, though not impressive. There are egg dishes and sandwiches, but you are paying for the view. You can get the same food cheaper other places, but then you'd miss the view.

An alternative to The Coffee Shack is **Oven and Butter** (Hwy. 11 between mile markers 109 and 110, *makai* side, Captain Cook, 808/323-2003, http://ovenandbutter.com, Mon.-Sat. 7am-5pm, Sun. 8am-2pm, $11-14). The operation started off at farmers markets and was so well liked that community members urged them to transition into a brick-and-mortar establishment. Breakfast (served 7:30am-11am) is hearty dishes like biscuits and gravy ($12.45) and kalua pork hash

($13.95), all made in house and with local ingredients. The highlight of lunch (11am-2pm) are the sandwiches such as the Reuben ($12.95) and locally smoked ham and cheese ($11.95), all of which are served on fresh artisan bread. The views aren't as good as those from The Coffee Shack, but Oven and Butter doesn't feel as overpriced and the wait for a table is definitely shorter at this grab-and-go establishment.

★ **Mi's Italian Bistro** (81-6372 Mamalahoa Hwy. between mile markers 110 and 111, *mauka* side, Kealakekua, 808/323-3880, www.misitalianbistro.com, Tues.-Sun. 4:30pm-8:30pm, reservations a must, $18-35) is one of the better restaurants on the island. Even though the strip mall location doesn't seem ideal, the restaurant itself feels quaint and romantic. Service is attentive. The chef ensures that you order the perfect dish and pair it with the right wine. For appetizers, try the marinated beets with candied macadamia nuts. The mains come in good-size portions. Try a dish with local veal or beef, but save room for the award-winning tiramisu or flourless chocolate torte.

A good foodie choice is **Annie's Island Fresh Burgers** (79-7460 Mamalahoa Hwy./Hwy. 11 between mile markers 112 and 113, 808/324-6000, www.anniesislandfreshburgers.com, Kealakekua, daily 11am-8pm, happy hour 3pm-5pm, $15). The meat is local, the salads have local organic lettuce and local vine-ripened tomatoes, and there are vegan options in addition to the numerous hamburgers with all kinds of toppings and savory sauces. The french fries are a must. Beer is available on draft.

Donkey Balls and Surfin Ass Coffee Company (79-7411 Mamalahou Hwy. between mile markers 113 and 114, *mauka* side, Kainaliu, 808/322-1475, www.

alohahawaiianstore.com, Mon.-Sat. 8am-6pm, Sun. 9am-6pm) are not the same donkey balls as those you see in stores throughout Kailua. These donkey balls are better. Donkey balls are dark/white/milk chocolate-covered coffee beans, and they are addictive! Buy a few bags to take with you as a snack or to bring home. There are samples available and the staff is friendly. The coffee drinks are fantastic and huge, so order small.

The outdoor beer garden of ★ **Rebel Kitchen** (79-7399 Mamalahoa Hwy. between mile markers 113 and 114, *mauka* side, Kainaliu, 808/322-0616, www.rebelkitchen.com, Mon.-Sat. 11am-8pm, Sun. 11am-4pm, $10-$16) likely will catch your eye, as it's often packed at night and on weekends. The menu isn't huge, but it doesn't need to be because what they offer is fresh and fast. The salads look like your usual run-of-the-mill offerings, but the dressing is tangy and flavorful with hints of ginger and sesame and even the grilled veggie salad has tons of crunch to it. Most importantly, the prices are more reasonable when you compare them to similar offerings in the Kona and Kohala resort areas. Beer and wine are available.

An institution in town, **Teshima Restaurant** (79-7251 Mamalahoa Hwy./Hwy. 11 between mile markers 113 and 114, *mauka* side, Kainaliu, 808/322-9140, www.teshimarestaurant.com, daily 6:30am-1:45pm and 5pm-9pm, $8-20) has been serving it up the same for years and it works well. It's a casual Japanese-style diner run for generations by the Teshima family, who opened it as a general store in 1929 and then a restaurant in 1940. Get a bento box ($9), to go or to stay. It comes with meat, egg roll, fried fish, and additional sides. Meals from fish to teriyaki beef come with a lot of extras, ensuring that you'll leave completely satisfied.

Getting There and Around

AIR

The **Kona International Airport** (KOA) is just north of Kailua-Kona on Highway 19. The drive from the airport to Kailua is only about 20 minutes. The open-air airport is small, although it can get crowded due to the sheer number of travelers moving through it. Arrive early because the check-in and security lines can get quite long. If you are dropping someone off or coming to the airport to pick someone up, it's free to park in the lot if you are there less than 20 minutes.

Hawaiian Airlines (www.hawaiianair.com) offers interisland flights that tend to board minutes before their scheduled departure times. There are many daily direct flights to Honolulu and a few to Maui; however, to get to the other islands, it is often necessary to travel through Honolulu. From Kona, it is possible to fly directly to the Mainland on airlines such as Alaska Airlines, American Airlines, Delta Airlines, and United Airlines.

SHUTTLE

If you're not renting a car, many of the resorts will arrange a pickup for you (for a fee). If you would like to schedule your own shared ride service, try **SpeediShuttle** (808/329-5433, www.speedishuttle.com, beginning at $14 per person for minimum 2 people). It is a shared ride, although they charge more if you're not traveling with two people. For a private taxi you can expect to pay $25 to Kailua and upward of $60 to the Kohala resorts.

BUS

Via **Hele-On Bus** (www.heleonbus.org, 808/961-8744, $2 per ride, $1 each for luggage, large backpacks, bikes) it is possible, with a little planning, to make it from the Kona side to the Hilo side and from Kona north to Kohala as far as Hawi. Check the website for bus stop locations as well as specific directions on options for taking the bus to/from the Kona airport.

Kohala

Look for ★ to find recommended sights, activities, dining, and lodging.

Highlights

★ **Hamakua Macadamia Nut Factory:** Nibble on macadamia nuts of every variety imaginable while you watch the workings of the factory (page 69).

★ **Pololu Valley Lookout and Beach:** This view of the coastline is spectacular. It's worth driving to the road's end and simply staring for a few minutes, or taking a steep hike down to the secluded beach (page 72).

★ **Puako Tide Pools:** Teeming with sealife, this watery wonderland offers some of the best snorkeling and diving on the island (page 75).

★ **Hapuna Beach State Recreation Area:** With pristine white sands and turquoise waters perfect for snorkeling, bodyboarding, and swimming, this is one of the best beaches on the island (page 75).

★ **Spencer Beach Park:** a favorite for families, this beach is a comfortable camping spot with facilities, shade, and sand (page 76).

★ **Mahukona Beach Park:** Here you'll find an underwater treasure of ruins from the plantation days—a good opportunity for beginning snorkelers (page 76).

© AVALON TRAVEL

The Kohala district, also known as the Gold Coast, is the peninsular thumb in the northwestern portion of the Big Island.

At its tip is Upolu Point, only 30 miles from Maui across the 'Alenuihaha Channel. Kohala was the first section of the Big Island to rise from beneath the sea. The long-extinct volcanoes of the Kohala Mountains running down its spine have been reduced by time and the elements from lofty, ragged peaks to rounded domes of 5,000 feet or so. Kohala is divided into North and South Kohala. North Kohala, an area of dry coastal slopes, former sugar lands, a string of sleepy towns, and lush and deeply incised valleys, forms the northernmost tip of the island. South Kohala boasts *the* most beautiful swimming beaches on the Big Island, along with world-class hotels and resorts.

South Kohala is a region of contrast. It's dry, hot, tortured by wind, and scoured by countless old lava flows. The predominant land color here is black, and this is counterpointed by scrubby bushes and scraggly trees, a seemingly semiarid wasteland. This was an area that the ancient Hawaiians seemed to have traveled through to get somewhere else,

yet Hawaiians did live here—along the coast—and numerous archaeological sites dot the coastal plain. Still, South Kohala is stunning with its palm-fringed white-sand pockets of beach, luxury resorts, green-landscaped golf courses, colorful planted flowers, and inviting deep-blue water. You come here to settle into a sedate resort community, to be pampered and pleased by the finer things that await at luxury resorts that are destinations in and of themselves. Of the many scattered villages that once dotted this coast, only two remain: Puako, now a sleepy beach hideaway, and Kawaihae, one of the principal commercial deepwater ports on the island. In Kawaihae, at the base of the North Kohala peninsula, Highway 19 turns east and coastal Route 270, known as the Akoni Pule Highway, heads north along the coast.

North Kohala was the home of Kamehameha the Great. From this fiefdom he launched his conquest of all the islands. The shores of North Kohala are rife with historical significance, and with beach parks where

Kohala

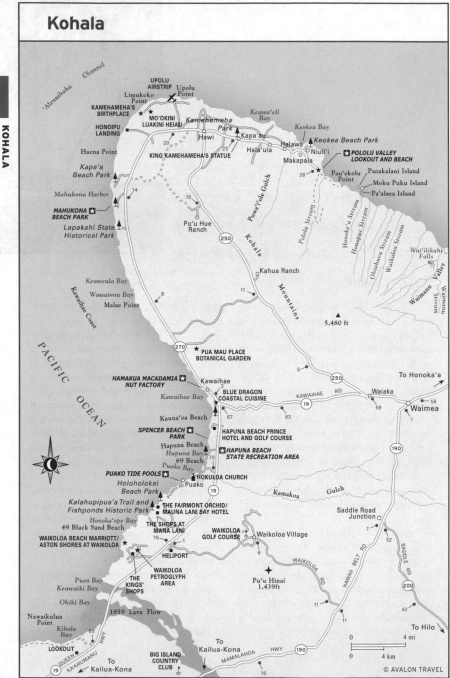

'Alenuihaha Channel

Limukoko Point

UPOLU AIRSTRIP

Upolu Point

KAMEHAMEHA'S BIRTHPLACE

HONOIPU LANDING

MO'OKINI LUAKINI HEIAU

Kamehameha Park

Keawa'eli Bay

Keokea Bay

Keokea Beach Park

Hawi

Kapa'au

Haena Point

KING KAMEHAMEHA'S STATUE

Hala'ula

Halawa

Niuli'i

POLOLU VALLEY LOOKOUT AND BEACH

Kapa'a Beach Park

Makapala

Pau'ekolu Point

Paoakalani Island

Moku Puku Island

Pa'alaea Island

Mahukona Harbor

MAHUKONA BEACH PARK

Pu'u Hue Ranch

Puwa'i'ole Gulch

Pololu Stream

Honoke'a Stream

Honopue Stream

Ohiahua Stream

Waikaloa Stream

Wai'ilikahi Falls

Lapakahi State Historical Park

250

Kohala

Keaweula Bay

Wawaionu Bay

Malae Point

Kawaihae Coast

Kahua Ranch

11

Kohala Mountains

5,480 ft

PACIFIC OCEAN

270

PUA MAU PLACE BOTANICAL GARDEN

5

To Honoka'a

250

HAMAKUA MACADAMIA NUT FACTORY

Kawaihae

Kawaihae Bay

BLUE DRAGON COASTAL CUISINE

KAWAIHAE RD

Waiaka

19

Waimea

56

59

1

Kauna'oa Beach

67

63

SPENCER BEACH PARK

HAPUNA BEACH PRINCE HOTEL AND GOLF COURSE

Hapuna Beach

Hapuna Bay

69 Beach

HAPUNA BEACH STATE RECREATION AREA

190

Puako Bay

PUAKO TIDE POOLS

Holoholokai Beach Park

HOKULOA CHURCH

Puako

19

Kamakoa

Gulch

Kalahupipua'a Trail and Fishponds Historic Park

THE FAIRMONT ORCHID/ MAUNA LANI BAY HOTEL

Saddle Road Junction

Honoka'ope Bay

49 Black Sand Beach

THE SHOPS AT MANA LANI

75

WAIKOLOA GOLF COURSE

Waikoloa Village

7

52

WAIKOLOA BEACH MARRIOTT/ ASTON SHORES AT WAIKOLOA

HELIPORT

6

SADDLE RD

Pueo Bay

Keawaiki Bay

THE KINGS' SHOPS

WAIKOLOA PETROGLYPH AREA

Pu'u Hinai 1,439ft

WAIKOLOA RD

190

HAWAII BELT RD

200

Ohiki Bay

11

To Hilo

Nawaikulua Point

Kiholo Bay

1859 Lava Flow

11

42

LOOKOUT

83

QUEEN HWY

19

KAAHUMANU

To Kailua-Kona

To Kailua-Kona

BIG ISLAND COUNTRY CLUB

MAMALAHOA

HWY

190

16

0   4 mi

0   4 km

© AVALON TRAVEL

few ever go. Among North Kohala's cultural treasures is Lapakahi State Historical Park, a must-stop attraction offering a walk-through village and "touchable" exhibits that allow you to become actively involved in Hawaii's traditional past. Northward is Kamehameha's birthplace and within walking distance is Mo'okini Luakini, one of the oldest *heiau* in Hawaii and still actively ministered by the current generation of a long line of *kahuna*.

Hawi, the main town in North Kohala, was a sugar settlement whose economy turned sour when the last of the seven sugar mills in the area stopped operations in the mid-1970s. Hawi is making a big comeback, along with this entire northern shore, which has seen an influx of small boutiques and art shops. The main coastal road winds in and out of numerous small gulches, crosses some one-lane bridges, and ends at Pololu Valley lookout, where you can overlook one of the premier taro-growing valleys of old Hawaii. A walk down the steep *pali* into this valley is the Hawaii you imagined from movies and reruns of *Lost*.

ORIENTATION
South Kohala: Resort Area

Distinctive for its abundance of large resorts and rental properties, white-sand beaches lined with coconut trees, and its proximity to the airport, the Waikoloa and Mauna Lani areas are geared to meet the needs of tourists. This small area holds enough beaches and restaurants to keep you occupied for days. With three shopping centers located within the resorts, you really never have to leave the premises.

This coast's fabulous beaches are known not only for swimming and surfing, but for tide pooling and awe-inspiring sunsets as well. There are little-disturbed and rarely visited archaeological sites, expressive petroglyph fields, and the best-preserved portion of the Ala Kahakai National Historic Trail. Note: The Waikoloa Beach Resort area *(makai)* is drastically different than the Waikoloa Village area *(mauka)*. Waikoloa Village is where many

individuals who work at the resorts live. You won't find beaches there!

Kawaihae

Kawaihae is a pass-through port town with a gas station and some restaurants worthy of a stop. Some dive outfitters are based out of the harbor; they often take their clients to the waters of South Kohala or Kona, although the nearby waters are just as nice and are less crowded.

Hawi to the End of the Road

Located on the northwest tip of the island, these communities are nearly perfect small towns offering walkable main streets filled with excellent restaurants, art galleries, and coffee shops. The beaches here are rocky but offer breathtaking views of the coast and, if you're lucky, of Maui too. Unlike the southern part of the Kohala district, northern Kohala doesn't look like a lava-filled landscape from outer space. Instead, although it is quite dry in this region, there are gorgeous large trees providing shade from the sun. Spend the day strolling the streets of Hawi, explore the backroads and waters of Kohala on an ATV or kayak, watch the sunset at Pololu Valley, and then finish your day with dinner at one of the many foodie restaurants in Hawi or dancing to live music at the nearby Blue Dragon restaurant in Kawaihae.

PLANNING YOUR TIME

The only reason to plan your time in Kohala is so that you remember to leave that perfect beach you've been lounging on for days. The afternoons in Kohala can cloud over, so plan your day accordingly. If you are spending an entire week in Kohala, as many do, take the time to explore the assorted beaches, such as the well-regarded Hapuna Beach State Recreation Area or a resort beach, which you are free to visit because all beaches must have public access points even for nonguests. Experienced divers and snorkelers should head to the Puako tide pools for a multitude of sealife or to Mahukona Beach Park to discover

South Kohala

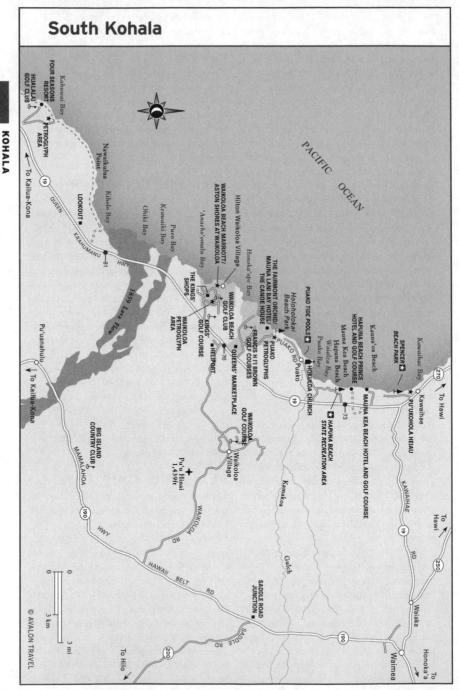

PACIFIC OCEAN

FOUR SEASONS RESORT

HUALALAI GOLF CLUB

PETROGLYPH AREA

Kahuwai Bay

To Kailua-Kona

Nawaikulua Point

LOOKOUT

Kiholo Bay

19 QUEEN

KAAHUMANU HWY

81

Ohiki Bay

Keawaiki Bay

Puako Bay

'Anaeho'omalu Bay

Honoka'ope Bay

Hilton Waikoloa Village

WAIKOLOA BEACH MARRIOTT/ ASTON SHORES AT WAIKOLOA

THE KINGS' SHOPS

WAIKOLOA BEACH GOLF CLUB

WAIKOLOA GOLF COURSE

KINGS' GOLF COURSE

WAIKOLOA PETROGLYPH AREA

HELIPORT

QUEENS' MARKETPLACE

76

THE FAIRMONT ORCHID/ MAUNA LANI BAY HOTEL/ THE CANOE HOUSE

FRANCIS H I'I BROWN GOLF COURSES

PUAKO PETROGLYPHS

Holoholokai Beach Park

PUAKO TIDE POOLS

PUAKO RD Puako

MOKULOA CHURCH

HAPUNA BEACH PRINCE HOTEL AND GOLF COURSE

Kauna'oa Beach

Mauna Kea Beach

Hapuna Beach

Waialea Bay

Puako Bay

MAUNA KEA BEACH HOTEL AND GOLF COURSE

SPENCER BEACH PARK

Kawaihae Bay

270

To Hawi

PUUKOHOLA HEIAU

Kawaihae

KAWAIHAE RD

HAPUNA BEACH STATE RECREATION AREA

73

19

WAIKOLOA GOLF COURSE

Waikoloa Village

BIG ISLAND COUNTRY CLUB

Pu'u Hinai 1,439ft

WAIKOLOA RD

Kamakoa Gulch

To Hawi

To Hawi

1859 Lava Flow

Pu'uanahulu

To Kailua-Kona

MAMALAHOA HWY

190

HAWAII BELT RD

SADDLE ROAD JUNCTION

SADDLE RD

200

To Hilo

190

250

Waiaka

Waimea

To Honoka'a

0 3 km

0 3 mi

© AVALON TRAVEL

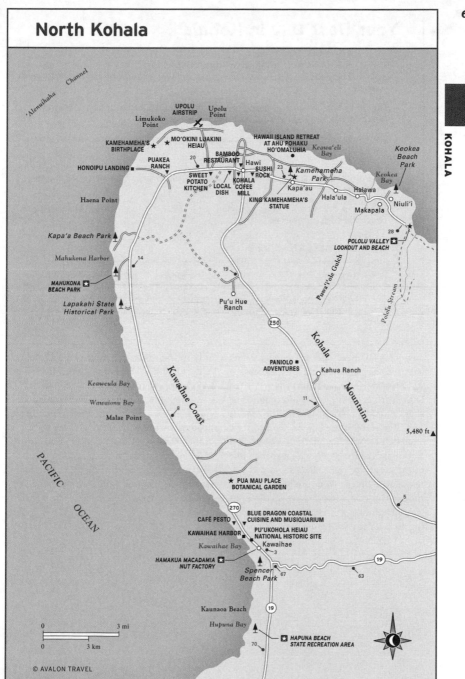

North Kohala

'Alenuihaha Channel

Limukoko Point

UPOLU AIRSTRIP

Upolu Point

KAMEHAMEHA'S BIRTHPLACE

MO'OKINI LUAKINI HEIAU

HAWAII ISLAND RETREAT AT AHU POHAKU HO'OMALUHIA

Keawa'eli Bay

Keokea Beach Park

HONOIPU LANDING

PUAKEA RANCH

BAMBOO RESTAURANT

20

Hawi

SUSHI ROCK

23

Kamehameha Park

Keokea Bay

SWEET POTATO KITCHEN

LOCAL DISH

KOHALA COFFEE MILL

Kapa'au

Halawa

Niuli'i

Haena Point

KING KAMEHAMEHA'S STATUE

Hala'ula

Makapala

Kapa'a Beach Park

28

Mahukona Harbor

14

POLOLU VALLEY LOOKOUT AND BEACH

MAHUKONA BEACH PARK

19

Lapakahi State Historical Park

Pu'u Hue Ranch

Pauwa'a'ole Gulch

Pololu Stream

250

Kohala

Keaweula Bay

PANIOLO ADVENTURES

Kahua Ranch

Mountains

Wawaionu Bay

Malae Point

8

11

5,480 ft

Kawaihae Coast

PUA MAU PLACE BOTANICAL GARDEN

PACIFIC OCEAN

5

270

CAFÉ PESTO

BLUE DRAGON COASTAL CUISINE AND MUSIQUARIUM

KAWAIHAE HARBOR

PU'UKOHOLA HEIAU NATIONAL HISTORIC SITE

Kawaihae Bay

Kawaihae

3

19

HAMAKUA MACADAMIA NUT FACTORY

Spencer Beach Park

67

63

Kaunaoa Beach

19

Hupuna Bay

70

HAPUNA BEACH STATE RECREATION AREA

0   3 mi

0   3 km

© AVALON TRAVEL

Your Best Day in Kohala

- Start your day on the **Ala Kahakai National Historic Trail.** Pick a point on the trail and go for a short walk, leaving plenty of time to stop at any number of beaches (especially the secret ones).

- Stop to sample all sorts of flavors of macadamia nuts and brittle at the **Hamakua Macadamia Nut Factory** on your way north to Hawi.

- Visit the galleries and shops in **Hawi** and eat lunch at one of the excellent restaurants in town.

- Try an adventure like **ziplining.**

- Drive to the lookout at **Pololu Valley** to watch the sunset and witness one of the best views on the island.

- Finish your day with dinner and dancing at the **Blue Dragon Coastal Cuisine & Musiquarium** in Kawaihae.

RAINY-DAY ALTERNATIVE

Most people come to Kohala and never leave the beach, so there aren't many daytime indoor activities in the area. Thus, if it's raining in Kohala, take a peek to the south to Kona and then look *mauka* toward Waimea and see if you can spot any clouds in either direction—and then head to where there are none. If it's raining everywhere on the island, your best bet is to drive the 15 minutes to nearby Waimea or Kona to spend some time inside one of the museums or movie theaters.

an unofficial underwater museum of debris left from the plantation and railroad days.

There are some great trails best visited in the early morning or late afternoon—the short Kalahupipua'a Trail near the Mauna Lani Bay Hotel, the Malama Trail to view ancient petroglyphs, or the Ala Kahakai National Historic Trail, which spans most of the length of the Kohala region. If you need more breaks from the beach, hop in the car and take a scenic drive up the coast (from Highway 19 to Highway 270), watching for whales peeking out from the ocean

(only in the winter) on your way to Pololu Valley for sunset. Even though the distance is short, you can take your time with this drive, stopping at the Hamakua Macadamia Nut Factory on the way and then wandering through the shops in Hawi. Or, use the afternoon for several short jaunts to the north for some of the best lunch places on the island or for ziplining the canopy or even for traveling to Waimea, which is only about 20 minutes away from the Kohala Coast and has cooler weather.

Sights

KAWAIHAE
Pu'ukohola Heiau National Historic Site

While Pu'uhonua O Honaunau is the "city of refuge," **Pu'ukohola Heiau National Historic Site** (Hwy. 270 between mile markers 2 and 3, 808/882-7218, www.nps.gov/puhe, gate hours 7:45am-4pm, park open 24 hours, free), which means "the temple on the hill of the whale," was a place of war. Today, it is one of the best-preserved and most significant temple sites in Hawaii. A walk around the park will take you about 30-45 minutes. Call 808/206-7056 for a self-guided cell phone audio tour or ask a ranger in the visitors center for a tour ($2 suggested donation) if one is available. You can also call ahead to reserve a tour, and I encourage you to do just that as the rangers are a true wealth of information about all things Hawaii. If you're bringing kids, ask the ranger for the Junior Ranger activity book, which comes with a free pin.

Visit early in the morning for the best chance of seeing blacktip reef sharks. Also keep a lookout for birds, as the park ranger guarantees you will see at least 10 different kinds during your visit.

★ Hamakua Macadamia Nut Factory

The **Hamakua Macadamia Nut Factory** (Maluokalani St., off Hwy. 270 between mile markers 4 and 5, 808/882-1690, www.hawnnut.com, daily 9am-5:30pm) might become your happy place (unless you have a nut allergy—then please don't go here). Imagine a room full of macadamia nuts of every variety imaginable, all available to sample for free. Candy corn, brittles, and coffee can be sampled as well. If you're planning on purchasing some nuts to take home, the prices are comparable to the local grocery stores. Or if you really love mac nuts, buy one of the four-pound bags—a good deal for about $40 depending on the variety. You can also watch the interior workings of the factory or try to crack a macadamia nut yourself.

Pu'ukohola Heiau National Historic Site

Pua Mau Place Botanical Garden

This 12-acre garden doesn't get much traffic, but it's quite a sight for plant enthusiasts. The one-hour self-guided tour through **Pua Mau Place Botanical Garden** (Ala Kahua Dr., off Hwy. 270 near mile marker 6, 808/882-0888, www.puamau.org, daily 9am-4pm, adults $15, seniors $13, children 6-16 $5) takes you through the landscaped garden, an unlikely location here in arid Kohala. The focus is on flowering plants, ones that thrive and flourish in a windy and arid environment. While many plants have been established, some of the showiest are the hibiscus, plumeria, and date palm. With so much sunshine and so little rain, this is a harsh environment, and only certain types of plants survive. A greater challenge for the plants is that no pesticides are sprayed and brackish water is used for irrigation. Only the hardy make it, but those that do seem to love it. Heavy mulch guides you along the well-signed paths; plant numbers correspond to a book you take on your self-guided tour. Whimsy is added by the giant bronze sculptures of insects that dot the garden here and there, the aviary, and the Magic Circle, a circle of stones reminiscent of megalithic stone monuments like Stonehenge. The garden is open for private functions such as weddings. Note: At the time of printing, the garden was for sale. Please call ahead before visiting to ensure it is still open.

HAWI TO THE END OF THE ROAD

Lapakahi State Historical Park

Want to experience Hawaii as early settlers did 600 years ago? A visit to **Lapakahi State Historical Park** (Hwy. 270 between mile markers 13 and 14, daily 8am-4pm, gate closes 3:30pm, free), a reconstructed historical village, is a good place for kids and history buffs. The self-guided tour is one of the better ones on the island because the pamphlet available at the small visitors center in the parking lot is user-friendly, and the trail is well marked and maintained. The trail, made up of two 0.5-mile loops, takes about 45 minutes. As you walk clockwise around the numbered stations, you pass canoe sheds and a fish shrine dedicated to Ku'ula, to whom the fishermen always dedicated a portion of their catch. A salt-making area demonstrates how the Hawaiians evaporated seawater by moving it into progressively smaller "pans" carved in the rock. There are numerous home sites along the wood-chip trail. Particularly interesting to kids are exhibits of games like *konane* (Hawaiian checkers) and *'ulu maika* (a form of bowling using stones) that the children are encouraged to try. Throughout the area, numerous trees, flowers, and shrubs are identified, and as an extra treat, migrating whales come close to shore December-April.

Upolu Airport Road Scenic Drive to Kohala Historical Sites State Monument

At mile marker 20, turn off Highway 270 down a one-lane road to Upolu airstrip. You'll know you're on Upolu Airport Road when you see the wind farm on your right. You really need a Jeep to do the scenic drive. Follow the road until it reaches a dead end at the runway. Turn left onto a *very* rough dirt road, which may not be passable. This entire area is one of the most rugged and isolated on the Big Island, with wide windswept fields, steep sea cliffs, and pounding surf. Pull off at any likely spot along the road and keep your eyes peeled for signs of cavorting humpback whales, which frequent this coast November-May. After bumping down the road for about two miles (count on at least 45 minutes if you walk), turn and walk five minutes uphill to gain access to **Mo'okini Luakini Heiau.**

In 1962, Mo'okini Heiau was declared a National Historic Landmark. Legend says that the first temple at Mo'okini was built as early as AD 480. This incredible date indicates that Mo'okini must have been built immediately upon the arrival of the first Polynesian explorers, who many scholars maintain arrived in large numbers a full two centuries later. Regardless of its age, the integrity of the remaining structure is remarkable and shows great skill in construction.

When you visit the *heiau* (temple), pick up a brochure from a box at the entrance; if none are available, a signboard nearby gives general information. The entire *heiau* is surrounded by a stone wall erected for its protection in 1981. In one corner of the enclosure is a traditional Hawaiian structure used in some of the temple ceremonies. On occasion, this building is blown down by the strong winds that lash this coast. Notice the integration of the stone platform. This thatched structure is perfectly suited to provide comfort against the elements. Look through the door at a timeless panorama of the sea and surf. Notice that the leeward stones of the *heiau* wall are covered in lichens, giving them a greenish cast and testifying to their age. A large, flat stone outside the wall was used to prepare victims for the sacrificial altar. The only entrance to the *heiau* itself is in the wall roughly facing southwest. Inside is an enclosure used by the person responsible for finding and catching the human sacrifices that were offered at the temple.

This was once a closed temple for the *ali'i*

only, but the *kapu* was lifted in 1977 so that others may visit and learn. Be respectful, as this temple is still in use, and stay on the designated paths, which are cordoned off by woven rope. Along the short wall closest to the sea is a "scalloped" altar where recent offerings of flowers are often seen. Inside the *heiau* are remnants of enclosures used by the *ali'i* and space set aside for temple priests. The floor of the temple is carpeted with well-placed stones and tiny green plants that give a natural mosaic effect.

A few minutes' walk south of the *heiau* along this coastal dirt track is **Kamehameha's birthplace,** called **Kamehameha 'Akahi 'Aina Hanau.** Rather unpretentious for being of such huge significance, the entrance to the area is at the back side, away from the sea. Inside the low stone wall, which always seems to radiate heat, are some large boulders believed to be the actual "birthing stones" where the high chiefess Kekuiapoiwa, wife of the warrior *ali'i* Keoua Kupuapaikalananinui, gave birth to Kamehameha sometime around 1758. There is much debate about the actual year and place of Kamehameha's birth, and some place it elsewhere in 1753, but it was to the Mo'okini Heiau nearby that he was taken

Lapakahi State Historical Park

for his birth rituals, and it was there that he performed his religious rituals until he completed Pu'u Kohola Heiau down the coast at Kawaihae around 1791. This child, born as his father prepared a battle fleet to invade Maui, would grow to be the greatest of the Hawaiian chiefs—a brave, powerful, but lonely man, isolated like the flat plateau upon which he drew his first breath. The temple's ritual drums and haunting chants dedicated to Ku were the infant's first lullabies. He would grow to accept Ku as his god, and together they would subjugate all of Hawaii. In this expansive North Kohala area, Kamehameha was allowed unencumbered vistas and sweeping views of neighboring islands—unlike most Hawaiians, whose outlooks were limited by the narrow, confining, but secure walls of steep-sided valleys. Only this man with this background could rise to become "The Lonely One," high chief of a unified kingdom.

Together, Mo'okini Heiau, King Kamehameha's birthplace, and several other nearby historic sites make up the seven-acre **Kohala Historical Sites State Monument.** In 2005, Kamehameha Schools bought a large tract of land surrounding Kamehameha's birthplace and Mo'okini Luakini Heiau in order to protect the environs from residential and commercial development that might disturb the sacred nature of these cultural sites.

Note: You'll have to return to Highway 270 the way you came because the road is closed off on the south end (but there is a small dirt turnaround there).

★ Pololu Valley Lookout and Beach

If you are looking for the *Lost* experience on the Big Island, the **Pololu Valley Lookout and Beach** (Hwy. 270 where the road ends) is it. Park your car in the lot at the end of the highway; grab your bathing suit, tent, some food and water; and hike the one-mile trail to the beach (about 30 minutes down and 45 minutes up for a novice hiker). If you're not interested in the hike, the view itself is worth driving to the road's end and simply staring for a few minutes. If you do walk down, the beach at the bottom has wonderful blackish sand, but the shoreline can be rocky and the waves hit hard depending on the day.

It's about 12 miles from Pololu Valley to Waipi'o Valley, with five deep-cut valleys in between, including the majestic Waimanu, the largest. It's not possible to drive to Waipi'o

Pololu Valley Lookout

here, but a super hiker could likely make it between the two.

Locals swear that you don't need a permit to stay here, and it's not patrolled at night—but don't worry, no safety issues have ever been reported. Pitch your tent on top of one of the small green hills and it's likely that you will have the place to yourself, or you won't notice if anyone else is there. There are no facilities (even at the parking lot), so make sure to bring enough food and water for your visit. Enjoy a nighttime dip in the ocean, but take care because the tide can be rough.

Beaches

SOUTH KOHALA: RESORT AREA
Anaeho'omalu Bay (A Bay)

A long, narrow strip of inviting salt-and-pepper sand, **Anaeho'omalu Bay,** or **A Bay** (Hwy. 19 at mile marker 76, daily 6am-7pm), the beach that fronts hotels such as the Waikoloa Beach Marriott Resort and Hilton Waikoloa Village, briefly was split into two parts by the March 2011 tsunami, but through some engineering magic has been made whole again. Enter through the Waikoloa Beach Resort area and park behind Queens' MarketPlace. Although the beach is used by the resort hotels, it is accessible for nonguests via a huge parking lot (where the Hele-On buses wait). All the standard water sports are possible here, and rentals for equipment are available from a kiosk in front of the Marriott. Also in front of the Marriott are lounge chairs that are open to the public. The public restrooms and showers are near the parking lot.

Holoholokai Beach Park and Malama Trail

A shaded park with a grassy area, **Holoholokai Beach Park** (Holoholokai Beach Park Rd., daily 6:30am-6:30pm) makes a nice place to picnic or to fish away the afternoon. There are better places to access to the ocean, but you might want to jump in after walking the Malama Trail to view the **Puako Petroglyphs,** approximately 3,000 individual rock carvings considered some of

Anaeho'omalu Bay

the finest and oldest in Hawaii. The trail is 1.4 miles round-trip (about a 45-minute walk), but avoid going midday when the unshaded trail can be extremely hot. A good walker can do the trail in slippahs, but others may want to wear closed-toe shoes. If you're short on time, just walk the first part of the paved trail (about 5 minutes from the parking lot) to view some of the more photograph-able petroglyphs. Bathrooms and drinking fountains are available in the parking lot. To get there, from Highway 19 (between mile markers 73 and 74) turn onto Mauna Lani Drive, turn right at the first turn on the roundabout to North Kaniku Drive, and then turn right onto Holoholokai Beach Park Road.

Kalahupipua'a Trail and Fishponds Historic Park

The short, peaceful, paved **Kalahupipua'a Trail** (Mauna Lani Bay Hotel, daily 6:30am-6:30pm), which can be connected with the larger shoreline trail system, the **Ala Kahakai National Historic Trail,** passes through ancient fishponds (still stocked with fish) and the Eva Parker Woods Cottage Museum, originally constructed in the 1920s as part of a larger oceanfront estate. To get there, from Highway 19 (between mile markers 73 and

74) turn onto Mauna Lani Drive and gain access through the Mauna Lani Bay Hotel, or for public access follow Mauna Lani Drive and turn left on Pauoa Road; look for the public-access lot on the right side.

If you continue to walk south on the Kalahupipua'a Trail for a few more minutes, you'll end up at **Makaiwa Bay,** a white-sand beach that is a great spot for snorkeling, especially for beginners (the signage is so good here that there is a diagram indicating where to go snorkeling in the water based on your level of expertise). Behind the beach is the Mauna Lani Beach Club (the parking lot is not open to the public before 4:30pm, but you can walk there via the trail), housing the upscale restaurant **Napua** (1292 S. Kaniku Dr., 808/885-5022, daily 11am-4pm and Tue.-Fri. 5pm-9pm, lunch $14-16, dinner $18-40). If you walk through the beach and up the stairs at the end of the beach, you'll be on **Ala Kahakai National Historic Trail,** which passes some amazing-looking homes. You can continue on this scenic path to 49 Black Sand Beach.

49 Black Sand Beach

A little-known, clean and quiet salt-and-pepper sand beach with little shade and calm

ancient fishponds located on the Kalahupipua'a Trail

water, **49 Black Sand Beach** (Honokaope Pl., Mauna Lani Resort Area, daily 7am-7pm) makes for a nice place to get away. The parking lot, including shower and bathroom facilities, is only a minute away from the sand, making this spot a good place to go if you don't want the hassle of parking and trekking to a beach.

To get there from Highway 19, between mile markers 73 and 74 turn onto Mauna Lani Drive; continue around the roundabout and turn right onto North Kaniku Drive, then left on Honokaope Place. Check in with the security guard to get a beach pass.

69 Beach (Waialea Bay)

The name of the beach is mostly what gets curious onlookers to visit it, but they are usually happy they made the trip. The **69 Beach on Waialea Bay** (Hwy. 19 between mile markers 70 and 71, daily 7am-7:30pm) is pleasant: a long, narrow stretch of white sand, lots of shade, and excellent snorkeling. Restroom and shower facilities are available and there are several picnic areas. This sometimes-crowded beach isn't the best in the area, but you won't be disappointed if you spend an afternoon here.

To get to 69 Beach from Highway 19, between mile markers 70 and 71 turn *makai* onto Puako Beach Drive and take the first right onto old Puako Road and then the first left after that; follow the road into the parking area. Note: Nonresidents must pay a $5 fee to park at the beach; however, the same parking receipt is good for both 69 Beach and Hapuna Beach.

★ Puako Tide Pools

One of the most developed fringing reefs on the island, the **Puako tide pools** (Puako Beach Dr., off Hwy. 19 between mile markers 70 and 71) are an underwater wonderland offering some of the best snorkeling and diving on the island. Once you are in the water, look for submerged lava tubes and garden eels hiding under the sandy ocean bottom. There are no facilities or rental

companies located here, so bring in what you need, including equipment and snacks.

Access is available at several different points along the shorefront, but the easiest point may be right before the road dead-ends; from Highway 19 between mile markers 70 and 71 turn *makai* onto Puako Beach Drive and follow the road through the village—even though there is a Dead End sign—and head toward the dead end and turn *makai* into the dirt parking area located right before the "road ends in 500 ft." sign.

★ Hapuna Beach State Recreation Area

Locals allege that the **Hapuna Beach State Recreation Area** (Hwy. 19 near mile marker 69, daily 7am-8pm) is one of the top beaches in the world, and that assertion might be true. Even on weekdays the large parking lot fills up early as locals and tourists alike rush to this white-sand beach to get a choice spot (especially since there is little shade). The turquoise waters are perfect for snorkeling, bodyboarding, and swimming. There is a lifeguard on duty, and the picnic areas, some of which are shaded, have great views of all the action on the beach. If you forgot your snorkel gear, towels, boogie boards, or chairs, you can rent from the **Three Frogs Cafe** (on the grassy area near the parking lot, grill daily 10am-4pm, $10, rentals daily 10am-4pm, cash only). The grill offers tacos, hot dogs, fries, shaved ice, and fruit smoothies. Note: There is a $5 parking fee for nonresidents that is used for beach conservation; given this fee, many beach users have decided to usurp the system by parking on the street outside the lot or by parking at the free lot at the nearby Hapuna Beach Prince Hotel. If you do pay the parking fee, you can use the same parking receipt at nearby 69 Beach.

Kauna'oa Beach

All beaches in Hawaii are public; it's knowing how to access them that is the trick. The Mauna Kea Beach Hotel's beach, **Kauna'oa Beach** (Hwy. 19 near mile marker 68), is another example where you merely have to ask a security guard for a pass to park in the public lot at the hotel. Technically, there are even different bathroom and shower facilities for the public users versus the hotel guests, but since it's the same beach, there is a lot of intermingling, including public use of lounge chairs reserved for guests. Once you're in, you'll want to stay for the entire day. The water is perfect for swimming and there is a long stretch of white sand as well as a grassy area ideal for a picnic or just lounging with a book.

To get to Kauna'oa Beach, from Highway 19 turn *makai* onto Mauna Kea Beach Drive near mile marker 68 and ask the guard if you can have a parking permit for the public beach.

★ Spencer Beach Park

A top family beach and one of the best camping spots on the Big Island (you need a permit), **Spencer Beach Park** (Hwy. 270 between mile markers 2 and 3, 6am-11pm) gets crowded on weekends and holidays. It shares an entrance with Pu'ukohola Heiau National Historic Site. There are picnic pavilions with barbecues, lots of shade, a sandy beach with calm waters, restroom and shower facilities, and a general congenial atmosphere. It's more popular among locals than tourists, probably given the fact that nearby Hapuna Beach provides a more idyllic beach setting. However, this is one of the best public spaces on the Big Island and a top pick if you are someone who likes to people-watch while lounging in the shade.

HAWI TO THE END OF THE ROAD
★ Mahukona Beach Park

There is no sand at this beach; instead, **Mahukona Beach Park** (Hwy. 270 between mile markers 14 and 15) is a modern-day ruin.

Spencer Beach Park

It was a shipping port during the plantation days, and you can still see the decrepit structure of the Hawaii Railroad Company (from 1930) standing in the parking lot. History or archaeology buffs or Instagrammers will want to take a quick detour just to see the modern ruins that are above ground (and snap some selfies). Snorkelers can delight in an underground adventure not so much for the fish, but for plantation and shipping artifacts scattered below the surface. To enter the water, look for the ladder at the old dock. There are no facilities in this section of the beach park; instead, at the fork in the road veer left to the campground area, where there are portable bathrooms. It's not a great campsite, but the picnic area is nice and sheltered.

Water Sports

The Waikoloa resort area and Anaeho'omalu Bay (A Bay) are not as much of an apex of ocean activities as other areas in the region. Each resort tends to offer ocean and beach equipment rental to its guests, and most also offer quick instruction for snorkeling and stand-up paddling. Fees for activities and rentals tend to be higher when purchased through hotels. You'd be better off going directly to the source to get a better price.

DIVING AND SNORKELING

Given that there is a harbor in Kawaihae, it seems like a natural location for diving and snorkeling tours; however, there isn't much activity here because most tourists prefer Kona. There really is no reason to avoid diving and snorkeling here—in fact, the benefits are that it is less crowded than the Kona Coast and the water is just as full of remarkable marine life.

Those with experience snorkeling or diving should explore the Puako tide pools, one of the most developed fringing reefs on the island. One can spend the entire day surveying sealife. There aren't rental agencies here so it is imperative to rent before you come. Alternatively, Mahukona Beach Park with its shallow water presents a good opportunity for beginners to get their feet wet and discover some nearby underwater treasure (or garbage, depending how you look at it).

If you want to join a tour, **Kohala Divers** (Hwy. 270 in Kawaihae Shopping Center, 808/882-7774, www.kohaladivers.com) has a reputation for good service and quality equipment. Kohala Divers offers a PADI open-water certification course ($530). Experienced divers can book a trip such as the popular two-tank morning charter ($139 per person), a two-tank night dive ($149), or a shorter one-tank dive ($100). Both diving and snorkeling equipment is available to rent.

The other option is **Mauna Lani Sea Adventures** (66-1400 Mauna Lani Dr., 808/885-7883, http://maunalaniseaadventures.com), although it doesn't specialize in scuba diving. For certified divers, two-tank dives with gear ($170) are offered and one-tank night dives ($125) are offered a few times a week depending on interest and must

Mahukona Beach Park

be booked over the phone. PADI-certified courses are also available ($800).

BODYBOARDING, SURFING, AND STAND-UP PADDLEBOARDING

The Kohala Coast is a good place to try out your bodyboarding and stand-up paddling skills because the waves here tend not to be too big or rough. Conversely, these conditions are not ideal for surfing. Experienced surfers head to the beach at Pololu Valley, but you have to really want to surf there since a visit requires carrying your board down (and more importantly, up) the steep trail.

Ocean Sports (Queens' MarketPlace and beach shack on Anaeho'omalu Bay, 808/886-6666, www.hawaiioceansports.com) offers rentals for all your ocean needs. Perhaps one of the best deals is on Sunday, Wednesday, and Friday from 10am to 2pm, when for $35 per person you receive unlimited rentals and discounts on their catamaran adventure. This isn't a bad deal considering a stand-up paddleboard is usually $50 for an hour. You must return at the end of each hour with your equipment and can only take it out again if no one else is waiting. If you need some help getting started, they offer beach boys (who are like lifeguards) to aid you in short classes. Snorkeling is $30 for 45 minutes ($10 for an extra person), and stand-up paddling is $40 for 30 minutes of instruction.

KAYAKING

After years of closure, the Kohala ditch tours are back with **Flumin' Kohala** (55-517 Hawi Rd., 808/933-4294, www.fluminkohala.com, adults $135, children $75). The Kohala Ditch is a 110-year-old system of irrigation tunnels and channels that supplied water to plantations during the heyday of the sugar industry. This three-hour adventure tour, offered four times daily (8am, 9am, 12:15pm, and 1:15pm), takes visitors on a 3-mile kayak float through the ditch system. The float is leisurely, so don't expect anything similar to white-water rafting. This slow-paced tour is led by local guides who share stories of Hawaiian history and folklore. This tour is not good idea for those who identify as claustrophobic.

BOAT TOURS

During winter Kawaihae Harbor is a prime location for whale-watching. Leaving from here will save you some time on the road, as this harbor is closer to the majority of the resorts and also tends to be less crowded than Honokohau. Boat trips range from snorkeling and/or diving adventures to whale- and dolphin-watching rides to sunset open-bar cruises.

Extending their monopoly on the water, **Ocean Sports** (Whale Center in Kawaihae Harbor, 61-3657 Akoni Pule Hwy./Hwy. 270, 808/886-6666, www.hawaiioceansports.com) touts a champagne sunset cruise on a sailing catamaran. It is a good deal ($129 adults, $64.50 children, *kama'aina* rates available) for those who like to combine drinking with cruising. The open bar (including a sunset champagne toast) comes with lots of appetizers, and for an extra $25 you can renew your vows on board! The Sunset Sail ($129 adults, $59.50 children) is similar to the champagne cruise, but with less food and no champagne. In summer (April-November), Ocean Sports offers a 3.5-hour morning dolphin snorkel trip ($147 adults, $73.50 children) complete with lunch and an open bar (that they assure is only available after the snorkeling is complete). In winter (December-April) one can combine drinking and whale-watching during the Whales & Cocktails cruise ($119 adults, $59.50 children). Check availability online; the schedules change with the seasons.

Mauna Lani Sea Adventures (66-1400 Mauna Lani Dr., 808/885-7883, http://maunalaniseaadventures.com) similarly has gotten in on the drinking-on-water market with their sunset sails ($99 plus tax adults, $45 plus tax children) that include whale-watching during the winter months.

Hiking and Biking

HIKING

Guided hikes aren't a big business in Kohala because there aren't too many established trails here, but the Kohala Mountains do offer some splendid scenery if you decide to explore on your own or join **Hawaii Forest and Trail** (808/331-8505, www.hawaii-forest. com, adults $169 plus tax, children $139 plus tax). This top-rated tour company offers an all-day hiking experience along the Kohala Ditch trail to Kapoloa Waterfall at the back of Pololu Valley and another hiking trek to other waterfalls in the area. It also takes guests on its six-wheel Pinzgauer vehicle into rugged former sugarcane lands for views of waterfalls and the coast. The hiking portion is pretty minimal (only 1.5 miles), making this tour accessible to anyone comfortable walking that distance over uneven terrain.

BIKING

Highway 19 extending north of the airport provides a nice, flat stretch of road. It's an ideal place to ride fast, and you'll see many serious bikers doing just that. Otherwise, renting a bike simply to ride around the resort area can make for a nice afternoon. Riders wishing to follow the Kona **Ironman route** will want to continue from Highway 19 to Highway 270 north to Hawi to experience the steep climb. Beware: As you travel north on Highway 270 there is not much of a shoulder for bike riding.

For do-it-yourself rentals in the area, **Bikeworks Beach and Sport** (Queens' MarketPlace, 808/836-5000, www.bikeworkshawaii.com) has a nice selection of ultra-deluxe road bikes ($75 per day), deluxe bikes ($60), and cruisers ($25) and has compiled a great list of suggested rides on their website.

If you're aching for a guided or group-riding tour, consider **Velissimo Tours** (808/327-0087, www.cyclekona.com, $125-145 per person), which offers four different day trips. Some trips are for beginners while others are for more experienced riders, like the ride up the Kohala Mountain Range. Both mountain and road bikes are available. Velissimo also offers week-long bicycling tours that include accommodations ($3,200) for those who want to cycle around the entire island.

Adventure Sports

ATV TOURS

ATV Outfitters (Hwy. 270 between mile markers 24 and 25, 808/889-6000, www.atvoutfittershawaii.com, adults $129-149, children 5-11 $80-249) offers an extreme way to experience the Kohala backcountry. There are three options of varying duration, each available twice daily: a historical tour (1.5 hours), the waterfall and rainforest tour (2 hours), and a deluxe ocean and waterfall adventure (3 hours). Prices vary depending on if you are driving the ATV or if you are merely along for the ride. Drivers with passengers must be at least 25 years old. Each tour will take you to out-of-the-way places along the coast and up into the rain forest on former Kohala sugar plantation land. You'll ride over backroads and fields, through lush gullies to waterfalls, come to the edge of ocean cliffs, or dip down to a pebble beach. These fully equipped machines let you get to places that you wouldn't be able to reach otherwise. Safe and reliable, the four-wheelers are easy to operate even for those who have had no experience on a motorcycle. Helmets, gloves, and goggles are supplied and instruction is given. Wear

The King's Trail

A conglomeration of several trails, the **Ala Kahakai National Historic Trail** system stretching over half the island was formalized in 1847 as a way to increase access for missionaries and transportation of goods. But even before that time these trails were the method ancient Hawaiians used to travel the island; they linked together the kingdom of Hawaii's major districts. Thus, the trails present sites of significant events in Hawaiian history, from the arrival of the Polynesians to the islands to the arrival (and subsequent killing) of Captain Cook in Hawaii. Historically, the trail began in the northern part of Kohala (at Upolu Point) and extended into south Puna (at Waha'ula Heiau). Much of this route is not visible anymore due to modern-day construction and/or lava covering it up.

Nowadays, the trail is most visible and walkable between Kawaihae and Pu'uhonua O Honaunau (south of Captain Cook). The National Park Service is working on improving the usability of these trails, but for now, there is about a 15-mile section that one can easily follow. If you start at Spencer Beach Park, you can follow the trail south along the coast. Another well-marked section starts at the Mauna Kea Beach Hotel, where you can travel south toward Hapuna Beach or north to a secret beach that can only be accessed via the trail. Since the trail is a combination of a historical shore trail and the *ala loa* (king's trail or long trail), you will see different signage depending on where you are (many of the signs read Ala Kahakai, though) and in some places it seems like there are two parallel trails. One of the nicest sections of the trail starts near the Mauna Lani Bay Hotel and Bungalows and takes you through ancient fishponds to some beautiful beaches, and then passes by million-dollar homes. The trail can be easily accessed in sections for a stroll of an hour or two, or you can try a larger portion of the trail from Spencer Beach Park to Hapuna Beach (about three miles one-way) if you are looking for a half-day or a whole-day activity. This route will take you through two desolate hidden beaches (Mau'umae Beach and a beach literally called "secret beach") that make for excellent stops.

long pants and closed-toe shoes. Mention the website for a discount; reservations are recommended, as the tours fill up quickly.

ZIPLINING

The ziplining business (also known as the business of suspending oneself on a line in the forest canopy) is flourishing on the Big Island. With an excellent reputation, **Kohala Zipline** (808/331-3620, www.kohalazipline. com, $169 plus tax per adult, $139 plus tax per child) offers the only full-canopy zipline tour on the Big Island. Decide how much of your day you want to spend all strapped up: three hours or a full day. The full-day tour ($249 plus tax per person) includes lunch and waterfall swimming. Tours are offered nearly every half hour from 7:30am to 3pm; if you're on a tight schedule, book ahead of time because tours fill up. You'll probably be able to find an opening if you don't book in advance, but the options might be limited.

HELICOPTER TOURS

The majority of helicopter tours leave from the heliport just south of the Waikoloa resort area or from a heliport next to the Hilo airport. Companies tend to focus on tours to see lava at Hawai'i Volcanoes National Park, and the longer or deluxe tours will circle the island to get a glimpse of Waipi'o Valley and waterfalls in Kohala. These tours are expensive, but if you have the funds do it, people always say that it was their favorite part of the trip—though not people who suffer from motion sickness. Tip: Wear a dark color (like black), otherwise your clothing will be reflected in the helicopter's windows and thus will show up in your photos.

Sunshine Helicopters (808/882-1233 or 800/622-3144, www.sunshinehelicopters. com), one of the larger companies with service on each island, runs a 40-minute Kohala Mountain and Hamakua Valley tour ($169 per person with online discount) and a two-hour

Volcano Deluxe tour that circles the island ($520 per person with online discount or $510 for the early-bird tour).

Another large operation is **Blue Hawaiian Helicopters** (808/886-1768 in Waikoloa, 800/786-2583, www.bluehawaiian.com), which operates tours from both the Kona and Hilo sides with two helicopter options— the A-Star and the Eco-Star. The Eco-Star is touted as "the first touring helicopter of the 21st century," meaning that its seats are more comfortable, it is quieter, and it has larger windows for a less obstructed view than the A-Star. Most importantly, it costs more. From the Kona side, there are three tour options: a 90-minute Kohala Coast Adventure ($213 for A-Star, $259 for Eco-Star), the standard trip to see the waterfalls of the region; the two-hour Big Island Spectacular ($396, $495), an all-encompassing trip that circles the island to witness all its highlights; and the two-hour Big Island-Maui Trip ($440, $495), a quick jaunt over to Maui to view Haleakala Crater and then a glimpse of the Kohala waterfalls on the way back. This particular tour has a six-person minimum.

Golf

The resorts in South Kohala offer half a dozen of the best golf courses in the state, and they are all within a few miles of each other.

Like rivers of green, the links-style **Kings' Golf Course** (600 Waikoloa Beach Dr., 808/886-7888, http://waikoloabeachgolf.com), designed by Tom Weiskopf and Jay Morrish, and the **Beach Golf Course** (808/886-6060), a Robert Trent Jones Jr. creation, wind their way around the hotels and condos of Waikoloa Beach Resort. Both have plenty of water and lava rock hazards, and each has its own clubhouse. Lessons, a golf clinic, and a half-day golf school can be arranged through both courses. Prices are reasonable, ranging $95-145. Off-property guests pay about $35 more per round than Waikoloa Beach Resort guests. Discounts are available after 2pm and for nine-hole rounds after 8:30am. Family golf days, where children under 17 ($25) play nine holes of quality time with their parents, are a great deal for both children and adults ($50). Multi-round packages also available.

Surrounding the Mauna Lani Bay Hotel are the marvelous **Francis H. I'i Brown North Course** and **Francis H. I'i Brown South Course,** whose artistically laid-out fairways, greens, and sand traps make them modern landscape sculptures. The 18-hole courses are carved from lava, with striking ocean views in every direction. Call the pro shop (808/885-6655) for information, tee times, clinics, and lessons. Discounts are available for booking online (www.maunalani.com/g_rates.htm). Resort guests pay $120-170 depending on the time of day and time of year (prices go up $10 in the winter months), while nonguests can expect to pay at least $225 for a round.

The Mauna Kea's classic, trendsetting **Mauna Kea Golf Course** (808/882-5400, www.princeresortshawaii.com/mauna-kea-golf-course/) was designed by the master, Robert Trent Jones Sr., and has been voted among America's 100 greatest courses and one of Hawaii's finest. Deceptive off the tee, it's demanding at the green. It lies near the ocean and has been joined by the more spread-out **Hapuna Golf Course** (808/880-3000, www.princeresortshawaii.com/hapuna-golf.php), designed by Arnold Palmer and Ed Seay, which has been cut into the lava up above the hotels and highway. Both 18-hole courses give even the master players a challenge. Rates for the Mauna Kea course range $165-235 for resort guests depending on the time of day (discounts given for twilight play) and $270 for nonguests. The Hapuna course ranges $80-130 for guests and nonguests pay $150. "Stay and play" discount packages are available from both hotels.

Shopping and Entertainment

SHOPPING
South Kohala: Resort Area

The two main shopping areas in Waikoloa, **Kings' Shops** and **Queens' MarketPlace,** are across the street from one another on Waikoloa Beach Drive. The Kings' Shops are high-end stores such as Louis Vuitton, Coach, Tiffany, and the tiniest Macy's that you will ever see. Across the street, the Queens' MarketPlace offers typical mall selections, such as Lids, Claire's, and Quiksilver, as well as a food court (daily 7:30am-9:30pm).

Hawi to the End of the Road

Hawi and the adjoining Kapa'au are cute towns with a small main street (it's actually Hwy. 270) lined with shops, galleries, and restaurants. It's definitely worth making a short detour here, parallel parking your car and strolling from store to store. The entire walk will take you less than two hours. Yes, there is some Hawaiiana here, but this area has an artist colony feel to it, lending to goods that are higher quality than the standard kitsch you'll find in Kona or Hilo.

ENTERTAINMENT

All the resort hotels in the area have bars with live music on the weekends and sometimes also weekday evenings. The Waikoloa Beach area hosts daily events at the Queens' MarketPlace, Kings' Shops, Hilton Waikoloa Village, and Waikoloa Beach Resort. Many of the events are free and can be found on the resort's website (www.waikoloabeachresort. com). Many of the events are ideal for children—such as Hawaiian storytelling. One notable event is the weekly free concert with Big

Island slack-key guitarist John Keawe. I urge you to attend that show. He plays other places on the island during the week, but you usually have to pay to see him.

For something a little more local, go to **Sansei Seafood Restaurant and Sushi Bar** (201 Waikoloa Beach Dr. in Queens' MarketPlace, 808/886-6286, www.dkrestaurants.com) for weekend karaoke coupled with cheap sushi and drink deals.

North of the resort area in Kawaihae, the **Blue Dragon Coastal Cuisine & Musiquarium** (Hwy. 270 between mile markers 3 and 4, 808/882-7771, www.bluedragonhawaii.com) has the best of both worlds: live music and dancing. It's one of few places on the island where people get dressed up for a night out. No, it's not a club, it's more like an old-time big band dance hall—classy and romantic with excellent cocktails.

In Hawi, **Bamboo Restaurant** (Hwy. 270, Hawi, 808/889-5555, www.bamboorestaurant. info) has live music on the weekends. **Kohala Coffee Mill** (55-3412 Akoni Pule Hwy./Hwy. 270, Hawi, 808/889-5577) also features local artists throughout the week in its small café.

The larger resorts all hold **lu'au** on alternating days during the week (see calendar online at www.waikoloabeachresort.com). They mostly feel like factory luau—getting people in and out and fed quickly. While it is more convenient to simply attend a luau at your hotel, you might want to venture out for a more Cirque de Soleil-style experience at **The Fairmont Orchid** (www.fairmont.com/orchid). This lu'au is more expensive than its counterparts, but it's a true VIP experience and the food is better than at other luau.

Food

SOUTH KOHALA: RESORT AREA

All the resorts in the area have at least one restaurant located on the premises. These restaurants, for the most part, are fine but not notable and tend to be more expensive than off-site restaurants. If you don't want to travel too far away from your hotel or condo, but still want to eat out, there are some worthwhile options nearby.

With postcard views of A-Bay and daily live music, the **Lava Lava Beach Club** (69-1081 Ku'uali'i Pl, Waikoloa, 808/ 769-5282, www.lavalavabeachclub.com, Mon.-Fri. 11am-10pm, Sat.-Sun. 10am-10pm, happy hour 3pm-5pm, $15-30) draws a large crowd. Dinner reservations are a must (you can make them online); however, there is open seating at the bar or at a few chairs located in the sandy area (for those who like to get their feet wet). The food is good enough here, but often you can hear guests complaining about the prices; still, the fun atmosphere and beachfront views keep the place very crowded.

This would be a number one spot on the Mainland, but given the immense amount of great sushi on the Big Island, **Sansei Seafood Restaurant and Sushi Bar** (201 Waikoloa Beach Dr., Queens' MarketPlace, 808/886-6286, www.sanseihawaii.com, dinner Sun.-Thurs. 5:30pm-10pm, Fri. and Sat. 5:30pm-1am, rolls $4-18, appetizers $4-17, entrées $18-30) is simply good. What is of note here is the amazing specials and the fact that it is open much later than almost any other restaurant around. The early-bird special offers 50 percent off sushi, appetizers, and entrées 5pm-6pm on Sunday and Monday. Come early, as tables fill up the moment the clock strikes 5pm. Friday and Saturday there is late-night karaoke (free for 21 and over, 10pm-1am) with drink specials and 50 percent off sushi and appetizers.

If you're seeking something on the lighter side, **Juice 101** (68-1330 Mauna Lani Dr., The Shops at Mauna Lani, 808/887-2244, www.juicebar101.com, daily 6am-5pm) is just the ticket. As their name implies, they have fresh juice squeezed from fruits and greens as well as smoothies. Try the kale smoothie and acai

lu'au at The Fairmont Orchid

bowl to energize you for the day. If that's not your thing, enjoy the breakfast bagels and a cup of coffee. Lunch is available, and kid-friendly too, with options such as grilled cheese. It's more a takeout place than a dine-in joint, but they do have free wireless Internet.

A new addition to The Shops at Mauna Lani, ★ **The Blue Room** (68-1330 Mauna Lani Dr., The Shops at Mauna Lani, 808/887-0999, daily 11am-9pm, $18-32) is modeled after the Blue Room (of course) at 'Iolani Palace, the royal residence located in downtown Honolulu. The interior is decorated with beautiful historical photos of important women of Hawaiian history and the outdoor patio has a nice mixture of native plants that celebrate the land and sea. The vision of the owners was to create a Parisian café that serves high-end local drive-in food. This fusion of styles may sound confusing, but it works. The mains, such as the lau lau roasted pork, are good, but the appetizers like the Kauai shrimp, foie gras, and shrimp spring rolls are the real highlight. I recommend coming for their happy hour (daily 3pm-5pm) or just considering ordering a dinner of several appetizers—leaving room for their flourless chocolate cake. Service is excellent.

Another new addition to The Shops at

Mauna Lani is **Under the Bodhi Tree** (68-1330 Mauna Lani Dr., The Shops at Mauna Lani, 808/895-2053, www.underthebodhi. net, daily 7am-7pm, $6-15) a dream-come-true small café for the vegan/vegetarian/gluten-free/raw crowd. Their banana bread French toast breakfast ($12) is excellent; they also serve hearty egg omelets and large bowls of oatmeal. Lunch consists of locally sourced specials of day, salads, and sandwiches. The best deal here is their happy hour (daily 2pm-5pm), which includes a few different meal deals like soup, side salad, and on-tap kombucha for the bargain rate of $15.

Amid the usual humdrum of resort restaurants, **The Canoe House** (68-1400 Mauna Lani Dr., Mauna Lani Bay Hotel, 808/885-6622, www.maunalani.com/dining/canoe-house, Mon.-Sat. 5:30pm-8:30pm, $42) is a standout. The menu is thoughtful, using local ingredients (as much as possible) to create beautiful, well-executed dishes, and the wine list is extensive. I recommend any of the fresh fish or the rack of lamb. And the view! Right on the ocean, this restaurant makes for an ideal romantic evening. If you want to splurge try the "Captain's Table" blind tasting menu for $100 per person, or $160 with wine pairings.

The Blue Room restaurant is modeled off the 'Iolani Palace.

KAWAIHAE

There is a surprisingly large number of restaurants in this small town, which attracts the overflow of resort visitors seeking food outside the bounds of their hotel. Thus prices are somewhat higher than what you'd expect. There is a harbor right in town, and many restaurants offer fresh seafood.

One of the most fun eating experiences on the Big Island, the ★ **Blue Dragon Coastal Cuisine & Musiquarium** (Hwy. 270 between mile markers 3 and 4, 808/882-7771, www.bluedragonhawaii.com, Thurs.-Sun. 5:30pm-11pm, $18-35) is always crowded with locals and visitors alike dancing away the evening while breaking for bites of the coastal cuisine. If I could award Michelin stars (as it turns out, I can't) I'd give one to chef Noah, who I'm sure we will be reading more about in the future. From the lillikoi julep cocktail to the "live" salad (you'll have to order it to see) to the pork chop cooked in a clove bride with guava sauce to the coocunt pancetta "mash up" with flourless chocolate cake and mango sauce—chef Noah presented me with one of the best and most interactive meals of my life. And…the price point is surprisingly right. Reservations are a must, although sometimes you can get a seat at the small bar. Additionally, the restaurant offers transportation ($35 per person through **Big Island Party Bus**), so you should feel welcome to have that second or fourth julep cocktail as you dance the night away.

An addition to the Blue Dragon family is **Dragon Wagon** (Hwy. 270 between mile markers 3 and 4, Wed.-Sun. 11am-4pm, $4-7) a food truck located in the restaurant's parking lot. The offerings include small bites like six different kinds of sliders ($4 each) and pork belly musabi ($4). But there is also (and somewhat randomly) gourmet hot dogs ($6) and seasoned french fries ($4). This newly opened food truck is a great addition to the area but still is working out some kinks—like where eaters should sit that isn't directly in the sun.

Also in the Blue Dragon parking lot (61-3616 Kawaihae Rd) is the ★ **Original Big Island Shave Ice Company** (808/895-6069, www.obisic.com, Tues.-Sat. 11:30am-5:30pm, Sun. 1:30pm-5:30pm). Shave ice here (small $3, regular $4) is a revelation—shaved ultra-thin and topped with real fruit flavors like mango and guava, this food truck might just win the unofficial Big Island shave ice competition. For those of you who like a little ice cream on your shave ice, not a problem: Add ice cream flavors such as sweet potato or mac nut for just an extra $1.25. My favorite is the azuki bean toppings on a li hing mui ice.

The other choice close by is **Café Pesto** (Kawaihae Center, 808/882-1071, www.cafepesto.com, daily 11am-9pm, pizzas average $13 for a 9-inch wood-fired pizza, dinner mains $18-35), which feels entirely like your hometown Italian restaurant meets Hawaii. The menu is a little all over the place, from pizza and calzones to fish and Thai-style food. I'd stick with the Italian side of the menu. Reservations are recommended.

Located in the parking lot in front of Da Fish House, **Lunch Wagon** (61-3665 Akoni-Pule Hwy, Mon.-Fri. 10:30am-2:30pm, $10) is a food truck with an uncreative name, but some of the best fresh fish in the area—and the price is right. You order at the window and wait (patiently) at a shaded outdoor table for your name to be called. The fresh fish plate of the day (usually with choice of ahi, mahimahi, or ono) is served with two sides ($10). Skip the expensive resort lunch and grab a to-go plate from the Lunch Wagon to bring back to the beach.

HAWI TO THE END OF THE ROAD

Hawi is the spot where ex-New Yorkers or restaurant veterans come to open restaurants, and you will reap the benefits of their decision. Nearly every restaurant in the area offers something better than the next. In fact, one of your biggest hardships in Hawaii will be finding time to eat everywhere in town.

You'll think you're in Pahoa (the hippie enclave of the Big Island) when you see the menu at **Sweet Potato Kitchen** (55-3406 Akoni Pule Hwy./Hwy. 270, Hawi, Mon.-Fri. 9am-3:30pm, $6-12). This (mostly) gluten-free, vegan, farm-to-table restaurant serves up breakfast and lunch delights such as maple and mac-nut granola and "forbidden" shitake congee. Don't come hungry, because this one-woman (sometimes two) show gives new meaning to the idea of "slow food." Yet if you have the time and your hunger levels can hold out, it's worth the wait, especially for the freshly made tonics and chais. Note: Seating is all outdoors and there is no restroom here.

Best known for their *liliko'i* (passion fruit)-infused drinks, **Bamboo Restaurant** (Hwy. 270, Hawi, 808/889-5555, www.bamboorestaurant.info, Tues.-Sat. 11:30am-2:30pm and 6pm-8pm, Sun. brunch 11:30am-2:30pm, happy hour Tues.-Thurs. 4pm-6pm, $20) is a Hawi mainstay offering classic dishes like chicken, fish, and vegetarian options such as polenta, served with a hint of Hawaiiana—meaning that the standard dishes are seasoned with teriyaki sauce, coconut milk, and passion fruit sauces galore. The food is good enough, but the restaurant is located in an early 1900s building that provides a wonderful ambience for a hot afternoon, and the overall experience is worthwhile. There is live music on Saturday nights.

A few doors down from Bamboo Restaurant, **Local Dish** (55-3419 Akoni Pule Hwy./Hwy. 270, Hawi, Thurs.-Mon. 11am-4pm, $15) is the Jewish deli you've been looking for in Hawaii. Classic deli sandwiches, like Reubens, are served on locally made bread. There are even a few vegetarian options such as their grilled portobello mushroom sandwich. Locals in town are a bit sour that this place replaced a popular deli spot, but Local Dish still entices both locals and weary tourists passing through town.

Next door to Local Dish, one of the few authentic Mexican restaurants on the island, **Mi Ranchito** (55-3419 Akoni Pule Hwy./Hwy. 270, Hawi, Mon.-Sat. 11am-8pm, $9-16), is a true taquería and one of the best choices if you're looking for something a little less pricey than the majority of Hawi restaurants. The price is right and the portions are huge. Vegetarian and gluten-free options are available. You won't see the restaurant from the street; it is in the interior of the building where Local Dish is located.

If you're looking for a quick to-go treat while strolling the streets, stop in to **Kohala Coffee Mill** (55-3412 Akoni Pule Hwy./Hwy. 270, Hawi, 808/889-5577, Mon.-Fri. 6am-6pm, Sat.-Sun. 7am-6pm, $7-10) for an ice cream cone or a cookie or take a seat outdoors and listen to one of the live music performances that tend to pop up on any given day. This is a laid-back coffee shop with beverages such as ice-cold chai as well as breakfast bagel sandwiches. Salads and hamburgers are available for lunch.

A treat for those who love sushi and even those who do not, the rolls at **Sushi Rock and Trio** (55-3435 Akoni Pule Hwy./Hwy. 270 in Hawi Town, 808/889-5900, www.sushirockrestaurant.net, Mon.-Thurs. noon-3pm and 5:30pm-8pm, Fri.-Sat. noon-3pm and 5:30pm-9pm, Sun. 11am-3pm and 5:30pm-8pm, $17) truly are a fusion of traditional sushi combinations and local ingredients, such as purple sweet potatoes with ahi and goat cheese. Rolls can be ordered individually or by platter, such as the Ali'i, which includes 32 premium rolls. Feel free to ask the chef to pick your rolls if you can't decide for yourself. The platters are a good deal—the larger the better if you're with friends. The new addition to this restaurant is **Trio,** which originally existed as a semi-separate restaurant with a completely different menu (by the same owner) that now is combined with the sushi menu. If you love sushi, but your partner likes macaroni and cheese, you can avoid the usual dinner fight and dine at one table. The addition of the non-sushi items has changed the ambience of the restaurant for the worse, in my opinion, but Sushi Rock still remains one of the only dinner options in Hawi and thus retains its crowds.

A bit farther up the road in Kapa'au, **Minnie's** (54-3854 Akoni Pule Hwy./Hwy.

270, Kapa'au, 808/889-5288, Mon.-Thurs. 11am-8pm, Fri. 11am-3pm and 5pm-8:30pm, $9) is a surprising find for visitors—although a lot of locals will call it their favorite place in town. The plate lunch, the most expensive item on the menu at $15, includes the fresh fish of the day, two scoops of rice, and one additional side—big enough for two fairly hungry people. I recommend the plate (even just for one person), but if you're craving a burger or even a veggie sandwich, Minnie's has those too. You can enjoy this unpretentious food inside or on the porch watching the cars roll their way to the Pololu overlook.

Getting There and Around

CAR

If you're heading back to the airport from the Kohala Coast, the **last gas station** you'll pass before you get to the airport is the **Shell station** in the **Kings' Shops** in the Waikoloa resort area. The problem is that it's still about 20 miles from the airport, but if you top your tank off you should be okay. There isn't a close gas station south of the airport either. The closest station is probably at Costco in Kailua and it isn't open early in the morning or late at night. If you're heading north from Waikoloa, your next gas station is about 15 miles away in Kawaihae.

TAXI

Not so much a taxi per se, **Big Island Party Bus** (www.bigislandpartybus.com, 808/345-0000) offers groups the option of fitting a large number of people into a van without having to worry about parking, drinking, or dark roads late at night. This is a great option if you are traveling with a large group or multiple families and want a pickup for dinner or even to create your own adventure to a different part of the island.

BUS

It is possible, with some good planning, to make it from the Kona side to the Hilo side and from Kona to Kohala on the **Hele-On Bus** (www.heleonbus.org, 808/961-8744, $2 per ride, $1 each for luggage, large backpacks, bikes).

The North Kohala-to-South Kohala bus is a commuter route for those who work at the resorts. It only runs once daily Monday-Saturday, leaving from Kapa'au at 6:20am, making stops south of Highway 270 (such as in Hawi and Kawaihae) and then on Highway 19 at all the resorts, ending at the Hilton Waikoloa Village. The bus returns north from the Hilton Waikoloa Village at 4:15pm, arriving in Kapa'au at 5:35pm.

A second option gets you farther south to Kona and east to Waimea, but unfortunately only runs Monday-Friday. The bus leaves from Kapa'au at 6:45am and travels south on Highway 270 to the junction of Highway 19, where it goes east to Waimea, arriving at the Parker Ranch Shopping Center and continuing to the Keauhou Shopping Center (in south Kona). From the Parker Ranch Shopping Center, it is possible to connect on a different bus to the Hamakua Coast and Hilo.

Ka'u

Ka'u is known for the route that takes visitors between Kona and Hawai'i Volcanoes National Park. But hidden off the main highway are magnificent, secluded beaches of all sizes and colors—from white to black to green.

Some require a greater sense of adventure than others, not to mention more than the average rental car. A four-wheel- or all-wheel-drive vehicle will serve you well here.

Formed from the massive slopes of Mauna Loa, the Ka'u district presents some of the most ecologically diverse land in the islands. It stretches 50 miles from north to south and almost 30 miles from east to west, housing the longest undeveloped coastline in the state. At the bottom of Ka'u is Ka Lae, the southernmost tip of the state of Hawai'i. It's also the southernmost point in the United States. Many establishments in the area are happy to remind you of this fact and provide you with excellent photo opportunities.

Ka Lae was probably the first landfall made by the Polynesian explorers on the islands. A variety of archaeological remains, particularly around the coastal spots, show the island's immigration history. Much more recently, Ka'u was sugar country. The vestiges of this era can be seen in sleepy former plantation towns that don't even know how quaint they are. Today, Ka'u is known for its macadamia nut and coffee farms. Some locals argue that Ka'u coffee is much better than its Kona counterpart. Nightlife in Ka'u is somewhat lacking, but it doesn't matter much because you will be exhausted from the long walk (or bumpy drive) to a secret beach. It's worth packing it in early to get a morning start at the Saturday swap meet in Ocean View or a walk through the lava tubes of Kula Kai Caverns.

While Ka'u's main towns, Ocean View, Na'alehu, and Pahala, are little more than pit stops, the real charms of the region are tucked away down secondary roads that are hardly given a look by most unknowing visitors. You can discover deserted beaches, turtles basking on the shore, a Tibetan Buddhist temple, an electricity farm sprouting windmill generators, and a less-visited section of Hawai'i Volcanoes National Park. The upper slopes

---

Previous: Wood Valley Temple; Green Sand Beach. **Above:** southernmost point in the United States.

Look for ★ to find recommended
sights, activities, dining, and lodging.

Highlights

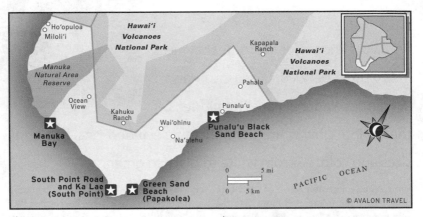

★ **South Point Road and Ka Lae (South Point):** Drive down scenic South Point Road to Ka Lae, the southernmost place in the United States, for a 50-foot jump into the ocean (page 96).

★ **Manuka Bay:** Getting to Manuka Bay is a four-wheel-drive adventure—but the secluded white-sand beach is worth it (page 98).

★ **Green Sand Beach (Papakolea):** A semiprecious stone called olivine gives the soft sand here its distinctive green tinge (page 100).

★ **Punalu'u Black Sand Beach:** You're almost guaranteed to see turtles basking in the sun at this popular, easily accessed beach (page 101).

Ka'u

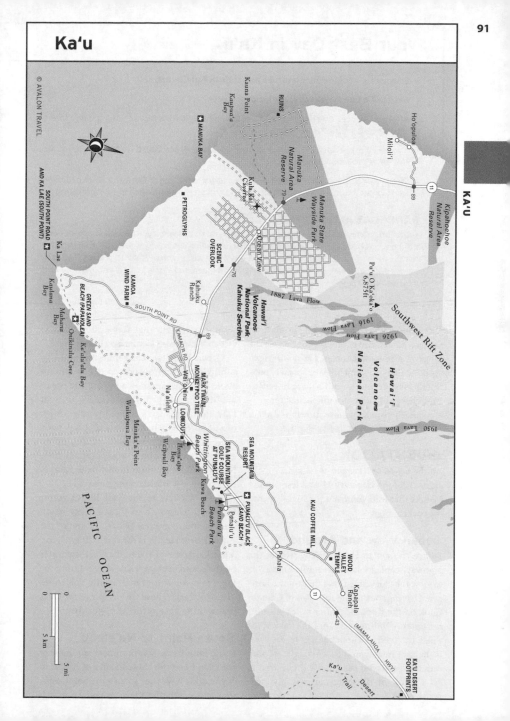

© AVALON TRAVEL

Kauna Point
Kaupua'a
Bay

RUINS ■

✚ MANUKA BAY

Manuka
Natural Area
Reserve

Kipahoehoe
Natural Area
Reserve

Ho'opuloa

Milioli'i

Manuka
Natural Area
Reserve

■ PETROGLYPHS

Kahuku
Caverns

Manuka State
Wayside Park

11

89

Ocean View

79

SCENIC
OVERLOOK

76

Hawai'i
Volcanoes
National Park
Kahuku Section

Pu'u O Kaloka'o
6,875ft

Southwest Rift Zone

Ka Lae

✚

SOUTH POINT ROAD
AND KA LAE (SOUTH POINT)

Kaulana
Bay

KAMOA
WIND FARM

Kahuku
Ranch

1887 Lava Flow

1926 Lava Flow

1916 Lava Flow

Hawai'i
Volcanoes
National Park

GREEN SAND
BEACH (PAPAKOLEA)

SOUTH POINT RD

69

Onikiniki Cove

Ke'alu' alu
Bay

KAMOA RD

Wai'ohinu

MARK TWAIN
MONKEYPOD TREE

Na'alehu

1950 Lava Flow

Muhona
Bay

Waikapuna Bay

Manaka'a Point

Honu'apo
Bay

Waipuli
Bay

LOOKOUT

Whittington
Beach Park

SEA MOUNTAIN
GOLF COURSE
AT PUNALU'U

SEA MOUNTAIN
RESORT

Kawa Beach

✚ PUNALU'U BLACK
SAND BEACH

Punalu'u
Beach Park

Punalu'u

KAU COFFEE MILL

Pahala

WOOD
VALLEY
TEMPLE

Kapapala
Ranch

11

43

(MAMALAHOA HWY)

PACIFIC OCEAN

KA'U DESERT
FOOTPRINTS

Ka'u
Trail

Desert

0 ———— 5 km

0 ———— 5 mi

Your Best Day in Ka'u

- Start with an early-morning lava tube tour at **Kula Kai Caverns.**

- Head to **Ka Lae** (South Point) and jump off the cliff.

- After you recover, travel farther down South Point Road for a hike or a bumpy ride to the **Green Sand Beach** for a swim.

- If you want to just relax, head straight to the **Punalu'u Black Sand Beach,** where you are guaranteed to see some turtles.

- Stop in at **Hana Hou** (the southernmost restaurant in the United States) for lunch or dinner. Don't forget the award-winning pie. If it's a Friday night you might catch some live local music.

RAINY-DAY ALTERNATIVE

The Ka'u district is one of the driest on the island, so rain is unlikely. If you happen to experience a downpour, all is not lost. Try booking a lava tube tour with **Kula Kai Caverns or visiting the Ka'u Coffee Mill.** A third option is to drive to Wood Valley with the **Wood Valley Temple** as your destination. Wood Valley is already lush and green, and a little rain will only make it seem more extraordinary.

and broad pasturelands are the domain of hunters, hikers, and *paniolo,* who still ride the range on sure-footed horses. Those willing to abandon their cars and hike the sparsely populated coast or interior of Ka'u are rewarded with views of landscapes untouched for generations. Time in Ka'u moves slowly and *aloha* still forms the basis of day-to-day life.

ORIENTATION

All the towns of Ka'u and the district's main sights lie along Highway 11 or a few smaller byways that lead you from the highway into the backcountry.

Ocean View and Around

Before you get to Ocean View, stop at the highway scenic lookout near mile marker 75 to view the black lava flows that fill the horizon. Driving south from the town of Captain Cook on the Kona side, after miles of uninterrupted winding road (not the easiest for those inclined to carsickness) Ocean View is the first town you'll pass—a sight for sore eyes for those who need to use the restroom, get a drink, or fill up on surprisingly inexpensive gas. Services are located in two small

shopping centers that flank the highway: Ocean View Town Center and Pohue Plaza.

Ocean View is a conglomeration of five subdivisions that pushes up the mountain about six miles and down toward the ocean another three. The highest lots are at about 5,000 feet. This is an unincorporated town of self-sufficient individuals that has been carved out of rough volcanic rubble with an overlay of trees and bush. Many families move here to build retirement homes or the homes they could not afford on the Kona side.

Besides a visit to the Kula Kai Caverns, there is little to do in Ocean View itself. Because there are few lights, it's one of the island's best locations for stargazing. Ocean View has some of the highest asthma rates on the island because it's downwind from the vog (volcanic smog) of Hawai'i Volcanoes National Park. Those with respiratory issues may want to pass by this area quickly.

South Point to Na'alehu

South Point is the southernmost landmass of the island and the United States of America. If you don't have time to visit the point itself, you can catch the view as you approach

Ocean View and Around

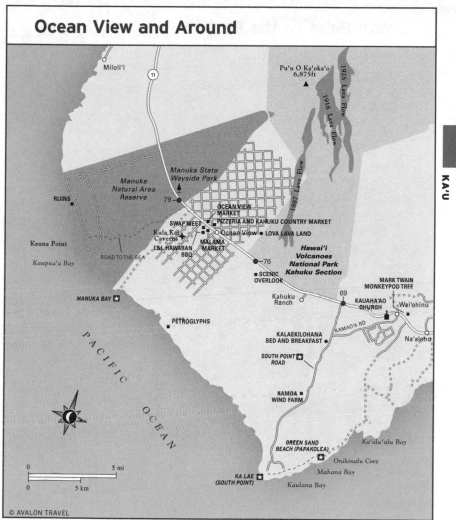

Miloli'i

11

Pu'u O Ka'oka'o
6,875ft

1926 Lava Flow

1916 Lava Flow

1887 Lava Flow

Manuka State
Wayside Park

Manuka
Natural Area
Reserve

RUINS

79

OCEAN VIEW
MARKET

SWAP MEET

PIZZERIA AND KAHUKU COUNTRY MARKET

Kula Kai
Caverns

Ocean View

LOVA LAVA LAND

MALAMA
MARKET

L&L HAWAIIAN
BBQ

Hawai'i
Volcanoes
National Park
Kahuku Section

Kauna Point

Kaupua'a Bay

ROAD TO THE SEA

76

SCENIC
OVERLOOK

MARK TWAIN
MONKEYPOD TREE

MANUKA BAY

Kahuku
Ranch

69

KAUAHA'AO
CHURCH

Wai'ohinu

PETROGLYPHS

KAMAO'A RD

Na'alehu

KALAEKILOHANA
BED AND BREAKFAST

SOUTH POINT
ROAD

PACIFIC

OCEAN

KAMOA
WIND FARM

GREEN SAND
BEACH (PAPAKOLEA)

Ka'alu'alu Bay

Onikinalu Cove

Mahana Bay

KA LAE
(SOUTH POINT)

Kaulana Bay

0   5 mi
0   5 km

© AVALON TRAVEL

the area from the west side of the island. Look for the massive windmills dotting the landscape. As you drive east of South Point you'll pass by the Kahuku section of Hawai'i Volcanoes National Park, a newer and less-traveled portion of the park that offers wonderful birding opportunities. Cashing in on its proximity to South Point, the closest town, Na'alehu, is best known as the place that has all the "southernmost" restaurants, bars, and bakeries. It has some of the better

culinary delights in the area. Check out the overhanging monkeypod trees forming a magnificent living tunnel in front of some of the former plantation managers' homes as you pass through on Highway 11.

Highway 11 South of Hawai'i Volcanoes National Park

As you climb north up the coast you'll pass through **Punalu'u,** an important port during the sugar boom of the 1880s. Notice

South Point to the Park

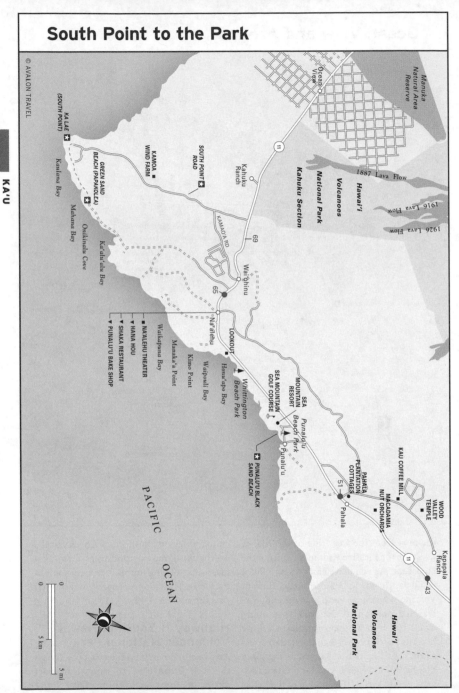

© AVALON TRAVEL

KA'U

KA LAE (SOUTH POINT)

Kaulana Bay

GREEN SAND BEACH (PAPAKOLEA)

KAMOA WIND FARM

SOUTH POINT ROAD

Kahuku Ranch

Hawai'i Volcanoes

National Park

Kahuku Section

Manuka Natural Area Reserve

Ocean View

1887 Lava Flow

1916 Lava Flow

1926 Lava Flow

Onkimalu Cove

Maluna Bay

Ka'alu'alu Bay

KAMA'OA RD

69

Wai'ōhinu

65

Nā'ālehu

LOOKOUT

PUNALU'U BAKE SHOP

SHAKA RESTAURANT

HANA HOU

NĀ'ĀLEHU THEATER

Waikapuna Bay

Manakā'a Point

Kimo Point

Waipouli Bay

Honu'apo Bay

Whitington Beach Park

SEA MOUNTAIN GOLF COURSE

SEA MOUNTAIN RESORT

Punalu'u Beach Park

Punalu'u

PUNALU'U BLACK SAND BEACH

PAHALA PLANTATION COTTAGES

51

Pahala

KAU COFFEE MILL

MACADAMIA NUT ORCHARDS

WOOD VALLEY TEMPLE

43

Kapapala Ranch

11

Hawai'i Volcanoes

National Park

PACIFIC OCEAN

0

5 km

0

5 mi

the tall coconut palms in the vicinity and the fishpond behind the beach, both unusual for Kaʻu. Punaluʻu means "diving spring," named after freshwater springs found on the floor of the bay—making for some cold ocean water. Native divers once paddled out to sea, then dove with calabashes that they filled with freshwater from the underwater springs. This was the main source of drinking water for the region.

The string of flat-topped hills in the background are the remains of volcano cones that became dormant about 100,000 years ago. In sharp contrast with them is **Loʻihi Seamount,** 20 miles offshore and about 3,000 feet below the surface of the sea. This very active submarine volcano is steadily building and should reach the surface in just a few tens of thousands of years. Opportunists suggest investing in real estate there now.

Some 22 miles southwest of the main section of Hawaiʻi Volcanoes National Park is **Pahala,** clearly marked off Highway 11. The Hawaiʻi Belt Road flashes past this hamlet, but if you drive into it, you'll find one of the best-preserved examples of a classic sugar town in the islands. Not long ago, the hillsides around Pahala were blanketed by fields of cane and dotted with camps of plantation workers. Today, the huge mill is gone, and only the whir of a modern macadamia nut-processing plant now breaks the stillness. At least 40 farms now produce Kaʻu coffee in hillside plantations above Pahala; while not as well-known as Kona coffee, it's gaining a reputation for itself.

PLANNING YOUR TIME

Most visitors spend at most a day in this area as they travel between Kona and Hawaiʻi Volcanoes National Park. The best way to experience Kaʻu is as a road trip: start either on the west or east side of the district and stop at successive places of interest along Highway 11.

Kaʻu often is the hottest part of the island, and is thus best experienced early in the morning while the day is still cool. The best midday adventures are those that involve cooling off. The most accessible beach is the shaded Punaluʻu Black Sand Beach. It's often crowded with locals picnicking and camping as well as visitors flocking to get a look at the many turtles that make it home. (I can't guarantee much in life, but I promise you'll see a turtle here.)

Those eager for solitude can use four-wheel-drive cars to reach secluded beaches via the very rough Road to the Sea or Manuka Bay Road or to venture up the mountain into the Kahuku Section of Hawaiʻi Volcanoes National Park. If hot-weather off-roading doesn't suit you, make a reservation with Kula Kai Caverns to spelunk with a guide through one of the most complex lava tube systems in the world.

For those on the culinary tour of the island, Kaʻu houses the essential stops of the Kaʻu Coffee Mill in Pahala for free samples galore of macadamia nuts as well as the Hana Hou restaurant and Punaluʻu Bake Shop, both in Naʻalehu. Their macadamia nut pie, sweet breads, and *malasadas* are welcome treats on the way back to the national park or Kona.

KAʻU

Sights

OCEAN VIEW AND AROUND
Kula Kai Caverns

Part of the Kanohina Lava Tube system—one of the most complex lava systems in the world—the **Kula Kai Caverns** (Hwy. 11 between mile markers 78 and 79, 808/929-9725, www.kulakaicaverns.com) are only 1,000 years old. There are other places on the island to view lava tubes (and many of these sites are free), but you won't regret this tour. The enthusiastic and extremely knowledgeable guides provide you with information not only about the formation of this particular tube, but about the geological formation of the greater area. The standard tour ($20 adults, $10 children) moves slowly and lasts about 40 minutes. You're in wide-open space as you move through the caverns. There are some uneven spots, but the paths are well lit. Those who are not claustrophobic should try the "crawl tour" ($60), which takes you on your hands and knees through some additional tunnels, or the "two-hour tour" ($95 adults, $65 children) to explore even more tunnels in the labyrinth. Advance reservations are required to gain entrance into the gated community where the tunnels are located.

SOUTH POINT TO NA'ALEHU
★ South Point Road and Ka Lae (South Point)

South Point is exactly what you think it is—the southernmost landmass of the island and the United States of America. It lies at a latitude 500 miles farther south than Miami and 1,000 miles below Los Angeles. Known in Hawaiian as Ka Lae, it was probably the first landfall made by the Polynesian explorers on the islands. Most people drive down **South Point Road** (off Hwy. 11 between mile markers 69 and 70) so that they can say they've been there and then to do one of the most thrilling activities possible on the Big Island—jump off Ka Lae and make the 50-foot drop into the ocean. Luckily, there is a ladder available to get you back to the top. On your way down South Point Road to Ka Lae, look at the Kamoa Wind Farm—where windmills go to

the southernmost point in the United States

die—and the mostly functioning Pakini Nui Wind Farm towering overhead.

The sign to South Point Road will be obvious off Highway 11. Follow the road south for 12 miles for some of the best photo opportunities on the Big Island. The drive down South Point is now paved and easy for any car, although it is narrow, so watch for oncoming cars and pull off to the side if necessary. The road splits somewhat—stay to the right. Where the road ends you'll surely see many other cars parked and you should also park here. Unless you're pressed for time, don't be so quick to turn back just yet. From Ka Lae most visitors continue on to the **Green Sand Beach** just a few minutes east of the point.

Mark Twain Monkeypod Tree

All the guidebooks list the **Mark Twain Monkeypod Tree** (Hwy. 11 near mile marker 66) in Wai'ohinu as an attraction, but it's really just a medium-size tree surrounded by a fence, not really worth a stop. Just stick your head out the window if you happen to see the faded sign that indicates the location of the tree. The story goes that Mark Twain planted the original tree in 1866, but it was blown down during a hurricane in 1957. The tree that now stands grew from a shoot from the original tree trunk.

Na'alehu Theater

The **Na'alehu Theater** (Hwy. 11, corner of Na'alehu Spur Rd.) is a unique sight for those interested in plantation architecture or urban decay. It is part of a group of theaters that were constructed in the 1930s by a Japanese entrepreneur (the other two extant are the Kona Theater in Captain Cook and the Aloha Theatre in Kainaliu Town). At the height of the plantation days these theaters served as the centers of entertainment and news for their communities. Allegedly, at one time, each plantation community had its own theater. Nowadays, the graffiti on the exterior of the building says it all: "save me." The community hopes that the building will eventually be restored and turned into a community theater, but until then, this modern ruin deserves some marveling (solely from the exterior).

HIGHWAY 11 SOUTH OF HAWAI'I VOLCANOES NATIONAL PARK
Ka'u Coffee Mill

While the **Ka'u Coffee Mill** (96-2694

The Dalai Lama visited the Wood Valley Temple in 1980.

Wood Valley Rd., 808/928-0550, http://kaucoffeemill.com, daily 8:30am-4:30pm) is educational in the sense that the storefront offers a history of growing, processing, and roasting coffee in this region, it also offers my favorite things: plenty of free samples of coffee and **Hamakua Macadamia Nuts.** Upon walking in, you might be thinking, "Wait, these free samples look familiar!" That's very observant of you: Indeed, you have seen these samples before. The Ka'u Coffee Mill is a sister store to the glorious Hamakua Macadamia Nut Factory in North Kohala. This location is different from the North Kohala one; here, the story is coffee, with a tour around the coffee mill. There the story is mac nuts with a view into the processing plant. The customer service and knowledgeable staff are excellent here.

Wood Valley Temple

Just a few miles north of the Black Sand Beach you'll find the turnoff to **Pahala** town. There is little to do or see here; however, the village presents one of the best-preserved examples of a classic sugar town in the islands. Head into town on the main road from the highway and continue to the stop sign at Pikake Street. Turn right. Pikake takes you to the edge of town; continue straight up the road about five miles until you come to the forest. At the forest, follow the paved road left. You've arrived in Wood Valley—a hidden forest of eucalyptus trees in the back of town.

Here you'll find the **Wood Valley Temple.** It's the first building on your right, marked by colorful prayer flags. Park and walk up to the temple to see the gold Buddha. You'll feel like you're anywhere but Hawaii. The retreat facility at one time housed a Japanese Shingon Mission. When the Shingon sect moved to a new facility in Kona, this building was abandoned and given to Wood Valley Temple. The grounds, hallowed and consecrated for decades, already held a Nichiren temple, the main temple here today, which was dismantled in 1919 at its original location and rebuilt on its present site to protect it from lowland flooding. The Dalai Lama visited in 1980 to dedicate the temple and again in 1994, when he addressed an audience of more than 3,500 people. Programs vary, but people genuinely interested in Buddhism come here for meditation and soul-searching. Services are at 7am and 6pm are led by the Tibetan monk in residence. Visitors are welcome, but are asked to enter the compound as quietly as possible.

Beaches

OCEAN VIEW AND AROUND
★ Manuka Bay

If you're tired of the busloads of tourists at other beaches, this is the spot for you. You will think you are lost as you traverse the lava rocks on your way to the beach at **Manuka Bay** (Hwy. 11 near mile marker 83). The white-sand beach is secluded (more reminiscent of Mexico than Hawaii). You can explore ancient petroglyphs on the north side of the bay. Another activity is foraging for salt: collect it in a ziplock bag, take it home, and let it dry—do-it-yourself Hawaiian sea salt.

Watch out for bees; on a recent visit they were swarming in abundance.

A four-wheel-drive vehicle is a must. This adventure is as much about off-roading as it is about the beach. Near mile marker 83, turn right onto a dirt road on the *makai* side of the highway. The road is unmarked; look for a sign about respecting the area where the unmarked Manuka Bay road meets Highway 11. If you get to Manuka State Wayside Park, you've gone too far. Once on the road, always veer to the right if the road forks. The ride can be a long and difficult, but it is worth it.

Ka'u Scenic Drive or Bike

Views of the coast and rolling green hills are everywhere on this road from Na'alehu.

The drive northeast on Highway 11 from Na'alehu to Hawai'i Volcanoes National Park is one of the prettiest drives on the Big Island, with splendid views of the coast and rolling green hills on the *mauka* side of the road. As lovely as this drive is, it's also worth considering the upper road through the hills. This drive is slower than the highway route but the views are spectacular and the road is now paved, making it an easy journey. If you're a biker, consider riding this route; it offers some challenging hills and very little car traffic. You'll feel like you have the entire island to yourself.

The drive can start from either direction—from the north in Pahala (about 22 miles south of Hawai'i Volcanoes National Park) or from the south in Na'alehu. It is somewhat easier to start in Na'alehu because the route is obvious from there. The drive starts on Ka'alaiki Road, directly to the left of the Punalu'u Bake Shop. Drive up the hill (passing a cemetery on your left) and continue up the hill veering right. Continue on this road for nearly 45 minutes, passing ranches, a large metal ball (the southernmost FAA radar used for air-traffic control), coffee plantations, and macadamia nut trees. The drive ends at the western part of Pahala town. There, you can turn either left or right to get through the town and back to Highway 11. The easier way is to turn left and drive about 0.6 mile. Then make a sharp right onto Pikake Street (which is likely unmarked) and left onto Kamani Street, which leads back to Highway 11. If you turn left (or north) onto Pikake Street (instead of turning right to get onto the highway), Pikake turns into Wood Valley Road, on which you can extend your drive and check out the Ka'u Coffee Mill and Wood Valley Temple.

Road to the Sea

Another excellent four-wheeling route is the six-mile-long Road to the Sea. It's not for the faint of heart (or for those who get carsick). Amazingly, people live on this road and make the commute daily. At Highway 11, between mile markers 79 and 80, turn *makai* onto the dirt road. The short drive can take almost 45 minutes, but the journey is worth it. You

arrive at a secluded green-and-black-sand beach where you can swim and snorkel. Be careful: the water depth drops off quickly.

Before you reach the beach at the end of the road, you'll notice a clear turnoff to another bad road. This road leads to Manuka Bay. It's even rougher than the Road to the Sea, requiring a powerful four-wheel-drive vehicle with a lot of clearance. If you can make it part of the way on the turnoff road, it's not too far to get out of the car and walk to the rest of the way to Manuka Bay.

SOUTH POINT TO NA'ALEHU
★ Green Sand Beach (Papakolea)

Ever seen green sand? It's what results when lava containing olivine, a green semiprecious stone, becomes weathered by wind and time. Visit the **Green Sand Beach at Papakolea** (off South Point Rd. from Hwy. 11 between mile markers 69 and 70) to see it for yourself. Don't expect to see something bright green—it's more of a green tinge. Getting to the beach is a journey in itself, so some visitors like to make a day out of it (or at least a half day).

To get to the beginning of the road/trail to the beach, take South Point Road to the end and then drive toward the left on the paved road when you see the sign for "Green Sand Beach" (and an arrow pointing to the left). You'll know when to stop when you see other cars parked in a makeshift parking area. From here, you can walk the rest of the way to the beach. (Please do so: People driving past this point have caused severe erosion of the land.)

Recently, a few tour companies have begun shuttling visitors to the beach for a small fee.

If you decide not to hitch a ride, pay for a ride, or drive it yourself, from the parking area to the beach is an easy 45-minute walk, less than three miles; just stay to the left. Bring lots of water, a hat, and some sunscreen; there's no shade and the sun gets hot. You'll know you've arrived at the beach when you see an eroded cinder cone at the edge of the sea. Getting down to the beach takes some skill—go slow and use the path that has already been carved out. Watch your footing to ensure that you don't slip. The beach is soft (and greenish), but it can get windy and the waves can get rough. People camp unofficially here, but there is a slim chance of getting kicked out. There are no facilities, so plan ahead.

HIGHWAY 11 SOUTH OF HAWAI'I VOLCANOES NATIONAL PARK
Whittington Beach Park

Located three miles north of Na'alehu, **Whittington Beach Park** (Hwy. 11 near mile marker 60) is a great spot for a picnic or stretching your legs. The turnoff to the park is well marked from the main highway. On the

The olivine in the soil makes the sand appear green at the aptly named Green Sand Beach.

north (or left) side of the parking lot are tide pools that are protected from the powerful waves—an ideal area for snorkeling and swimming. It's also a great place to see turtles. On the right side (past the picnic tables) is a sugar plantation ruin, the remnants of an old dock. A rail line from the Ka'u cane lands terminated here for shipment of raw sugar to be processed elsewhere. Camping is possible with a county permit. The well-maintained facilities include restrooms, a drinking fountain, and a covered picnic area, making it a good place to pitch a tent.

Kawa Beach

Kawa Beach (Hwy. 11 between mile markers 58 and 59) is Hawaiian Homeland territory, and therefore it's essential that you are friendly to those who reside on that land. This black-sand beach is nearly secluded, much quieter than its better-known counterpart, Punalu'u, down the road, There are no signs to alert you to the turnoff, just a bunch of Kanaka Maoli flags (*kanaka maoli* means "true people" in the Hawaiian language) and signs that say "take back Hawaii." The

unmarked road is obvious, but the gate is locked so that cars cannot use it. Park outside the gate on the highway and it will take you about 30 minutes to walk back to the beach. When you arrive, you'll be happy you did. Locals surf here (it was apparently an ancient surfing spot), but amateurs should be cautious of the waves.

★ Punalu'u Black Sand Beach

I can guarantee that you will see turtles lazily basking in the sun at **Punalu'u Black Sand Beach** (Hwy. 11 between mile markers 56 and 57). So will the busloads of tourists that you'll have to compete with to take a picture. It is the most easily accessible and nicest beach in the area, so it gets busy, especially on weekends. Park on either the right side of the beach near the picnic stands, bathroom, and showers, or on the left side closer to the beach itself. On the left side, there are drinks for sale on the weekends and a lovely pond, filled with lily pads and ducks (the area is maintained privately). Camping is allowed here; on holiday weekends local families take full advantage of the opportunity.

Recreation

FISHING

The Ka'u coast, with its impressive jagged coastline, offers excellent conditions for shore fishing. If you are at South Point or Road to the Sea you'll likely see locals with their huge trucks and extremely long and flexible rods fishing for *ulua*, a general term for reef fish of several varieties that usually weigh between 10 and 100 pounds. You don't need a permit to fish in this area, but you'll need to respect the locals as fishing (and especially night fishing) can be a territorial endeavor, and your efforts in the same spot might not be welcomed. There aren't any rental places around here so you'll need to bring your own equipment.

HIKING
Ocean View and Around
MANUKA STATE WAYSIDE PARK

Once a privately owned botanical garden, the 13.4-acre **Manuka State Wayside Park** (Hwy. 11 near mile marker 81) features over 150 species of trees. It's a must-see for plant enthusiasts, but not a necessary stop for those with limited time. Signs identify the flora you'll see over the two-mile loop around the park. The trail is easy and takes about 60-90 minutes to complete. There's a small lava pit around the halfway point. Don't forget the mosquito spray!

South Point to Na'alehu

KAHUKU SECTION OF HAWAI'I VOLCANOES NATIONAL PARK

The newly opened **Kahuku section of Hawai'i Volcanoes National Park** (Hwy. 11 between mile markers 70 and 71, entrance gate opens at 9am and closes at 3pm) was purchased in 2003 from the Kahuku Ranch (parts also are owned by the Nature Conservancy). This 116,000-acre portion of the park looks completely different from its main section. Originally preserved as ranchland, it wasn't ravaged by lava and so includes lots of large old trees and native Hawaiian species. There are a few different options for visiting this section of the park: by car, bike, on your own by foot, or on a guided hike. If you drive, you can begin at the turnoff for the park. Take note that while the scenic drive option begins on a graded gravel road suitable for all vehicles, it soon turns into a four-wheel-drive-only path. With views of Ka Lae down below and rolling pastures up above, this 12-mile round-trip drive presents an excellent opportunity to spot native forest birds and rare yellow-flowering ohia lehua trees. This route is also possible by bike—fantastic training for you budding ironmen and ironwomen. If you are a do-it-yourself hiker, there are five trail options: the shortest is a strenuous 0.4-mile loop up a cinder cone, the longest a 4.7-mile loop with a 520-foot elevation change up the west edge of the 1887 lava flow.

Guided hikes do not require reservations and are free. There is no ranger station here, but at the bottom of the road (where it intersects with Hwy. 11) is an information board with postings about the park and its offerings. Check the park website (www.nps.gov/havo) for a schedule of the guided hikes that explore rare plants in this old-growth forest. They are offered always on Saturdays about twice a month at both 9:30am and 12:30pm. The website is up-to-date with good descriptions of which tours are offered.

GOLF

Those who play the **Sea Mountain Golf Course** (Hwy. 11 between mile markers 56 and 57, 808/928-6222, daily 7am-1pm, $22-25) prefer it to nearby courses in Volcano and Hilo—perhaps due to the outstanding ocean views. Punalu'u Beach is nearby for a dip when you're finished with the round. Green fees are inexpensive (relatively speaking), with discounts for tee times before 9am on weekdays. Bring your own snacks and drinks—there's no snack bar in sight.

Entertainment and Events

ENTERTAINMENT

Nights are quiet in Ka'u. If you're looking for live music, sporadically **Hana Hou** restaurant (95-1148 Na'alehu Spur Rd., Na'alehu, 808/929-9717, www.hanahourestaurant.com) has live performances with a prix fixe menu ($20) and is BYOB. There is no schedule, so call the restaurant in advance, as reservations usually are necessary for these events.

The hours posted indicate that **Shaka Restaurant** (Hwy. 11, Na'alehu, 808/929-7404, daily 10am-8pm, $10) closes later on the weekends depending on the crowd. On most Friday nights, however, you'll find live music and Saturday karaoke doesn't even start until 8:30pm. It's on the west side of the center of Na'alehu.

EVENTS

Because Ka'u is eager to attract visitors, new events pop up frequently. Check the listings in the blog of the *Ka'u Calendar* (http://kaunewsbriefs.blogspot.com), the local newspaper.

The weeklong **Ka'u Coffee Festival** (www.kaucoffeefest.com) takes place each May. This event celebrates the local coffee, which some argue is better than Kona coffee and deserves more recognition. The festival is set up like a county fair, with coffee tastings and demonstrations, recipe competitions, farm tours, and live local music. There's even a Miss Ka'u Coffee Pageant (it's a big deal—it's a qualifier for the state competition). Most events are free, while a few like the pageant and coffee/farm tours are fairly priced at $10-20.

Food

OCEAN VIEW

In Ocean View, most people head straight to the **Pizzeria** (425 Lotus Blossom Ln., Ocean View Town Center, 808/929-9677, Sun.-Thurs. 11am-7pm, Fri.-Sat. 11am-8pm, $18, cash only). Pizzas are tasty, if overpriced. There are also salads and subs on the menu. Vegetarian options are available, and you are free to BYOB (from one of the small grocery stores around the corner). They only accept cash and local checks.

For a long time there weren't any late-night food options in Ocean View for those nighttime drives back from Volcano to the Kona side. The local chain restaurant, **L & L Hawaiian Barbeque** (92-8701 Mamalahoa Hwy./Hwy 11 next to the Malama Market, Ocean View, 808/929-8888, daily 7am-9pm, $7) now fills the hungry stomachs of many weary drivers. As many locals will say, "the food is unexpectedly good" given that it truly is fast food. It might not be anyone's first choice of cuisine, but their cheap breakfasts, burgers, and plate lunches not only offer your typically large fast-food portions, but also quick service at incredibly low prices.

On the other side of town you'll find **Ka-Lae Garden Thai Food** (92-8395 Mamalahoa Hwy./Hwy 11 between mile markers 76 and 77, Ocean View, Wed.-Sun. 11am-7pm, $10). You can smell the "authenticity" of the Thai cuisine from the moment you enter the simple storefront that also sells a few grocery items. The menu warns "Our Thai food is not fast food" and this is true not only because everything from the green and red curries to the papaya salad are made from scratch, but also because, at times, there is only one person cooking and also taking orders. The wait is worth it, though, and so is the option to have brown rice with your meal.

Markets

Most days, beginning around 11am until they are sold out (probably around 5pm), you'll see a table with a large banner offering "Steak Lunch" in the parking lot at the **Malama Market** (92-8701 Hawai'i Belt Rd./Hwy. 11, Pohue Plaza, *makai* side, 808/939-7560, daily 6:30am-8pm). Nothing beats the smell of fresh barbecue in a parking lot. Your nose isn't fooling you; the smell is a good indication of the actual taste. The large portions of this local-style cuisine—beef, macaroni salad, and white rice (all for $6)—will keep you satiated. The market also has a good selection of fresh fruits and vegetables as well as some prepared food (including breakfast, which sells out fast) and Redbox DVD rentals. Its excellent bathroom is also a useful stop.

The **Ocean View Market** (Hwy. 11, *mauka* side, diagonally across from Malama Market, 808/929-9843, daily 6am-9pm) is open an hour later than Malama Market. It offers a fairly good stock of groceries (including organic and gluten-free products) as well as beer and wine.

SOUTH POINT TO NA'ALEHU

Na'alehu claims all the "southernmost" restaurants, bars, and bakeries in the United States. Your first stop into southern-dom is **Shaka Restaurant** (Hwy. 11, on the west side of the center of town, Na'alehu, 808/929-7404, daily 8am-8pm, $9-20). This southernmost bar in the United States (the title of southernmost restaurant was already taken) is mediocre at best, but offers large portions at good prices. The menu is American and local food (grilled chicken, fries, fresh catch). The large TVs are blasting with sports games or CNN. Make a quick pit stop—you won't find another one for quite a while.

You'll easily find the **Punalu'u Bake Shop** (Hwy. 11 near Ka'alaiki Rd., central Na'alehu, 808/929-7343, www.bakeshophawaii.com, daily 9am-5pm, $3-10) from its smell and the large tourist buses parked in its lot. Peek into the kitchen and head into the bake shop to pick up a treat. Offerings include *malasadas* (Portuguese doughnuts), coconut turnovers, and sweet bread in flavors like taro and guava. There's also a lunch with vegetarian options. If the indoor seating is too crowded or loud, try the picnic tables outside. It's also a great pit stop (they advertise their bathrooms along with their pastries).

Directly across the street from the Punalu'u Bake Shop is **Hana Hou** (95-1148 Na'alehu Spur Rd., 808/929-9717, www.hanahourestaurant.com, Sun.-Thurs. 8am-7pm, Fri.-Sat. 8am-8pm, $12), your best choice for eating in the Ka'u district. Delicious burgers ($12) are served on homemade buns. Specials are usually locally focused (like the catch of the day), and the rotating homemade desserts like macadamia nut cheesecake are always mouthwatering. Service can be slow, but BYOB is allowed, which can make the wait more bearable. There is sometimes live music on weekends.

Getting There and Around

BUS

Since Ka'u is right smack in the middle between the east and west sides of the island, it's quite easy and relatively quick to travel to either side of the island from here. The **Hele-On Bus** (www.heleonbus.org, 808/961-8744, $2 per ride, $1 each for luggage, large backpacks, bikes) only makes one eastbound trip daily (except Sunday) from Ocean View via Volcano to Hilo (the full route). It leaves Ocean View from the parking lot across from the Malama Market at 6:40am, arriving in Hilo at 9:20am. The bus then leaves Hilo at 2:40pm and returns to the same spot in Ocean View at 5:15pm.

It also is possible to travel west from Pahala to Ocean View to Kona (including the airport) and as far as the resorts in Kohala. The Hele-On bus from Mauna Kea Beach in Kohala leaves daily at 7:15am and Monday-Saturday only at 2:30pm, passing by the Kona airport and arriving in Ocean View and Pahala about four hours later. The return trips from Pahala to Kohala are Monday-Saturday only at 8am and daily at 3:30pm. Check the Pahala-to-South Kohala bus schedule on the website for more information.

Hawai'i Volcanoes National Park

Highlights

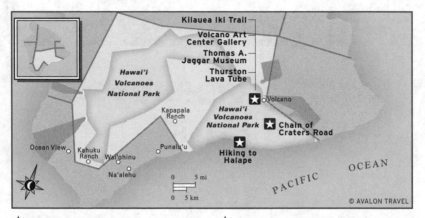

★ **Volcano Art Center Gallery:** This is one of the finest art galleries in the entire state, boasting the best the islands have to offer (page 113).

★ **Thomas A. Jaggar Museum:** This state-of-the-art museum offers a fantastic multimedia display of the amazing geology and volcanology of the area. At night you can watch the lava glow from the viewing area (page 115).

★ **Thurston Lava Tube:** Ferns and moss hang from the entrance of this remarkable natural tunnel. It's as if the very air is tinged with green (page 116).

★ **Chain of Craters Road:** Every bend of this road offers a panoramic vista. The grandeur and power of the forces that have been creating the earth from the beginning of time are right before your eyes (page 117).

★ **Kilauea Iki Trail:** This trail takes you from the top of the crater with its lush tropical vegetation to the crater floor, which still breathes volcanic steam (page 124).

★ **Hiking to Halape:** Your rewards for this strenuous hike are sugary sand and a sheltered lagoon—by far the most remote and pristine beach on the island (page 124).

The indomitable power of Hawai'i Volcanoes National Park is apparent to all who come here.

Wherever you stop to gaze, realize that you are standing on a thin skin of cooled lava in an unstable earthquake zone atop one of the world's most active volcanoes.

Established in 1916 as the 13th U.S. national park, Hawai'i Volcanoes National Park now covers 333,000 acres. Based on its scientific and scenic value, the park was named an International Biosphere Reserve by UNESCO in 1980 and awarded World Heritage Site status in 1987 by the same organization, giving it greater national and international prestige. This is one of the top visitor attractions in the state.

With a multitude of ways to access the park—by foot, by car, by bike, and by helicopter—Hawai'i Volcanoes National Park truly does offer something for everyone. Even non-nature lovers are impressed by the environmental oddities offered here, such as the vastly different landscapes situated next to each other. Within moments one can pass through a tropical rain forest to what appears like a lunar landscape. Even if this doesn't impress, it will be hard to tear yourself away from the lava flow or glow. It's surreal.

In conjunction with a visit to the park, you'll surely pass through Volcano Village, known for the cadre of artists and scientists that live there. With wineries, farmers markets, restaurants, and galleries, it can feel like the Sonoma of Hawaii and not just somewhere to pass through on the way to somewhere else.

ORIENTATION
Hawai'i Volcanoes National Park

Practically speaking, you'll find the main entrance to the park off Highway 11 near mile marker 28; however, the park itself extends far to the north and the south of the main entrance. The upper end of the park is the summit of stupendous Mauna Loa, the most massive mountain on earth. Mauna Loa Road branches off Highway 11 and ends at a footpath for the hale and hearty who trek to the 13,679-foot summit. The park's heart is Kilauea Caldera, almost three miles across, 400 feet deep, and encircled by 11 miles of Crater Rim Drive. At the park visitors center you can give yourself

---

Previous: Hawai'i Volcanoes National Park offers some of the best hiking on the island; entrance to Thurston Lava Tube. **Above:** Lava flows in Hawai'i Volcanoes National Park.

Hawai'i Volcanoes National Park

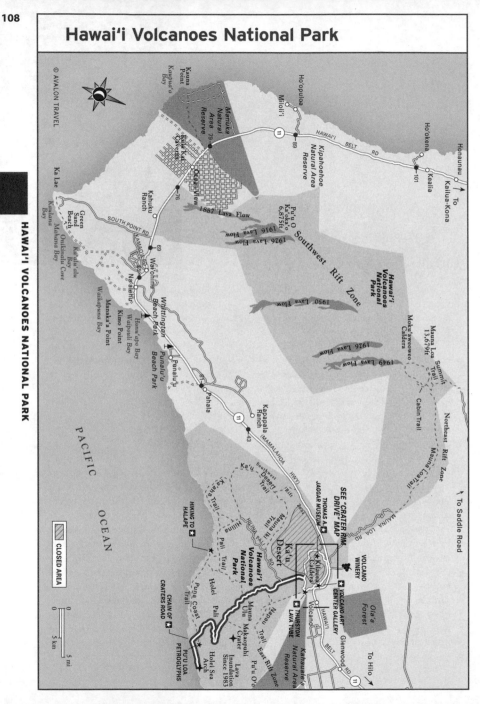

© AVALON TRAVEL

Kaunā Point
Kaupua'o Bay

Ka Lae

Ka'ū
Kahilama Bay

Green Sand Beach

Ka'alu'alu Bay

Onilkinla Cove

Mahana Bay

Waikapuna Bay

Manakā'a Point

Kimo Point

Waiōpai Bay

Honu'apo Bay

Nīnole

Waiōhinu

Nā'ālehu

Ho'opuloa

Miloli'i

Ho'okena

Honaunau

To Kailua-Kona

Keahalia

101

89

HAWAI'I BELT RD

11

Kīpāhoehoe Natural Area Reserve

Māmalu Natural Area Reserve

Ocean View

Kula Kai Caverns

Kahuku Ranch

76

SOUTH POINT RD

KAMA'OA

69

SOUTH POINT

1887 Lava Flow

Pu'u O Ka'oka'o 6,875ft

1916 Lava Flow

1926 Lava Flow

1950 Lava Flow

Southwest Rift Zone

Hawai'i Volcanoes National Park

Moku'āweoweo Caldera

Mauna Loa 13,679ft Summit

1926 Lava Flow

1949 Lava Flow

Summit Trail

Cabin Trail

Northeast Rift Zone

Mauna Loa Trail

To Saddle Road

MAUNA LOA RD

Whittington Beach Park

Punalu'u Beach Park

Punalu'u

Pāhala

87

43

11

Kapāpala Ranch

(MĀMALAHOA HWY.)

Ka'ū Desert Trail

Southwest Rift

Ka'ū Desert

Mauna Iki Trail

Hilina Pali Trail

HILINA PALI RD

THOMAS A. JAGGAR MUSEUM

SEE "CRATER RIM DRIVE" MAP

Kīlauea Caldera

VOLCANO WINERY

VOLCANO ART CENTER GALLERY

THURSTON LAVA TUBE

Volcano

HAWAI'I BELT

Glenwood RD

To Hilo

11

Ola'a Forest

Kahauale'a Natural Area Reserve

East Rift Zone

Pu'u 'Ō'ō

Lava Inundation Since 1983

Mauna Ulu

Makaopuhi Crater

Nāpau Trail

Holei Pali

Puna Coast Trail

CHAIN OF CRATERS ROAD

PU'U LOA PETROGLYPHS

Holei Sea Arch

HIKING TO HALAPE

Hawai'i Volcanoes National Park

Pali Trail

PACIFIC

OCEAN

CLOSED AREA

0   5 km

0   5 mi

Crater Rim Drive

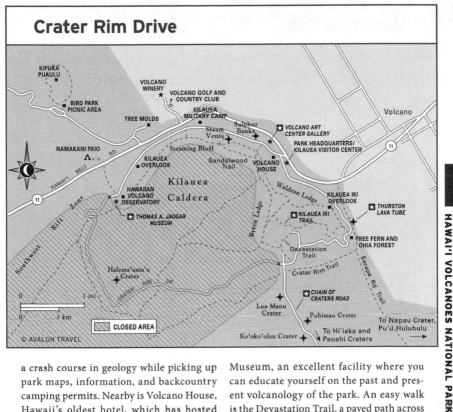

KIPUKA PUAULU

VOLCANO WINERY

VOLCANO GOLF AND COUNTRY CLUB

BIRD PARK PICNIC AREA

KILAUEA MILITARY CAMP

TREE MOLDS

Volcano

Sulphur Banks

Steam Vents

VOLCANO ART CENTER GALLERY

NAMAKANI PAIO

PARK HEADQUARTERS/ KILAUEA VISITOR CENTER

RD

Steaming Bluff

11

HAWAI'I BELT

KILAUEA OVERLOOK

Sandalwood Trail

VOLCANO HOUSE

11

Rift Zone

Kilauea Caldera

Waldron Ledge

KILAUEA IKI OVERLOOK

HAWAIIAN VOLCANO OBSERVATORY

THURSTON LAVA TUBE

THOMAS A. JAGGAR MUSEUM

KILAUEA IKI TRAIL

Byron Ledge

TREE FERN AND OHIA FOREST

Southwest

Devastation Trail

Escape Rd Trail

Halema'uma'u Crater

Crater Rim Trail

CRATER RIM DR

CHAIN OF CRATERS ROAD

0   1 mi

0   1 km

Lua Manu Crater

Puhimau Crater

To Napau Crater, Pu'u Huluhulu

CLOSED AREA

© AVALON TRAVEL

Ko'oko'olau Crater

To Hi'iaka and Pauahi Craters

HAWAI'I VOLCANOES NATIONAL PARK

a crash course in geology while picking up park maps, information, and backcountry camping permits. Nearby is Volcano House, Hawaii's oldest hotel, which has hosted a steady stream of adventurers, luminaries, royalty, and heads of state ever since it opened its doors in the 1860s. Just a short drive away is a pocket of indigenous forest, providing the perfect setting for a bird sanctuary. In a separate section of the park is 'Ola'a Forest, a pristine wilderness area of unspoiled flora and fauna.

Crater Rim Drive circles Kilauea Caldera past steam vents, sulphur springs, and tortured fault lines that always seem on the verge of gaping wide and swallowing the landscape. On the way you can peer into the mouth of Halema'uma'u Crater, home of the fire goddess, Pele. You'll also pass Hawaiian Volcano Observatory, which has been monitoring geologic activity since the turn of the 20th century. Adjacent to the observatory is the Thomas A. Jaggar Museum, an excellent facility where you can educate yourself on the past and present volcanology of the park. An easy walk is the Devastation Trail, a paved path across a desolate cinder field where gray, lifeless trunks of a suffocated forest lean like old gravestones. Within minutes is Thurston Lava Tube, a magnificent natural tunnel overflowing with vibrant fern grottoes at the entrance and exit.

The southwestern section of the park is dominated by the Ka'u Desert—not a plain of sand, but a semiarid slope of lava flow, cinder, scrub bushes, and heat that's been defiled by the windblown debris and gases of Kilauea Volcano and fractured by the sinking coastline. It is a desolate region, an area crossed by a few trails that are a challenge even to the sturdy and experienced hiker. Most visitors, however, head down the Chain of Craters Road, down the *pali* to the coast, where the road ends abruptly at a hardened flow of lava and from where visitors can

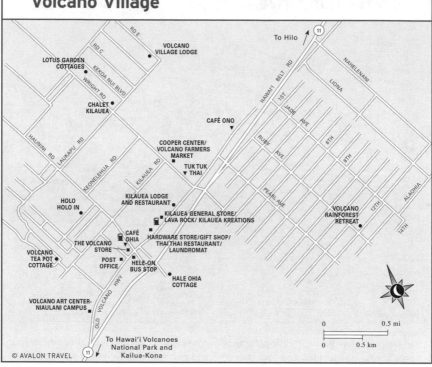

Volcano Village

glean information about current volcanic activities from the small ranger station and try to glimpse the ongoing volcanic activity in the distance.

Volcano Village

Driving north on Highway 11, you will pass by the park's entrance before reaching the main part of Volcano town (if you are driving from Hilo, you pass the town first). Although there are residential communities on both sides of the road, the *mauka* side is the center of Volcano town. Nearly every restaurant and shop is on the short Old Volcano Road—the inner road that parallels Highway 11 through town. The golf course area, where the Volcano Winery is also housed, is on Highway 11 between mile markers 30 and 31 just south of the park.

PLANNING YOUR TIME

It's best to decide in advance how much time you want to spend at the park and whether you're visiting by car, by foot, or by bike. Regardless of your plan, your first stop should be the visitors center to check with a park ranger about any new closures in the park, new safety advisories, or a special program going on that day. Start early. The park looks entirely different in the early morning—the colors are different and it is much quieter before the busloads of tourists start to arrive. Lastly, pack a lunch. The food options in the park are minimal. Better to bring a great sandwich with you so that you don't have to return to town midday to get fed.

It is possible to see the park's "greatest hits" in one long day if you drive from sight to sight on Crater Rim and then Chain of Craters Road. You'll even have time to get

Your Best Day in the Volcano Area

- Wake up early and walk the **Crater Rim Trail.**

- Stop at the **visitors center** to chat with a park ranger (before it gets crowded).

- Visit the **Thurston Lava Tube** and hike the **Kilauea Iki Trail.**

- Get back in the car and drive the **Chain of Craters Road,** stopping at a lookout to have your packed lunch.

- In the later afternoon, after a brief rest, stop by the **Volcano Winery** for a tasting.

- Have an early dinner in **Volcano Village** or at the **Volcano House.**

- Return to the park to watch the glow from the **Thomas A. Jaggar Museum.**

- If you're not too tired, go bowling at **Kilauea Military Camp** or visit the **Lava Lounge** for some karaoke with the locals.

RAINY-DAY ALTERNATIVE

I'll try to break it to you as gently as possible: It can rain at Hawai'i Volcanoes National Park. Sometimes it's a spritz and you can continue on with only getting slightly damp, and other times it can rain hard and outdoor activity is not really possible. There are a few indoor places you can go while waiting for sunshine.

From facials to pedicures to traditional *lomilomi* massages, **Hale Ho'ola: Hawaiian Healing Arts Center and Spa** does it all and does it well, and at half the cost of spas on the Kona side. What makes this a truly great rainy-day activity is that you can call at the last minute and owner Suzanne Woolley will try to accommodate you.

Art enthusiasts will love **2400 Fahrenheit Glass Blowing,** just a few minutes north of Hawai'i Volcanoes National Park. Even if glassblowing isn't taking place, this gallery makes for a worthy stop.

If the weather still hasn't cleared up, try the **Volcano Winery** for a tasting, or drive to Hilo. Often the weather in Hilo can be drastically different from that in Volcano (you can see the clouds moving as you drive north on Highway 11).

out and walk around, have a leisurely dinner, and then come back to catch the glow at night. There are a handful of fairly easy hikes that only take 2-3 hours. If you're planning on doing one or more of those hikes (such as Kilauea Iki), you might want to give yourself an extra day in the park. Two days at Hawai'i Volcanoes National Park will allow you to see all the major sights and accomplish at least two beginner- to medium-level hikes. At least three days in the park will be necessary to get into the backcountry and, maybe more importantly, to get back out.

In this age of Internet, you can see the park without physically being there. If want to check conditions before you head into the park (i.e., is it worth driving to the park at night), there are several useful websites you can use to check **lava status** (http://volcano. wr.usgs.gov/kilaueastatus.php for general status updates, http://volcanoes.usgs.gov/ hvo/cams/HMcam for the Thomas A. Jaggar Museum viewing area) and **trail closures** (www.nps.gov/havo/closed_areas.htm).

The National Park Service also offers the free *Your Guide to Hawai'i Volcanoes National Park* app for iPhone users, available for download from iTunes.

Exploring the Park

Admission to Hawai'i Volcanoes National Park (www.nps.gov/havo) is $15 per vehicle (good for multiple entries over a seven-day period), $25 for a Hawaii Tri-Park Annual Pass, $8 per individual (walkers and bikers), and free to those 62 and over with a Golden Age, Golden Eagle, or Golden Access passport. These "passports" are available at the park headquarters and are good at any national park in the United States. Note: There are several weekends throughout the year when the park is free. Check the park's website to see if your visit coincides with one of these times. Also note, the price for admission will be increasing yearly through 2017; for instance, in 2016 it is $20 per vehicle to enter the park and in 2017 it will be $25.

THE VOLCANOES
Kilauea

Continuously active since 1983, Kilauea dominates the heart of Hawai'i Volcanoes National Park. Many of the park's sights are arranged one after another along **Crater Rim Drive,** which circles **Kilauea Caldera.** Most of these sights are the "drive-up" variety, but plenty of major and minor trails lead off here and there.

Expect to spend a full day atop Kilauea to take in all the sights, and never forget that you're on a rumbling volcano. Kilauea Caldera, at 4,000 feet, is about 10°F cooler than the coast. It's often overcast, and there can be showers. Wear walking shoes and bring a sweater or windbreaker, maybe even a change of clothes. Binoculars, sunglasses, and a hat will also come in handy.

People with respiratory ailments, those with small children, and pregnant individuals should be aware that the fumes from the volcano can cause problems. That sour taste in your mouth is sulphur from the fumes. Stay away from directly inhaling from the sulphur vents and don't overdo it, and you should be fine.

Mauna Loa

It's a little discombobulating at times—you're sweating in the hot lava fields of the park and in the background you see the snowcapped Mauna Loa. Reaching 13,680 feet in elevation, this magnificent peak is a mere 116 feet shorter than its neighbor Mauna Kea, which is the tallest peak in the Pacific (and by some accounts, the tallest in the world).

Mauna Loa holds its own impressive statistics. It is the most massive mountain on earth, containing some 19,000 cubic miles of solid, iron-hard lava, and it's estimated that this titan weighs more than California's entire Sierra Nevada mountain range. In fact, Mauna Loa (Long Mountain), at 60 miles long and 30 miles wide, occupies the entire southern half of the Big Island. Unlike Mauna Kea, Mauna Loa has had some recent volcanic activity, spilling lava in 1949, 1950, 1975, and 1980.

The summit of Mauna Loa, with its mighty **Moku'aweoweo Caldera,** is all within park boundaries. Mauna Loa's oval Moku'aweoweo Caldera is more than three miles long and 1.5 miles wide and has vertical walls towering 600 feet. At each end is a smaller, round pit crater. From November to May, if there is snow, steam rises from the caldera. This mountaintop bastion is the least-visited part of the park because this land is remote and still largely inaccessible.

Plans for future use of this area include opening up several hundred miles of trails and Jeep tracks to hiking and perhaps other activities, as well as creating additional campsites and cabins; these uses will undoubtedly take years to come to fruition. For now, it is possible to drive or bike the 10-mile Mauna Loa Road to the trailhead at over 6,600 feet, hike nearly 20 miles to the summit, and stay overnight at some true backcountry cabins before you head back down.

VISITORS CENTER AREA
Kilauea Visitor Center

As they say in the *Sound of Music,* "Let's start at the very beginning, a very good place to start," in other words, the park's **Kilauea Visitor Center** (808/985-6000, daily 9am-5pm) and headquarters. It's the first building you pass on the right after you enter through the gate. By midmorning it's jammed, so try to be an early bird. The center is well run by the National Park Service, which offers a free film about geology and volcanism, with tremendous highlights of past eruptions and plenty of detail on Hawaiian culture and natural history. It runs every hour on the hour starting at 9am. Once a day at 11:30am the 1959 Kilauea Iki eruption video is shown in the auditorium; it's a must-see for those planning on hiking that trail. Free ranger-led tours of the nearby area are also given on a regular basis, and their start times and meeting places are posted near the center's front doors. Also posted are After Dark in the Park educational interpretive program activities, held two or three times a month on Tuesdays at 7pm. If you are visiting with kids, ask the rangers about the free **Junior Ranger Program.** They'll give each child a park-related activity book, pin, and patch.

The museum section of the visitors center looks like it was constructed at least 20 years ago before museums got technological updates, but it still offers relevant information about the geology of the area, with plenty of exhibits on flora and fauna. If you are interested in these topics, a quick stop here will greatly enrich your visit. A walk around the museum will only take about a half hour. If you're looking for more volcano-specific information, you'll find that at the Thomas A. Jaggar Museum a few minutes up the road.

The small gift shop in the visitors center has park posters, postcards, T-shirts, sweatshirts, raincoats, and lots of books and maps to help navigate you through the park, as well as a selection of kid-friendly volcano-related toys.

Many day trails leading into the caldera from the rim road are easy walks that need no special preparation. Before you head down the road, ask for a trail guide from the rangers at the visitors center, fill up your water bottle, and use the public bathroom.

Volcano House

Even if your plans don't include an overnight stop, go into **Volcano House,** across the road from the visitors center, for a look. A stop at the lounge provides refreshments and a tremendous view of the crater. Volcano House still has the feel of a country inn. This particular building dates from the 1940s, but the site has remained the same since a grass hut was perched on the rim of the crater by a sugar planter in 1846. He charged $1 a night for lodging. A steady stream of notable visitors has come ever since: almost all of Hawaii's kings and queens dating from the middle of the 19th century, as well as royalty from Europe. Mark Twain was a guest, followed by Franklin Roosevelt. More recently, a contingent of astronauts lodged here and used the crater floor to prepare for walking on the moon. Since 1986 the hotel has been under local management as a concessionaire to the National Park Service.

★ Volcano Art Center Gallery

Across the parking lot from the visitors center is the **Volcano Art Center Gallery** (808/967-7565, http://volcanoartcenter.org, daily 9am-5pm except Christmas), which occupies part of the original 1877 Volcano House. A new show featuring one of the many superlative island artists is presented monthly, and there are always ongoing demonstrations and special events. Artworks on display are in a variety of media, including canvas, paper, wood, glass, metal, ceramic, fiber, and photographs. There is also a profusion of less expensive but distinctive items like posters, cards, and basketry made from natural fibers collected locally. One of the functions of the art center is to provide interpretation for the national park. All of the 300 or so artists who exhibit here do works that in some way

EXPLORING THE PARK

HAWAI'I VOLCANOES NATIONAL PARK

relate to Hawaii's environment and culture. The Volcano Art Center is one of the finest art galleries in the entire state, boasting works from the best the islands have to offer. Definitely make this a stop.

As a community-oriented organization, the Volcano Art Center sponsors classes and workshops in arts, crafts, and yoga, the Kilauea Volcano Wilderness Runs, and a season of performing arts, which includes musical concerts, hula, dance performances, and stage plays. Some involve local performers, while others headline visiting artists. Performances, classes, and workshops take place at the Kilauea Theater at the military camp, at the hula platform within the park, or in Volcano at the Niaulani campus building. Tickets for performances are sold individually at local outlets or you can buy a season ticket. For current information and pricing, call the Volcano Art Center office (808/967-8222) or check its website for what's happening.

Crater Rim Trail is an easy walk that passes by many of the park's sights.

CRATER RIM DRIVE

The 11-mile road that circles the Kilauea Caldera and passes by nearly all the main sights in the park is **Crater Rim Drive.** For the past few years a part of the road has been closed due to elevated levels of sulphur dioxide gas. You can still drive on the road, but you can't usually complete the entire circle. However, don't let this deter you. A large part of the road is still open, and there are so many intriguing nooks and crannies to stop at along Crater Rim Drive that you'll have to force yourself to be picky if you intend to cover the park in one day.

Along this road you will travel from a tropical zone into desert, and then through a volcanic zone before returning to lush rain forest. The change is often immediate and differences dramatic. Since you can't circle the caldera, the following sights are listed in two sections: those to the right of the visitors center and those to the left of the visitors center. The sights to the left of the visitors center can also be reached by turning left immediately after you pass through the entrance gate of the park.

To the Right of the Visitors Center
SULPHUR BANKS

You can easily walk to **Sulphur Banks** from the visitors center along a 10-minute paved trail. Your nose will tell you when you're close. Alternatively, walk the 0.6-mile trail from the Steam Vents parking lot. A boardwalk fronts a major portion of this site. As you approach these fumaroles, the earth surrounding them turns a deep reddish brown, covered over in yellowish-green sulphur. It's an amazing sight, especially in the morning when the entire area seems to look pink. The rising steam is caused by surface water leaking into the cracks, where it becomes heated and rises as vapor. Kilauea releases hundreds of tons of sulphur gases every day. This gaseous activity stunts the growth of vegetation. And when atmospheric conditions create a low ceiling, the gases sometimes cause the eyes and nose to water.

STEAM VENTS

Within a half mile you'll come to the **Steam Vents,** which are also fumaroles, but without sulphur. In the parking lot there are some vents covered with grates, and if you walk just two minutes from the parking lot toward the caldera on the gravel trail, you'll see how the entire field steams. It is like being in a sauna or getting a wonderful free facial. There are no strong fumes to contend with here, just other tourists. If you walk back toward the caldera, you'll see a gravel trail that follows the caldera around. This is the **Crater Rim Trail,** and you can walk it from here to many of the sights, including the Thomas A. Jaggar Museum—an easy 20-minute walk (one-way) through the woods from here.

KILAUEA MILITARY CAMP

If you continue in the same direction on the road, you'll pass the **Kilauea Military Camp.** It's where military families come to vacation. Although it looks like it's not open to the public, many parts of it actually are open to nonmilitary personnel, including the post office, the Lava Lounge bar, the cafeteria, the bowling alley, and the Kilauea Theater, which is used for community events.

KILAUEA OVERLOOK

Some distance beyond the Kilauea Military Camp is **Kilauea Overlook,** as good a spot as any to get a look into the caldera, and there are picnic tables near the parking lot. Here too is **Uwekahuna (Wailing Priest) Bluff,** where the *kahuna* made offerings of appeasement to the goddess Pele. A Hawaiian prayer commemorates their religious rites. Unless you're stopping for lunch or making your own offering, it's perhaps better to continue on to the observatory and museum, where you not only have the view outside but get a scientific explanation of what's happening around you.

★ THOMAS A. JAGGAR MUSEUM

The **Hawaiian Volcano Observatory** (http://hvo.wr.usgs.gov) has been keeping tabs on the volcanic activity in the area since the turn of the 20th century. The actual observatory is filled with delicate seismic equipment and is closed to the public, but a lookout nearby gives you a spectacular view into the eye of **Halema'uma'u Crater** (House of Ferns), Pele's home. From here, steam rises and, even more phenomenally spectacular, a lake of molten lava forms. The lava has been rising and falling over the last few years, and when it does rise, it puts on one of the best

the glow from the Halema'uma'u Crater

HAWAI'I VOLCANOES NATIONAL PARK

EXPLORING THE PARK

Don't Take the Lava Home!

Legend has it that taking lava rock from Hawaii will bring you bad luck. **Pele,** the goddess of fire, does not like when her rocks leave Hawaii. (Although rumor has it that the legend was actually started by rangers at the national park who wanted to stop people from picking up rocks.) Every year the park receives lava rocks returned to them by mail with notes of explanation handwritten by the recipients of bad luck. I am not saying whether or not I think this legend holds true, but I can say it's best not to take the rock.

If you so happen to take something and want to send it back, you can send it to **Hawai'i Volcanoes National Park** (P.O. Box 52, Hawaii National Park, HI 96718). They have a pile of returned rocks. If you want your rock to return with a ceremony of forgiveness, with just a $15 donation you can send your rock to Rainbow Moon (Attn: Lava Rock Return, P.O. Box 699, Volcano, HI 96785). Your rock will be returned to its source wrapped in a ti leaf. In addition, Rainbow Moon will happily send you an email to confirm that your rock was returned appropriately.

nighttime shows you'll ever see. You can check the webcam (http://volcanoes.usgs.gov/hvo/cams/hmcam) located within the crater to see what the lava is doing and decide if it's worth heading back there at night to watch its performance.

This is a major stop for all passing tourists and tour buses. Information plaques in the immediate area tell of the history and volcanology of the park. One points out a spot from which to observe the perfect shield volcano form of Mauna Loa—most times too cloudy to see. Another reminds you that you're in the middle of the Pacific, an incredible detail you tend to forget when atop these mountains.

Next door to the observatory, the state-of-the-art **Thomas A. Jaggar Museum** (808/985-6049, daily 10am-8pm, admission free) offers a fantastic multimedia display of the amazing geology and volcanology of the area, complete with a miniseries of spectacular photos on movable walls, topographical maps, inspired paintings, and video presentations. The expert staff constantly upgrades the displays to keep the public informed on the newest eruptions. The 30-45 minutes it takes to explore the teaching museum will enhance your understanding of the volcanic area immeasurably. There is also a gift shop here, much like the one at the visitors center, which carries sweatshirts and raincoats that visitors

are, at times, desperate to get their hands on. Drinking water and bathrooms are available here. From the Jaggar Museum the rest of the Crater Rim Road is closed, thus it's necessary to turn around and go back the way you came.

To the Left of the Visitors Center
KILAUEA IKI OVERLOOK

The first parking lot you'll pass on the right is the gateway to **Kilauea Iki** (Little Kilauea). In 1959, lava spewed 1,900 feet into the air from a half-mile crack in the crater wall (there is an amazing picture showcasing this occurrence on a board in the parking lot). It was the highest fountain ever measured in Hawaii. Within a few weeks, 17 separate lava flow episodes occurred, creating a lake of lava. In the distance is the cinder cone, **Pu'u Pua'i** (Gushing Hill), where the lava flowed from its brownish-red base in 1959. The cone didn't exist before then. If you look down from the overlook into the crater floor you'll see something that resembles a desolate desert landscape that is still steaming in spots. Unbelievably, you can fairly easily walk across this on the Kilauea Iki trail. Surrounding the crater is a rain forest filled with native birds and plants.

★ THURSTON LAVA TUBE

Just up the road from the overlook is the remarkable **Thurston Lava Tube,** otherwise called Nahuku, which resembles a Salvador Dalí painting. As you approach, a signboard gives you the lowdown on the geology and flora and fauna of the area. The paved trail starts as a steep incline that quickly enters a fern forest. All about you are fern trees, vibrantly green, with native birds flitting here and there. As you approach the lava tube, it seems almost man-made, like a perfectly formed tunnel leading into a mine. Ferns and moss hang from the entrance, and if you stand just inside the entrance looking out, it's as if the very air is tinged with green. The tunnel is fairly large and shouldn't be a problem for those who suffer from mild claustrophobia. The walk through the tube takes about 10 minutes, undulating through the narrow passage. At the other end, the fantasy world of ferns and moss reappears, and from there the trail leads back past public restrooms to the parking lot. The entire tunnel is lit and paved; however, for some extra fun take a flashlight to visit the unlit portion. As you walk up the stairway to exit the tube, you'll see on your left an open gate that looks into the darkness: This small unlit section *is* open to the public at their own risk. If you're good on your feet, take a quick look.

★ CHAIN OF CRATERS ROAD

The 37-mile round-trip **Chain of Craters Road** that once linked the park with Kalapana village on the coast in the Puna district was severed by an enormous lava flow in 1995 and can now only be driven to where the flow crosses the road beyond the Holei Sea Arch. It's pretty amazing when you get to the end of the road, though, where lava literally covers the pavement and you can see now-obsolete street signs in the distance.

Remember that the volcanic activity in this area is unpredictable, and that the road can be closed at a moment's notice. As you head down the road, every bend—and they are uncountable—offers a panoramic vista. There are numerous pull-offs; plaques provide geological information about past eruptions and lava flows. The grandeur, power, and immensity of the forces that have been creating the earth from the beginning of time are right before your eyes. Although the road starts off in the 'ohi'a forest, it opens to broader views and soon cuts diagonally across the *pali* to reach the littoral plain. Much of this section of the road was buried under lava flows from 1969 to 1974.

When the road almost reaches the coast,

Thurston Lava Tube

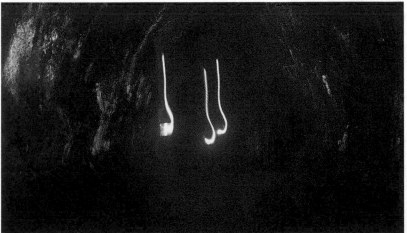

look for a roadside marker that indicates the Puna Coast Trail. Just across the road is the Pu'u Loa Petroglyph Field trailhead. The lower part of the road is spectacular. Here, blacker-than-black sea cliffs, covered by a thin layer of green, abruptly stop at the sea. The surf rolls in, sending up spumes of seawater. In the distance, steam billows into the air where the lava flows into the sea. At road's end you will find a barricade and an information hut staffed by park rangers throughout the afternoon and into the evening. Read the information and heed the warnings. The drive from atop the volcano to the end of the road takes about 45 minutes and drops about 3,700 feet in elevation.

While hiking to the lava flow is not encouraged, park staff do not stop you from venturing out. They warn you of the dangers and the reality ahead. Many visitors do make the hike, but there is no trail. The way is over new and rough lava that tears at the bottom of your shoes. Many hike during the day, but if you go in the evening when the spectacle is more apparent, a flashlight with several extra batteries is absolutely necessary. To hike there and back could take three to four hours. If you decide to hike, bring plenty of water. There is no shade or water along the way, and the wind often blows along this coast. Do not hike to or near the edge of the water, as sections of lava could break off without warning. Depending on how the lava is flowing, it may or may not be worth the effort.

Craters

As you head down Chain of Craters Road you immediately pass a number of the depressions for which the road is named. First on the right side is **Lua Manu Crater,** a deep depression now lined with green vegetation. Farther is **Puhimau Crater.** Walk the few steps to the viewing stand at the crater edge for a look. Many people come here to hear the echo of their voices as they talk or sing into this pit. Next comes **Ko'oko'olau Crater,** then **Hi'iaka Crater** and **Pauahi Crater.** Just beyond is a turnoff to the east, which follows a short section of the old road. This road ends at the lava flow, and from here a trail runs as far as **Napau Crater.**

The first mile or more of the Napau Trail takes you over lava from 1974, through forest *kipuka,* past lava tree molds, and up the treed slopes of **Pu'u Huluhulu.** (A *kipuka* is a piece of land that is surrounded by lava but has not been inundated by it, leaving the original vegetation and land contour intact.) From this

Ohelo berry bushes grow back quickly after a landscape has been devastated by lava.

cone you have a view down on Mauna Ulu, from which the 1969-1974 lava flow disgorged, and east toward **Pu'u O'o** and the active volcanic vents, some seven miles distant. Due to the current volcanic activity farther along the rift zone, you will need a permit to day-hike beyond Pu'u Huluhulu; the trail itself may be closed depending on where the volcanic activity is taking place. However, the trail does continue over the shoulder of **Makaopuhi Crater** to the primitive campsite at Napau Crater, passing more cones and pit craters, lava flows, and sections of rain forest.

Roadside Sights

For several miles, Chain of Craters Road traverses lava that was laid down about 40 years ago; remnants of the old road can still be seen in spots. There are long stretches of smooth *pahoehoe* lava interspersed with flows of the rough *'a'a*. Here and there, green pokes through a crack in the rock, bringing new life to this stark landscape. Everywhere you look, you can see the wild "action" of these lava flows, stopped in all their magnificent forms. At one vantage point on the way is **Kealakomo,** a picnic overlook where you have unobstructed views of the coast. Stop and enjoy the sight before proceeding. Several other lookouts and pull-offs have been created along the road to call attention to one sight or another. Soon the road heads over the edge of the *pali* and diagonally down to the flats, passing sections of the old road not covered by lava. Stop and look back and realize that most of the old road has been covered by dozens of feet of lava, the darkest of the dark.

The last section of road runs close to the edge of the sea, where cliffs rise up from the pounding surf. Near the end of the road is the **Holei Sea Arch,** a spot where the wave action has undercut the rock to leave a bridge of stone. Enjoy the scene, but don't lean too far out trying to get that perfect picture!

Pu'u Loa Petroglyphs

The walk out to **Pu'u Loa Petroglyphs** is delightful, highly educational, and takes less than one hour. As you walk along the trail (1.5 miles round-trip), note the *ahu,* traditional trail markers that are piles of stone shaped like little Christmas trees. Most of the lava field leading to the petroglyphs is undulating *pahoehoe* and looks like a frozen sea. You can climb bumps of lava, 8-10 feet high, to scout the immediate territory. Mountainside, the *pali* is quite visible and you can pick out the most recent lava flows—the blackest and least vegetated. As you approach the site, the lava changes dramatically and looks like long strands of braided rope.

The petroglyphs are in an area about the size of a soccer field. A wooden walkway encircles most of them and helps ensure their protection. A common motif of the petroglyphs is a circle with a hole in the middle, like a doughnut; you'll also see designs of men with triangular heads. Some rocks are entirely covered with designs, while others have only a symbolic scratch or two. These carvings are impressive more for their sheer number than the multiplicity of design. If you stand on the walkway and trek off towards the two o'clock position, you'll see a small hill. Go over and down it, and you will discover even better petroglyphs, including a sailing canoe about two feet high. At the back end of the walkway a sign proclaims that Pu'u Loa meant Long Hill, which the Hawaiians turned into the metaphor "Long Life." For countless generations, fathers would come here to place pieces of their infants' umbilical cords into small holes as offerings to the gods to grant long life to their children. Concentric circles surrounded the holes that held the umbilical cords. The entire area, an obvious power spot, screams in utter silence, and the still-strong mana is easily felt.

The Big Island has the largest concentration of petroglyphs in the state, and this site holds the greatest number. One estimate puts the number at 28,000.

OTHER PARK ROADS
Hilina Pali Road

About two miles down the Chain of Craters

Road, **Hilina Pali Road** shoots off to the southwest (to the left) over a narrow, roughly paved road all the way to the end at Hilina Pali Lookout—about nine miles. Soon after you leave the Chain of Craters Road, the vegetation turns drier and you enter the semi-arid Ka'u Desert. The road picks its way around and over old volcanic flows, and you can see the vegetation struggling to maintain a foothold. On the way you pass the **Mauna Iki trailhead,** Kulanaokuaiki Campground, and the former Kipuka Nene Campground—closed to help the *nene* recover their threatened population. You should see geese here, but leave them alone and don't feed them.

The road ends right on the edge of the rift, with expansive views over the benched coastline, from the area of current volcanic flow all the way to South Point. From here, one trail heads down the hill to the coast while another pushes on along the top of the cliff and farther into the dry landscape. At the *pali* lookout is a pavilion and restrooms, but no drinking water. This is not a pleasure ride, as the road is rough, but it is passable. For most it probably isn't worth the time, but for those looking for isolation and a special vantage point, this could be it. If you drive just slightly past the turnoff for Hilina Pali Road, you'll arrive at **Devil's Throat,** a pit crater formed in 1912. It's not directly off the road, so you'll have to park your car at the small gravel area by the side of the road, cross the street, and walk back about 50 feet to catch a glimpse.

Mauna Loa Road

About 2.5 miles south of the park entrance on the Highway 11, **Mauna Loa Road** turns off to the north. This road will lead you to the Tree Molds and a bird sanctuary, as well as to the trailhead for the Mauna Loa summit trail. As an added incentive, traveling just a minute down this road leaves 99 percent of the tourists behind.

Tree Molds is an ordinary name for an extraordinary area. Turn right off Mauna Loa Road soon after leaving the Belt Road and

follow the signs for five minutes. This road runs into the tree molds area and loops back onto itself. At the loop, a signboard explains what occurred here. In a moment, you realize that you're standing atop a lava flow, and that the scattered potholes were entombed tree trunks, most likely the remains of a once-giant koa forest. The lava stayed put while the tree trunks burned away, leaving the 15- to 18-foot-deep holes. Realizing what happened here and how it happened is an eye-opener.

Kipuka Puaulu is a sanctuary for birds and nature lovers who want to leave the crowds behind, just under three miles from Highway 11 up Mauna Loa Road. The sanctuary is an island atop an island. A *kipuka* is a piece of land that is surrounded by lava but has not been inundated by it, leaving the original vegetation and land contour intact. A few hundred yards away, small scrub vegetation struggles, but in the sanctuary, the trees form a towering canopy a hundred feet tall. The first sign takes you to an ideal picnic area called Bird Park, with cooking grills; the second, 100 yards beyond, takes you to **Kipuka Puaulu Loop Trail.** As you enter the trail, a bulletin board describes the birds and plants, some of the last remaining indigenous fauna and flora in Hawaii. Please follow all rules. The dirt trail is self-guided, and pamphlets describing the stations along the way are available from a box near the start of the path. The loop is only one mile long, but to really appreciate the area, especially if you plan to do any bird-watching, expect to spend an hour minimum.

Along the trail, you are privileged to see some of the world's rarest plants, such as a small bush called *'a'ali'i*. In the branches of the towering *'ohi'a* trees you might see an *'elepaio* or an *'apapane,* two birds native to Hawaii. Common finches and Japanese white-eyes are imported birds that are here to stay. There's an example of a lava tube, a huge koa tree, and an explanation of how ash from eruptions provided soil and nutrients for the forest. Blue morning glories have taken over entire hillsides. Once considered a pest and aggressively eradicated, they have recently been given a reprieve and are now considered good ground cover—perhaps even indigenous. When you do come across a native Hawaiian plant, it seems somehow older, almost prehistoric. If a precontact Hawaiian could come back today, he or she would recognize only a few plants and trees seen in this preserve. To hear the birds at their best, come in early morning or late afternoon.

Mauna Loa Road continues westward and gains elevation for approximately 10 miles. It passes through thick forests of lichen-covered koa trees, cuts across **Kipuka Ki,** and traverses the narrow **Ke'amoku Flow.** At the end of the pavement, at 6,662 feet, you will find a parking area and lookout. If the weather is cooperating, you'll be able to see much of the mountainside; if not, your field of vision will be restricted. A trail leads from here to the summit of Mauna Loa. It takes two long and difficult days to hike. Under no circumstances should it be attempted by novice hikers or those unprepared for cold alpine conditions. At times, this road may be closed due to extreme fire conditions.

Ka'u Desert Footprints

A trailhead for the **Ka'u Desert Trail** is about eight miles south of the park entrance along Highway 11, between mile markers 37 and 38. There isn't a parking lot here; just park your car on the side of the road on the gravel. There are usually one or two other cars there. You don't have to pay to walk on this trail since the trailhead isn't through the park entrance.

It's a short 20-minute hike from this trailhead to the **Ka'u Desert Footprints.** The 1.6-mile round-trip trek across the small section of desert is fascinating, and the history of the footprints makes the experience more evocative. Because of deterioration, the footprints are faint and difficult to see.

The predominant foliage is *'ohi'a,* which contrasts with the bleak desert surroundings. You pass a wasteland of *'a'a* and *pahoehoe* lava flows to arrive at the footprints. A metal fence in a sturdy pavilion surrounds the prints, which look as though they're cast in cement. They're in fact formed from pisolites: particles of ash stuck together with moisture, which formed mud that hardened like plaster. The story of these footprints is far more exciting than the prints themselves, which are eroded and not very visible.

In 1790, Kamehameha was waging war with Keoua over control of the Big Island. One of Keoua's warrior parties

Tree Molds area off Mauna Loa Road

of approximately 80 people attempted to cross the desert while Kilauea was erupting. Toxic gases descended upon them, and the warriors and their families were enveloped and suffocated. They literally died in their tracks. (Although romanticism would have it otherwise, the preserved footprints were probably made by a party of people who came well after the eruption or perhaps at some time during a previous eruption.) This unfortunate occurrence was regarded by the Hawaiians as a direct message from the gods proclaiming their support for Kamehameha.

Hiking and Biking

HIKING

There are over 150 miles of hiking trails within the park. One long trail heads up the flank of Mauna Loa to its top; a spiderweb of trails loops around and across Kilauea Caldera and into the adjoining craters; and from a point along the Chain of Craters Road, another trail heads east toward the source of the most recent volcanic activity. But by far the greatest number of trails, and those with the greatest total distance, are those that cut through the Ka'u Desert and along the barren and isolated coast. Many have shelters, and trails that require overnight stays provide cabins or primitive campsites.

Because of the possibility of an eruption or earthquake, it is *imperative* to check in at park headquarters, where you can pick up current trail information and excellent maps. In fact, a hiking permit is required for most trails outside the Crater Rim Drive area and the coastal stretch beyond the end of Chain of Craters Drive. New fees recently have been implemented for all **backcountry and front-country campsites,** including Kulanaokuaiki Campground, and are $10 per site per night. Permits can be obtained in person from the Backcountry Office at the **Visitor Emergency Operations Center** (located on Crater Rim Dr. in the building with two rock-based columns) from 8am to 4pm daily. The earliest you may obtain a permit is the day prior to your hike. They do not accept reservations or issue permits in advance.

Much of the park is hot and dry, so carry plenty of drinking water. Wear a hat, sunscreen, and sunglasses, but don't forget rain gear because it often rains in the green areas of the park. Stay on trails and stay away from steep edges, cracks, new lava flows, and any area where lava is flowing into the sea.

If you will be hiking along the trails in the Kilauea Caldera, the free park maps are sufficient for navigation. To aid with hikes elsewhere, it's best to purchase and use larger and more detailed topographical maps. One that is readily available and of high quality is the *Hawai'i Volcanoes National Park* map by Trails Illustrated, which is available at the gift shop at the visitors center.

Self-Guided Easy Hikes

If you find yourself only having one day to venture through Hawai'i Volcanoes National Park, there are several short hikes that will offer you a glimpse of what it's like to live next to an active volcano.

VOLCANO ART CENTER'S NIAULANI CAMPUS TRAIL

Just outside the park in Volcano Village is a four-acre old-growth tropical rain forest growing in volcanic ash from the 18th century. Some of the trees at the Volcano Art Center (19-4074 Old Volcano Rd., Volcano, 808/967-8222) are at least 200 years old and more than 65 feet tall. The **Niaulani Campus Trail,** which is filled with placards explaining the area and art, is a flat 0.7-mile loop. Bird lovers will delight in this opportunity to see native birds. If you get there early, you can participate in an hour-long **yoga** class on Monday at 7:30am or stop by to unwind on Thursdays at 5:30pm after a day of hiking.

CRATER RIM TRAIL

Although a large part of Crater Rim Drive is currently closed due to the sulphur dioxide (vog) from Halema'uma'u, it is possible to hike along the **Crater Rim Trail.** If you park at the Thomas A. Jaggar Museum and hike along the Crater Rim toward the visitors center, you will have unparalleled views of the vast Kilauea Caldera. Along the way you pass through desert-like conditions with sparse vegetation, eventually giving way to lush native tropical forests. You will also encounter the **Steam Vents,** where the water heated by the volcanic rises up from cracks in the earth. The hike along the Crater Rim Trail to/from the Thomas A. Jaggar Museum to the visitors center is approximately 2.5 miles and can take anywhere from 45 minutes to an hour. Parts of it are shaded; other sections cross an open field. The trailhead for this Crater Rim hike is to the left of the museum and parking lot, across the street from the visitors center (next to Volcano House). Parts of the trail have been paved and provide a good place for road or mountain biking.

SULPHUR BANKS TRAIL

From the visitors center parking lot you can get a good glimpse of some interesting volcanic geology. The **Sulphur Banks Trail** is a short and easy hike that offers intriguing sights. Bright yellow mineral deposits of sulphur line the trail as volcanic gases spew from the earth; this trail may remind some people of the volcanic vents in Yellowstone. Interpretive signs offer explanations of the volcanic activities so it's easy to understand what you're seeing. To get to this trail, walk to the left of the visitors center past the Volcano Art Center. A paved trail will lead you through a grassy field with a *heiau* (temple) and down a hill. If you see signs warning you that you may encounter volcanic gases, you're

going the right way. It's 0.5 mile one-way from the visitors center to the Sulphur Banks. If you want to make it into a longer hike, you can cross the road and connect to the Crater Rim Trail by the Steam Vents and hike all the way to the Thomas A. Jaggar Museum.

EARTHQUAKE TRAIL

If you head left from the visitors center (behind the Volcano House facing the caldera) on the Crater Rim Trail, you'll walk one mile round-trip toward **Waldron Ledge** on the **Earthquake Trail,** so named due to the damage this area incurred during the 1983 6.6 magnitude earthquake. Waldron Ledge offers one of the best views in the park, and the trail, which is paved and wheelchair- and stroller-accessible as well as bike friendly, presents an easy walk.

DEVASTATION TRAIL

Farther up Crater Rim Drive, most visitors hike along the one-mile round-trip **Devastation Trail,** which could aptly be renamed Regeneration Trail. The mile it covers is fascinating; it's one of the most-photographed areas in the park. It leads across a field devastated by a tremendous eruption from **Kilauea Iki.** The area was once an *'ohi'a* forest that was denuded of limbs and leaves, then choked by black pumice and ash. The vegetation has regenerated since then, and the recuperative power of the flora is the subject of ongoing study. Notice that many of the trees have sprouted aerial roots trailing down from the branches: This is total adaptation to the situation, as such roots don't normally appear. As you move farther along the trail, tufts of grass and bushes peek out of the pumice and then the surroundings become totally barren.

Self-Guided Moderate Hikes

If you're willing and able to complete more moderate hikes and want to experience the volcano with your own two feet, then attempt one or both of these hikes. Both hikes can easily be completed in one day.

★ KILAUEA IKI TRAIL

The **Kilauea Iki Trail** takes you from the top of the crater and lush tropical rain forest of native vegetation and native birds to the bottom of the crater floor, which is devoid of vegetation and still breathes volcanic steam. This is a moderate four-mile loop because you descend and ascend 400 feet to and from the crater floor. It takes on average three hours to complete.

The trail for this hike is clearly marked. The parking lot for Kilauea Iki is the first one on the right on the Chain of Craters Road. It's usually packed. From the parking lot go right and follow the Kilauea Iki sign, which will keep you to the left. As you hike along the rim, look to the left and down at the various railed-off lookouts. Below you is where you'll be as you descend the trail to the crater floor. Essentially you are passing along the rim and then descending across the barren landscape before returning back up through the trees.

Upon ascending the trail out of the crater floor, you will pass by the **Thurston Lava Tube** parking lot. This is a worthy addition to the hike to see a lava tube, but it is also one of the most popular stops with tour buses so it can get crowded. Note: Your car was not stolen; you are in the Thurston Lava Tube parking lot, not the lot you parked in. Keep walking through the parking lot to the next parking lot where you left your car.

The best time to do this hike is first thing in the morning, for several reasons. It's cooler in the morning and a more pleasant hike in the floor of the crater. When it's cooler it's also easier to spot all the steam vents, which are an active reminder that the crater could erupt again at any time. Finally, the birds are also much more active in the morning. Look for them along the crater rim as they search for insects to keep their bellies filled. Pick up a trail guide for this particular trail at the visitors center or download it from the park's website for further descriptions of the sights you'll pass on your way.

PU'U HULUHULU TRAIL

Another notable hike that can be completed in just two or three hours is the 2.5-mile round-trip **Pu'u Huluhulu Trail** to Mauna Ulu. This hike is for those who like adventure, since the trail isn't marked well. Follow the signs along the Chain of Craters Road. Turn left where the road splits and there will be a sign for Mauna Ulu. Follow the road and the signs until the road ends. The trailhead will be to the left of the parking lot. This moderate hike will take you to the summit of a steaming volcanic crater that can also provide you with 360-degree panoramic views of the park; on a clear day you can even see the ocean. The trail crosses lava flows from the 1970s, and you'll see young plants sprouting out from cracks in the lava. Follow the trail to Pu'u Huluhulu (Hairy Hill), a crater that has an island of vegetation *(kipuka)* that didn't burn during the 1970s flows. It's a short hike to the top of the *pu'u* (hill), which gives you a good view of Mauna Ulu, the big mountain right in front of you. You can't hike past Pu'u Huluhulu without a permit, but you can follow the old flows up toward the top of Mauna Ulu. There aren't official trail markers to the top but it's easy to pick your own way up the young lava and return the way you came back to the trail. From the top of Mauna Ulu you can peer into the crater, which is hundreds of feet deep, and imagine what it must have been like when lava was spewing from it up to 1,700 feet into the air. A trail guide is available at the visitors center or online on the park's website.

Self-Guided Advanced Hikes

For experienced hikers who want to do some overnight camping and hiking, the park has several options for backcountry wilderness trips.

★ HIKING TO HALAPE

A large section of the park has trails that run along the coast, providing access to several beaches that offer premier camping. By far one of the most remote and pristine beaches on the island is **Halape.** Getting here is something you have to earn, though.

The absolute closest you can get by vehicle is the **Hilina Pali Trailhead,** from where it is an eight-mile descent to the beach across hot, dry, rugged terrain. The first two miles are straight down the *pali* (cliff) with multiple switchbacks to get you safely to the bottom. Halape is the sandiest beach along the coast, but there are also other beautiful places to access the ocean that aren't quite as sandy. One stunning option: After descending the switchbacks to the bottom of Hilina Pali, take the trail to the right toward Ka'aha. This is a nice bay that offers lots of room to explore all the way to the *pali* that extends to the ocean. Some nice tide pools here offer unique snorkeling and swimming. If you keep to the left, the trail will lead you to Halape after six extremely hot miles that include some more steep ascents and descents—but your reward is a sugary beach and a sheltered lagoon that offer you sand and protection from the raw ocean that crashes just past the lagoon. This spot is popular, so you're likely see other campers, but you'll never see the crowd you would in the more accessible sections of the park. Bathroom facilities are available here. There is water available at the backcountry sites, but it must be treated before drinking because it is from a cistern of collected rainwater. Before you go, make sure to ask a ranger if there is water available; at times there is a drought.

The park requires backcountry permits to camp in these sections. They are available from the Backcountry Office at the Visitor Emergency Operation Center. There is a limit to the number of people they allow at any given time, so plan accordingly and know to get your permits ahead of time before you begin your trek.

If you have the option for someone to pick you up, the best route with the most variety is to hike down from Hilina Pali, spend a night or two at Halape, and then enjoy a nice flat hike out by heading toward Keahou and Apua, both of which have shelter and water.

This route covers a longer distance, but it is not as steep as the route you came on.

HIKING TO MAUNA LOA'S SUMMIT

The most extreme hike of them all, Mauna Loa offers a unique experience to climb to the summit of the island's largest volcano. This trip will take you to elevations of almost 14,000 feet, so be prepared for altitude sickness and changes of weather. Winter conditions can occur any time of the year here. It has snowed here in May! (Yes, it snows in Hawaii.) There are cabins available to stay in along the way; they require a permit from the Backcountry Office that you can only get the day before your hike. The Pu'u 'Ula'ula (Red Hill) cabin contains 8 bunks, and the Mauna Loa summit cabin has 12 bunks. Visitors are allowed a three-night maximum stay per site. Pit toilets are available at the cabins as well as drinking water (although check with park rangers about the water level). Don't forget to treat the water. No water is available on the trails themselves.

There are two trail options for your hike: via the Mauna Loa Road trailhead (an hour drive from the Kilauea Visitor Center) or the Mauna Loa Observatory trailhead (a two-hour drive via Saddle Road), which is not in the park. The **Mauna Loa Road trail** ascends 6,600 feet over 18 miles. Depending on your hiking speed, it will take 4-6 hours to hike the 7.5 miles from the trailhead to the Pu'u 'Ula'ula cabin. Then, it's 8-12 additional hours to hike the 11.5 miles from the Pu'u 'Ula'ula cabin to the Mauna Loa summit cabin.

The **Mauna Loa Observatory Trail** climbs 1,975 feet over 3.8 miles up the volcano's north slope until it reaches the rim of the Moku'aweoweo Caldera (the summit). From here, the Mauna Loa summit cabin is 2.1 miles. In all, it takes about 4-6 hours to hike from the Observatory trailhead to the Mauna Loa summit cabin. However, the hike back from the Mauna Loa summit cabin to the Mauna Loa Observatory trailhead is much quicker—only about three hours.

In summary, you have a few options for

this hike. If you have friends on the ground (or means to hire a taxi), you can start from the Mauna Loa Road trailhead and finish at the Mauna Loa Observatory trailhead (for a quicker exit). But again, you'll need someone to pick you up or arrange to leave a car at the trailhead. Otherwise, most hikers choose to hike from the Mauna Loa Observatory to the Mauna Loa summit cabin and return to the observatory for a challenging but manageable hike. A great resource for this hike is available here at www.kinquest.com/misc/travel/trailguide.php. The guide on this site provides a mile-by-mile description of what you'll see.

Note: Mauna Loa is at a high altitude, so it is *imperative* to wait at least 24 hours between scuba diving and ascending Mauna Loa in order to avoid getting the bends.

Guided Hikes

When picking a guided hike of the park, the most important factors to consider are: How many people will be on the tour? If the minimum isn't met, will the tour get canceled? How much hiking and walking will you actually be doing? Will the hiking be for beginners or more advanced walkers?

Ranger-led hikes are a great way to explore the park for free with certifiably experienced guides. The **Exploring the Summit hike** is offered daily at 10:30am and 1:30pm. This 45-minute walk over a paved trail meets in front of the Kilauea Visitor Center and takes guests around the rim while the ranger lectures on Hawaiian history and geology. Check the bulletin board outside the visitors center for daily postings of additional hikes. Often, there is at least one additional hike (on some specific topic) each day.

Several private tour guides happily take groups around the park on hikes. Dr. Hugh Montgomery, the owner and president of **Hawaiian Walkways** (800/457-7759, www.hawaiianwalkways.com) receives excellent reviews for his guided hikes in the national park ($190 per person). Hugh is truly an expert on Hawaiian flora and fauna and offers a lot of personal attention to his small groups,

making his tours a great choice for hikers of any level.

★ **Friends of Hawaii Volcanoes National Park** (808/985-7373, http://fhvnp. org/institute/private-tours, $250-450 per group) is a nonprofit organization that uses all the proceeds from their tours to support projects and programs at the national park. That makes you feel pretty good! Even better, the tour guides are retired park rangers and wildlife biologists. Not to mention, these tours are a pretty good deal for a group of people. Since the tours are all on-demand, your group (up to 6 people) can decide between 4-8 hour excursions and moderate or extreme hikes. Transportation is not provided; the tour guide gets in your car(s) with you. This tour is a great way to support the park and customize exactly what you'd like to see with the added expertise of someone familiar with the area.

Similarly, Warren Costa, aka ★ **Native Guide Hawaii** (808/982-7575, www.nativeguidehawaii.com, $300 for one person or $150 per person for two or more) will personally pick you up (and return you safely) after guiding you through the park on a hike that includes narration on Hawaiian culture, legends, and geology of the park. Warren is concerned with not only teaching about the environment, but also raising awareness about how the environment relates to Hawaiian culture. Tours have a maximum of six guests, and children are welcome.

BIKING

Biking is permitted in the park on paved roads, paved sections of the Crater Rim Trail, and on some dirt trails. The park has created an excellent *Where to Bicycle* brochure that is available at www.nps.gov/havo/planyourvisit/bike.htm.

The suggested bike rides include a moderate 11-mile loop to circle the rim, a moderate 18-mile round-trip ride on Hilina Pali Road, a challenging 36-mile round-trip Summit to Sea ride following the path of Mauna Ulu eruption, and a challenging 11.5-mile loop up (climbing 2,600 feet!) and down Mauna Loa Road. The guide includes several short off-shoots from the Mauna Loa Road for those who want to do some mountain biking.

If you don't have a bike with you or are not an experienced rider, or you're simply looking for a different way to see the park, take a guided bike tour of the park with **Bike Volcano** (808/934-9199, www.bikevolcano.com, $110-134 per person and from $105 to ride in the van). What makes this a great way to see the park is that it takes some cars off the road and the ride is all downhill and truly easy for anyone (including youngsters and those of us who are out of shape). There are snacks at several stops on the tour. Half-day (3 hours and 8.5 miles) and full-day (5 hours and 15 miles) tours are available. Experienced riders

may be bored or frustrated by the slow pace. The ride stops at all the major sights along the Crater Rim, where the tour guide, who is trained in geology and Hawaiian culture, gives informative talks about the park. Bike Volcano offers several pickup points for riders (including from Hilo), or riders may meet at the Kilauea Visitor Center.

Another company that does a similar basic bike tour of the park, but picks up from both Hilo and the Kona side, is **Nui Pohaku** (808/937-0644, www.nuipohaku.com, $139-239). The tour guides among the different companies tend to know each other, so the actual tour and information given aren't that different. The main difference is that Nui Pohaku uses older bikes than the other companies.

Tours

BUS TOURS

If you have rented a car, there isn't much of a reason to take a tour bus around the park unless you really want to be able to ask questions of someone semi-knowledgeable while you're sightseeing. Otherwise, this guide as well as the brochures available at the park visitors center should provide you with enough information for your journey.

Guided tour bus trips to the park tend to be best and most utilized by day-trippers to the park—either those flying in from another island for the day or those traveling from the Kona side who don't want to worry about driving back to Kona late at night. These guided tours are also great for visitors who might need translation into languages other than English.

The most ubiquitous tour company of them all, **Roberts Hawaii** (866/898-2519, www.robertshawaii.com, $79 per adult, $54.50 per child) offers pickup from Hilo and then a full-day journey to the park with stops at the Mauna Loa Macadamia Nut Factory (in Hilo) and the major sights in the park. Roberts

has been doing this tour for a long time and has the schedule down pat. They know what they're doing, but you likely won't get much personal attention or willingness to alter their schedule. There is a 15 percent discount if you book online.

The Hilo-based **Kapoho Kine Adventures** (25 Waianuenue Ave., Hilo, 808/964-1000, www.kapohokine.com) offers a range of lengthy full-day tours to the park with possible pickup from the Kona side, a trip over the Saddle Road, and then a second (or third) pickup from Hilo before heading to the park. The entire tour, from pickup to drop-off, is 12 hours long. The tour is $299 (plus tax) with Kona pickup, $219 if you meet in Hilo or at the park. If a 12-hour tour sounds like no fun while you're on vacation, they also offer a shorter (10-hour) Evening Lava Expedition tour with later pickup that visits a Kona coffee farm for lunch and then heads to the park for a tour, dinner at Volcano House, and sunset at the Jaggar Museum for some lava viewing ($99 children, $119 adults plus tax).

The crème de la crème, for those leaving

from the Kona side, is **Hawaii Forest and Trails** (808/331-8505, www.hawaii-forest.com, $179 children, $209 adults plus tax), with an ecofriendly ethos, extremely in-the-know tour guides, and flexibility with their small groups. This 12-hour round-trip adventure, which includes continental breakfast and lunch, is mainly a tour of the main park sights with stops along the Kaʻu Coast for some sightseeing. Although you'll mostly stay on the bus during this tour, there are several less-than-a-mile walks—ideal for those who do want to do some walking in the park.

A twilight trip is also available and offers something a little different from the usual twilight excursion. The tours leave later in the afternoon and travel to the park via the Saddle Road, making stops at **Mauna Kea State Park** and near Hilo to explore the **Kaumana Cave** before arriving to the park around sunset to witness the lava flow from Puna or the glow from near the Thomas A. Jaggar Museum.

HELICOPTER TOURS

A dramatic way to experience the awesome power of the volcano is to take a helicopter tour. The choppers are perfectly suited for the maneuverability necessary to get an intimate bird's-eye view. The pilots will fly you over the areas offering the most activity, often dipping low over lava pools, skimming still-glowing flows, and circling the towering steam clouds rising from where lava meets the sea. When activity is really happening, tours are jammed, and prices, like lava fountains, go sky-high. Remember, however, that these tours are increasingly resented by hikers and anyone else

trying to have a quiet experience, and that future regulations might limit flights over the lava area.

Also, these tours are not without danger, as helicopters have crashed near lava flows during commercial sightseeing flights. Nonetheless, if you are interested, contact one of the helicopter companies located in Hilo or Kona. Alternatively, fixed-wing plane tour companies also offer flights over the volcano area from both Hilo and Kona.

Sunshine Helicopters (808/882-1233 or 800/622-3144, www.sunshinehelicopters. com), leaving from Hapuna on the Kona side, offers a two-hour Volcano Deluxe tour that circles the island ($520-$595 per person with online discount or $510 for the early-bird tour).

Another large operation is **Blue Hawaiian Helicopters** (808/886-1768 in Waikoloa, 800/786-2583, www.bluehawaiian.com), which operates tours from both the Kona and Hilo sides with two helicopter options—the A-Star and the Eco-Star. The Eco-Star is touted as "the first touring helicopter of the 21st century," meaning that its seats are more comfortable, it is quieter, and it has larger windows for a less obstructed view than the A-Star. Most importantly, it costs more. From the Kona side, there is a two-hour Big Island Spectacular ($396/$495), an all-encompassing trip that circles the island to witness all its highlights, including a quick flyover of the park. From the Hilo side, the one-hour Circle of Fire Plus Waterfalls Tour ($196/$241) will take you over the waterfalls near Hilo on the way to Hawaiʻi Volcanoes National Park.

Entertainment

After a long day at the park, you might be too tired to do anything, but there are several opportunities for "nightlife" in Volcano.

The **Lava Lounge** (808/967-8333) at Kilauea Military Camp in the park offers not only cheap drinks, but karaoke most Thursday nights, live music sometimes on the weekends, and big parties for holidays like Halloween and St. Patrick's Day. If you want an activity to go along with your drinking, the **Bowling Alley** across the street from the Lava Lounge has five old-school lanes and rents shoes. You don't have to drink while you bowl, and actually if you want alcohol you need to purchase it at the Lava Lounge and bring it to the bowling alley.

The **Volcano Art Center** (808/967-8222, volcanoartcenter.org) organizes monthly poetry slams (usually on a Friday night toward the end of the month), frequent music concerts (not just Hawaiian music), and demonstrations of Hawaiian culture such as hula. Check the website for additional information.

The **After Dark in the Park** program (Kilauea Visitor Center, Tues. 7pm, park entrance fee applies plus recommended $2 donation) presents talks by experts in the fields of volcanology, geology, and Hawaiian culture. Check the schedule (www.nps.gov/havo/planyourvisit/events_adip.htm) for more information. Note: It's not always a lecture; sometimes there are slack-key guitarists or choral groups performing. In addition, some months additional programs are added on Wednesday nights. Check the bulletin board just outside the Kilauea Visitor Center for additional information of what's happening in the park.

Food

VOLCANO VILLAGE

I wish the dining experience in Volcano—with its captive audience of tourists who are starving after a long day of touring the park—were so much better than it actually is. There are a few options, but they tend toward mediocre and overpriced, so keep your expectations low. If you're not too hungry, are in the area for a few days, or are simply in the mood for a drive, it might be worth heading to Hilo (40 minutes away) to seek better options. The choices in Volcano are listed from south to north on Old Volcano Road. They are all within minutes of one another.

The newest restaurant in the village, **'Ohelo Café** (19-4005 Haunani Rd., 808/339-7865, daily 11:30am-2:30pm and 5:30pm-9:30pm, $15-35), is a good option in the Volcano Village food desert. The best bang for your buck comes from the wood-fired pizzas ($13-15), which are served at both lunch and dinner. The daily burger (offered lunch only, $14) has good flavor, but I'd skip their plate lunch because it's a bit overpriced for "local food."

In the back side of the same complex, the food at **Eagle's Lighthouse Cafe** (corner of Old Volcano Rd. and Haunani Rd., Mon.-Sat. 7am-5pm, $10) (formally known as Café Ohia) is reasonably priced. There never seem to be enough people working here for as crowded as it gets. But the crowds are here for a reason: homemade breads, pastries, and lunch specials. For $9.75 you have your choice of deli sandwich with Hawaiian-style sides. The portions are large. If you're not too hungry, try the Portuguese bean soup. It's a nonvegetarian hearty stew that will warm you up during the sometimes chilly Volcano days. There is no indoor seating, so either take your sandwiches to go into the park or enjoy them outside on picnic tables. Since the wait can get long, the staff encourages patrons to head next door to the grocery store and grab a beer to enjoy outside.

The most romantic and rustic option in town is the long-standing **Kilauea Lodge** (19-3948 Old Volcano Rd., 808/967-7366, www.kilauealodge.com, daily 7:30am-2pm and 5pm-9pm, lunch $12, dinner $32). The food is expensive, but the setting seems to match. The large fireplace sets the mood for this truly lodge-like setting, with game animals adorning the ceiling and featured on the menu. Vegetarian choices are limited here. The meat dishes are prepared well and come with satisfying sides like mashed potatoes, but overall, the meat dishes are better in the restaurants of Waimea. Foodies and those who like to drink might try their *li hing mui* (salted dried plum)-rimmed cocktails, like *liliko'i* (passion fruit) margaritas. Eating isn't a requirement for drinking here. If you solely want drinks, you can simply walk in, cozy up on the couch in front of the fireplace, and order away. Reservations are a must for dinner, and if you want to surprise your dinner guest, call ahead to ask for your name on the menu.

The food truck craze has finally made it to this side of the island. ★ **Tuk Tuk Thai** (19-4030 Wright Rd. in the Cooper Center parking lot, 808/747-3041, www.tuk-tukthaifood.com, Tues.-Sat. 11am-6pm, $12) is truly the best choice around (if they're open). The standard (American-style) Thai dishes are available: fried rice, curry, pad thai noodles—all with a choice of tofu, chicken, or shrimp. It's not clear to me why they don't stick around for dinnertime (they'd make a killing!), so I recommend picking it up early for dinner and taking it back to your vacation rental to reheat later. Portions are huge. If you're in a rush or starving during your hike, you can call ahead and they will have your order ready upon arrival.

Some locals say that **Thai Thai** (19-4084 Old Volcano Rd., 808/967-7969, www.

lavalodge.com/thai-thai-restaurant.html, daily 11:30am-9pm, $11-26) is their favorite Thai food place on the island. The food is all spicy and authentic, with traditional dishes such as soups, rice noodles, and curries. Beer, wine, and plenty of gluten-free and vegetarian options are offered, and a children's menu is available. The restaurant is attached to a gift shop with tourist items and toiletries. Call ahead; sometimes they don't follow their posted hours.

Right before the road comes to a dead end, you'll find Ira Ono's place (that's what the locals call it): **Café Ono** (19-3834 Old Volcano Rd., 808/967-7261, www.volcanogardenarts.com, gallery Tues.-Sun. 10am-4pm, café 11am-3pm, $14). It's the kind of place that you either love or hate. The menu lists only four or five mains, drinks, and a few desserts each day. But the food tastes like something you could have made but you probably would have seasoned better. The service is quick enough. The setting is lovely, with a few tables in the back of the art gallery and more outdoors among the trees.

Markets

The small **Volcano Store** (Old Volcano Rd., daily 5am-7pm) is pretty much the equivalent of a bodega. From fresh *musubi* to chips, some frozen foods, books, local jams, wine, and some of the nicest flower bouquets around, it somehow has everything you might need in a small space, including an ATM inside. What it does not have is a great selection of food for camping. Prices are a little bit more expensive than the larger stores in Hilo or Kona.

Down the street, the **Kilauea General Store** (19-3872 Old Volcano Rd., 808/967-7555, Mon.-Sat. 7am-7:30pm, Sun. 7am-7pm) has fewer goods than the Volcano Store, but still has wine, an ATM, and dry goods like bread and jam (actually, their jam is made in-house) as well as DVDs to rent. There is also an in-house sub shop open at lunchtime, and fresh coffee is on hand all day long.

The Sunday morning **Volcano Farmers Market** (19-4030 Wright Rd. at the

Cooper Center, http://thecoopercenter.org/ FarmersMarketVolcano.html, Sun. 6:30am-10am) is attended by what seems like every single resident of Volcano Village. It serves as an important community event. It entails the usual farmers markets accoutrements like produce and plants, but it also has jams, chocolate brittle, and prepared foods. Come early for breakfast (really early!—most vendors are sold out by 8am) and stay to chitchat with the locals.

HAWAI'I VOLCANOES NATIONAL PARK

The newly reopened **Volcano House** (1 Crater Rim Dr., 808/756-9625, www.hawaiivolcanohouse.com) includes two side-by-side eating options: **Uncle George's Lounge** (daily 11am-10pm, $13) and ★ **The Rim Restaurant** (daily breakfast buffet 7am-10am, $18 per adult, $9 per child, lunch 11am-2pm, $15, dinner 5:30pm-9pm, $20-30), both with priceless views of the nearby crater. The lounge offers a more casual and intimate setting with pupus like kalua pork and pineapple pizza ($12) and a Big Island burger ($14) offered throughout the day. Local beers on draft are a good deal here. The restaurant is almost fancy. You'd probably want to change out of your rain-soaked pants and muddy hiking shoes to feel comfortable dining here. Reservations are a must, especially if you're booking during sunset—and that's precisely when you should dine to watch the colors change over the crater. Entrees are expensive but have the presentation one would expect for those prices—although you're likely going to too distracted by the views to actually look at the food. I'd skip the stuffed Big Island chicken ($24) for something tastier like the Hilo coffee-rubbed lamb ($39). An extensive wine list is also available.

While the facility doesn't *look* open to the public, the Kilauea Military Camp (808/438-6707) eateries **Lava Lounge** (Mon.-Sat. 4pm until no one is there, Sun. open at 2pm in football season) and **Crater Rim Café** (Mon.-Fri. 6:30am-1pm, Sat.-Sun. 6:30am-11am, daily 5pm-8pm) indeed are open to anyone and are the best way to mingle with park employees—especially at the Lava Lounge, where after a few drinks, they are thrilled to speak with anyone who doesn't work at the park. The café serves breakfast, lunch, and dinner (à la carte and buffet options) and often has special events or themed meals for holidays. The Lava Lounge only offers a few options, entirely of the bar food variety, such as chicken wings and garlic fries. But yes, they do have a full bar and lots of beer on draft.

Getting There and Around

While it's not possible to travel inside the park on public transportation, you can get to and from the park with **Hele-On Bus** (www.heleonbus.org, 808/961-8744, $2 per ride, $1 each for luggage, large backpacks, bikes). The bus travels twice in the morning and once in the evening, starting at the Kilauea Visitor Center, passing through Volcano Village, and then traveling north on Highway 11 to Hilo.

The bus leaves from Hilo twice in the morning and three times in the afternoon. The trip takes about 1.5 hours depending on how many people are getting on and off (sometimes it can be a lot). It is possible from Hilo to make connections to the Kona side, Waimea, and the Hamakua Coast. Or, once a day the bus continues on to Ka'u, where it also is possible to make connections to the Kona side.

Puna

There is something magical about Puna. The pace of life on the Big Island is slow, but somehow, it moves even slower here, where free spirits spend Sunday afternoon drumming at Kehena Beach, soaking in warm tide pools, and practicing yoga.

Formed from rivers of lava spilling from Mauna Loa and Kilauea again and again over the last million years or so, Puna is the most volcanically active part of the island. The molten rivers stopped only when they hit the sea, where they fizzled and cooled, forming a chunk of land that bulges into the Pacific—marking the state's easternmost point at Cape Kumukahi.

Highway 11 (the Hawai'i Belt Road) cuts through the center of Puna, running uphill straight toward the town of Volcano. Along the way, this road passes through well-established villages, some of the largest and best-known flower farms in the state, and scattered residential subdivisions.

Pahoa, the major town in this region, was at one time the terminus of a rail line that took commodities and people to Hilo. This was timber country and later sugarcane land, but since the mills have closed, it has turned to producing acres of anthuriums and papayas.

Down the hill from town, you can stroll through the rock forest at Lava Tree State Monument before you head farther east into the brilliant sunshine of the coast. The anthurium and papaya farms are oases of color in a desert of solid black lava.

Southward is a string of beaches that are truly off the beaten path. You can also visit natural areas where the sea tortured the hot lava into caves, tubes, arches, and even a natural hot bath. Camp, swim, surf, or just play in the water to your heart's delight, but realize that there are few places to stop for food, gas, or supplies.

ORIENTATION
Highway 11 between Volcano and Hilo
The crossroads of the east side of the island, in the heart of Kea'au, the first town south of Hilo on Highway 11, is a strip mall at the intersection where the road splits to travel

Previous: Ahalanui Beach Park; Kaimu Beach. **Above:** Isaac Hale Beach Park.

Look for ★ to find recommended
sights, activities, dining, and lodging.

Highlights

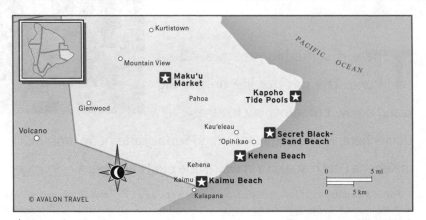

★ **Kapoho Tide Pools:** The landscape here is impressive, with tide pools surrounded by lava rocks and an ocean backdrop, but even better is the world under the water—it's a great spot for beginner snorkelers (page 142).

★ **Secret Black-Sand Beach:** You can bask in the sun all day long at this deserted beach, beyond it you'll find even more secret sand (page 143).

★ **Kehena Beach:** On Sundays Punans and like-minded visitors gather on Kehena Beach to drum and swim naked in the ocean. The vibe is friendly and you won't feel out of place if you are clothed (page 144).

★ **Kaimu Beach:** Here you can watch how a beach becomes a black-sand beach—from the waves hitting the black boulders and over time breaking them down into smaller pieces and, eventually, sand (page 144).

★ **Maku'u Market:** It's part food truck fair, part farmers market, and part antiques swap meet—and you don't have to get here at the crack of dawn to be part of the action (page 145).

Puna

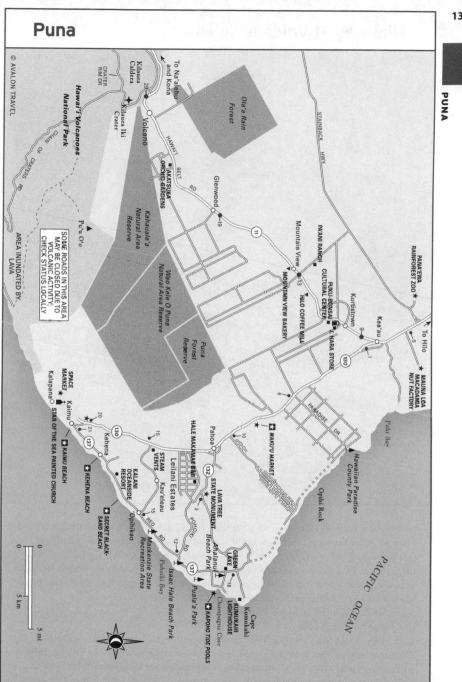

© AVALON TRAVEL

SOME ROADS IN THIS AREA
MAY BE CLOSED DUE TO
VOLCANIC ACTIVITY;
CHECK STATUS LOCALLY.

AREA INUNDATED BY
LAVA

Pu'u O'o

Hawai'i Volcanoes
National Park

CHAIN OF CRATERS RD

CRATER
RIM DR

Kilauea
Caldera

Kilauea Iki
Crater

Volcano

To Na'alehu
and Kona

29

HAWAI'I BELT RD

AKATSUKA
ORCHID GARDENS

Glenwood

Kahaualeʻa
Natural Area
Reserve

Wao Kele O Puna
Natural Area Reserve

Ola'a Rain
Forest

STAINBACK HWY

19

11

Puna
Forest
Reserve

Mountain View

PA'ANI RANCH

MOUNTAIN VIEW BAKERY

HILO COFFEE MILL

FUKU-BONSAI
CULTURAL CENTER

HARA STORE

Kurtistown

Kea'au

9

130

PANA'EWA
RAINFOREST ZOO

To Hilo

5

MAUNA LOA
MACADAMIA
NUT FACTORY

1

6

PARADISE DR

Hawaiian Paradise
County Park

Puhi Bay

SPACE
MARKET

Kaimu

Kalapana

STAR OF THE SEA PAINTED CHURCH

20

21

130

Kehena

137

KAIMU BEACH

KEHENA BEACH

SECRET BLACK-
SAND BEACH

'Opihikao

15

KALANI
OCEANSIDE
RESORT

STEAM
VENTS

HALE MAKAMAE B&B

Pahoa

MAKU'U MARKET

10

132

LAVA TREE
STATE MONUMENT

Leilani Estates

Kauʻeleau

15

RED RD

POHOIKI RD

Mackenzie State
Recreation Area

Pohoiki Bay

Isaac Hale Beach Park

12

3

137

Ahalanui
Beach Park

Pualaʻa Park

GREEN
LAKE

18

KAPOHO TIDE POOLS

Champagne Cove

KUMUKAHI
LIGHTHOUSE

Cape
Kumukahi

Opihi Rock

PACIFIC OCEAN

0   5 km

0   5 mi

Highway 11 Volcano to Hilo

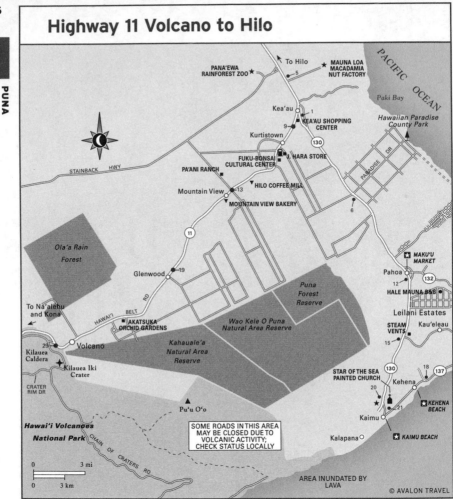

SOME ROADS IN THIS AREA
MAY BE CLOSED DUE TO
VOLCANIC ACTIVITY;
CHECK STATUS LOCALLY

AREA INUNDATED BY
LAVA

© AVALON TRAVEL

on to Pahoa, north to Hilo, or south toward Volcano. Before the sugar mill closed in 1984, this was a bustling town. Today, numerous subdivisions have mushroomed, becoming bedroom communities to Hilo. Highway 130 heads southeast from here to the steamy south coast, while Highway 11 heads southwest and passes through the mountain villages of Kurtistown, Mountain View, Glenwood, and Volcano at approximately 10-mile intervals, then enters Hawai'i Volcanoes National Park. Although only two lanes, Highway 11 (the

Hawai'i Belt Road), is straight, well surfaced, and scrupulously maintained. Worthy attractions in the area include the Kazumura Cave in Glenwood, reputedly the longest lava tube system in the world, and the indoor Fuku-Bonsai Cultural Center.

Pahoa

Arriving in Pahoa town, you're entering into lower (or south) Puna district. It has a reputation for both fields filled with marijuana plants and petty crime. This second assessment seems to me unwarranted; I have been to Pahoa numerous times without incident. Pahoa isn't a necessary stop on a tour of Puna, although the main street is lined with quaint shops, and because there are few restaurants or grocery stores and no banks outside of town, it's a good place to get supplies. The evenings offer some of the best barhopping on the island.

In late 2014 through early 2015, residents of Pahoa were on watch. The Kilauea volcano eruption changed directions and began flowing towards Pahoa town, threatening to cross the highway and separate lower Puna from the rest of the island. The National Guard was called in to assist with public safety. Then, amazingly, Pele changed her mind and the lava flow stopped just at the boundary of the Pahoa Transfer Station. Although mostly cooled now, the lava spectacle can still be seen down the road on Apa'a Street where lava entered through a chain-link fence and then just...stopped.

Highway 132 and the Red Road (Highway 137)

To most visitors, this southeastern part of the island feels both physically and mentally out of the way. But it's the best and easiest place to have an adventure without trespassing. Some of the island's best snorkeling is within minutes of the highway. In August 2014, Tropical Storm Iselle devastated the lower Puna area. Before the storm, a lush canopy of *albizzia* trees surrounded Highway 132, creating a fairy-tale backdrop to your road trip. Sadly, the majority of these trees were knocked down by the storm.

Highway 137, aka the Red Road, aka Kapoho-Kalapana Road, meets Highway 132 at the "Four Corners" intersection and continues south and then west to Kaimu Beach, where the Kalapana lava flow of 1990 covered the road. Stop at Kaimu Beach to witness the formation of one of the newest black-sand beaches on the island. Highway 137 is nicknamed the Red Road because crushed red lava rock was used to build it; most of it is now covered by black asphalt.

PLANNING YOUR TIME

For too long visitors have left Puna untouched. But this region is a must-see for those who want to get away from tour buses. Try to visit Pahoa on the weekend when the markets take place. Even on a weekday, it's easy to spend a very full day hopping from beach to tide pool and then catching a bite to eat during happy hour at Kaleo's Bar and Grill. The good news for those looking for some peace and quiet is that there is no cell phone service in much of this area! Make sure to plan ahead for a day without a phone.

A tour of the area should start with Highway 132 and then circulate south and then west on Highway 137 (the route looks like a backward C) so that you can end your evening, especially if it's a Wednesday, at Uncle Robert's Awa Bar where locals and visitors congregate for music and a farmers market. To stay on Highway 132, keep to the left when the road forks (if you go to the right you'll end up on Pahoa-Pohoiki Road).

If you stop at all the sights and beaches on the Red Road (Highway 137), it will take you the entire day (or longer if you decide to make longer stops for snorkeling). Even if you don't stop, the road itself makes for a great hour-long drive, passing through coastal rain forest, hugging the ocean, and presenting picturesque photo ops.

It's not worth going out of your way to make stops on Highway 11 between Volcano and Hilo unless it is raining or you need a few minutes to stretch your feet. If you are traveling south on Highway 11, stock up on supplies in Kea'au. You won't find another larger grocery store until you reach Ocean View, more than an hour away.

Highways 132 and 137: The Red Road

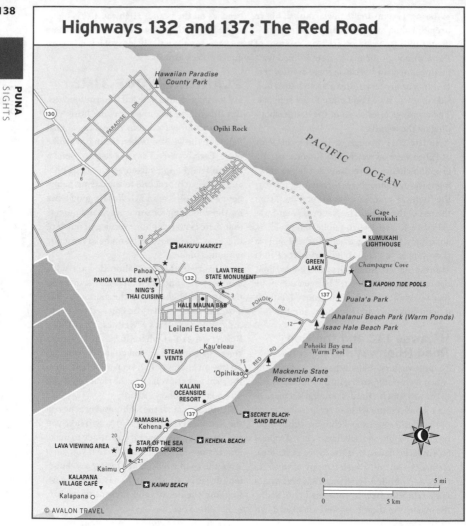

Sights

HIGHWAY 11 BETWEEN VOLCANO AND HILO
Akatsuka Orchid Gardens

It can be hard to find a parking spot at **Akatsuka Orchid Gardens** (Hwy. 11 between mile markers 22 and 23, 808/967-8234, www.akatsukaorchid.com, daily 9:30am-5pm, free), an indoor warehouse filled with orchids, not because it's that crowded, but because the lot is filled with huge tour buses from the cruise ships. It isn't a must-see but it's good for a quick stop. The flowers here make good souvenirs; many are prepackaged to take on the plane and have already passed the agricultural check.

Kazumura Cave

Kazumura Cave is the world's longest lava tube, the deepest cave in the United States, and the eighth-longest cave in the world. A few tour companies will take you deep into the cave, but the best guide is Harry Schick with **Kazumura Cave Tours** (Hwy. 11 near mile marker 22, 808/967-7208, http://kazumuracave.com, Mon.-Sat. 8am-6pm by appointment, starting at $30 per person), who explains lava tube geology in depth. Three tours range 2-6 hours (shorter tours for beginners, longer ones for experienced cavers). Reservations must be made in advance. Children over 11 years old are welcome on the tours. The walking isn't too challenging, but it's not always a flat surface. You must be able to climb the ladders that are used to get from room to room.

Pa'ani Ranch

The **Pa'ani Ranch** (N. Kulani Rd. off Hwy. 11 between mile markers 13 and 14, 808/968-7529, www.paaniranch.com, daily 8am-5:30pm) is the perfect stop for *keiki* (children). There's a zipline course ($125) geared for children, horseback riding ($90), and ATV rides ($90). The guides are truly focused on accommodating children. The Lil' Wrangler program is for 2-8-year-olds ($72 per person for 1.5 hours, children under 5 must have an adult with them) and includes a wagon ride, pond fishing, a hand-led pony ride, and a petting zoo.

Fuku-Bonsai Cultural Center

Ever since you saw *Karate Kid* (the original version with Ralph Macchio), haven't you wanted a bonsai tree? The **Fuku-Bonsai Cultural Center** (Hwy. 11 between mile markers 9 and 10, 808/982-9880, www.fukubonsai.com, Mon.-Sat. 8am-4pm, free) offers a bonsai starter package for $25; it includes a 30-minute class to get you started as a bonsai master with your very own plant

to keep. The handcrafting of each tree (and there are many of them scattered along the property) is unbelievable. All plants are approved to take back to the Mainland and shipping services also are offered. The road to the center is a bumpy one. Follow the signs from Highway 11—it's about a five-minute drive from there.

HIGHWAY 132 AND THE RED ROAD (HIGHWAY 137)
Lava Tree State Monument

Lava Tree State Monument (Hwy. 132, open daylight hours, free) was a rain forest before its giant trees were covered with lava, like hot dogs dipped in batter. The encased wood burned, leaving hollow stone skeletons behind. Today, you can stroll through this lichen-green rock forest yourself. The flat, 0.7-mile trail loops through the lava molds of 'ohi'a trees covered by a lava flow in the 1790s. This park is 2.7 miles southeast of Pahoa on the left side of the road after you pass the intersection of Pahoa-Pohoiki Road. It makes for a nice quick stop (or a place for a picnic), but don't go out of your way if you have already seen the lava trees around Hawai'i Volcanoes National Park. Facilities include nice bathrooms and picnic tables.

Cape Kumukahi

Kumukahi means "First Beginnings." This is the most eastern point in the chain of islands and the first place the air hits after it has traveled thousands of miles across the ocean, leading locals to maintain that Cape Kumukahi has the cleanest air in all of the state (and maybe even the Northern Hemisphere). It's the site of the Kumukahi Lighthouse, which was built in 1934 (although some histories say 1928 or even 1938) and looks more like a utility tower. To get there, at the junction of Highway 132 and Highway 137, called the "Four Corners" intersection, go east on Highway 132, which becomes a rental-car-friendly dirt road, Kumukahi Lighthouse Road, that ends at the lighthouse.

Walk east from the lighthouse over uneven lava to the ocean. There is a somewhat hidden four-wheel-drive road over the lava; you can follow that path. As you get closer to the edge, if you veer slightly right you'll see a cairn marking a trail and a tide pool with a lava roof. It's almost like a cave, but open on both sides. Walk down a few lava rocks into the tide pool, being careful not to slip. Beware of large waves.

Green Lake

Along Highway 130 on the way toward Highway 137, off to the right is a hill covered with trees. This is Green Mountain. At its center is Green Lake (Hwy. 137 just south of the Hwy. 132 intersection), one of the few natural lakes in the state. On the short hike to the lake you'll pass through some beautiful scenery, including fruit trees and huge monkeypod trees. Some say that Green Lake was formed by a volcanic crater and is as deep as the ocean. Rumor has it that in the 1970s Jacques Cousteau and a team of divers tried to find the bottom and couldn't. Today, the lake is covered in algae that makes the water unwelcoming for swimming.

To get to Green Lake, look on the right side of the road between mile markers 8 and 9 for the obvious Green Lake sign on the fence. For entry call Smiley (808/965-5500 or 808/430-3071, $5 per person). Green Lake is not a must-see if you only have one day in the area but is recommended if you're spending several days.

MacKenzie State Recreation Area

Most tourists don't visit **MacKenzie State Recreation Area** (on Hwy. 137 two miles west of Isaac Hale Beach Park, daily 7am-7pm) because there isn't beach access, and most Hawaiians use it only for fishing. They won't be here after dark because they believe it's haunted. They say their ancestors still roam the King's Trail by night. Camping is allowed with a permit, but it's not a great place to camp unless you're hunting ghosts.

Lava Tree State Monument

The King's Trail

Part of the Ala Kahakai National Historic Trail, which is most visible throughout the Kona side, the **King's Trail** (Hwy. 137 before mile marker 18, 4.3 miles west from MacKenzie State Recreation Area) connects important historical and religious sites throughout the island. It was used in the late 1800s to herd cattle to port. Much of it has been paved over or completely destroyed by lava. This is one of few places on the east side of the island where you can still see it. To find the trail, look for a cleared area on the *makai* side of Highway 137 with lots of rocks. Walk about 10 feet from the road (over the rocks) and you'll see the stones in the shape of a path, remnants of the King's Trail.

Star of the Sea Painted Church

Like an inspired (but less talented) Michelangelo, Father Everest Gielen painted the ceiling of **Star of the Sea Painted Church** (Hwy. 130 between mile markers

the Star of the Sea Painted Church

Heidler, an artist from Atlanta. The artwork itself can is gaudy but sincere, with wild blues, purples, and oranges. The ceiling is adorned with symbols, portraits of Christ, the angel Gabriel, and scenes from the Nativity. Behind the altar, a painted perspective gives the impression that you're looking down a long hallway at an altar that hangs suspended in air. Originally located near Kalapana, the church was moved to this location so that it wouldn't be destroyed by lava.

Steam Vents

The **steam vents** (Hwy. 130 near mile marker 14, 808/965-2112, www.heavenlykingdom.net) have gone through several iterations, from a public scenic stop to an in-the-know spot in the back of a house. Today, they can be visited in a sauna, with seats to maximize the steaming experience. The place is run by The Kingdom of Heaven, a religious organization. They do not charge for the experience but suggest a donation of $20 per steam. Bathers are often unclothed. If you're only interested in taking a look (but not going in), feel free to stop. Ask the innkeeper to take you to the large hole in the back (one of the largest on the Big Island).

19 and 20, daily 9am-4pm), working mostly at night by oil lamp. He was transferred to Lana'i in 1941, leaving the work unfinished until it was completed in 1964 by George

Beaches

HIGHWAY 132 AND THE RED ROAD (HIGHWAY 137)
Champagne Pond

The crystal-clear **Champagne Pond** (off Kumukahi Lighthouse Rd.) is a naturally occurring warm pond heated by the volcano underneath. It's warm, but not hot. You'll see turtles lounging about, but will need snorkeling equipment to view the amazing life under the water.

To get there, at the junction of Highway 132 and Highway 137, called the "Four Corners" intersection, go east on Highway 132, which becomes a rental-car-friendly dirt road, Kumukahi Lighthouse Road, that ends at the lighthouse. At the end of Kumukahi Lighthouse Road to your right is a rough four-wheel-drive road to the public entrance of the pond. The private entrance is through a nearby paved unnamed road to the Kapoho Beach Lots subdivision area. You need a code to get through the gate—get it by renting a property there or knowing someone who lives there. If you don't have a four-wheel-drive car, you can walk to the pond about 45 minutes over the rough road. Keep the ocean on your left and it will be obvious when you've arrived to the ponds (they are next to an A-frame house).

Want to See Some Lava Flow?

The lava flow of 2015 began to flow into the transfer station and then suddenly stopped.

I mean, that's why you came to Hawai'i, right? I am sorry to say that you can't see it all the time. For years, the **viewing area on Highway 130** (follow the signs and veer right when the road splits; it's right before it reaches Hwy. 137) was reliably the place to be after sunset. Months (even years) will go by when it's visible every night, and then it disappears. At the time of printing, the lava flow was not visible from the Kalapana lava viewing area or from Pahoa town. So even if some assertive tour guide tells you that he or she will take you there, call the Kalapana lava viewing hotline (808/967-8862) first to see if there is actual lava flowing, or check online (http://www.nps.gov/havo/planyourvisit/lava2.htm).

★ Kapoho Tide Pools

Surrounded by lava rocks with a magnificent ocean backdrop, the **Kapoho tide pools** (daily 7am-7pm, $3 suggested donation) offer some of the best snorkeling on the Big Island. The landscape is impressive, but the world under the water is even better, filled with colorful fish. It's like you're in an aquarium. This is a great spot for beginners because the water is very shallow. Experts can swim farther out to experience greater depths. Pay attention to where you put your belongings on the lava rock—when the tide gets high your things will get wet. Wear water shoes even if you're not snorkeling to avoid getting cut on the lava rocks or coral and bring a Band-Aid or two just in case. There are no facilities here.

On Highway 137, 1.1 miles south from the Highway 132/Highway 137 intersection, turn left onto Kapoho Kai Road, which is marked and paved. Continue straight on the coconut-tree-lined road and park in the designated area. To walk to the pools, follow the arrows painted on to the road; turn left at Wai'opae Road where the road forms a T. Follow the signs to the State Marine Park.

Ahalanui Beach Park (Warm Ponds)

Although the official name of this beach park is **Ahalanui Beach Park** (Hwy. 137 between mile markers 10 and 11, daily 7am-7pm), everyone just calls it "the warm ponds." The water is warm but not hot, very inviting on a cloudy day. This isn't a hidden pond, it's a public one—cement surrounds it and stairs lead down into it. The water is not too deep and there is a lifeguard on duty, so it gets quite crowded with families. Ocean water mixes in on the right side of the pond. It's a great place to watch locals playing music and the waves crashing. Some have expressed concerns about the cleanliness of the water; a longtime lifeguard in the area suggests that the best time to bathe is when the tide is moving (and the water isn't stagnant). Do not enter into the water if you have an open cut, as it could get infected. The park has picnic tables, showers, and portable toilets in the parking lot.

Isaac Hale Beach Park and Warm Pool

On your left as you enter **Isaac Hale Beach Park** (off Hwy. 137, daily 7am-7pm) you will see a field where the community holds festivals and sports activities. From Highway 137, turn *makai* at the Isaac Hale sign directly across from Pohoiki Road. The main road forms a T, and to the left there are nice covered picnic areas with barbecues on the ocean side of the street. On the *mauka* side of the street there is a children's playground area. If you turn right at the T, park in the lot near the boat ramp. You'll see lots of locals hanging around. Sometimes there are food trucks. Just to the right of the boat ramp (in front of the private home with the No Trespassing signs) is a very

small *keiki* tide pool. If you continue walking on the dirt path into the forest between the tide pool and house, about 20 yards back on your right side you'll see a warm pond nestled behind the trees. Facilities include a shower near the boat ramp and bathrooms in the parking lot. Camping is allowed with a county permit, but not recommended.

For bodyboarding, surfing, and stand-up paddleboarding, Issac Hale Beach Park is your best bet. For this reason, the park can get very crowded on weekends and in the summer.

★ Secret Black-Sand Beach

Chances are that you'll be alone or among only a few other people at the **secret black-sand beach** on Highway 137. If you set your odometer as you pass MacKenzie State Recreation Area, the secret black beach is exactly two miles west of the recreation area's entrance. You'll pass under a canopy of trees and the path to the beach is on the ocean or *makai* side of the road where the road curves and it looks like there is room for a car to park—if you're lucky there might be one parked there, which will alert you where to stop. The other marker to look for is two trees that look like they have fallen horizontally. Pass through the horizontal trees

Ocean water mixes into this warm pond at Ahalanui Beach Park.

or go around them to the right—if you look closely you'll see that there is a trail worn from previous users. Head back through the forest toward the ocean and after two minutes you'll have arrived to the black-sand beach.

Enjoy the virtually deserted beach by basking in the sun all day long (you'll have to bask, as there is no shade). But there is more! To the right it looks like there is a natural wall. Climb up (it's not too hard and there is a clear path) to see small tide pools and an even more black sand on the other side.

★ Kehena Beach

On Sundays, you can hear the drumming at **Kehena Beach** (Hwy. 137) from the road. This is the day locals and like-minded visitors gather to drum, partake of *pakalolo* (marijuana), and swim naked in the ocean. (There are kids here, but it might not be a kid-friendly stop). The beach is sandy with lots of shaded areas, but the water is rough and warrants caution, although it doesn't seem to deter anyone from swimming or bodyboarding. The vibe is friendly and you won't feel out of place if you are clothed. On other days of the week, you might find only a few people lounging on the beach.

Kehena Beach is 5.4 miles west of

MacKenzie State Park or 1.1 miles west of the King's Trail stop (set your odometer). Look on the *makai* side of the road for a parking area facing the ocean. The entrance to the beach is to the left via a short dirt trail. The downhill trek can be tricky.

★ Kaimu Beach

Legend (from the 1990s) says that **Kaimu Beach** (Hwy. 137 where the road dead-ends) was once sandy with beautiful coconut trees . . . until the Kalapana lava flow covered over it. Along the path down to the beach, an information board shows what the beach looked like before the lava. Small coconut trees have been planted by locals over the last 20 years in an effort to rebuild, and a new public art exhibit continues to grow among the budding trees. At the shoreline, waves hit black boulders, breaking them down over time into smaller pieces and, eventually, sand. This is the origin of a black-sand beach. It's not a great place to sit and you can't really swim here (the waves are rough), so most people just take in the gorgeous view with a walk—you can also enjoy a public art installation along the walkway to the beach which provides a beautiful contrast to the black landscape. At night, when the lava is

Ever since Kaimu Beach was destroyed by the Kalapana lava flow, locals have been planting coconut trees to encourage its recovery.

flowing into the ocean, you can also see the glow in the distance.

Kaimu Beach is 9 miles southwest of MacKenzie State Park or 5.6 miles from Kehena Beach. Park in the spots on the *makai* side of the road or in the lot on the *mauka* side (there are bathrooms there behind the restaurant) and follow the path to the left of the vendors out to the beach. The walk will take you about five minutes; it's not paved, but it's easy. The lava may have destroyed the area, but not cell phone service. The open lava field has created a direct route from the nearby cell phone tower: your phone service has been restored!

Shopping

HIGHWAY 11 BETWEEN VOLCANO AND HILO

A small beacon of light on Highway 11 between Hilo and Volcano, the **J. Hara Store** (17-343 Volcano Rd./Hwy. 11 near mile marker 11, 808/966-5462, www.jharastore. com, Mon.-Sat. 6am-8pm, Sun. 7am-7pm) is truly a local institution. It somehow packs everything into a small space: produce, hunting gear, liquor, and first-aid items (really a must if you're going to sell hunting gear and liquor together). In the same parking lot complex is a gas station owned by **7-Eleven** (open 24 hours). It's notable for the Spam *musubi,* a local delicacy of rice and Spam wrapped in nori (like a sushi roll). These to-go sandwiches are delightful and cheap (just $1). Pick one up to bring with you for a day at the national park or just eat it right away (it's better served hot).

PAHOA
★ Maku'u Market

The **Maku'u Market** (Hwy. 130/Kea'au-Pahoa Rd. near mile marker 8, Sun. 8am-2pm) is part food truck fair, part farmers market, part antiques market. Unlike at many other markets, you don't have to get here at the crack of dawn to be part of the action. In fact, many vendors start their mornings off at other nearby markets (like the one in Volcano) and then make their way here afterward. The prepared food selection here is tops, with everything from

The Maku'u Market near Pahoa is a must-stop for foodies.

Indian to Greek to local-style barbecue. The produce selection is extensive and you'll find fruits here that are hard to find at other markets, such as the coveted mangosteen fruit. Bring the family, as there is always some form of live entertainment under the picnic shelter. Also bring a raincoat or umbrella: Rainstorms are common here, but they offer a good opportunity to hang out under the covered shelter and make new friends and try new foods.

HIGHWAY 132 AND THE RED ROAD (HIGHWAY 137)
SPACE Market

No, not outer space: it's the **Seaview**

Performing Arts Center for Education (SPACE) market (at Uncle Robert's Awa Bar, where Hwy. 137 ends at Kaimu Beach, Sat. 7am-noon). This market definitely reflects the laid-back, off-the-grid culture of lower Puna, and likewise, it's one of the more interesting markets on the island. It's not too big—a straight walk through will only take you a few minutes, but if you stay and linger you'll be guaranteed some excellent people-watching time. Grab a raw wheat-free delight (I am serious) and some coconut turmeric tea (it is surprisingly delicious—both spicy and sweet) and head to the back covered picnic area. Produce is for sale as well as local crafts (think feather earrings and knitted bikinis).

Entertainment and Events

PAHOA

If you're looking for nightlife, Pahoa town offers enough townie bars for a barhop or crawl (your choice). Start at **Kaleo's Bar and Grill** (15-2969 Pahoa Village Rd., 808/965-5600, http://kaleoshawaii.com, daily 11am-9pm), where there is live music and creative cocktails, before moving to **Black Rock Café** (15-2872 Pahoa Village Rd., 808/965-1177, daily 7am-9pm) for cheap beer by the pitcher and a live cover band, and end your night at **Lava Shack** (15-2471 Pahoa Village Rd., 808/965-6644, daily 2pm-2am, happy hour daily 2pm-7pm), which stays open later than almost anywhere else on the Big Island, for some free pool and more cheap beer.

If you're looking to learn more about the history of the area stop by the small **Pahoa Village Museum** (15-2931 Pahoa Village Rd., 808/430-1573, Mon.-Sat. 11am-6pm). Besides showcasing cultural artifacts, the space is also used as a coffee shop as well as a meeting place for events and workshops. The website isn't too useful, but check out their Facebook page for additional information on upcoming events.

HIGHWAY 132 AND THE RED ROAD (HIGHWAY 137)

You never know who is going to show up at ★ **Uncle Robert's Awa Bar** (on Hwy. 137 where the road ends at Kaimu Beach). One local mentioned a recent sighting of a legendary musician who stopped by to play guitar. It's usually open by midafternoon, so grab a stool at this open-air bar to have some kava or 'awa, as they say in Hawaiian. If you're a first timer, go easy on the kava; although it relaxes you (ancient Hawaiians used it for medicinal purposes), drinking lots of it has diuretic properties. As the night goes on, Uncle Robert's turns into a local hangout joint with music playing well into the night. Wednesday nights (4pm-9pm) are particularly good nights to stop by here when the market (food and craft vendors) is taking place as well as performances from better-known local bands. Come early, as the parking areas start filling up by 4pm. The bar also serves as a somewhat unofficial lava flow information kiosk. A small "exhibit" showcases photos of the area over the last 50 years, including some pictures of the lava flow of the 1990s that destroyed the area.

Food

HIGHWAY 11 BETWEEN VOLCANO AND HILO

The "stone cookies" at **Mountain View Bakery** (Old Volcano Rd. between mile markers 14 and 15, 808/968-6353, Mon.-Fri. 6:30am-1pm, Sat. 7:30am-1:30pm, cash only) are like a biscotti, tastier when dipped in a cup of coffee.

Most people think of Kona when they think of coffee on the Big Island, but there is in fact some mighty good coffee on the Hilo side. The **Hilo Coffee Mill** (17-995 Volcano Rd./Hwy. 11 between mile markers 12 and 13, 808/968-1333, www.hilocoffeemill.com, Mon.-Fri. 7am-4:30pm except Wed. 7am-2pm, Sat. 7am-4pm) sells its own coffee and tea. Tours and tastings (about 20 minutes long) are available on demand. Hour-long comprehensive farm and facility tours (call for a reservation) are also available, On Saturdays 8am-1pm the Hilo Coffee Mill is the home of a farmers market (it also includes flea and craft items) that is mostly active early in the morning.

The crossroads of east Hawaii, **Kea'au Shopping Center** (16-586 Old Volcano Rd., where Hwy. 11 meets Hwy. 130 toward Pahoa) presents a plethora of options. Quick and cheap, **Lemongrass Restaurant** (808/982-8558, Mon.-Sat. 10am-9pm) serves standard Asian fast food. Locals like it because it has a lunch special. Across Kea'au-Pahoa Road, the small outdoor **Kea'au Market** (Tues.-Fri. 8am-5pm, Sat. 8am-3pm) includes food stands of nearby restaurants.

Markets

In addition to a slew of restaurants, Kea'au Shopping Center also is the location of the large chain supermarket **Foodland** (daily 6am-10pm). If you're looking for gluten-free and vegan foods check out **Kea'au Natural Foods** (808/966-8877, www.keaaunaturalfoods.com, Mon.-Fri. 8:30am-8pm, Sat. 8:30am-7pm, Sun. 9:30am-5pm). They carry their own brand of vitamins, which brings down the price, and have prepackaged small bags of bulk nuts and trail mixes.

PAHOA

All establishments are located on Main Government Road, also called Pahoa Village Road. Beware of the locations of restaurants on Google Maps as some establishments have noted that they are not placed correctly on the map.

One visitor said it best: "Why wouldn't you want to have beer with breakfast?" At **Black Rock Café** (15-2872 Pahoa Village Rd., 808/965-1177, daily 7am-9pm, $8), you can. But it's more than likely that you'll have a fun night out, especially on weekends with live music. The menu is little more than standard bar fare—salads, chicken sandwiches, and burgers—but keep your expectations low and you'll be pleasantly surprised.

The atmosphere at **Sirus Coffee Connection** (15-2874 Pahoa Village Rd., 808/965-8555, Mon.-Sat, 7am-6pm, Sun. 7am-3pm) is not super cozy, but you could definitely spend a few hours here with a book and a cup of coffee. They have free Wi-Fi, which is a big deal for locals living off the grid. Breakfast and lunch sandwiches are available (with vegetarian options), as are sweet treats. They also have gluten-free bread.

★ **Tin Shack Bakery** (15-1500 Akeakamai Loop, 808/965-9659, Mon.-Sat. 6am-3pm, $8) is as close as you'll get to feeling like you're in (new) Brooklyn and not in Hawaii. Set in a converted warehouse "shack" building, this coffee shop/bakery is cool, almost too conventionally cool for Pahoa. At the same time, and standard for Pahoa, there are nonstop vegan and gluten-free options for breakfast and lunch here. Pick up some of their homemade pastries to take with you on your road trip around the region.

Luquin's Mexican Restaurant (15-2942

Pahoa Village Rd., 808/965-9990, www. luquinsmexicanrestaurant.com, daily 7am-9pm, happy hour 3pm-6pm, $10-20) feels like a restaurant off the side of the road in Mexico. The food is good enough and the portions are large. Gluten-free (corn tortilla) and vegetarian options (tofu enchiladas) are on the menu. Enjoy beer on draft and pitcher specials. There's also Wi-Fi.

The Big Island has some of the best Thai restaurants outside of Thailand itself, and **Ning's Thai Cuisine** (15-2955 Pahoa Village Rd., 808/965-7611, Mon.-Sat. noon-9pm, Sun. 5pm-9pm, $15) is up there with the pack. Try the pineapple curry or the *massaman* curry and you won't be sorry, If you like your food spicy, ask for it hot. Vegetarian options are abundant.

★ **Kaleo's Bar and Grill** (15-2969 Pahoa Village Rd., 808/965-5600, http://kaleoshawaii.com, daily 11am-9pm, $12-20) is one of the more romantic restaurants in Pahoa town. The extensive menu will leave you asking how they do it all. Somehow, they serve Asian food, local food, burgers, fish, and Italian cuisine and do it all well. The portions are huge (there's an $8 charge to split one dish). The sandwiches and wraps are a very good value (you'll have leftovers). There are vegetarian and gluten-free options. There is often live music on weekends. At the bar, locals will engage you in conversation over a cocktail stirred up by the friendly bartenders.

Markets

The **Malama Market** (15-2660 Pahoa Rd., 808/965-2105, 6am-10pm) has everything you need: a deli counter, fresh *poke*, wine, liquor, Redbox DVD rentals, and an ATM.

Island Naturals Market and Deli (15-1403 Pahoa Village Rd., 808/965-8322, www. islandnaturals.com, Mon.-Fri. 7am-8pm, Sat.-Sun. 7am-7pm) has a coffee and smoothie bar as well as an excellent hot bar (they charge per pound) with many gluten-free and vegan options. Beer and wine (nonorganic and organic varieties) are available and on sale for 20 percent off every Friday.

HIGHWAY 132 AND THE RED ROAD (HIGHWAY 137)

How far would you go for an organic, mostly local, very vegetarian-friendly meal? Some islanders drive over an hour to the all-you-can-eat buffets at ★ **Kalani Oceanside Retreat** (12-6860 Kalapana-Kapoho Beach Rd./Hwy. 137, 808/965-0468, www.kalani. com, breakfast daily 7:30am-8:30am, $13; lunch daily noon-1pm, $15; dinner daily 6pm-7:30pm, $24, *kama'aina* discounts available). The options range from fish to chicken to tofu and tempeh—there are raw-food and gluten-free options too. You only have about an hour to eat, as the restaurant is open for specific dining windows, and trust me; you will feel very full when it's over.

Kalapana Village Café (12-5037 Pahoa Kalapana Rd. where Hwy. 137 ends at Kaimu Beach, 808/965-0121, Mon.-Fri. 7am-7pm, Sat.-Sun. 8am-9pm, $8, *kama'aina* discounts available) looks like a hole-in-the-wall, but you'll be thrilled when you take the first bite of your food. There are vegetarian salads made from local produce, hamburgers, and large portions of french fries and onion rings. There's lovely outdoor seating.

Getting There and Around

CAR

To get to Pahoa stay on Highway 130 heading south from Hilo or Kea'au. Turn right before the complex with the Longs Drugs (this road isn't marked but turns into Main Government/Pahoa Village Road). Continue on Main Government/Pahoa Village Road as it curves to the left. After a mile, you will begin to drive through the main part of town. If you miss the right turn from Highway 130, continue on the highway for 1.5 miles and turn right on Kapoho Road. You are now entering the town from the south side.

BUS

The Hele-On bus route from the Glenwood area to Hilo is the same as the Ka'u (Volcano) route and is not very well serviced. The Hilo-Pahoa route has numerous buses (nearly hourly) and you can travel as far as Pohoiki (near Isaac Hale Beach Park). Remember, if you want to travel from Pahoa to Volcano or Kona, for instance, you will need to transfer buses in Hilo.

The **Hele-On Bus** (www.heleonbus.org, $2 per ride, $1 each for luggage, large backpacks, bikes) follows the Pahoa-Hilo route schedule, stopping in Pahoa at 5:25am, 8:15am, and then almost every 1.5 hours (check the schedule) to 8:45pm on its way to Hilo. The ride to Hilo takes about 70 minutes and makes all intermediate stops on the way. There are three buses (8:50am, 1:35pm, 7:45pm) from Pahoa town south to the Red Road area (south Puna with beaches) and back north on Highway 130 toward Pahoa. The entire route takes about an hour.

Hilo

H
ilo is hip. It has dive bars, walkable streets, historic buildings, cheap rents, two universities, and, most important, it's an underrated foodie mecca.

It has the potential to be the new Brooklyn or the new Portland or maybe a Berkeley or Ann Arbor. But Hilo has resisted change and happily retains itself as a relic of old Hawai'i.

Hilo has the second-largest population in the state (after Honolulu). It is a classic tropical town, the kind described in books like Gabriel García Márquez's *Love in the Time of Cholera*. Many of the downtown buildings date to the early 1900s, when the plantation industry was booming and the railroad took workers and managers from the country to the big city of Hilo. You can walk the central area comfortably in an afternoon, but the town does sprawl some due to the modern-day construction of large shopping malls and residential subdivisions in the outlying areas.

In Hilo the old beat, the old music, and that feeling of a tropical place where rhythms are slow and sensual still exist. Nights are alive with sounds of the tropics, namely coqui frogs, and the heady smells of fruits and flowering trees wafting on the breeze. Days epitomize tropical weather, with predictable afternoon showers during the winter and spring months.

Hilo's weather makes it a natural greenhouse; botanical gardens and flower farms surround it like a giant lei. Black-sand beaches are close by waiting for you to come cool off. To counterpoint this tropical explosion, Mauna Kea's winter snows backdrop the town. Hilo is one of the oldest permanently settled towns in Hawaii, and the largest on the windward coast of the island. Don't make the mistake of underestimating Hilo, or of counting it out because of its rainy reputation. 'Akaka Falls is less than 30 minutes from downtown Hilo, but there is a lot to see on the way right off the highway, including an incredible four-mile scenic drive that winds through a rain forest that smells overwhelmingly like papayas.

ORIENTATION
Downtown Hilo and the Bayfront

You'll know you are nearing downtown when

Previous: Richardson's Beach Park; Kayakers take advantage of the calm water and spectacular views of the Hilo Bay. **Above:** Rainbow Falls.

Look for ★ to find recommended
sights, activities, dining, and lodging.

Highlights

★ **Coconut Island:** A favorite picnic spot for decades, Coconut Island offers the best panorama of the city, bay, and Mauna Kea beyond (page 160).

★ **Rainbow Falls and Boiling Pots:** The 80-foot Rainbow Falls is true to its name, its mists throwing flocks of rainbows into the air. At the potholed riverbed of Boiling Pots, river water cascades from one bubbling whirlpool tub into the next (page 162).

★ **Onomea Scenic Drive (Four-Mile Scenic Drive):** Along this four-mile route you'll see jungle that covers the road like a living green tunnel, the Hawaii Tropical Botanical Garden, and one fine view after another (page 163).

★ **'Akaka Falls State Park:** In addition to the falls, this park offers a pristine valley and an accessible foray into the island's beautiful interior (page 164).

★ **Richardson's Beach Park:** Head to this black-sand beach for terrific snorkeling, swimming, or just snoozing in the shade (page 165).

★ **Honoli'i Beach Park:** This beach is one of the finest surfing spots on this side of the island. Even if you're not a surfer, it's worth coming here to watch the local talent hit the big waves (page 166).

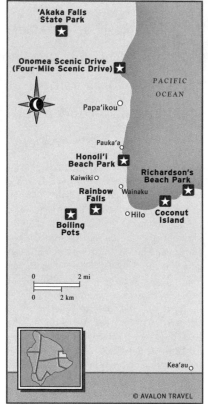

Hilo and Around

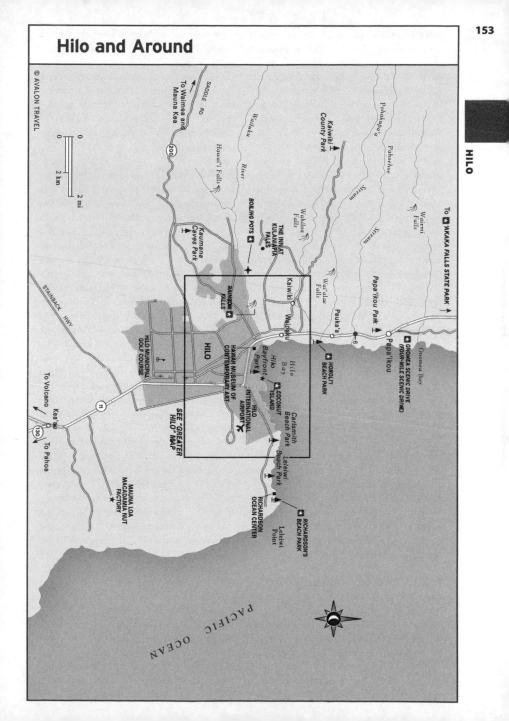

© AVALON TRAVEL

0   2 mi
0   2 km

To Waimea and
Mauna Kea

SADDLE RD

Wailuku River

Hawai'i Falls

STAINBACK HWY

To Volcano

Keaau

To Pahoa

Kaumana
Caves Park

BOILING POTS

THE INN AT
KULANIAPIA
FALLS

Wahilea Falls

Kaiwiki

Kaiwiki
County Park

Pohakupua'a

Puhoehoe

Wai'ama
Falls

Stream

Stream

To ʼAKAKA FALLS STATE PARK

ONOMEA SCENIC DRIVE
(FOUR-MILE SCENIC DRIVE)

Papaʼikou Park

Onomea Bay

Papaʼikou

Pauka'a

Wai'aluae
Falls

RAINBOW
FALLS

Waiakea

HILO

HILO MUNICIPAL
GOLF COURSE

HAWAII MUSEUM OF
CONTEMPORARY ART

Bayfront
Park

Hilo
Bay

Hilo

COCONUT
ISLAND

HILO
INTERNATIONAL
AIRPORT

SEE "GREATER
HILO" MAP

HONOLI'I
BEACH PARK

Carlsmith
Beach Park

Leleiwi
Beach Park

RICHARDSON
OCEAN CENTER

RICHARDSON'S
BEACH PARK

Leleiwi
Point

MAUNA LOA
MACADAMIA NUT
FACTORY

PACIFIC OCEAN

you start seeing parking spaces that require parallel parking. The central downtown area is made up of Kamehameha Avenue (also called Bayfront), Kilauea Avenue (which turns into Keawe Street), and Kinoole Street—parallel streets running north to south bounded on the east by Mamo Street and on the west by Waianuenue Avenue before one has to cross over a bridge to another section of Hilo.

This area is much denser than any other part of town and easily walkable. Within this area you'll find the bus station, Hilo Farmers Market, cafés, restaurants, grocery stores, and tourist shops. While this isn't where you would come to jump in the water, this area is where you'll see cruise ship passengers walking around (with the ship in the distance towering over the town) picking up souvenirs.

Greater Hilo

Thanks to our old friend urban sprawl, Hilo begins almost right after the Kea'au Shopping Center on Highway 11. Hilo has greatly expanded from its original roots by transforming its farmlands (and the settlements of native Hawaiians) into the area on Highway 11 that now houses the Hilo International Airport, Walmart, Target, and the Prince Kuhio Mall. Where Highway 11 meets the ocean, you'll find the town's secret jewels: its beaches. Travel east on Kalaniana'ole Avenue, where beaches are situated one after another, easily recognizable from the road by their official county park signs. Although these beaches are easily accessible, you'll be entering into a coastal wonderland that couldn't feel farther from the suburban enclave just up the road.

North Hilo to 'Akaka Falls

Pass over the "Singing Bridge" leaving downtown Hilo and soon after you're in the North Hilo district traveling on Highway 19 toward the Hamakua Coast. This route, one of the prettiest on the island with its ocean views, passes by several old plantation towns that are still residential communities that do not offer anything of interest to tourists. Just

seven miles out of Hilo, you'll pass the sign for Four-Mile Scenic Drive. You should turn onto it immediately; it's the old route that parallels the highway. Back on the highway as you drive north, you'll arrive at the town of Honomu, the gateway to 'Akaka Falls. From here it's still necessary to climb *mauka* on Highway 220 (about 20 minutes) until you reach the entrance to this must-see sight.

PLANNING YOUR TIME

While many visitors to the Big Island stay only on the Kona side, those who know the island well and appreciate its diversity split their time between the Kona and Hilo sides. Hilo, being the largest city and main hub on the east side, is the logical place to use as a base. The city is bite-size, but you'll need a rental car to visit most of the sights around town. Hilo itself has plenty to keep a traveler busy for a number of days. First, spend time exploring the natural beauty of the city and its close-by botanical gardens, its bay and beaches, and the pretty waterfalls only a few minutes from downtown. Both Rainbow Falls and the potholed riverbed of Boiling Pots are Instagram-able, and perhaps best when there's plenty of rain to make them perform at their best. Take an hour or two to walk under the giant banyan trees that canopy Banyan Drive, stroll through the relaxing Lili'uokalani Gardens, and walk the bridge to Coconut Island for a perfect view of the bay and waterfront with snowcapped Mauna Kea as a backdrop. While you are out that way, continue on down Kalaniana'ole Avenue for a morning or afternoon in the water at one of the small beaches along the Keaukaha strip.

Hilo is an old town. Reserve a morning or afternoon for a walking tour of town, viewing its well-kept historic buildings, and then spend a few hours at both the Pacific Tsunami Museum, where you will learn about the brutal waters that destroyed much of Hilo's Bayfront, and the Lyman Museum and Mission House, where the life of early missionaries to Hawaii comes alive. A bit

Downtown Hilo and the Bayfront

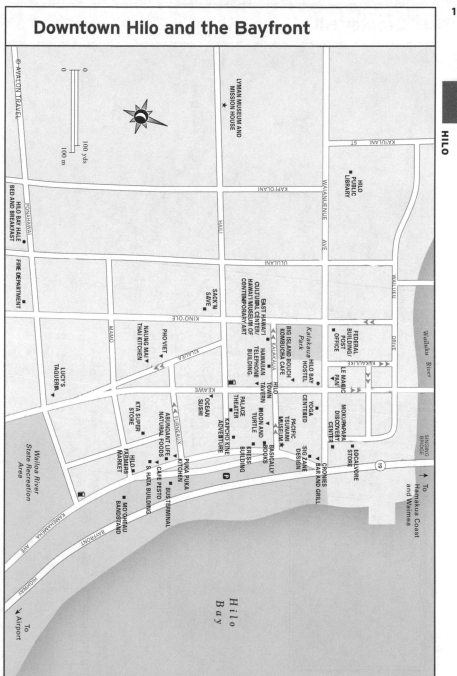

© AVALON TRAVEL

0

0

100 yds

100 m

LYMAN MUSEUM AND
MISSION HOUSE ★

HILO
PUBLIC
LIBRARY

KAIULANI ST

KAPI'OLANI

WAIANUENUE AVE

HAILI

'ULULANI

WAILUKU

KEKAULIKE

DRIVE

Wailuku River

SINGING
BRIDGE

AVALON TRAVEL

HILO BAY HALE
BED AND BREAKFAST

PONAHAWAI

FIRE DEPARTMENT

SACK'N
SAVE

EAST HAWAI'I
CULTURAL CENTER/
HAWAI'I MUSEUM OF
CONTEMPORARY ART

KINO'OLE

BIG ISLAND BOUCH
KOMBUCHA CAFE

HAWAIIAN
TELEPHONE
BUILDING

KALAKAUA

Kalākaua
Park

HILO BAY
HOSTEL

FEDERAL
BUILDING/
POST
OFFICE

LE MAGIC
PAN

MOKUPAPAPA
DISCOVERY
CENTER

LOCALVORE
STORE

MAMO

PHO VIET

NAUNG MAI
THAI KITCHEN

KILAUEA

KEAWE

TOWN

HAWAIIAN
TAVERN

MOON AND
TURTLE

YOGA
CENTERED

PACIFIC
TSUNAMI
MUSEUM ★

CRONIES
BAR AND GRILL

LUCY'S
TAQUERIA

KTA SUPER
STORE

OCEAN
SUSHI

FURNEAUX

PALACE
THEATER

KAPOHO KINE
ADVENTURE

KRESS
BUILDING

BASICALLY
BOOKS

SIG ZANE
DESIGN

19

To
Hamakua Coast
and Waimea

Wailoa River
State Recreation
Area

KAMEHAMEHA AVE

BAYFRONT

ABUNDANT LIFE
NATURAL FOODS

HILO
FARMERS
MARKET

PUKA PUKA
KITCHEN

S. HATA BUILDING

CAFE PESTO

BUS TERMINAL

P

MO'OHEAU
BANDSTAND

HIGHWAY

To
Airport

Hilo
Bay

Greater Hilo

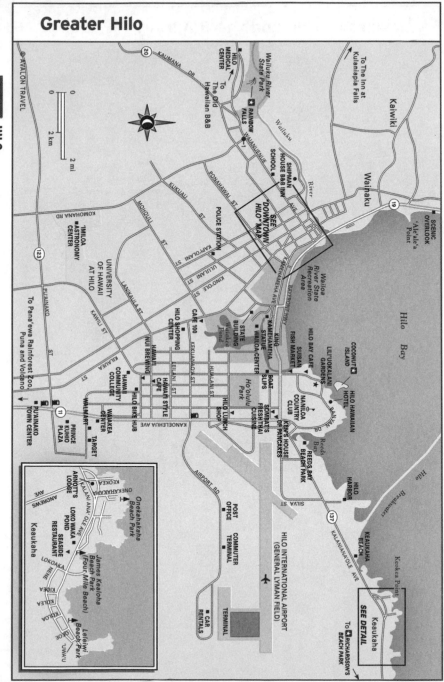

© AVALON TRAVEL

0
2 km
0
2 mi

To The Inn at
Kulaniapia Falls

Kaiwiki

Wainaku

KAUMANA DR

20

HILO
MEDICAL
CENTER

To
The Old
Hawaiian B&B

Wailuku River
State Park

RAINBOW
FALLS

Wailuku

Wailuku

SHIPMAN
HOUSE B&B INN

WAIANUENUE

SCHOOL

River

19

SCENIC
OVERLOOK

'Ale'ale'a
Point

KUKUAU
ST

PONAHAWAI ST

POLICE STATION

SEE
DOWNTOWN
HILO MAP

KAMEHAMEHA AVE

Waloa
River State
Recreation
Area

KOMOHANA RD

'IMILOA
ASTRONOMY
CENTER

123

MOHOULI
ST

KAPIOLANI ST

ULUILANI ST

KINOOLE ST

BAYFRONT HWY

Hilo Bay

To Pana'ewa Rainforest Zoo,
Puna and Volcano

PUAINAKO

UNIVERSITY
OF HAWAII
AT HILO

LANIKAULA ST

KAWILI ST

CAFE 100

HILO SHOPPING
CENTER

STATE
BUILDING

Waiakea
Pond

KEKUANAOA ST

KING
KAMEHAMEHA
STATUE

WAILOA CENTER

HILO BAY CAFE

SUISAN
FISH MARKET

LILI'UOKALANI
GARDENS

COCONUT
ISLAND

HILO HAWAIIAN
HOTEL

ST

KUKILAU
ST

NUI BREWING

HAWAII
COMMUNITY
COLLEGE

HAWAII
STYLE
CAFE

LEILANI ST

HULIHI ST

Ho'olulu
Park

BOAT
SLIPS

SOMBAT'S
FRESH THAI
CUISINE

NANILOA
COUNTRY
CLUB

KEN'S HOUSE
OF PANCAKES

BANYAN DR

11

PUAINAKO
TOWN CENTER

PRINCE
KUHIO
PLAZA

WALMART

HILO BIKE
HUB

WAIAKEA
CENTER

TARGET

KANOELEHUA AVE

HILO LUNCH
SHOP

Reeds
Bay

REEDS BAY
BEACH PARK

HILO
HARBOR

KEAUKAHA
BEACH

Hilo
Breakwater

Keokea Point

AIRPORT RD

POST
OFFICE

COMMUTER
TERMINAL

SILVA ST

HILO INTERNATIONAL AIRPORT
(GENERAL LYMAN FIELD)

KALANIANAOLE AVE

137

Keaukaha

SEE DETAIL

To ★ RICHARDSON'S
BEACH PARK

ARNOTT'S
LODGE

KEKEA

ANDREWS
AVE

KALANI ANA OLE AVE

ONEKAHAKAHA

Onekahaha
Beach Park

Keaukaha

LOKO WAKA
POND

SEASIDE
RESTAURANT

James Kealoha
Beach Park
(Four Mile Beach)

LOKOAKA

NENE

KIKEA

KULEA

KOLOA

'UWA'U

Leleiwi
Beach Park

TERMINAL

CAR
RENTALS

Your Best Day in Hilo

- Wake up early and come to **Honoli'i Beach Park** to surf or to watch the surfers.

- If it's a Wednesday or Saturday, head to the **Hilo Farmers Market** to see the wide range of fruits that grow on the island.

- Take a **walking tour of downtown Hilo** to see the architecture of early-20th-century Hawaii.

- Stop in the **Hawaii Museum of Contemporary Art, Pacific Tsunami Museum,** or the **Lyman Museum.**

- In the afternoon, relax at one of the many black-sand beaches just 10 minutes from downtown, such as **Richardson's Beach Park.**

- Have dinner at one of Hilo's undervalued foodie joints: **Puka Puka Kitchen, Sombat's Fresh Thai Cuisine, or Hilo Bay Cafe.**

- For a low-key night, catch an art film or a performance at the **Palace Theater.**

- For a high-energy night, meander over to **Kim's Karaoke Lounge** for drinks, pupu, and, of course, karaoke.

- Late at night go where the locals go to end the evening: **Ken's House of Pancakes.**

RAINY-DAY ALTERNATIVE

Hilo is a great place to spend a rainy day, given the large number of museums and movie theaters. Here are a few other ideas, and they are mostly free and kid friendly.

Right on the Bayfront, it's easy to totally miss the **Mokupapapa Discovery Center for Hawaii's Coral Reefs.** This newly renovated museum is great for spending a few minutes perusing its information about reefs and fish of the Northwestern Hawaiian Islands.

out of town is the Pana'ewa Rainforest Zoo, also good for a couple of hours to view tropical animals in a natural environment, and the opportunity to see some of the thick and luxuriant forest cover that surrounds the city. For exploration from Hilo, it's an hour's drive down to the steamy Puna Coast, about the same up to the stark lava lands of Hawai'i Volcanoes National Park or along the wet and wonderful Hamakua Coast to time-lost Waipi'o Valley, and a bit longer for a trek to the top of the Mauna Kea to see the astronomical observatories and experience a sunset from the heights.

Before the shift of tourism to the drier Kona side of the island, Hilo was the Big Island's major visitor destination. This old town and steamy tropical port still holds many attractions, from missionary homes to forest waterfalls to landscaped tropical gardens to diminutive beaches with great snorkeling options.

DOWNTOWN HILO AND THE BAYFRONT

Lyman Museum and Mission House

A few short blocks above downtown Hilo, the **Lyman Museum and Mission House** (276 Haili St., 808/935-5021, www.lymanmuseum. org, Mon.-Sat. 10am-4:30pm, $10 adults, $8 seniors, $3 children, $17 family, $5 students) showcases the oldest wood building on the Big Island, originally built in 1839 for David and Sarah Lyman, some of the first Christian missionaries on the island. The museum is a Smithsonian affiliate with a bit of everything, from fine art to mineral and gem collections to exhibits on habitats of Hawaii. The first-floor Earth Heritage Gallery holds a mineral and rock collection that's rated one of the best in the entire country, and by far the best in Polynesia. The museum also holds a substantial collection of archival documents and images relating to Hawaii's history.

Next door is the Lyman Mission House, which opened as a museum in 1931. The furniture is authentic "Sandwich Isles" circa 1850. Some of the most interesting exhibits are of small personal items, such as a music box that still plays and a collection of New England autumn leaves that Mrs. Lyman had sent over to show her children what that season was like. Upstairs are bedrooms that were occupied by the Lyman children. Mrs. Lyman kept a diary and faithfully recorded eruptions, earthquakes, and tsunamis. Scientists still refer to it for some of the earliest recorded data on these natural disturbances. The master bedroom has a large bed with pineapples carved into the bedposts, crafted by a ship's carpenter who lived with the family for about eight months. The bedroom mirror is an original, in which many Hawaiians received their first surprised look at themselves. Guided tours of the Lyman Mission House are included with museum admission and are given twice a day (11am and 2pm) by experienced and knowledgeable docents who relate many intriguing stories about the house and its occupants.

Pacific Tsunami Museum

Hilo suffered a devastating tsunami in 1946 and another in 1960. Both times, most of the waterfront area of the city was destroyed, but the 1930 Bishop National Bank building survived, owing to its structural integrity. Appropriately, the **Pacific Tsunami Museum** (130 Kamehameha Ave., 808/935-0926, www.tsunami.org, Tues.-Sat. 10am-4pm, $8 adults, $7 seniors, $4 students) is now housed in this fine art deco structure and dedicated to those who lost their lives to the devastating waves that raked the city. The museum has numerous permanent displays, an audiovisual room, computer linkups to scientific sites, and periodic temporary exhibitions. The most moving displays of this museum are the photographs of the last two terrible tsunamis that struck the city and the stories told by the survivors of those events. Stop in for a look. It's worth the time.

Mokupapapa Discovery Center for Hawaii's Coral Reefs

This newly renovated museum right on the Bayfront, the **Mokupapapa Discovery Center for Hawaii's Coral Reefs** (76 Kamehameha Ave., Suite 109, 808/933-8195, www.papahanaumokuakea.gov, Tues.-Sat. 9am-4pm, free) has a few interactive features and life-size models of wildlife, and is filled with information about the science, culture, and history of the Northwestern Hawaiian Islands and their marine life. Besides the fact that is has a great restroom (so hard to find public restrooms on Bayfront!), this center offers a perfect place to bring kids for an hour of learning masked as fun. Since the center is indoors, this visit also makes for a great pop-in on the chance that you catch yourself in a Hilo rainstorm.

Around Banyan Drive

If your Hilo hotel isn't situated along Banyan Drive, go there. This bucolic, horseshoe-shaped road skirts the edge of Waiakea Peninsula, which sticks out into Hilo Bay. Lining the drive is an almost uninterrupted series of banyan trees forming a giant canopy. Skirting its edge are the Lili'uokalani Gardens, a concentration of hotels, and Reed's Bay.

This peninsula was once a populated residential area, an offshoot of central Hilo. Like much of the city, it was destroyed during the tsunami of 1960. Park your car at one end and take a stroll through this park-like atmosphere. Or arrive early and join other Hilo residents for a morning jog around the loop.

The four dozen banyans that line this boulevard (the first planted in 1933, the last in 1972) were planted by notable Americans and foreigners, including Babe Ruth, President Franklin D. Roosevelt, King George V, Hawaiian volcanologist Dr. Thomas Jaggar, Hawaiian princess Kawananakoa, pilot Amelia Earhart, Cecil B. DeMille, and then-senator Richard Nixon. A placard in front of most trees gives particulars. Time has taken its toll here, however, and as grand as this drive once was, it is now a bit overgrown and unkempt in spots, with much of the area needing a little sprucing up.

LILI'UOKALANI GARDENS

The **Lili'uokalani Gardens** are formal Japanese-style gardens located along the west end of Banyan Drive. Meditatively quiet, they offer a beautiful view of the bay. Along the footpaths are pagodas, torii gates, stone lanterns, and half-moon bridges spanning a series of ponds and streams. Along one side sits a formal Japanese teahouse, where women come to be instructed in the art of the tea ceremony. Few people visit this 30-acre garden, and if it weren't for the striking fingers of black lava and the coconut trees, you could easily be in Japan.

Lili'uokalani Gardens, a formal Japanese-style garden, offers idyllic views of the bay.

★ COCONUT ISLAND

Coconut Island (Moku Ola) is reached by footbridge from a spit of land just outside Liliʻuokalani Gardens. It was at one time a *puʻuhonua* (place of refuge) opposite a human sacrificial *heiau* on the peninsula side. Coconut Island has restrooms, a pavilion, and picnic tables shaded by tall coconut trees and ironwoods. It's been a favorite picnic spot for decades; kids often come to jump into the water from stone abutments here, and older folks come for a leisurely dip in the cool water. The only decent place to swim in Hilo Bay, it also offers the best panorama of the city, bay, and Mauna Kea beyond.

Wailoa River State Recreation Area

To the east of downtown is **Waiakea Pond,** a brackish lagoon where people often fish, although that might not be such a great idea given the rumored levels of pollution. The **Wailoa River State Recreation Area,** which encompasses the lagoon, is a 132-acre preserve set along both sides of this spring-fed pond. City residents use this big, broad area for picnics, pleasure walks, informal get-togethers, fishing, and launching boats. On the eastern side are picnic pavilions and

barbecue grills. Arching footbridges cross the river and connect the halves.

Stop at the **Wailoa Center** on the western side for tourist information and cultural displays such as exhibits by local artists (808/933-0416, Mon.-Tues. and Thurs.-Fri. 9am-4:30pm, Wed. noon-4:30pm). The walls in the upstairs gallery of this 10-sided building are used to display works of local artists and cultural/historical exhibits, changed on a regular basis. On the lower level hang astonishing pictures of the 1946 and 1960 tsunamis that washed through the city. The Wailoa Center sits in a broad swath of greenery, an open, idyllic, park-like area that used to be a cramped, bustling neighborhood known as Shinmachi. It, like much of the city, was almost totally destroyed during the tsunami of 1960. Nearby stands the **Tsunami Memorial** to the residents of this neighborhood who lost their lives in that natural disaster.

Also close by is the county **Vietnam War Memorial,** dedicated to those who died fighting that war, and a **statue of King Kamehameha,** a new version of which graces the town of Kapaʻau at the northern tip of the island.

East of Waiakea Pond and across Manono

Coconut Island is a favorite for local kids.

Street you'll see **Ho'olulu Park,** with the Civic Center Auditorium and numerous athletic stadiums. This is the town's center for organized athletic events, large cultural festivals, the yearly **Merrie Monarch Festival** (www.merriemonarch.com), and the annual county fair.

GREATER HILO
Mauna Loa Macadamia Nut Factory

Mauna Loa Macadamia Nut Factory (16-701 Macadamia Road, 808/966-8618, www.maunaloa.com, Mon.-Fri. 8:30am-5pm) is several miles south of Hilo off Highway 11, nearly at Kea'au. Head down Macadamia Road for about three miles, through the 2,500-acre plantation, until you come to the visitors center. Inside is an informative free video explaining the development and processing of macadamia nuts in Hawaii. Walkways outside the windows of the processing center and chocolate shop let you view the process of turning these delicious nuts into tantalizing gift items; this is best viewed from August through January when most of the processing is done. Then return to the snack shop for macadamia nut goodies like ice cream and cookies, and to the gift shop for samples and an intriguing assortment of packaged macadamia nut items. While you're here, step out back and take a self-guided tour of the small garden, where many introduced trees and plants are identified.

Pana'ewa Rainforest Zoo

Not often can travelers visit a zoo in such a unique setting, where the animals virtually live in paradise. The 150 animals at this 12-acre zoo are endemic and introduced species that would naturally live in such an environment. While small and local, the zoo is a delight and the only natural tropical rain forest zoo in the United States of America. The road to the **Pana'ewa Rainforest Zoo** (800 Stainback Hwy., 808/959-9233, www.hilozoo.com, daily 9am-4pm, closed Christmas and New Year's Day, free) is a trip

in itself, getting you back into the country. On a typical weekday, you'll have the place much to yourself. The zoo, operated by the county Department of Parks and Recreation, has a petting zoo every Saturday from 1:30pm to 2:30pm and it's a hoot (no pun intended). Your kid will have the time of his/her life. Admission is free, although donations to the nonprofit Friends of the Pana'ewa Zoo, which runs the gift shop at the entrance, are appreciated.

Here you have the feeling that the animals are not "fenced in" so much as you are "fenced out." The collection of about 75 species includes ordinary and exotic animals from around the world. You'll see pygmy hippos from Africa, a rare white Bengal tiger named Namaste, a miniature horse and steer, Asian forest tortoises, water buffalo, monkeys, and a wide assortment of birds like pheasants and peacocks. The zoo hosts many endangered animals indigenous to Hawaii, like the *nene,* Laysan duck, Hawaiian coot, *pueo,* Hawaiian gallinule, and even a feral pig in his own stone mini-condo. There are some great iguanas and mongooses, lemurs, and an aviary section with exotic birds like yellow-fronted parrots and blue and gold macaws. The zoo makes a perfect side trip for families and will certainly delight the little ones.

To get to the zoo from Hilo, take Highway 11 (Hawai'i Belt Road) south toward Volcano. About 2.5 miles past Prince Kuhio Shopping Plaza look for the Zoo sign on a lava rock wall, just after the sign reading "Kulani 19." Turn right on Mamaki.

'Imiloa Astronomy Center

Located on the upper campus of University of Hawai'i at Hilo, the **'Imiloa Astronomy Center** (600 Imiloa Pl., 808/969-9700, www.imiloahawaii.org, Tues.-Sun. 9am-5pm, adults $17.50, children 5-12 $9.50, senior, military, and *kama'aina* discounts available) opened in 2006 dedicated to the integration of science and indigenous culture. The word *'imiloa* means "exploring new knowledge," and the center educates visitors by separating its exhibits into "origins" and "explorations." Although in another place, the combination of studying astronomy and voyages may not make as much sense, here in Hawaii the two matters are linked given that the ancient Polynesians used the stars to wayfind from Polynesia to Hawaii and back.

In addition to the exhibits, a planetarium hosts daily kids' programs as well as Friday night laser light shows. Special events and workshops frequently occur at the center. Check the website for more information and for the Hawaiian word of the day. Say it at the register and get a $2 discount for each individual who speaks the word.

★ Rainbow Falls and Boiling Pots

A few miles out of town as you head west on Waianuenue Avenue, two natural spectacles within Wailuku River State Park are definitely worth a look. A short way past Hilo High School a sign directs you to **Rainbow Falls,** a most spectacular yet easily visited natural wonder. You'll look down on a circular pool in the river below that's almost 100 feet in diameter; cascading into it is a lovely waterfall. The 80-foot falls deserve their name because as they hit the water below, their mists throw flocks of rainbows into the air. Underneath the falls is a huge cavern, held by legend to be the abode of Hina, mother of the god Maui. Most people are content to look from the vantage point near the parking lot, but if you walk to the left, you can take a stone stairway to a private viewing area directly over the falls (be careful; it can be slippery). Here the river, strewn with volcanic boulders, pours over the edge. Follow the path for a minute or so along the bank to a gigantic banyan tree and a different vantage point. The falls may be best seen in the morning when the sunlight streams in from the front.

Follow Waianuenue Avenue for two more miles past Hilo Medical Center to the heights above town. A sign to turn right onto Pe'epe'e

Falls Street points to the **Boiling Pots.** Few people visit here. Follow the path from the parking lot past the toilets to an overlook. Indented into the riverbed below is a series of irregularly shaped depressions that look as though a peg-legged giant left his prints in the hot lava. Seven or eight resemble naturally bubbling whirlpool tubs as river water cascades from one into the next. This phenomenon is best after a heavy rain. Turn your head upriver to see **Pe'epe'e,** a gorgeous, five-spouted waterfall. Although signs warn you not to descend to the river—it's risky during heavy rains—locals hike down to the river rocks below to sunbathe and swim in pools that do not have rushing water. Be careful because it can get slippery; flash floods can and have occurred here.

Kaumana Cave

In 1881, Mauna Loa's tremendous eruption discharged a huge flow of lava. The river of lava crusted over, forming a tube through which molten lava continued to flow. Once the eruption ceased, the lava inside siphoned out, leaving the tube now called **Kaumana Cave** (Rte. 200). Follow a steep staircase down into a gray hole draped with green ferns and brightened by wildflowers. Smell the scent of the tropical vegetation. You can walk only a few yards into the cave before you'll need a strong flashlight and sturdy shoes. I'm not kidding: it's really dark and wet in there. A headlamp is ideal. Most people take the left "fork" at the bottom of the stairs instead of the right one—the right one involves more crawling over uneven tight surfaces.

To get to Kaumana Cave from downtown Hilo, turn left on Waianuenue Avenue. Just past mile marker 1 stay to the left onto Kaumana Drive (Saddle Rd.). Kaumana Cave is on the right just past mile marker 4. There are many reports of GPS leading people to the wrong location, so follow the directions here and look for the sign. Also, there have been break-ins reported in the parking area, so take proper precautions.

NORTH HILO TO 'AKAKA FALLS
★ Onomea Scenic Drive (Four-Mile Scenic Drive)

Highway 19 heading from Hilo to Honoka'a has magnificent inland and coastal views one after another. Most people find the **Onomea Scenic Drive** when coming north from Hilo. Only five minutes from the city, you'll come to Papa'ikou town. Just past mile marker 7 and across the road from the Papa'ikou School, a road posted as the scenic drive dips down toward the coast. Take it. (If you are coming from the Kona side you'll see a sign between mile markers 10 and 11). Almost immediately, signs warn you to slow your speed because of the narrow winding road and one-lane bridges, letting you know what kind of area you're entering. Start down this meandering lane past some modest homes and into the jungle that covers the road like a living green tunnel. Prepare for tiny bridges crossing tiny valleys. Stop, and you can almost hear the jungle growing. Along this four-mile route are sections of an ancient coastal trail and the site of a former fishing village. Drive defensively, but take a look as you pass one fine view after another. This road runs past the Hawaii Tropical Botanical Garden and a couple of places for quick eats before heading up to higher ground to rejoin Highway 19 at Pepe'ekeo.

If you're coming from Hilo, just a few minutes (or 1.5 miles) along the Onomea Scenic Drive is the **Hawai'i Tropical Botanical Garden** (27-717 Old Mamalahoa Hwy., 808/964-5233, www.hawaiigarden.com, daily 9am-5pm, last entry 4pm, adults $15, children 6-16 $5). Remember that the entrance fee not only allows you to walk through the best-tamed tropical rain forest on the Big Island but helps preserve this wonderful area in perpetuity.

The gardens were established in 1978 when Dan and Pauline Lutkenhouse purchased the 25-acre valley, and they have been open for viewing since 1984. Mr. Lutkenhouse, a retired San Francisco businessman, personally

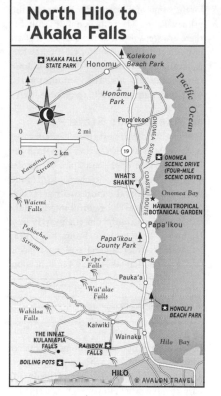

North Hilo to 'Akaka Falls

performed the work that transformed the valley into one of the most exotic spots in all of Hawaii. The locality was amazingly beautiful but inaccessible because it was so rugged. Through personal investment and six painstaking years of toil aided by only two helpers, he hand-cleared the land, built trails and bridges, developed an irrigation system, acquired more than 2,000 different species of trees and plants, and established one mile of scenic trails and a water lily lake stocked with *koi* and tropical fish. Onomea was a favorite spot with the Hawaiians, who came to fish and camp.

These inviting gardens, a "living museum" as they call it, will attract lovers of plants and flowers, and those looking to take really great photographs. The loop through the garden is about a mile long, and the self-guided tour takes about 90 minutes. As you walk, listen for the songs of the native birds that love this primeval spot. The walk is not difficult, but there are steps down to the gardens that are not wheelchair accessible. Golf carts ($5) are available to help those who need it down the boardwalk, and then nonmotorized wheelchairs are allowed in the garden itself.

★ 'Akaka Falls State Park

Everybody's idea of a pristine Hawaiian valley is viewable at **'Akaka Falls State Park** (on Hwy. 220, gate open 7am-7pm, $5 per car or $1 per pedestrian, no charge for Hawaii residents), one of the most easily accessible forays into Hawai'i's beautiful interior. Take the Honomu turnoff from Highway 19 onto Highway 220 to get here. From the parking lot, walk counterclockwise along a paved "circle route" that takes you 0.4 mile in about a half hour. The footpath does require some physical exertion. Along the way, you're surrounded by heliconia, ti, ginger, orchids, azaleas, ferns, and bamboo groves as you cross bubbling streams on wooden footbridges. Many varieties of plants that would be in window pots anywhere else are giants here, almost trees. An overlook provides views of **Kahuna Falls** spilling into a lush green valley below. The trail becomes an enchanted tunnel through hanging orchids and bougainvillea. In a few moments you arrive at **'Akaka Falls.** The mountain cooperates with the perfect setting, forming a semicircle from which the falls tumble 442 feet in one sheer drop, the tallest single-tier waterfall in the state. After heavy rains, expect a mad torrent of power; during dry periods marvel at liquid-silver threads forming mist and rainbows.

Beans

If you define a beach as a long expanse of white sand covered by a thousand sunbathers and their beach umbrellas, then Hilo doesn't have any. If a beach, to you, can be a smaller, more intimate affair where a good number of tourists and families can spend the day on pockets of sand between fingers of black lava, then Hilo has a few. Hilo's beaches are small and rocky—perfect for keeping crowds away. The best beaches all lie to the east of the city along Kalaniana'ole Avenue, an area known as the Keaukaha Strip, which runs six miles from downtown Hilo to its dead end at Leleiwi Point. Not all beaches are clearly marked, but even those that aren't are easily identified by the cars parked along the road.

DOWNTOWN HILO AND THE BAYFRONT
Hilo Bayfront Park

A thousand yards of gray-black sand that narrows considerably as it runs west from the Wailoa River toward downtown, **Hilo Bayfront Park** (along Kamehameha Ave.) at one time went all the way to the Wailuku River and was renowned throughout the islands for its beauty. Commercialism of the waterfront ruined it: By 1960, so much sewage and industrial waste had been pumped into the bay that it was considered a public menace, and then the great tsunami came. Reclamation projects created the Wailoa River State Recreation Area at the east end, and shorefront land became a buffer zone against future inundation. Few swimmers come to the beach because the water is cloudy and chilly, but the sharks don't seem to mind! The bay is a perfect spot for canoe races, and many local teams come here to train. Notice the judging towers and canoe sheds of local outrigger canoe clubs. Toward the west end, near the mouth of the Wailuku River, surfers catch long rides during winter, entertaining spectators. There is public parking along the eastern half near the canoe clubs or at the Wailoa River mouth where the fishing boats dock.

GREATER HILO

Although these beaches are outside of the downtown area, they are really only a few minutes from downtown, and all of them are within minutes of one another. With only one exception, all the beaches are either black-sand beaches or have no sand, just a grassy area fronting the beach.

Reeds Bay Beach Park

Technically part of Hilo Bay, **Reeds Bay Beach Park** (at the end of Banyan Dr.) is a largely undeveloped area on the east side of the Waiakea Peninsula. The water here is notoriously cold because of a constantly flowing freshwater spring at its innermost end, hence the name Ice Pond. Mostly it's frequented by fishers and locals having a good time on weekends and holidays, and some sailors park their private boats here. Restrooms, water, and shower facilities are available.

Keaukaha Beach at Carlsmith Beach Park

Keaukaha Beach at Carlsmith Beach Park, located on Puhi Bay, is the first in a series of beaches as you head east on Kalaniana'ole Avenue. Look for Baker Avenue and pull off to the left into a rough parking area. This is a favorite spot with local people, who swim at Cold Water Pond, a spring-fed inlet at the head of the bay. A sewage treatment plant fronts the western side of Puhi Bay. Much nicer areas for swimming and snorkeling await you just up Kalaniana'ole Avenue, but this beach does have a restroom, shower, pavilion, and weekend lifeguard.

Onekahakaha Beach Park

Farther up the road, **Onekahakaha Beach Park** has it all: safe swimming, a small white-sand beach, lifeguards, and amenities. Turn left onto Onekahakaha Road and park in the lot of Hilo's favorite family beach. Swim in the large, sandy-bottomed pool protected by a man-made breakwater. Outside the breakwater the currents can be fierce, and

drownings have been recorded; there is a lifeguard on duty during the weekends. Walk east along the shore to find an undeveloped area of the park with many small tidal pools. Beware of sea urchins.

James Kealoha Beach Park (Four Mile Beach)

James Kealoha Beach Park, also known locally as **Four Mile Beach,** is next. People swim, snorkel, and fish here, and during winter it's a favorite surfing spot. Stay to the left side of the beach since it's more protected than the right side, which can get rough with strong currents during times of high surf.

Just offshore is an island known as Scout Island because local Boy Scouts often camp there. This entire area was known for its fishponds, and inland, just across Kalaniana'ole Avenue, is the 60-acre Loko Waka Pond. This site of ancient Hawaiian aquaculture is now a commercial operation that raises mullet, trout, catfish, perch, tilapia, and other species. There is a restroom here but no other amenities.

Leleiwi Beach Park

A favorite local spot for scuba divers thanks to its plentiful sealife, **Leleiwi Beach Park** lies along a lovely residential area carved into the rugged coastline. This park, unlike the majority of them, has a full-time lifeguard, which is good because the shore here is open to the ocean and currents may be strong.

★ Richardson's Beach Park

Adjacent to Lelewi Beach Park is Richardson Ocean Park, known locally as **Richardson's Beach Park.** A seawall skirts the shore, and a tiny cove with a black-sand beach is the first in a series. This is a terrific area for snorkeling, with plenty of marine life, including *honu* (green sea turtles). Walk east to a natural lava breakwater. Behind it are pools filled and flushed by the surging tide. The water breaks over the top of the lava and rushes into the pools, making natural whirlpool tubs. This is one of the most picturesque swimming areas on the island and is often crowded with families since it offers a lot of shade and a full-time lifeguard on duty. Full amenities are available.

NORTH HILO TO 'AKAKA FALLS
★ Honoli'i Beach Park

Traveling north a few miles out of Hilo brings you to **Honoli'i Beach Park** (Hwy. 19 between mile markers 4 and 5). Turn right onto Nahala Street, then left onto Kahoa, and follow it around until you see cars parked along the road. The water is down a steep series of steps, and while the black-sand beach is not much appreciated for swimming, it is known as one of the finest surfing spots on this side of the island. If you're not a seasoned surfer, no worries: there is a "kiddie" area, as well as two lifeguards if any issues should arise. I highly recommend just coming for a quick viewing session to see the local talent try their hand at big waves. Restroom facilities and showers are available.

Kolekole Beach Park

Kolekole Beach Park (Hwy. 19 near mile marker 14) is popular with local people, who use its pavilions for all manner of special occasions, usually on weekends. A pebble beach fronts a treacherous ocean. The entire valley was inundated with more than 30 feet of water during the great 1946 tsunami. The stream running through Kolekole comes from 'Akaka Falls, four miles inland. Take care while wading across it—the current can be strong and push swimmers out to sea. Local kids take advantage of the ocean's pull to try their hand at bodyboarding. Amenities include portable bathrooms, grills, electricity, picnic tables, pavilions, and a camping area (county permit required); no drinking water is available.

To get to Kolekole Beach Park, look for the tall bridge a few minutes north of Honomu, where a sign points to a small road that snakes its way down the valley to the beach park below. Slow down and keep a sharp eye out, as the turnoff is right at the south end of the bridge and easy to miss.

Richardson's Beach Park

Water Sports

Although all water sports are possible in Hilo, it's more difficult to rent equipment on this side of the island, probably because fewer tourists come to Hilo to engage in water sports.

CANOEING AND KAYAKING

Hilo Bay is home to many outrigger canoe clubs. In fact, it's a pretty big club sport on this side of the island. If you glance out onto Hilo Bay almost any day you'll see numerous canoes and kayaks rowing by. Most canoes on the bay are owned by clubs and they do not rent out their watercraft. It may be possible to find a canoe rental if you hang out near the launch area on Bayfront and ask around. But for now, there are no businesses renting out canoes or kayaks (a business opportunity awaits!).

DIVING AND SNORKELING

Nearly all the beach parks on Kalaniana'ole Avenue offer worthy snorkeling and diving, but the best spots are at Leleiwi Beach Park

and Richardson's Beach Park. Because everyone knows those are the best spots, they can become crowded. However, if you swim out just a little bit you'll leave the crowds behind and it will just be you and the turtles.

Nautilus Dive Center (382 Kamehameha Ave., 808/935-6939, www.nautilusdivehilo. com, Mon.-Sat. 9am-5pm) offers introductory diving courses ($85 per person), three- to five-day scuba certification ($360 per person), and more advanced courses. Rentals are $35 per day and discounts are available for longer rental periods. If you're looking for a guide, they do that too. For $85 you can arrange a charter tour that includes a two-tank dive.

SURFING AND STAND-UP PADDLEBOARDING

There are some top surfing and stand-up paddleboarding destinations on this side of the island. The most popular is Honoli'i Beach Park, where surfers and boarders don't have to worry about getting in the way of swimmers. Hilo Bay also lacks swimmers, but the water is usually cold and murky. North of Hilo in

Honoli'i Beach Park

Hakalau it is possible to surf near the bridge, where waves can reach up to 16 feet. At the beach parks on Kalaniana'ole Avenue, such as Richardson's, it's also possible to surf if the weather is right, but these beaches all are prime stand-up paddleboarding haunts when the water is calm.

The hardest part of your surfing/boarding attempt might not be getting up, it might be finding a board if you just want to rent one. Your best bet for renting is **Orchidland Surfboards** (262 Kamehameha Ave., 808/935-1533, www.orchidlandsurf.com, Mon.-Sat. 9am-5pm, Sun. 10am-3pm).

Shopping

DOWNTOWN HILO AND THE BAYFRONT

The Bayfront area is most definitely set up to encourage shopping. Unfortunately, it doesn't always inspire shops to stay open late or to stay open at all. Don't be surprised if by 5pm downtown Hilo feels like a ghost town. Likewise, while there are a few stores that have kept their doors open for over 20 years, many more close every year. So don't be surprised if your favorite store from a past trip is nowhere to be found.

The majority of shops on the Bayfront cater to cruise ship passengers. It's difficult to distinguish one shop from another and the same Hawaiiana tchotchkes (made in China) that they offer. Nevertheless, one store that stands apart is **Basically Books** (160 Kamehameha Ave., 808/961-0144, www. basicallybooks.com, Mon.-Fri. 9am-6pm, Sat. 10am-5pm, Sun. 11am-3pm). This isn't where you get recently published best sellers; instead, it has a good selection of Hawaiiana, out-of-print books, and an unbeatable selection of maps and charts. You can get anywhere you want to go with these nautical charts, road maps, and topographical maps, including quadrangles for serious hikers. The store also features a good selection of travel books and national flags, as well as children's books and toys with Hawaii themes. The owners also publish books about Hawaii under the Petroglyph Press name.

Another long-standing store, **Sig Zane**

kayaking in Hilo Bay

Eating Local, Dressing Local

Before it was trendy, Big Islanders already were "eating local" and wearing locally made clothes more out of practicality than out of hipster-ness. It's very expensive to import food to the island (and why would you? The food here is delicious and grows easily!) and as you may have noticed, there is a lack of chain retail stores on the island and "free shipping" never applies to Hawaii orders (trust me, it doesn't). What is new on the Big Island is the marketing of these lifestyle choices.

Located towards the end of the line of stores on the Bayfront is **The Localvore Store** (60 Kamehameha Ave. 808/965-2372, www.bigislandlocalvorestore.com, Mon.-Fri. 9am-6pm, Sat. 9am-3pm), which is, as the name implies, an all-"local" boutique grocer. This Brooklyn-esque establishment couldn't meet all your grocery needs—but if you're into a grocery store addict or into "food porn" it sure is fun to peruse their artisanal organic fruit rolls in flavors like jackfruit, durian, or jabuticaba, along with the fresh turmeric, mamaki tea leaves, noni juice, local raw honey, local meats (including lamb!), and coffee-infused lip balms. And of course they sell vegan desserts.

King Kamehameha Market (144 Kamehameha Ave., Tues.-Sat. 10am-6pm) is an Etsy-style market infused with some Hawaiiana. The large warehouse space fills up with small booths of Big Island clothing and jewelry designers. It seems like they are still attracting new booths (sometimes it's not very crowded here), but this space definitely is worth a quick stop to see what the island fashionistas are creating.

Design (122 Kamehameha Ave., 808/935-7077, www.sigzane.com, Mon.-Fri. 9:30am-5pm, Sat. 9am-4pm), sells distinctive island wearables in Hawaiian/tropical designs. This store is the real deal. Sig Zane designs the fabrics, and Sig's wife, Nalani, is a *kumu hula* who learned the intricate dance steps from her mother, Edith Kanakaole, a legendary dancer who has been memorialized with a local tennis stadium that bears her name. You can get shirts, dresses, and pareu, as well as affordable T-shirts, *hapi* coats, and even futon covers. The shelves also hold leather bags, greeting cards, and accessories.

GREATER HILO

The majority of shopping for everyday living happens within the same four corners off of Highway 11. More importantly, this area serves as a main wayfinding point for giving directions to all other locations around town (including the airport, which is nearby).

Prince Kuhio Plaza (111 E. Puainako St., 808/959-3555, www.princekuhioplaza.com, Mon.-Thurs. 10am-8pm, Fri.-Sat. 10am-9pm, Sun. 10am-6pm) is the closest thing the Big Island has to a Mainland-looking indoor mall.

It's filled with mall stores like Macy's, Sears, and Sports Authority (Can't rent a canoe? Just buy one!). And yes, there is a food court filled with your standard pretzel shop, hot dogs on a stick, and a Cinnabon. Since no mall would be complete without a multiplex, you'll find a nine-screen movie theater here, too.

NORTH HILO TO 'AKAKA FALLS

The 'Akaka Falls road passes through the town of Honomu. In addition to the multitude of sarong shops dotting the main street (it's like the sarong capital of the world here), the non-sarong shops along the main street are worth a stop.

★ **Glass from the Past** (28-1672-A Old Mamalahoa Hwy., 808/963-6449, Mon.-Sat. 10:30am-5pm, Sun. 7am-12pm) has been in Honomu for 25 years, and its merchandise has been in the area for nearly a hundred years. As the store's name indicates, it carries antique glass. What's so interesting about this glass is that it is from the different area plantations— all of which had their own soda works and dairy. Each piece of glass tells a story about Hawai'i's past. Even if you're not going to make a purchase, stop in and talk with the shop owner, who scrounges the area to find his products. It's like a modern-day archaeological dig.

A few doors down, **Mr. Ed's Homemade Jams and Bakery** (808/963-5000, Mon.-Sat. 6am-6pm, Sun. 9am-4pm) stocks every imaginable type of jam made from local ingredients like jaboticaba, jackfruit, starfruit, and purple sweet potato. The baked goods get bad reviews, but come in and taste one of the hundreds of jams. Low-sugar as well as no-sugar options are available; they also ship jars to the Mainland if you don't want to check your luggage.

Entertainment

NIGHTLIFE

People in Hilo tend not to stay out late. Maybe it's because we like to get up early and surf or maybe it's because bars open and then quickly shut down due to noise complaints from neighbors. For the most part, bars have stopped opening in town.

Nevertheless, when driving around Hilo you'll surely see a lot of intriguing bars. Many of them are geared toward specific groups of locals. So there is one that serves Japanese clientele, and one that serves a Korean clientele, and one for Filipino clientele, and so on. If you're not from the island or with a local, you might feel a little out of place at some of these establishments, but that doesn't mean you shouldn't check them out.

A popular place with pupu included with alcohol purchase is **Bamboo Garden** (718 Kinoole St., 808/935-8952). Less popular than Kim's, this place doesn't always have a crowd. This would be the place to come if you're not looking for a scene and want to ease yourself into the world of Hilo bars.

Hilo Burger Joint (776 Kilauea, 808/935-8880, http://hiloburgerjoint.com, daily 11am-11pm, happy hour daily 4pm-6pm, $12) is your quintessential college-town bar. In addition to 20 varieties of Big Island beef burgers, there's a full bar with lots of beers on draft. Service can be slow at times. There's live music on the weekends starting at 7pm. During the NFL season they open early on Sundays and serve breakfast.

That sports bar you've been searching for to watch your team on the big-ish screen is **Cronies Bar and Grill** (11 Waianuenue Ave., 808/935-5158, www.cronieshawaii.com, Mon.-Thurs. 11am-9pm, Fri. 11am-10pm, Sat. 11am-9pm, Sun. 11am-8pm, $11-20). On the weekends, it's jammed with sports lovers rooting for their favorite teams. Cronies is tempting for its prime location right on Bayfront.

The **Hilo Town Tavern** (168 Keawe St., 808/935-2171, daily 11:30am-2am) fills a much-needed hole in downtown Hilo, where it seems like everything else closes by 5pm. You might find yourself meandering inside after hearing live music as you walk by. The bands are all local and the music styles vary, but for no cover, why not come for a listen and a drink? The back part of the bar has a pool table and more chairs, there is an outside patio, and the menu (which has changed several times since opening) now offers fifteen different types of sauces for chicken wings (starting at $6).

THE ARTS

Facing the peaceful Kalakaua Park, ★ **Hawaii Museum of Contemporary Art** (141 Kalakaua St., 808/961-5711, www.ehcc.org, Tues.-Sat. 10am-4pm First Fri. 5:30pm-9pm.), formally the East Hawaii Cultural Center, is a nonprofit organization that supports local arts and hosts varying festivals, performances, and workshops throughout the year, here and at other locations on the island. Monthly juried and non-juried art exhibits are shown on the main-floor gallery; a venue for various performing artists is upstairs. The bulletin board is always filled with announcements of happenings in the local art scene. Stop in as there is always something of interest on the walls and they have a perfectly curated museum shop featuring works of Big Island artists. The Big Island Dance Council, Hawaii Concert Society, Hilo Community Players, and Bunka No Izumi are all member groups.

Food

DOWNTOWN HILO AND THE BAYFRONT

Establishments are listed from east to west on each respective street beginning farther from the bay and ending on Bayfront (also known as Kamehameha Avenue).

Saimin, a noodle soup developed during Hawaii's plantation days, is just one of many dishes served at **Nori's Saimin and Snacks** (688 Kinoole St., 808/935-9133, http://www.norishilo.com, Sun. and Tues.-Thurs. 10:30am-10pm, Fri.-Sat. 10:30am-11pm, $12-16). Even though this Korean-style noodle house is featured in a Hawaiian Airlines ad, it doesn't get a lot of tourists. The daily specials range from fried chicken to pigs' feet soup to meatloaf, making it a little difficult to get a handle on Nori's culinary identity. But what is for certain is that the portions are large and inexpensive and there is Hello Kitty paraphernalia surrounding the Formica booths. If you want to taste a bunch of local dishes in one sitting, try the Big Plate with ahi tempura, fried noodles, kalbi ribs, teri beef, chicken sticks, *musubi,* and macaroni salad. I have seen a good eater attempt to eat this himself and he needed some help. It is a legitimately big plate. Try their self-proclaimed "famous" chocolate *mochi* cookies and cakes. I am skeptical of their fame, but you can't go wrong with a chocolate-*mochi* mix.

A gourmet anomaly in Hilo, **Short N Sweet Bakery and Café** (374 Kinoole St., 808/935-4446, www.shortnsweet.biz, Mon.-Fri. 7am-4:30pm, Sat.-Sun. 8am-3pm, $10) was proclaimed the maker of "America's most beautiful cakes" by *Brides* magazine in 2010. It was a well-deserved honor, but don't be mistaken: Short N Sweet is more than a bakery.

Their lunch menu of panini and salads is a welcome break from local cuisine, and their Sunday brunch menu is gaining in popularity thanks to their homemade smoked salmon bagels and quiches. Weekdays are stocked full of deals; ask about the early-bird special (7am-10am). Vegetarian and wheat-free options are available, along with wireless Internet.

Just Cruisin' Coffee (835 Kilauea Ave., 808/934-7444, Mon.-Fri. 5:30am-9pm, Sat.-Sun. 5am-8pm, $7) has wireless Internet, drive-through windows, and outdoor seating. But where Just Cruisin' Coffee excels is with their delectable chicken macadamia nut salad with pesto sandwich, along with hot breakfast sandwiches, cold brewed coffee, smoothies, and coffee milk shakes.

Named after a famous all-Japanese fighting battalion, **Cafe 100** (969 Kilauea Ave., 808/935-8683, http://cafe100.com, Mon.-Thurs. 6:15am-8pm, Fri. 6:15am-9pm, Sat. 6:15am-7:30pm, $7) is a Hilo institution. The Miyashiro family has been serving food at this indoor-outdoor restaurant since the late 1950s. Cafe 100 has turned the *loco moco* (a hamburger and egg atop rice smothered in gravy) into an art form. Offerings include the regular *loco moco,* teriyaki *loco,* Spam *loco,* hot dog *loco, oyako loco,* and, for the health conscious, the mahimahi *loco.* If your waistline, the surgeon general, and your arteries permit, this is *the* place to have one. Breakfast choices include everything from bacon and eggs to coffee and doughnuts, while lunches feature beef stew, a salmon mixed plate, and fried chicken, or an assortment of sandwiches from teriyaki beef to good old BLT. Make your selection and sit at one of the

Hilo Brewing

Hilo has its own microbrewery, **Hawai'i Nui Brewing** (275 E. Kawili St., 808/934-8211, www. hawaiinuibrewing.com, Mon.-Thurs. 12pm-5pm, Fri. 12pm-6pm, Sat. 12pm-4pm). A small operation—it produces about 1,200 barrels a year—in business since 1996, this brewery (formerly known as the Mehana Brewery) crafts five varieties of light beer with no preservatives, brewed especially for the tropical climate. Stop at the small tasting room/logo shop for a sample or gift any day except Sunday. If it's not too busy, someone may show you around.

picnic tables under the veranda to watch the people of Hilo go by.

An unassuming new restaurant located in the Pakalana Inn, the five-table ★ **Paul's Place Café** (132 Punahoa St., 808/280-8646, http://paulsplcafe.wix.com/paulsplacecafe, Tues.-Sat. 7am-3pm, $12) is delightful. Paul Cubio really cares that you, the diner, have the best experience possible at his little café. On one occasion, Chef Paul felt so badly that I had to wait for a table that he offered me a fresh smoothie while I waited and profusely apologized, even though I was the one who showed up without a reservation. A reservation isn't a must, but greatly helps given the limited seating; it's easier to get a seat later in the afternoon. There are only a few items on the menu, which has a mix of breakfast plates and fresh salads. This isn't a Spam breakfast-with-a-serving-size-for-eight kind of place. The eggs Benedict is dainty, but perfectly prepared. The Greek salad isn't large enough to split, but one can taste the flavors of each individual ingredient. The food is made with love.

If you've had enough of "local plates" then you'll be excited to find ★ **Lucy's Taqueria** (94 Kilauea Ave, 808/315-8246, www.lucystaqueria.com, Sun.-Thurs. 10:30am-9pm, Fri.-Sat. 10:30am-10pm, $6-12). This "authentic" Mexican restaurant is quick and delicious and if it could get even better…it uses (mainly) local ingredients including Big Island beef. It's kind of a do-it-yourself place—you order at a counter, grab your own salsa (chips are free), and later bus your own table—but this DIYness keeps the prices low without compromising the quality of the food. Breakfast is

served all day and you might need it after trying one of their margaritas, which are served in the separate bar area.

The competition for title of best Thai food on the Big Island continues at **Naung Mai Thai Kitchen** (86 Kilauea Ave., 808/934-7540, www.hilothai.com, daily 11am-9pm, $11-17), where the great lunch specials, pineapple curry, and vegan tapioca pudding give the other "best" Thai restaurants a run for their money. The space is intimate.

Next door to Naung Mai is the newly opened **Pho Viet** (80 Kilauea Ave., 808/935-1080, Mon.-Tues., Thurs.-Sat. 11am-8pm, $8), serving the traditional Vietnamese soup called *pho* (pronounced "fuh"): beef noodle or chicken noodle soup served with sprouts and lime on the side. The *pho* is *pho*-nomenal. Note: They don't do takeout.

At the end of Keawe Street in a beautiful historic building you'll find **Le Magic Pan** (64 Keawe St., 808/935-7777, Mon.-Sat. 7:30am-10:30am, daily 10:30am-2pm and 5pm-9pm, Sun. brunch 9am-11am, $10-15), and it's worth stopping by. The menu includes both dessert crepes (with Nutella and bananas) and savory crepes (like shrimp with pesto). The meals are surprisingly filling, and with live music filling the air of this stylish long-standing building, Le Magic Pan makes for a good date-night option.

Front and center on Bayfront, with a black-and-white checkerboard floor, linen on the tables, an open-air kitchen, a high ceiling with whirling fans, and the calming effect of ferns and flowers, is **Café Pesto** (308 Kamehameha Ave., 808/969-6640, www.

cafepesto.com, Sun.-Thurs. 11am-9pm, Fri.-Sat. 11am-10pm, reservations recommended, lunch $14, dinner $20), in the historic S. Hata Building. It offers affordable gourmet food in an open, airy, and unpretentious setting that looks out across the avenue to the bay. Pizzas from the 'ohi'a wood-fired oven can be anything from a simple cheese pie for $8.50 to a large Greek or chili-grilled shrimp pizza for $18; you can also create your own. Lunchtime features sandwiches, calzones, and pasta. For dinner, try an appetizer like Asian Pacific crab cakes or sesame-crusted Hamakua goat cheese. Heartier appetites will be satisfied with the main dinner choices, mostly $15-28, which might be mango-glazed chicken, island seafood risotto, or a combination beef tenderloin and tiger prawns with garlic mashed potatoes. Follow this with a warm coconut tart or liliko'i cheesecake. Café Pesto also has a brass-railed bar where you can order caffe latte or a glass of fine wine to top off your meal. A kids' menu is available.

For well-priced food in a cute (very local) setting, it's imperative to get to ★ **Puka Puka Kitchen** (270 Kamehameha Ave., 808/933-2121, lunch Mon.-Sat. 11am-2:30pm and dinner Thurs.-Sat. 5:30pm-8:30pm, $15). It's a must to get there early, otherwise the best dishes are gone. However, for late arrivals (after 2pm) the bento boxes are half price and quite a deal. The food is Middle Eastern-meets-Indian-meets-Hawaii—with Japanese writing on the menu. The sautéed lamb plate is delicious, with tender pieces of locally sourced meat served with a green salad and rice. Order the house garlic rice to create the perfect plate of flavors. Other choices are the ahi plate, curry dishes, and the pita sandwiches—all hearty options. I would not get the barbecued chicken or the falafel, as the other plates are done better. There are several vegetarian options on the menu and they accommodate special diets.

★ **Two Ladies Kitchen** (274 Kilauea Ave., 808/961-4766, Tues.-Sat. 10am-5pm) brings mochi to a whole new level, crafting it from sweet rice flour according to their secret family recipe. Each piece looks like a work of art. You can sense the sheer excitement when the sign comes up that reads "we still have strawberry mochi today." The strawberries are real, which leads to a second sign that reads "you can't bring them to the Mainland" (due to the agricultural inspection). You'll wish you could, though.

GREATER HILO

The menu at the ★ **Hilo Bay Café** (123 Lihiwai St., Hilo, 808/935-4939, www.hilobaycafe.com, Mon.-Thurs. 11am-9pm, Fri.-Sat. 11am-9:30pm, lunch $15, dinner $24) seems like it was written by a food writer. It has dishes such as vegetarian flax sweet potato burger and roasted free-range chicken breast stuffed with cilantro-cumin mascarpone. The names of the dishes certainly make it hard to pick just one. The menu changes with the season and the meat, fish, and produce are from local farmers. The food here tastes good and they make excellent cocktails that are classics with a Hawaii twist. Service is attentive and with their new location on the actual Hilo Bay (they were formerly in a strip mall) the café makes for an ideal place for a romantic evening. A children's menu is available and reservations are a must.

The **Hilo Lunch Shop** (421 Kalanikoa St., Hilo, 808/935-8273, www.hawaiianstylecafe.com, Tues.-Sat. 5:30am-1pm, $3) is a one-stop shop for local flavors. The friendly staff is happy to explain each dish even when the customer line is long. The restaurant is set up in okazuya style. There is a long buffet and as you walk down it you point to what you want and a nice server boxes it for you. Most items are around $1 per piece or under and the selections include nori chicken, tempura, cone sushi, fishcakes, and salads. You can mix and match as you like and still not pay over $10 for a lot of food. There is limited seating inside but most people take their food to go. Come early! They often are sold out before noon, which is a good thing since some of the food, unfortunately, tends to be served cold towards the end of service.

You might recognize **Hawaiian Style**

Café (681 Manono St., Hilo, 808/ 969-9265, daily 7am-2pm, Tues.-Thurs. 5pm-8:30pm, Fri.-Sat. 5pm-9pm, $12-20) from its sister brunch location in Waimea. This Hilo location serves up the same huge breakfasts with the added bonus of dinner five nights of week. Like breakfast, dinner portions are huge—but don't be embarrassed about not wanting to split a meal given the many homemade local-style choices. Try the ribs (lamb or kalbi) or one of the "family recipe" stews, and come before you're too hungry—waits can be long at times.

In same new strip mall area is **Miyo's** (564 Hinano St, Hilo, 808/935-2273, www.miyo-srestaurant.com, Mon.-Sat. 11am-2pm and 5:30am-8:30pm, reservations recommended, $13-17), which touts itself as "home-style Japanese cooking." Many mourned Miyo's closing its shop in its old location (it was set up like a Japanese teahouse and overlooked a pond), but its new location suits it and modernizes not only the service, but also the cuisine. The menu is short: combination plates or bento boxes of sashimi or tempura served with chicken or beef. This is a favorite local place for power lunches, so reservations may be necessary for lunch and dinner.

It's no exaggeration to say ★ **Sombat's**

Fresh Thai Cuisine (88 Kanoelehua, Hilo, 808/969-9336, www.sombats.com, Mon.-Fri. 10:30am-1:30pm and 5pm-8:30pm, Sat. 5pm-8:30pm, lunch $7, dinner $15) is probably some of the best Thai food you'll have outside of Thailand. Sombat, the owner and chef, grows the herbs in her garden in order to get her dishes flavored just right. Eaters can often see her in the restaurant chatting with guests and checking to make sure everything is up to par. The lunch special is an outstanding deal, with portions almost large enough to feed two people. Usually you choose between a curry and a noodle dish. Come early, as the special often sells out by 12:30pm and then only the à la carte options are available. Try the coco soup with ahi; it's large enough that it can feed two or more people. Keep in mind that hot in Hawaii is very, very hot on the Mainland. So you might want to order a level down.

Pancakes make up about one-tenth of the massive menu at ★ **Ken's House of Pancakes** (1730 Kamehameha Ave., Hilo, 808/935-8711, www.kenshouseofpancakes. com, 24 hours), an institution in Hilo, so don't let the pancake part throw you off. Year after year Ken's wins awards for "Best Diner on the Island," and the accolade is well deserved. There are so many good things about

the thickest and freshest smoothie you will ever have at What's Shakin'

Ken's it's hard to know where to start. To begin with, it's one of few places in Hawaii that is open 24 hours. Check the menu for nightly specials; Sunday is all-you-can-eat spaghetti night. Breakfast is available anytime, but you'll be torn between a three-egg omelet with Portuguese sausage and the short ribs. Or, go big and order the Sumo Loco: six scoops of rice, five ounces of Spam, gravy, and three eggs. If that seems like overdoing it, order off the kids' menu or from the "lighter stuff." Save room, if you are capable, for the homemade pies.

NORTH HILO TO 'AKAKA FALLS

The options in this area are few and far between, so plan accordingly.

Halfway through the Onomea Scenic Drive you'll come across the glorious oasis of ★ **What's Shakin'** (27-999 Old Mamaloahoa Hwy., Pepeʻekeo, 808/964-3080, daily 10am-5pm, smoothies $7, lunch $10). It might sound like a lot, $7 for a smoothie—but I can almost guarantee that it will be the best smoothie you'll ever have and it will be filling enough to split between two people. The fruit is all grown on the farm that houses this stand, and you can taste the freshness in every sip. The food, usually a daily special as well as their standard menu of nachos, salmon burgers, and burritos, is equally delicious with huge portions and several vegetarian options. Note: If you are coming from the Kona direction, you'll pass a different smoothie stand as you turn right onto the scenic drive—What's Shakin' is just two minutes up the road from there.

On Wednesday and Saturday mornings, stop by the corner of Kamehameha Avenue and Mamo Street for the **Hilo Farmers Market,** perhaps the best farmers market on the island. This is a lively affair, great for local color, where you can get healthy, locally grown produce and bouquets of colorful flowers at bargain prices. It's not all locally grown; ask where it comes from if that's important to you. Across the street at The Market Place and also a few steps up the road under the big tents are more vendors selling flowers, arts and crafts, and other gift items.

Getting There and Around

AIR

The **Hilo International Airport** (code ITO) is right in town—so much so that you can see the Hawaiian Airlines logo overhead on the planes that are about to land (it's like the beginning montage of *Hawaii Five-0*). The airport is currently only an international airport in theory. Most international flights have to connect through one of the other Hawaiian airports (like Honolulu) before arriving to Hilo.

After many years of no direct flights to the Mainland, United Airlines began direct service between Hilo and Los Angeles and the San Francisco Bay Area. These flights are only a few times a week and tend to be seasonal. Otherwise, the airport is mostly used by interisland flights serviced by **Hawaiian Airlines** (www.hawaiianair.com). To get to the other islands, it is often necessary to travel through Honolulu. Hawaiian Airlines offers one direct flight to Maui daily.

BUS

Hilo's **Mooheau Bus Terminal** (between Kamehameha Ave. and Bayfront Hwy.) is the only proper bus terminal on the island—it's so official that there is actually a **tourist information kiosk** located inside. From the bus terminal it is possible to get anywhere on the island by utilizing the **Hele-On Bus** (www.heleonbus.org, 808/961-8744, $2 per ride, $1 each for luggage, large backpacks, bikes). Buses make almost hourly trips to Waimea via the Hamakua Coast as well as to Puna. For Volcano, Kaʻu, Kona, and Kohala, a little bit more planning is necessary, as there are only 3-4 daily direct buses to these regions. Check the website for exact times.

There are four separate intra-Hilo routes; however, some of these routes overlap. All the buses pass through the downtown terminal, and by selecting the correct route (check the website or ask at the terminal) it is possible to travel to the in-town beaches, shopping areas, the University of Hawai'i at Hilo, and even the airport. During peak times you can catch a bus nearly every 20 minutes or so. By the evening it's more like every 40 minutes or every hour. If you're not going too far, it usually is quicker to walk to your destination than wait for the bus.

If you are without a rental car on a quick layover from a cruise ship or your trip to visit the volcano or you just really hate dealing with parking, a good option is **Hoppa-on Hoppa-off Hilo Tour Bus** (808/895-4188, http://www.hop-onhop-offhilobus.com, $20). The day pass gives you unlimited boarding and reboarding on this open-air "fun" bus. It's kind-of like those duck tours that other cities have, only without the part where the bus becomes a transformer and goes into the water. The route includes the majority of sights in the downtown Hilo area from Richardson Beach to the shops on Bayfront to Rainbow Falls. One could walk to and from many of these locations and take the public bus to the others that are a bit farther afield, but if you don't really want to think about where to go and you like someone giving you some narration, then this tour bus will meet your needs.

TAXI

There are nearly two dozen taxi companies in town. For service 24 hours a day try **Ace One Taxi** (808/935-8303), **AA Marshall's Taxi** (808/936-2654) or **WJJ Taxi & Tours** (808/938-8786). You can get most anywhere in town or to/from the airport for under $15. If you're interested in a shared-ride taxi, you must purchase prepaid vouchers. Call 808/961-8744 for additional information on where to purchase the coupon books. For shared rides, it's one coupon per person for traveling 1-4 miles and two coupons per person for traveling 4.1-9.0 miles. Farther afield, you might expect about $50 to Pahoa, $75 to Volcano, and $100 to Honoka'a.

Hamakua Coast, Waimea, and the Saddle Road

Look for ★ to find recommended
sights, activities, dining, and lodging.

Highlights

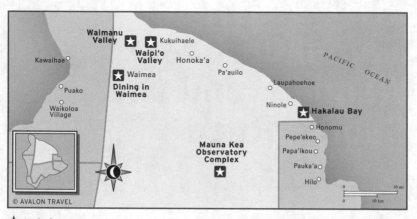

★ **Hakalau Bay:** Photographers and history buffs will be eager to visit the plantation-era ruins of Hakalau Mill, destroyed in the tsunami of 1946 (page 186).

★ **Waipi'o Valley:** Once a burial ground of Hawaiian royalty, this verdant valley is postcard perfect, with one of the best (if not the very best) views on the Big Island (page 187).

★ **Mauna Kea Observatory Complex:** View the heavens from the top of Mauna Kea, where astronomers expect an average of 325 crystal-clear nights per year (page 195).

★ **Waimanu Valley:** The hike down to Waipi'o and over the *pali* to the wild, verdant Waimanu Valley is one of the top treks in Hawaii (page 199).

★ **Dining in Waimea:** The birthplace of the Hawaii Regional Cuisine movement offers inspired dining in the heart of cowboy country (page 207).

You'll be surprised by how this northern slice of the island appears and feels so drastically different from the other regions.

The Hamakua stretch of the island, recently named the "Hilo-Hamakua Heritage Coast," draws visitors for its historical and cultural significance; there is not much beach to be had on this coast, and rough cliffs create difficult access to the ocean. Along the 50-mile stretch of Highway 19 from Hilo to Honoka'a, the Big Island grew its sugarcane for 100 years or more. Water was needed for sugar—a ton to produce a pound—and this coast has plenty. Present-day Hamakua is becoming known for its fertile growing land that is ideal for kava, mushrooms, vanilla, and macadamia nuts. Restaurants around the region source their ingredients from Hamakua, so indulge in some culinary delights on your drive around the coast.

With a population of around 2,250, Honoka'a (Rolling Bay) is the major town on the Hamakua Coast. The main street, Mamane Street, is filled with old false-front wooden buildings built in the 1920s and 1930s by Chinese and Japanese workers who left the sugar plantations to go into business for themselves. From Honoka'a, Highway 19 slips down the long Hamakua Coast to Hilo and Highway 240 heads north for nine miles to the edge of Waipi'o Valley, which you should not miss.

Waipi'o Valley (Curving Water) is the kind of place that is hard to believe unless you see it for yourself. It's vibrantly green, always watered by Waipi'o Stream and lesser streams that spout as waterfalls from the *pali* at the rear and to the side of the valley. The green is offset by a wide band of black-sand beach. From the overlook at the top of Waipi'o, you can make out the overgrown outlines of garden terraces, taro patches, and fishponds in what was Hawaii's largest cultivated valley.

Waimea, also known as Kamuela, is technically in the South Kohala district, but because of its inland topography of high mountain pasture on the broad slope of Mauna Kea, it is vastly different from the long Kohala coastal district. It also has a unique culture inspired by the range-riding *paniolo* (cowboys) of the expansive Parker Ranch. But

---

Previous: Go riding at one of Waimea's many ranches; Waipi'o Valley overlook. **Above:** Mauna Kea summit.

a visit here isn't one-dimensional. In town are homey accommodations, inspired country dining, and varied shopping opportunities. The town supports arts and crafts in fine galleries and has the island's premier performance venue. There's an abundance of fresh air and wide-open spaces, the latter not so easily found in the islands.

There is old lava along both sides of the road as you approach the broad tableland of the Saddle Road. Much of the lava here is from the mid-1800s, but some is from a more recent 1935 flow. Everyone with a sense of adventure loves this bold cut across the Big Island through a broad high valley separating the two great mountains, Mauna Loa and Mauna Kea. Heading up to the observatories at the top of Mauna Kea, the tallest peak in the Pacific, affords some truly stellar stargazing, while massive Mauna Loa offers one of the most extreme hikes on the island.

ORIENTATION
Hamakua Coast

Officially, the Hamakua Coast begins soon after the four-mile Onomea Scenic Drive out of Hilo and curls around to Waimea, but in reality the entire coastline should be named an official scenic drive. Even people who hate driving love this drive. This is the kind of road that asks for a convertible with a great soundtrack playing from the stereo. (This chapter is organized as if you are driving east to west on Highway 19 from Hilo along the Hamakua Coast toward Waimea. If you are coming from the Kona side, follow this chapter in reverse.)

The Hamakua Coast is a good example of appreciating the journey and not necessarily the end point. The entire drive, without stopping, takes only 45 minutes. But you can extend your trip by taking one of the many side roads that branch off the main highway. Unfortunately, the majority of these roads end up paralleling the highway and don't go far— mainly through the old housing areas from the plantation days.

If you are inclined to make stops along the way, there are several scenic points that allow you to soak in the magnificent ocean views down below. If you're looking for some longer excursions close to the road, stop at the Laupahoehoe Train Museum to peruse artifacts showcasing the history of the region, or visit some actual plantation artifacts (material culture for you academics out there!) at Hakalau Bay. If you really want to get out of the car and into the trees, hike one of the short trails of Kalopa Native Forest State Park, which is filled with native trees and birds, or try ziplining through the canopy of the World Botanical Gardens in Hakalau.

Honoka'a and Waipi'o Valley

Located on Highway 19 just 45 minutes west of Hilo and 20 minutes north of Waimea, Honoka'a is sort of a Hawaiian-style bedroom community. Follow the green sign pointing *makai* from Highway 19 to Mamane Street, the main street passing through the center of town that leads toward Highway 240 and Waipi'o Valley and the meeting points for the majority of organized Waipi'o trips. Mamane Street has a number of shops specializing in locally produced handicrafts, along with local-style restaurants, clothing and gift shops, and general merchandise stores and antiques shops. The town also holds a small health center, a post office, two banks, a movie theater, a public library, and a nine-hole golf course.

Highway 240 ends a minute outside of Kukuihaele at an overlook, and 900 feet below is Waipi'o (Curving Water), the island's largest and most southerly valley of the many that carve into the Kohala Mountains. A sacred land for ancient Hawaiians, the valley is a mile across and six miles from the ocean to its back end.

You can spend an hour in the sleepy Honoka'a town checking out the quaint handicraft boutiques and then stop back again at the end of the day after a visit to Waipi'o Valley for a happy hour cup of awa (kava) at the awa bar. And believe me, you'll be ready to relax after traveling by four-wheel-drive, horse, all-terrain vehicle, or your own two legs down the nearly vertical road to Waipi'o Valley.

Hamakua Coast, Waimea, and the Saddle Road

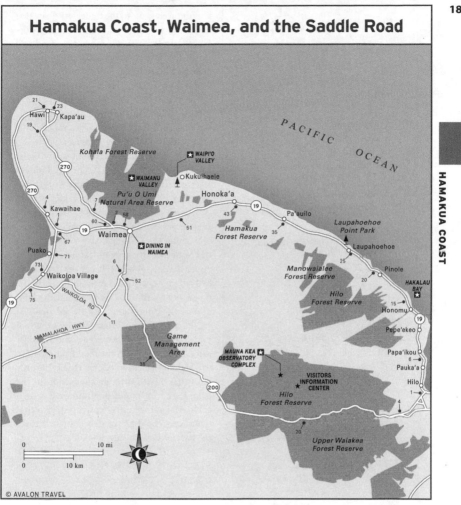

Waimea

Parker Ranch, founded early in the 19th century by John Palmer Parker, dominates the heart and soul of the region. Waimea revolves around ranch life and livestock, with herds of rodeos and "Wild West shows" scheduled throughout the year.

Waimea is also known as **Kamuela,** the Hawaiianized version of Samuel, after one of John Parker's grandsons. Kamuela is used as the post office address, so as not to confuse this town of Waimea with towns of the same name on the islands of Oʻahu and Kauaʻi.

In the last 30 years, Waimea has experienced real and substantial growth. In 1980 it had no traffic lights and was home to about 2,000 people. Now the population has grown more than threefold, there are three lights along the main highway, and there are occasional traffic jams. Waimea is modernizing and gentrifying, and its cowboy backwoods character is rapidly changing.

The town, at elevation 2,670 feet, is split

Hamakua Coast

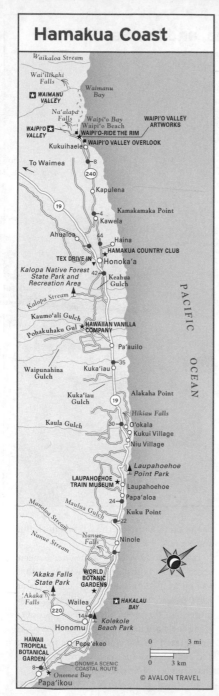

Waikaloa Stream
Wai'ilikahi Falls
★ WAIMANU VALLEY
Waimanu Bay
Na'alapa Falls
Waipi'o Bay
Waipi'o Beach
WAIPI'O VALLEY ARTWORKS
WAIPI'O ★ VALLEY
WAIPI'O-RIDE THE RIM
WAIPI'O VALLEY OVERLOOK
Kukuihaele
To Waimea
240
Kapulena
19
Kamakamaka Point
Kawela
Ahualoa
44
Haina
HAMAKUA COUNTRY CLUB
TEX DRIVE IN
Honoka'a
Kalopa Native Forest State Park and Recreation Area
42
Keahua Gulch
Kalopa Stream
Kaumo'ali Gulch
Pohakuhaku Gul
HAWAIIAN VANILLA COMPANY
Pa'auilo
Waipunahina Gulch
Kuka'iau
35
Kuka'iau Gulch
Alakaha Point
19
Hikiau Falls
Kaula Gulch
30
O'okala
Kukui Village
Niu Village
Laupahoehoe Point Park
LAUPAHOEHOE TRAIN MUSEUM
Laupahoehoe
Papa'aloa
24
Kuku Point
Manaloa Stream
Maulua Gulch
22
Nanue Stream
Nanue Falls
Ninole
'Akaka Falls State Park
WORLD BOTANIC GARDENS
'Akaka Falls
Wailea
★ HAKALAU BAY
220
14
Kolekole Beach Park
Honomu
HAWAII TROPICAL BOTANICAL GARDEN
Pepe'ekeo
8
ONOMEA SCENIC COASTAL ROUTE
Onomea Bay
Papa'ikou

PACIFIC OCEAN

0   3 mi
0   3 km

© AVALON TRAVEL

almost directly down the center—the east side is the wet side, and the west is the dry side. Houses on the east side are easy to find and reasonable to rent, while houses on the dry side are expensive and usually unavailable. You can literally walk from verdant green fields and tall trees to semi-arid landscape in a matter of minutes. This imaginary line also demarcates the local social order: upper-class ranch managers (dry), and working-class *paniolo* (wet).

Waimea is at the crossroads of nearly all the island's roads, the main ones being Highway 19 from Hilo (via the Hamakua Coast) and Highway 190 from Kailua-Kona. Highway 19 continues west through town, reaching the coast at Kawaihae, where it turns south and cuts along the Kohala Coast, passing by all the resorts on the way to Kailua-Kona. The upper road, Highway 190, connects Waimea to Kailua-Kona and the route looks much more like Marlboro Country than the land of *aloha,* with grazing cattle amid fields of cactus. On Highway 190 seven miles south of Waimea you'll find the turnoff to the Saddle Road (Highway 200), the road leading up to the Mauna Kea Observatory. This is the only road that travels through the middle of the island, and unlike in previous years when car-rental agreements explicitly stated that rental cars could not be driven on this road, the route is now paved and wide.

Mauna Kea and the Saddle Road

Slicing across the midriff of the island in a gentle arch from Hilo to the Mamalahoa Highway near Waimea is Highway 200, the Saddle Road. Access to both Mauna Loa and Mauna Kea is possible from the Saddle Road.

Along this stretch of some 55 miles you pass rolling pastureland, broad swaths of lava flows, arid fields that look a bit like Nevada, a *nene* sanctuary, trailheads for several hiking trails, mist-shrouded rain forests, an explorable cave, and spur roads leading to the tops of Mauna Kea and Mauna Loa. Here as well is the largest military training reserve in the state, with its live firing range, and the Bradshaw

Gulches and Traffic Delays

Driving the extremely scenic Highway 19 through the Hamakua Gulch, you'll see several signs for "gulches." A gulch is a deep ravine formed by erosion, sometimes with a stream running through it, and is usually larger than a gully. These gulches are also newly notable because they are the sites of huge traffic delays in the area. The county received funds to better secure the cliffs against rockslides, and as construction crews work their way down the coast placing netting onto the cliffs, traffic is reduced to one lane Monday-Friday 10am-3pm. Plan for some extra time if you are in a rush.

Army Airfield. What you won't see is much traffic or many people. It's a great adventure for anyone traveling between Hilo and Kona. Keep your eyes peeled for convoys of tanks and armored personnel carriers, which sometimes sally forth from the Pohakuloa Training Area, and also watch out for those who make this a high-speed shortcut from one side of the island to the other.

This road *is* isolated. If you do have trouble, you'll need to go a long way for assistance, but if you bypass it, you'll miss some of the best scenery on the Big Island. On the Kona side, the Saddle Road turnoff is about six miles south of Waimea along Highway 190, about halfway between Waimea and Waikoloa Road. From Hilo, follow Waianuenue Avenue inland. Saddle Road, Highway 200, also signed as Kaumana Drive, splits left after about a mile and is clearly marked. Passing Kaumana Caves Park, the road steadily gains elevation as you pass into and then out of a layer of clouds. Expect fog or rain.

About 28 miles out of Hilo and 25 miles up from the Kona side, a clearly marked spur road branches to the north; officially called the John A. Burns Way, but most often referred to as the Mauna Kea Access Road, it leads to the summit of Mauna Kea. You can expect wind, rain, fog, hail, snow, and altitude sickness. Intrigued? Proceed—it's not as bad as it sounds. In fact, the road, while steep, is well paved for the first six miles, and from there the road is graded gravel, banked, and usually well maintained but sometimes like a washboard, with the upper four miles paved so that dust is kept to a minimum to protect the sensitive "eyes" of the telescopes.

A four-wheel-drive vehicle is required beyond the visitors center, and if there's snow, the road may not be passable at all. (For current road conditions, call 808/935-6268.)

The Mauna Loa Observatory Road, a one-lane paved road with long stretches of potholes and rough patches, turns south off the Saddle Road between mile markers 27 and 28 and leads about 17 miles in a big zig and zag and gentle incline up to the Mauna Loa NOAA Atmospheric Observatory.

PLANNING YOUR TIME

If you came to Hawai'i not to sit on the beach, but instead to do a lot of sightseeing where it's not too hot, this region is ideal for you. Whether you're starting your trip from the east or west side of the island, you'll want to plan around being in **Waipi'o Valley** during the morning when the weather is better and when the majority of organized trips are set to leave. Unless you're going to do an overnight hiking trip through the valley, you really only need a day to see the valley and trek down it in whatever capacity.

Since the Hamakua Coast drive, without stops, is only 45 minutes, it can easily be completed in an afternoon even if you make several stops along the way. If you plan ahead, you can book reservations for a tasting at the **Hawaiian Vanilla Company** or **Hamakua Mushroom Tour and Tasting** and/or soaring through the **World Botanical Gardens** with **Zip Isle.** No planning is required to stop at any of the scenic overlooks or parks along the highway.

It's unfortunate that there isn't more to see in Waimea because there is so much good food

Waimea

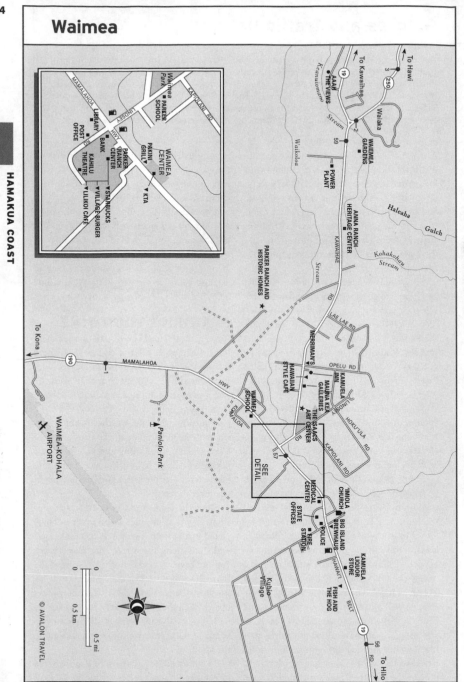

Waimea (Inset detail)

Waimea Park

PARKER SCHOOL

MAMALAHOA HWY

LINDSEY

KAPIOLANI RD

LIBRARY

POST OFFICE

BANK

KAHILU THEATRE

LILIKOI CAFE

VILLAGE BURGER

STARBUCKS

PARKER RANCH CENTER

WAIMEA CENTER

PAKINI GRILL

KTA

Main map

To Kawaihae

To Hawi

19

250

3

Keanuiomano Stream

Waiaka

2

Waikoloa

WAIMEA GARDENS

59

POWER PLANT

Haleaha

ANNA RANCH HERITAGE CENTER

Kohakohau Stream

Gulch

KAWAIHAE RD

PARKER RANCH AND HISTORIC HOMES

Stream

LAE LAE RD

To Kona

190

MAMALAHOA

1

MERRIMAN'S

HAWAIIAN STYLE CAFE

OPELU RD

KAMUELA INN

MAUNA KEA GALLERIES

THE ISAACS ART CENTER

LINCOLN ST

HOKU'ULA RD

KAMALOA

WAIMEA SCHOOL

HWY

KAMUELA

KAPIOLANI RD

SEE DETAIL

57

WAIMEA-KOHALA AIRPORT

Paniolo Park

MEDICAL CENTER

'IMIOLA CHURCH

BIG ISLAND BREWHAUS

STATE OFFICES

POLICE

FIRE STATION

MAMANE

Kuhio Village

KAMUELA LIQUOR STORE

FISH AND THE HOG

BELT

19

56

RD

To Hilo

0

0.5 km

0

0.5 mi

© AVALON TRAVEL

The Saddle Road

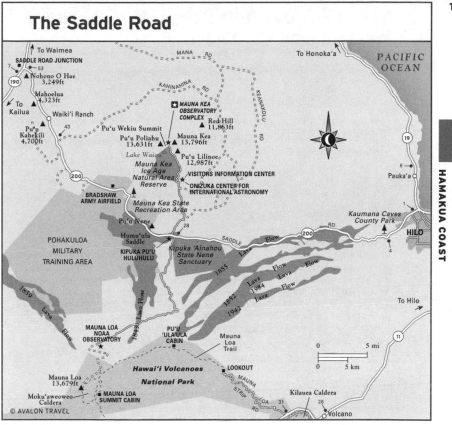

To Waimea
SADDLE ROAD JUNCTION
Nohono O Hae 3,249ft
Mahoelua 4,323ft
To Kailua
Waiki'i Ranch
Pu'u Kahekili 4,700ft
Pu'u Wekiu Summit
Pu'u Poliahu 13,631ft
Lake Waiau
Mauna Kea Ice Age Natural Area Reserve
BRADSHAW ARMY AIRFIELD
Pu'u Nene
POHAKULOA MILITARY TRAINING AREA
Humu'ula Saddle
KIPUKA PU'U HULUHULU
MAUNA LOA NOAA OBSERVATORY
Mauna Loa 13,679ft
Moku'aweoweo Caldera
MAUNA LOA SUMMIT CABIN
© AVALON TRAVEL
MANA RD
KAHINAHINA RD
MAUNA KEA OBSERVATORY COMPLEX
Red Hill 11,863ft
Mauna Kea 13,796ft
Pu'u Lilinoe 12,987ft
VISITORS INFORMATION CENTER
ONIZUKA CENTER FOR INTERNATIONAL ASTRONOMY
Mauna Kea State Recreation Area
Kipuka 'Ainahou State Nene Sanctuary
PU'U 'ULA'ULA CABIN
Hawai'i Volcanoes National Park
LOOKOUT
Mauna Loa Trail
KEANAKOLU RD
To Honoka'a
PACIFIC OCEAN
SADDLE RD
Lava Flow
1855
1984 Lava
1852
1942
Kaumana Caves County Park
HILO
To Hilo
Pauka'a
MAUNA STRIP RD
Kilauea Caldera
Volcano
HAMAKUA COAST
0 5 mi
0 5 km

that you'll want to stay all day. I recommend visiting Waimea as a way to cool off from the hot afternoons of the Kohala Coast or to pick up provisions on your way to Mauna Kea. Stroll through the stores at **Parker Square** or tour the **Anna Ranch Heritage Center** before heading to dinner.

Regardless of how much time you want to spend at the top of **Mauna Kea,** it's important to account for how much time it will take to get there. First there is traveling on the Saddle Road to the observatory access road, which can take about an hour from Waimea, depending on weather. The drive up to the visitors center takes another 30 minutes, after which it's an additional 40 minutes to the summit after you've spent time at the visitors center to acclimate to the altitude. If you're driving in the dark, these travel times can be much longer.

The point is, a trip to Mauna Kea is hardly a quick jaunt and especially is not quick if you're traveling on a group tour. Those planning on traveling to the summit to catch the sunset should leave a few hours ahead of time and even earlier if you might hike around the area first. After sunset, most visitors to Mauna Kea reconvene at the visitors center for an hour or two of star- and planet-gazing. Don't expect to head down before 8pm—it will be hard to walk away from the most awe-inspiring sky you might ever see.

Your Best Day in the Hamakua Coast, Waimea, and the Saddle Road

- Wake up early to catch the **view of Mauna Kea** from Waimea before the clouds come rolling in.

- Get breakfast at **Hawaiian Style Café** in Waimea.

- Head to **Waipi'o Valley** to join a group tour or venture down into the valley on your own.

- In the afternoon, take a drive east on Highway 19, stopping at **Hakalau Bay** to see some plantation ruins.

- Either head back the way you came or travel through Hilo and back over the **Saddle Road,** grabbing food and drinks for a picnic. Aim to arrive at the **Onizuka Center for International Astronomy** visitors information center on **Mauna Kea** just at sunset.

- Settle in for some **stargazing** that will astound you.

RAINY-DAY ALTERNATIVE

At some point during the day, rain or a mist is expected in Waimea—so don't let that throw you off. If it's really raining hard, you have a few options. The good news is, from Waimea you can see if it's raining down below in Kohala. If it's not, travel down the hill 20 minutes to soak up the sun.

If you want to stay in Waimea, visit the **Anna Ranch Heritage Center.** You can spend at least an hour or two touring on your own or with a guide. If you pay for the tour, for a few extra dollars you can get an "enhanced tour" that includes arts and crafts.

If you're on the Hamakua Coast, visit the **Laupahoehoe Train Museum** or the **Hawaiian Vanilla Company.**

Sights

HAMAKUA COAST
★ Hakalau Bay

There are residents of the Big Island who have never seen the abandoned plantation remnants in Hakalau Bay, a short detour off the highway. To get here from Highway 19, between mile markers 15 and 16 turn *makai* near the footbridge and follow the street around, going under the bridge and down toward the ocean and the park. Local kids come here to swim in the stream under the highway bridge (look up and you'll see that this bridge was once a train track and was turned upside down to be used as a road). Even if you're not interested in swimming in the murky water that flows into the ocean, photographers and history buffs will be eager to visit the ruins of Hakalau Mill, destroyed in the tsunami of 1946. Its remnants are scattered around the parking lot.

World Botanical Gardens

Touted as the state's largest botanical garden with over 5,000 different species, the **World Botanical Gardens** (Hwy. 19 at mile marker 16, *mauka* side, 808/963-5427, http://worldbotanicalgardens.com, daily 9am-5:30pm, self-guided tours adults $15, teens $7, children 5-12 $3, guided tours adults $57-187) is really the backdrop of the Zip Isle zipline that makes use of the botanical gardens. The entry fee to the gardens is included with the price of the zipline, and during the zip course itself you'll end up walking around a large portion of the gardens. When you are doing zipping, you can walk down to the river on a short trail or drive up to catch a glimpse of a waterfall. If you are planning to just come for the botanical gardens portion, your better bet might be to visit the Hawaii Tropical Botanical Garden in Onomea Bay down the road. The guided tours occur on a Segway and can take anywhere from 30 minutes to over two hours; the longer tours visit the falls.

Laupahoehoe Train Museum

Although small in size, the **Laupahoehoe Train Museum** (36-2377 Mamalahoa Hwy./ Hwy. 19 near mile marker 25, 808/962-6300, www.thetrainmuseum.com, Thurs.-Sun. 10am-5pm, Mon.-Wed. by appointment, adults $6, seniors $5, families $15) is big on the history of the Hamakua region. Interwoven with the history of the coastal train route, a 34-mile stretch with 21 stops that was destroyed by the 1946 tsunami, the museum offers abundant archival photos detailing what life on the Big Island looked like in the early 1900s. Next to the museum is a reconstructed train car and tracks. You only need about a half hour here, but it's worth stopping in if you have the time.

Laupahoehoe Point Park

This wave-lashed peninsula is a popular place for weekend family outings. A plaque at water's edge commemorates the tragic loss of 20 schoolchildren and their teacher, who were taken by the great tsunami of 1946. Afterward, the village was moved to the high ground overlooking the point. **Laupahoehoe Point Park** (Laupahoehoe Point Rd. off Hwy. 19 between mile markers 27 and 28) now occupies the low peninsula; it has nice shaded picnic tables, showers, electricity, and a county camping area. The park can get busy on the weekends with local families cooking out and playing tunes on their ukuleles. The sea is too rough to swim in, except perhaps by the boat launch ramp, but many anglers come here, along with some daring surfers. The road down to the park is narrow and winding and runs past several rebuilt homes and a restored Jodo Mission. It will take about 10 minutes to drive down to the park from the highway.

★ WAIPI'O VALLEY

Waipi'o, which means curved or arched waters, is known to Hawaiians as the Sacred Valley of the Kings. Locals know it as one of the best views on all of the Big Island—the valley really is postcard perfect, with a river running through deep green hills.

The valley itself has been inhabited by

Laupahoehoe Point Park

Culinary Delights of the Hamakua Coast

the vanilla pods of the Hawaiian Vanilla Company

Even those who are adamant in their hatred of mushrooms can't help but indulge in **Hamakua Mushrooms** (36-221 Manowaiopae Homestead Road, Laupahoehoe, 808/962-0305, http://hamakuamushrooms.com, Mon.-Fri. 9am-4pm). At one time, these exotic, buttery mushrooms were difficult to find on menus, but now one can find them at nearly every upscale restaurant on the island. If you can't get enough of these mushrooms or are just really interested in where your food comes from ("de-reifying food," as Marx would say…), you might enjoy this new tour and tasting. Tours are all indoors and include a cooking demo, mushroom tasting, and lots of video watching (Mon.-Fri. at 9:30am and 11:30am, lasts a little over an hour, adults $20 (plus tax), seniors $17.50, children 5-11 $10, students $10). The price is a bit steep, so if you're short on time and low on cash I'd recommend just stopping by their gift shop and picking up some fresh or dried mushrooms to try on your own.

The rock star of foodie tours is Jim Reddekopp, owner of **Hawaiian Vanilla Company** (43-2007 Paauilo Mauka Rd., Paauilo, 808/776-1771, www.hawaiianvanilla.com, Mon.-Sat. 10am-5pm). You may have seen him on The Food Network or Travel Channel. The company's gift shop, which Jim calls "an upscale Cracker Barrel," is mainly staffed by family members and is stocked full of vanilla products both of the culinary and lotion varieties. The tour, usually led by Jim, is the kind of hour (and a half) that will make you rethink your life. You'll leave wondering, "Should I quit my job and start a farm in Hawaii?"—Jim is that excited and inspirational. Three kinds of epiphany-inducing tours are available: the **Vanilla Experience Luncheon** (Mon.-Fri. at 12:30pm, adults $39, children under 12 $19) includes a vanilla-themed lunch (the highlight is the ice cream or sorbet depending on your lactose tolerance) and quick walk around the area; the **Farm Tour** (Mon.-Fri. at 1pm, $25 per person) includes a "Johnny Boy," the Arnold Palmer of the vanilla experience (half vanilla ice tea, half vanilla lemonade) and dessert plus tour of the farm; and the very special **Upcountry Tea** (Sat. at 3pm, $29 per person) includes vanilla tea (obviously), champagne toast, an appetizer, and several small courses, ending with dessert. The prices are right for this tour, Jim is hilarious, and the vanilla is sublime—you can't go wrong.

Hawaiians for over 1,200 years and is the site of many ancient temples and burial sites. Traditionally, the valley also held importance as a fertile ground for growing taro that is made into poi, a staple of the Hawaiian diet. Today, **Waipi'o Valley** (where Hwy. 240 ends) is home to waterfalls (the two most recognizable ones are Hi'ilawe and Hakalaoa), ancient fishponds close to the front of the valley, and, closer to the shore, sand dunes intermixed with old burial grounds.

Every culinary item known to the Hawaiians once flourished here; even Waipi'o pigs were said to be bigger than pigs anywhere else. In times of famine, the produce from Waipi'o could sustain the populace of the entire island. On the valley floor and alongside the streams you'll still find avocados, bananas, coconuts, passion fruit, mountain apples, guavas, breadfruit, tapioca, lemons, limes, coffee, grapefruit, and pumpkins. The old fishponds and streams are alive with prawns, wild pigs roam the interior, as do wild horses, and there are abundant fish in the sea. Carrying on the traditions of old, some farmers in the valley still raise taro, and this has once again become one of the largest taro-producing regions on the island and one of the principal production centers in the state.

Getting There

You can travel down into the valley in nearly every imaginable way: by horse, by ATV, by foot, by car, and so on. Spend some time considering which method of visiting Waipi'o meets your needs, depending on how much time you have, how much money you wish to spend, how much you want to plan ahead, and your physical prowess. For those who just want to catch a glimpse and a photo of the valley's glory from above without much effort, there is a lovely, easily accessible scenic overlook in front of the parking area (with restroom facilities).

The other important factor to consider is whether or not you want to actually go into the valley or simply travel around the rim. The majority of organized tours meet at stores in Kukuihaele, a small town just a few miles east of Waipi'o. As you drive west on Highway 240 from Honoka'a, when the road forks go toward the right (the sign will point to the right for Kukuihaele), follow the road and you will see the tour storefronts on the *makai* side of the road. Note: For many tours, reservations are needed. Very rarely can you just stop in and get on a tour—but if empty spaces are available due to no-shows you may be able to secure a spot at a discounted rate.

Waipi'o Valley overlook

ATV

As you can probably guess, **Ride the Rim** (check in at Waipi'o Valley Artworks, 48-5416 Kukuihaele Rd., Kukuihaele, 808/775-1450, www.ridetherim.com, morning and afternoon tours, $179 per adult ATV driver, $149 per adult buggy passenger, $99 per child buggy passenger) offers a three-hour tour around the rim (not the valley) through eucalyptus trees, stopping for a swim at a secluded waterfall. Riders must be over 16 years old and weigh between 100 and 350 pounds; however, those who can't drive can ride in an open-air buggy driven by a tour guide. This is a good way for families to tour together even if not everyone wants to get down and dirty with an ATV.

WAGON

Perhaps the most unexpected way to experience the valley is by mule-drawn wagon. This narrated cultural and historical tour organized by **Waipi'o Valley Wagon Tours** (meet at Last Chance Store, Kukuihaele, 808/775-9518, www.waipiovalleywagontours.com, Mon.-Sat., adult $60, senior $55, child 3-11 $30) allows you to get down into the valley without exhausting yourself. The tour is only 1.5 hours and that is a bit short given the amount of time it takes to actually get down into the valley. It's a good option for people short on time or families who want to travel together.

HIKING

It is possible to walk into the valley on your own. More complicated, however, is to walk the rim, as it is private property and tour companies lease rights to pass through it. Most people only take the journey into the valley as a means to the end—the end being the beach at the end of the road. To begin the vertical trek down into the valley, park your car in the lot at the end of Highway 240 or, inevitably, on the street. The road that walkers take down to the valley bottom and onward to the beach is the same paved road the cars use. Bring *plenty* of water and sunscreen for the walk—and a snack (I recommend picking up *malasadas* at Tex's in Honoka'a before you go—you'll thank me). You'll be sweaty and thirsty by the time you get to the bottom. And don't underestimate the downhill part of the journey—for many it's actually more challenging than the uphill part since it's quite hard on the knees. Give yourself about 45 minutes to get down and an hour to get back to the top. There are no

Waipi'o Valley

public restrooms in the valley and just the portable potties at the beach, so use the nicer facilities at the Waipi'o Overlook before you head down.

HORSEBACK

Waipi'o Ridge Stables (check in at Waipi'o Valley Artworks, 48-5416 Kukuihaele Rd., Kukuihaele, 808/775-1007, www.waipioridgestables.com, morning and afternoon 2.5-hour ride $85, morning 5-hour ride $165) can accommodate beginners, but it may be nerve-wracking since no training is provided. The horses are on auto-pilot, so there isn't much for you to do but enjoy the views. The important thing to note is that the ride is not through the valley, but through a eucalyptus forest to a great lookout spot. The ride is still nice and relaxing, but it doesn't offer the nonstop outstanding views that a ride through the valley might have. Also, while the wranglers are incredibly friendly and want to make you feel comfortable, they offer minimal background information about the area while you ride.

If touring the valley is what you want, your best option is **Na'alapa Stables** (check in at Waipi'o Valley Artworks, 48-5416 Kukuihaele Rd., www.naalapastables.com, Mon.-Sat. 9am and 12:30pm, $94). Known for their quality service and excellent guides who share stories of Hawaiian history and culture, this tour books up quickly, so make sure to plan ahead. Riders meet at Waipi'o Valley Artworks and then are transported down into the valley in the ranch's four-wheel vehicle. The road down to the valley is steep, so this trip might not be for the faint of heart. The entire tour is 2.5 hours, but actual horse time is not that long given the amount of time it takes to travel up and down into the valley. A printable coupon for $10 is available on their website.

Similarly, **Waipi'o on Horseback** (Hwy. 240 at mile marker 7, *mauka* side, 808/775-9888, www.waipioonhorseback.com, Mon.-Sat. 9:30am and 1:30pm, $90 plus tax,

discount if booked with ATV tour) is another valley trip that will get you there and near to the waterfalls. The ride through the valley is similar to those of other companies, but the guides do not seem as knowledgeable or as engaged with riders as guides at other companies.

FOUR-WHEEL-DRIVE AND SHUTTLE TOUR

The road leading down to Waipi'o is outrageously steep and narrow, averaging a 25 percent gradient. If you attempt it in a regular car, it'll eat you up and spit out your bones. More than 20 fatalities have occurred since people started driving it, and it has only been paved since the early 1970s. You'll definitely need four-wheel drive to make it; vehicles headed downhill yield to those coming up.

Not everyone can walk down to the valley on their own or has time or funds to join a tour. But residents of the area have asked me to nicely request that you do not drive down unless it is completely and utterly necessary. Residents have been advocating for the last few years to cut off tourist traffic to the valley, as the cars not only create a preventable traffic mess on the road but also inflict environmental havoc on the landscape.

If you want to be shuttled down to the bottom, the ★ **Waipi'o Valley Shuttle** (808/775-7121, www.waipiovalleyshuttle.com, Mon.-Sat., $59 adults, $32 children under 11, reservations recommended) makes a 90-minute descent and tour of Waipi'o Valley in air-conditioned, four-wheel-drive vans that leave from Waipi'o Valley Artworks in Kukuihaele, at 9am, 11am, 1pm, and 3pm Monday-Saturday. Along the way, you'll be regaled by beautiful legends and stories and shown the most prominent sights in the valley by drivers who live in the area. This is the easiest way into the valley, and the guides are locals who know what they're doing, as they've been at it since 1970. Sometimes drivers of this shuttle will give hikers a ride down to the valley floor or up the road to the overlook parking lot for a few bucks, if there's room in the vehicle.

Waipi'o: Then and Now

When Captain Cook came to Hawaii, 4,000 natives lived in Waipi'o; a century later only 600 remained. At the turn of the 20th century many Chinese and Japanese moved to Waipi'o and began raising rice and taro. There were schools, stores, a post office, churches, and a strong community spirit. Waipi'o was painstakingly tended. The undergrowth was kept trimmed and you could see clearly from the back of the valley all the way to the sea. In the 1940s, many people were lured away by a changing lifestyle and a desire for modernity. The tsunami in 1946 swept away most of the homes that remained; the majority of the residents pulled up stakes and moved away. For 25 years the valley was abandoned. The Peace Corps considered it a perfect place to build a compound to train volunteers headed for Southeast Asia. This too was later abandoned. Then in the late 1960s and early 1970s a few "back to nature" hippies started trickling in. Most only played Tarzan and Jane for a while and moved on.

Waipi'o is still unpredictable. In a three-week period from late March to early April of 1989, 47 inches of rain drenched the valley. Roads were turned to quagmires, houses washed away, and more people left. Part of the problem is the imported trees in Waipi'o. Until the 1940s, the valley was a manicured garden, but now it's heavily forested. All of the trees you will see are new; the oldest are mangroves and coconuts. The trees are both a boon and a blight. They give shade and fruit, but when there are floods, they fall into the river, creating logjams that increase the flooding dramatically. Waipi'o takes care of itself best when humans do not interfere. Taro farmers, too, have had problems because the irrigation system for their crops was washed away in the last flood.

Nowadays, those who live in the valley have learned to accept life in Waipi'o and genuinely love the valley. A few families with real commitment have stayed on and continue to revitalize Waipi'o. The valley now supports perhaps 40 residents. More people live topside but come down to Waipi'o to tend their gardens.

In the summer of 1992, the Bishop Museum requested an environmental impact survey on Waipi'o Valley because the frequency of visitors to the valley had increased tremendously. Old-time residents complained not only about the overuse of the valley but about the loss of their secluded lifestyle. As a result of the impact study, commercial tours are not allowed to go to the beach area on the far side of the stream, which is now open to foot traffic only.

The socio-ethnic battle for the valley continues. Some long-term residents, mostly but not exclusively of Hawaiian descent, have largely withdrawn the spirit of *aloha* from visitors. Their dissatisfaction is not wholly without basis: Some who have come to the valley have been disrespectful, trespassing on private property, threatening to sue landowners for injuries they themselves caused, or finding themselves stuck in a river that no one in their right mind would try to cross. Many wonderful, open, and loving people still live in the valley. Be respectful and stay on public property. If the sign says *Kapu* (which means "forbidden") or Keep Out, believe it. It is everyone's right to walk along the beach, the switchback that goes to Waimanu, and waterways. These are traditional free lands in Hawaii open to all people, and they remain so. With proper behavior from visitors, Waipi'o's *aloha* will return.

WAIMEA
Parker Ranch and Historic Homes

After a bit of reorganizing, the ubiquitous Parker Ranch organization has finally reopened a modified version of the ranch's **historic homes** (67-1435 Mamalahoa Hwy./ Hawai'i Belt Rd., 808/885-7311, www.parker-ranch.com, Mon.-Fri. 8:30am-3:30pm, free).

Dating from the 19th century, the Puuopelu house doubles as the organization's main headquarters. Grab a self-guided tour flier in the entryway and lead yourself through the small main room filled with historical furniture and Broadway memorabilia from Richard Smart's (the heir to the Parker Ranch) acting days. Next, visit the Mana Hale home, which was moved from its original location to this property, with relics from the early days of Parker Ranch. The two homes may only be of interest to history buffs, but I urge you to at least take the drive from the main road down to the site, as the views from the road and looking back at Mauna Kea are well worth the short detour.

The Isaacs Art Center

One of the preeminent galleries on the island is **The Isaacs Art Center** (65-1268 Kawaihae Rd., 808/885-5864, www.isaacsartcenter.org, Tues.-Sat. 10am-5pm). This art store/museum, part of Hawai'i Preparatory Academy, is worth a stop. An expansion into two distinct spaces is underway, but for now the museum and the store are intermixed, and the pieces dating from 19th- and 20th-century Hawaii and Asia are some of the finest (and priciest) on the island. Even if you don't have the means to afford fine art, the center's staff is happy to talk about each piece and give you a little lesson on Hawaiian art.

Anna Ranch Heritage Center

Dedicated to Anna Leialoha Lindsey Perry-Fiske, the "first lady of ranching" in Hawaii, the living-history museum at **Anna Ranch Heritage Center** (65-1480 Kawaihae Rd.,

Hwy. 19 near mile marker 58, 808/885-4426, www.annaranch.org, Tues.-Fri. 10am-3pm, guided tours 10am and 1pm by appointment (really, call ahead) $10, self-guided garden tour free) is a great entrée into what Hawaiian ranch life was like in the early 20th century. The property consists of the original house, a restored blacksmith area, and placards explaining the surrounding views of Waimea. Anna's house is nicely staged with lots of original artifacts, including parts of Anna's extensive hat and clothing collections. Fashion lovers will truly appreciate the collection. If you walk around the house yourself, you might only need about 30 minutes. The guided tour, on the other hand, can run nearly two hours. If you don't think you'll make it to one of the scheduled tours, call ahead to schedule a tour at a convenient time. Also, if you call ahead it may be possible to schedule an enhanced tour that includes activities for the kids: a lesson in lassoing, leather crafting, and a blacksmith demonstration.

MAUNA KEA
Onizuka Center for International Astronomy

This entire mountaintop complex, plus almost all of the land area above 12,000 feet,

Anna Ranch Heritage Center

is managed by the University of Hawai'i. Visitors are welcome to tour the observatory complex and stop by the visitors information center at the **Onizuka Center for International Astronomy** (808/961-2180, www.ifa.hawaii.edu/info/vis, daily 9am-10pm) at the 9,200-foot level. Named in honor of astronaut Ellison Onizuka, who was born and raised on the Big Island and died in the *Challenger* space shuttle tragedy in 1986, this center is a must-stop for stargazers. Inside are displays of astronomical and cultural subjects, informational handouts, computer links to the observatories on the hill above, and evening videos and slide shows, as well as a small bookstore and gift shop. At times, 11- and 16-inch telescopes are set up outside during the day to view the sun and sunspots; every evening they are there to view the stars and other celestial objects. The visitors center is about one hour from Hilo and Waimea and about two hours from Kailua-Kona. A stop here will allow visitors a chance to acclimate to the thin, high-mountain air—another must. A stay of one hour here is recommended before you head up to the 13,796-foot summit. The visitors center provides the last public restrooms before the summit and is a good place to stock up on water, also unavailable higher up.

Free stargazing is offered nightly 6pm-10pm, and there's a summit tour every Saturday and Sunday (weather permitting) at 1pm. These programs are free of charge. For either activity, dress warmly. Evening temperatures will be 40-50°F in summer and might be below freezing in winter, and winds of 20 miles per hour are not atypical. For the summit tour, you must provide your own four-wheel-drive transportation from the visitors center to the summit.

Going Up the Mountain

If you plan on continuing up to the summit, you must provide your own transportation and it must be a four-wheel-drive vehicle. People with cardiopulmonary or respiratory problems or with physical infirmities or weakness and women who are pregnant are discouraged from attempting the trip. In addition, those who have been scuba diving should not attempt a trip to the top until at least 24 hours have elapsed. These are serious warnings. As the observatories are used primarily at night, it is requested that visitors to the top come during daylight hours and leave within 30 minutes after sunset to minimize the use of headlights and reduce the dust from the road, both factors that might disrupt optimal viewing. It's suggested that on your way down you use flashing warning lights that let you see a good distance ahead of you while keeping bright white lights unused. However, as one security person has stated, safety is their primary concern for drivers, so if you feel you must use your headlights to get yourself down without an accident, by all means do so. Some rental companies have changed their rules regarding taking cars up to the summit and it is not allowed. Others have not wavered. Cars can have a difficult time handling the climb up, so decide for yourself if it is worth making the trip on your own. It is possible to hitch a ride from the visitors center to the summit with a nice passerby, but plan ahead to make sure that you also have a ride back! It would be a long cold walk down in the dark.

Alternatively, make arrangements for a **guided tour** to the top. These tours usually last seven to eight hours and run $175-200 per person. Tour operators supply the vehicle, guide, food, snacks, and plenty of warm clothing for your trip. They also supply telescopes for your private viewing of the stars near the visitors center after seeing the sunset from the top. From the Kona side, try **Hawaii Forest and Trail** (808/331-5805 or 800/464-1993, www.hawaii-forest.com). In Hilo, contact **Arnott's Hiking Adventures** (808/969-7097, www.arnott-slodge.com, discounts available for hotel guests). Take extra layers of warm clothing and your camera.

Mauna Kea: From Silversword to Snow

As you climb Mauna Kea (White Mountain), you pass through the clouds to a barren world devoid of vegetation. The earth is a red, rolling series of volcanic cones. You get an incredible vista of Mauna Loa peeking through the clouds and what seems like the entire island lying at your feet. In the distance the lights of Maui flicker.

Off to your right is **Pu'u Kahinahina,** a small hill whose name means Hill of the Silversword. It's one of the few places on the Big Island where you'll see this rare plant. The mountaintop was at one time federal land, and funds were made available to eradicate feral goats, one of the worst destroyers of the silversword and many other native Hawaiian plants.

Lake Waiau (Swirling Water) lies at 13,020 feet, making it the third-highest lake in the United States. For some reason, ladybugs love this area. This lake is less than two acres in size and quite shallow. Oddly, in an area that has little precipitation and very dry air, this lake never dries up or drains away, fed by a bed of melting permafrost below the surface.

Here and there around the summit are small caves, remnants of ancient quarries where Hawaiians came to dig a special kind of fired rock that is the hardest in all Hawaii. They hauled roughed-out tools down to the lowlands, where they refined them into excellent implements that became coveted trade items. These quarries, Lake Waiau, and a large triangular section of the glaciated southern slope of the mountain have been designated **Mauna Kea Ice Age Natural Area Reserve.**

A natural phenomenon is the strange thermal properties manifested by the cinder cones that dot the top of the mountain. Only 10 feet or so under their surface is permafrost that dates back 10,000 years to the Pleistocene epoch. If you drill into the cones for 10-20 feet and put a pipe in, during daylight hours air will be sucked into the pipe. At night, warm air comes out of the pipe with sufficient force to keep a hat levitating.

Mauna Kea was the only spot in the tropical Pacific thought to be glaciated until recent investigation provided evidence that suggests that Haleakala on Maui was also capped by a glacier when it was higher and much younger. The entire summit of Mauna Kea was covered in 500 feet of ice. Toward the summit, you may notice piles of rock—these are terminal moraines of these ancient glaciers—or other flat surfaces that are grooved as if scratched by huge fingernails. The snows atop Mauna Kea are unpredictable. Some years it is merely a dusting, while in other years, such as 1982, there has been enough snow to ski from late November to late July.

★ **MAUNA KEA OBSERVATORY COMPLEX**

Atop the mountain is a mushroom grove of astronomical observatories, as incongruously striking as a futuristic earth colony on a remote planet of a distant galaxy. The crystal-clear air and lack of dust and light pollution make the **Mauna Kea Observatory Complex** *the* best in the world. At close to 14,000 feet, it is above 40 percent of the earth's atmosphere and 98 percent of its water vapor. Temperatures hover around 40-50°F during the day, and there's only 9-11 inches of precipitation annually, mostly in the form of snow. The astronomers have come to expect an average of 325 crystal-clear nights per year, perfect for observation. The state of Hawaii leases plots at the top of the mountain, upon which various institutions from all over the world have constructed telescopes. Those institutions in turn give the University of Hawai'i up to 15 percent of their viewing time. The university sells the excess viewing time, which supports the entire astronomy program and makes a little money on the side. Those who work at the top must come down every four days because the thin air makes them forgetful and susceptible to making calculation errors. Scientists from around the world book months in advance for a squint through one of these phenomenal telescopes, and institutions from several countries maintain permanent outposts there.

The second telescope on your left is the

United Kingdom's **James Clerk Maxwell Telescope** (JCMT), a radio telescope with a primary reflecting surface more than 15 meters in diameter. This unit became operational in 1987. It was dedicated by Britain's Prince Philip, who rode all the way to the summit in a Rolls Royce. The 3.6-meter **Canada-France-Hawaii Telescope** (CFHT), finished in 1979 for $33 million, was the first to spot Halley's Comet in 1983.

A newer eye to the heavens atop Mauna Kea is the double **W. M. Keck Observatory.** Keck I became operational in 1992 and Keck II followed in 1996. The Keck Foundation, a Los Angeles-based philanthropic organization, funded the telescopes to the tune of over $140 million; they are among the world's most high-tech, powerful, and expensive. Operated by the California Association for Research in Astronomy (CARA), a joint project of the University of California and Cal Tech, the telescopes have an aperture of 400 inches and employ new and unique types of technology. The primary reflectors are fashioned from a mosaic of 36 hexagonal mirrors, each only three inches thick and six feet in diameter. These "small" mirrors have been carefully joined together to form one incredibly huge, actively controlled light reflector surface. Each of the mirror segments is capable of being individually positioned to an accuracy of a millionth of an inch; each is computer-controlled to bring the heavenly objects into perfect focus. These titanic eyeballs have already spotted both the most distant known galaxy and the most distant known object in the universe, 12 billion and 13 billion light years from earth, respectively. The light received from these objects today was emitted not long after the Big Bang that created the universe theoretically occurred. In a real sense, scientists are looking back toward the beginning of time!

In addition to these are the following: The **NASA Infrared Telescope Facility** (IRTF), online since 1979, does only infrared viewing with its three-meter mirror. Also with only infrared capabilities, the **United Kingdom Infrared Telescope** (UKIRT), in operation since 1979 as well, searches the sky with its 3.8-meter lens. Directly below it is the **University of Hawai'i 0.6-meter Telescope.** Built in 1968, it was the first on the mountaintop and has the smallest reflective mirror. Completed in 1970, the **University of Hawai'i 2.2-meter Telescope** was a huge improvement over its predecessor but is now the second-smallest telescope at the top. The **Caltech Submillimeter Observatory** (CSO) has been looking into the sky since 1987 with its 10.4-meter radio telescope. **Subaru** (Japan National Large Telescope) is a monolithic 8.3-meter mirror capable of both optical and infrared viewing. It is the most recently completed telescope on the mountain, fully operational since 2000. The **Gemini Northern 8.1-meter Telescope,** also with both optical and infrared viewing, is run by a consortium from the United States, United Kingdom, Canada, Chile, Argentina, and Brazil. Its southern twin is located on a mountaintop in Chile, and together they have been viewing the heavens since 1999. Situated to the side and below the rest is the **Submillimeter Array,** a series of eight 6-meter-wide antennae. About two miles distant from the top is the **Very Long Baseline Array,** a 25-meter-wide, centimeter wavelength radio dish that is one in a series of similar antennae that dot the 5,000-mile stretch between Hawaii and the Virgin Islands.

Currently, while the state is considering expansion of the complex to include additional telescopes and support facilities, a number of groups, including The Hawaiian-Environmental Alliance, are calling on the state to proceed in a culturally and environmentally friendly manner or to not proceed at all. This is a highly contested issue on the island.

VISITING THE TELESCOPES

At present, only the **Subaru Telescope** (www.naoj.org) allows visitors on organized tours, and you *must* reserve at least one week

The Thirty Meter Telescope

It's likely that sometime during your visit to the Big Island you'll see a sign or T-shirt reading "We are Mauna Kea" or you'll overhear a tour guide discussing this contentious issue. The Thirty Meter Telescope (TMT), a $1.4 billion project consisting of 492 segmented mirrors, would be the most powerful telescope on the planet constructed on one of the best stargazing places in the world—the summit of Mauna Kea. In 2009, immediately after it was announced that Mauna Kea would be the site of this telescope, opposition to its construction began. The conflict over the TMT isn't linear or easily explained as science versus religion versus environmental justice versus the educational-industrial-complex. But generally speaking, the argument on the "pro" construction side is that the building of this telescope, which allows for observations from near-ultraviolet to mid-infrared, is important for the advancement of science. Additionally, proponents argue that this project will create hundreds of construction jobs for locals and ultimately permanent jobs on the island. As controversy over the TMT has mounted, the TMT board established a (very) large scholarship and grant-making fund for Native Hawaiian students interested in the sciences and technology.

Nevertheless, opposition to the TMT has been fierce. Arguments against the project include: Mauna Kea is a sacred site to Native Hawaiians and construction of an additional telescope (yes, you'll note there already are some there and there were protests against those too) is considered sacrilegious; some are concerned that construction will cause ecological damage to the mountain (where will all the waste from construction and additional people on the mountain go?) as well as to the Mauna Kea aquifer; others point to the fact that the TMT is not paying a fair market value to the lease the land on the mountain (the University of Hawaii manages the telescopes on the mountain and they determine the amount); lastly, some think the TMT will plainly be an eyesore on the mountain.

Again, the "sides" of this debate aren't delineated between Native Hawaiians versus "the scientist"—this is a complicated story and one that evokes many emotions for islanders.

ahead of time through their website. These free, 40-minute tours are given at 10:30am, 11:30am, and 1:30pm only on Tuesdays, Wednesdays, and Thursdays and only 15 days out of the month. Tours are run in English and Japanese, with the first and last tours of the day usually in English. The tour schedule is posted two months in advance on the telescope's website. Transportation to the telescope is the visitor's responsibility. This tour is a brief introduction to the telescope itself and the work being performed. There is no opportunity to actually view anything through the telescope. All safety precautions pertaining to visiting the summit also apply to visiting this telescope for the tour.

While the Keck telescopes do not offer tours, the visitors gallery at the telescope base is open weekdays 10am-4:30pm for a 12-minute video, information about the work being done, and a "partial view of the Keck I

telescope and dome." Two public restrooms are also available to visitors. The same information and video are available in the lobby at the Keck headquarters in Waimea.

ALONG THE SADDLE ROAD
Pohakuloa

The broad, relatively flat saddle between Mauna Kea and Mauna Loa is an area known as **Pohakuloa** (Long Stone). At an elevation of roughly 6,500 feet, this plain alternates between lava flow, grassland, and semiarid desert pockmarked with cinder cones. About seven miles west of the Mauna Kea Access Road, at a sharp bend in the road, you'll find a cluster of cabins that belong to the Mauna Kea State Recreation Area. This is a decent place to stop for a picnic and potty break. No camping is allowed, but housekeeping cabins that sleep up to six can be rented (permits are required and can be obtained through the state of Hawaii's permits website: https:// camping.ehawaii.gov/camping). Nearby is a game management area, so expect hunting and shooting of wild pigs, sheep, and birds in season. A few minutes west is the Pohakuloa Training Area, where maneuvers and bomb practice can sometimes disturb the peace in this high mountain area. If the military is on maneuvers while you're passing through, be attentive to vehicles on or crossing the road.

Beaches

It seems as if this region should be a prime beach spot, but it isn't. Although the Hamakua district has some of the most spectacular ocean views to be had on the Big Island, there is little access to the water from the soaring cliffs. Waimea is completely landlocked, although it feels like the beach is so close because you can see it from town.

HONOKA'A AND WAIPI'O VALLEY
Waipi'o Beach

Stretching over a mile, **Waipi'o Beach** (access via Waipi'o Valley Rd.) is the longest black-sand beach on the island. A tall and somewhat tangled stand of trees and bushes fronts this beach, capping the dune. If you hiked the one-hour vertical road to get here you'll likely want to jump in immediately, but be careful: The surf here can be dangerous, and there are many riptides. If there is strong wave action, swimming is not advised. It is, however, a good place for surfing and fishing. There are two sections of the beach, and in order to get to the long expanse of beach across the mouth of the stream, you have to wade across. It's best to try closer to where the stream enters the ocean because there are fewer slippery boulders there. To compound matters, waves sometimes wash water up the mouth of the stream. If possible, go at low tide. Note there are no changing areas here. Portable bathrooms are located behind the beach near the parking area.

To get to the beach, you have to get down

Mauna Kea summit

the Waipiʻo Valley Road first. Whether you walk or drive down, when you get to the bottom turn at the first right instead of continuing straight into the valley and into private property. You'll find the next portion of your walk or drive to be muddy and filled with potholes. This road takes you directly to the beach. If you drove, park your car in the area under the trees, where there will likely be other cars. If you walked, it's often possible to hitch a ride back up with someone driving from the beach.

Hiking

This region is hike central, with many different kinds of hikes, from easy to difficult, with every type of scenery imaginable. Don't trespass on private land. Local residents don't want hikers wandering through their backyards on the way to find some hidden view. There are plenty of on-the-beaten-track and underutilized legal hikes in this area that will challenge you for days.

KALOPA NATIVE FOREST STATE PARK AND RECREATION AREA

This spacious natural area is five miles southeast of Honokaʻa, 12 miles north of Laupahoehoe, three miles inland on a well-marked secondary road, and at 2,000 feet in elevation. Little used by tourists or residents, **Kalopa Native Forest State Park and Recreation Area** (Kalopa Rd., off Hwy. 19 between mile markers 39 and 40, gate open daily 7am-8pm) is a great place to get away from the coast and up into the hills. Hiking is terrific throughout the park and adjoining forest reserve on a series of nature trails—but the trails are not marked clearly and are difficult to follow. Most of the forest here is endemic, with few alien species. Some of what you will see are ʻohiʻa, koa, the hapuʻu tree fern, and kopiko and pilo, both species of the coffee tree family. Near the entrance and camping area is an **arboretum** of Hawaiian and Polynesian plants. Beyond the arboretum is a 0.75-mile nature trail loop through an ʻohiʻa forest, and a 3-mile loop trail takes you along the gulch trail and back to camp via an old road. Next to the area where you park your car there is a board with pamphlets outlining the trails. Unfortunately, although the pamphlets are detailed, the sites marked on paper aren't all marked at the corresponding physical locations; still, if you feel like getting out of the heat, this is a worthy off-the-beaten-path place to explore. Birdlife here may not be as varied as it is higher up the mountainside, but you can catch sight of ʻelepaio, aukuʻu (a night heron), white-eyes, cardinals, and the Hawaiian hoary bat. The park offers day-use picnicking, tent camping, and large furnished cabins (state permit required) that can house up to eight people. Reserve online and print your permit through the website (http://camping.ehwaii.gov).

To get to Kalopa Native Forest State Park, turn mauka on Kalopa Road and follow the signs up to the park—it will take about 15 minutes. There is more than one way from the highway to the park, so don't worry if you end up turning mauka on a different road.

★ WAIMANU VALLEY

The hike down to Waipiʻo and over the pali to **Waimanu Valley** is considered by many one of the top three treks in Hawaii. You must be fully prepared for camping and in excellent condition to attempt this hike. Also, water from the streams and falls is not good for drinking due to irrigation and cattle grazing topside; hikers should bring purification tablets or boil or filter it to be safe. To get to Waimanu Valley, a switchback trail, locally called the Z Trail but otherwise known as the **Muliwai Trail,** leads up the 1,200-foot pali, starting about 100 yards inland from the west end of Waipi'o Beach. Although not long, this is by far the most difficult section of the trail. Waimanu was bought by the State of Hawaii some years ago, and the government is responsible for trail maintenance.

The trail ahead is decent, although it can be muddy because you go in and out of more than a dozen gulches before reaching Waimanu. In the third gulch, which is quite deep, a narrow cascading waterfall tumbles into a small pool right at trailside, just right for a quick dip or to dangle your feet. Another small pool is found in the fifth gulch. After the ninth gulch is a trail shelter. Finally, below is Waimanu Valley, half the size of Waipi'o but more verdant, and even wilder because it has been uninhabited for a longer time. Cross Waimanu Stream in the shallows where it meets the sea. The trail then continues along the beach and back into the valley for about 1.5 miles, along the base of the valley's far side, to the 300-foot-high Wai'ilikahi Falls. For drinking water (remember to treat it), walk along the west side of the *pali* until you find a likely waterfall. The Muliwai Trail to the Waimanu Valley floor is about 15 miles round-trip from the trailhead at the bottom of the *pali* in Waipi'o Valley, or 18 miles round-trip from Waipi'o Lookout.

Regardless of how long it takes you to complete this hike, it's quite the badge of honor. Some have been known to finish it in 24 hours and others take a few leisurely days at normal hiking speed. To stay overnight in Waimanu Valley, you must have a camping permit obtained through the Division of Forestry and Wildlife (http://camping.ehawaii.gov); permits are for up to six people ($12 Hawaii residents, $18 nonresidents). Sites that are not listed on the website are temporarily unavailable for camping or hiking. Before you go, check the news release section of the Division of Forestry and Wildlife website (http://hawaii.gov/dlnr) to make sure that the trail is not closed due to hazardous conditions such as rain and/or mud.

Kalopa Native Forest State Park and Recreation Area

MAUNA KEA

Hiking on **Mauna Kea** means high-altitude hiking. Although the height of the mountain (13,796 feet) is not necessarily a problem, the elevation gain in a short hour or two of getting to the top is. It takes time for the body to acclimatize, and when you drive up from the ocean you rob yourself of the chance to acclimatize easily. What you may expect to experience normally are slight dizziness, a shortness of breath due to reduced oxygen levels, and reduced ability to think clearly and react quickly. Some people are more prone to elevation problems, so if you experience more severe symptoms, get to a lower elevation immediately. These symptoms include prolonged or severe headache, loss of appetite, cramped muscles, prolonged malaise or weakness, dizziness, reduced muscle control and balance, and heart palpitations. Use your head, know your limits, and don't push yourself. Carry plenty of water (more than you would at a lower elevation) and food. Wear a brimmed hat, sunglasses, sunscreen, and lip balm, a

---

long-sleeved shirt and long pants, and sturdy hiking boots or shoes. Carry a jacket, sweater, and gloves, as it can be cold and windy at and near the top. Don't alter the natural environment and stay on established trails.

There are a few good trails on the mountain. About six miles above the Onizuka Center for International Astronomy Visitors Information Center, a dirt track heads off the access road to the west and downhill to a parking lot. From the parking area, it's about one mile farther west, over the saddle between two small cones, to Lake Waiau and its placid waters. This should take less than 30 minutes. On the way, you cross the Mauna Kea Humu'ula Trail, which starts at the third parking lot near the T intersection above and heads down the mountain to the visitors center. Taking the Humu'ula Trail to Lake Waiau should also take about 30 minutes. Continuing on down the Humu'ula Trail a couple of miles brings you past an ancient adze quarry site. Perhaps the most convenient hike is that to the true summit of the mountain. Start from the roadway across from the University of Hawai'i's 2.2-meter telescope, cross over the guardrail, and follow the rough path down into the saddle and steeply up the hill, a distance of less than half a mile.

THE SADDLE ROAD

Besides having the access road to Mauna Kea, the Saddle Road is a great place to explore by foot—especially on your way to Mauna Kea or on your way to/from the Hilo side and the Kona side.

Pu'u O'o Trail

Just after mile marker 24 on the way up from Hilo is the trailhead for the **Pu'u O'o Trail.** From the small parking lot along the road, this trail heads to the south about four miles where it meets Powerline Road, a rough four-wheel-drive track, and returns to the Saddle Road. This area is good for bird-watching, and you might have a chance to see the rare 'akiapola'au or 'apapane, and even wild turkeys. This area is frequently shrouded in clouds or fog, and it could rain on you. You may want to walk only partway in and return on the same trail, rather than making the circle.

Kipuka Pu'u Huluhulu

Bird-watchers or nature enthusiasts should turn into the **Kipuka Pu'u Huluhulu** parking lot, across the road from the Mauna Kea Access Road turnoff. A *kipuka* is an area that has been surrounded by a lava flow, but never inundated, that preserves an older and established ecosystem. The most recent lava around Pu'u Huluhulu is from 1935. At the parking lot you'll find a hunters' check-in station. From there, a hiking trail leads into this fenced, 38-acre nature preserve. One loop trail runs through the trees around the summit of the hill, and there is a trail that runs down the east side of the hill to a smaller loop and the two exits on Mauna Loa Observatory Road, on its eastern edge. Pu'u Huluhulu means Shaggy Hill, and this diminutive hill is covered in a wide variety of trees and bushes, which include *mamane, naio, 'iliahi* (sandalwood), koa, and *'ohi'a.* Some of the birds most often seen are the greenish-yellow *'amakihi,* the red *'i'iwi* and *'apapane,* and the dull brown and smoky-gray *'oma'o.* In addition, you may be lucky enough to spot a rare *'io,* Hawaiian hawk, or the more numerous *pueo,* a short-eared owl. The entire loop will take you 45 minutes or less, so even if you are not particularly drawn to the birds or the trees, this is a good place to get out of the car, stretch your legs, and get acclimatized to the elevation before you head up to Mauna Kea.

MAUNA LOA

The Saddle Road is the other choice, besides near Hawai'i Volcanoes National Park, for accessing **Mauna Loa** and its trails. The **Mauna Loa Observatory Road** turns south off the Saddle Road and zigs and zags up to the **Mauna Loa NOAA Atmospheric Observatory** at 11,140 feet, which you can see high on the hillside above as you progress along this road. According to the signboard below this small complex, measurements are gathered here for carbon dioxide, carbon monoxide, methane, CFCs, ozone, solar radiation, atmospheric dust, stratospheric aerosols, and temperatures, among other items. Even a two-wheel-drive vehicle could handle this road without problems, but driving it would abrogate your rental car contract. Use a four-wheel-drive rental vehicle that is approved for this road. Although it could be done faster, give yourself an hour to take in the surroundings, check out the distant sights, and reach the end of the road. Use your vehicle lights, particularly if there are low clouds, and straddle the reflective white line that runs down the center of this single-lane road all the way up to the observatory, pulling over only to let vehicles from the other direction get by. The atmospheric observatory is not open to the public, but you can park in a small parking lot below it at the end of the pavement.

About two miles in from the turnoff is a rock formation at the side of the road that, at a certain angle, looks remarkably like Charles deGaulle, former president of France—and you don't have to use your imagination much at all. As you continue, you get a fine, distant look at the observatories on top of Mauna Kea across the saddle, Pu'u Huluhulu below at the turnoff, and the military reservation beyond to the west. About four miles in, at a turn in the road, there is a gravel road that heads over the horizon to the west, an abandoned attempt at a highway shortcut to Kailua-Kona. About eight miles up, at a point where there are a number of telephone and television transmitter towers, the road makes a big zag and heads almost in a straight-line shot, following power poles to the observatory. Notice the different colors of lava that the road crosses and the amount of vegetation on each type. The older brown lava has some grasses and small bushes growing from it, while the newer black lava is almost totally barren. There are large areas of red lava as well, and some of that has been used as road base and paving material. You will see several collapsed lava tubes near the road as you make your way up. Still farther on, areas of ropy *pahoehoe* lava stick up through newer *'a'a* lava. Around mile 15, new pavement has been laid so your ride gets smoother even as the road goes through a series of roller-coaster waves as you approach the end of the road. Beyond the end of the pavement, an extremely rough Jeep track continues—best used as a hiking trail. This track zigzags up the mountainside, eventually ending near the crater rim after about seven miles. The **Mauna Loa Observatory Trail** leaves the gravel Jeep track several hundred yards beyond the end of the pavement and heads almost straight up the mountainside, crossing the Jeep trail several times. The Observatory Trail climbs 1,975 feet over 3.8 miles up the volcano's north slope until it reaches the rim of the Moku'aweoweo Caldera summit. From this point, the Mauna Loa summit cabin is 2.1 miles. It takes about 4-6 hours altogether to hike from the observatory trailhead to the Mauna Loa summit cabin. The hike back from the Mauna Loa summit cabin to the Mauna Loa Observatory trailhead is only about three hours because you're going downhill.

A helpful resource for this hike can be found at www.kinquest.com/misc/travel/trailguide.php. This site provides a guide with a mile-by-mile description of what you'll see while you hike.

The Mauna Loa summit cabin is available to stay in for free but requires a permit from the Kilauea Visitor Center in Hawai'i Volcanoes National Park; you can only get them the day before your hike. The Mauna Loa summit cabin has 12 bunks. Visitors are allowed a three-night maximum stay. Pit toilets are available at the cabin as well as drinking water. Don't forget to treat the water. There's no water available on the trail.

Mauna Loa is at a very high altitude, so wait at least 24 hours between scuba diving and ascending Mauna Loa in order to avoid getting the bends.

Other Recreation

HORSEBACK RIDING

All the available outfitters more or less have the same restrictions for riders: usually no children under 7 (the exact age might vary), and riders above 250 pounds must notify the tour operator prior to the ride of their exact weight. It is also important to be honest with the tour operator about your ability level, because some operators do not allow beginners on certain tours and others do not want advanced riders.

Views of the Kona and Kohala Coasts are abundant on **Paniolo Adventures** (Kohala Mountain Rd./Rte. 250 at mile 13.2, 808/889-5354, www.panioloadventures.com, tours range $69-175 depending on length). The company has a good reputation for being professional, knowing what they are doing, and enjoying their work. With six different rides ranging from picnic adventures to sunset trots, you'll likely find a ride that suits your skill level and your schedule. A favorite tour is the 1.5-hour sunset ride ($89), suitable for all experience levels.

Dehana Ranch (47-4841 Old Mamalahoa Hwy./Hwy. 19, 808/885-0057, www.dahanaranch.com, daily, $70-150) offers a menu of choices (from 1.5-hour to 2.5-hour rides) and is excellent at meeting the needs of riders. Most rides are through the ranch with lovely faraway views of Waipi'o and Mauna Kea. Whether you're looking to be the best caregiver to your child (like taking your kids or grandkids to Hawaii wasn't already enough?) or drop off your unruly children, Kids Camp at the ranch is a great place to visit. From July 1 to August 30 you can keep your kids busy from 9:30am to 3:30pm at the cost of $160 (includes lunch and riding lessons). Reservations need to be made one day in advance.

ZIPLINING

Zipline rides, also known as canopy tours, are booming on the Big Island, with each company competing with the next for the best course. Not all the courses are "certified" or have insurance, and accidents, although rare, have occurred with those who are not. Inquire about the company's credentials before you go. Companies in the area that have had a number of accidents are not included in these listings.

Zip Isle (Hwy. 19 at mile marker 16, *mauka* side, Hakalau, 808/963-5427, www.zipisle.com, daily 9am-5:30pm, $167 adults, $97 children *kama'aina* discounts available) is located in the World Botanical Gardens, the state's largest botanical garden. If you have gone ziplining in Costa Rica, this course isn't for you. The thrills are minimal, but the staff is friendly and knowledgeable, making this an ideal course for first-timers and children (minimum weight requirement of 70 pounds, although they are lenient on this). Also, the course was constructed in partnership with certified engineers in order to guarantee the utmost safety for zipliners. There are three tours daily and it's a good idea to reserve a week in advance.

GOLF

Golfing on the Big Island can be an adventure in itself due to the hilly and rocky terrain. For instance, carts aren't even allowed on the 15-acre course at the **Hamakua Country Club** (Hwy. 19 between mile markers 42 and 43, 808/775-7244, http://hamakuagolf.com, $15 for unlimited play, 17 and under free with paying adult) because of how steep it is. Open from sunrise to sunset, the course is small and you play the nine holes as much as you wish. Designed in the 1920s by Frank Anderson, the course works on the honor system, with a box for dropping off payment next to the course. Remember not to tell anyone on the Kona side that you just paid $15 to play golf—though they won't believe you even if you did tell.

Shopping

HONOKA'A AND WAIPI'O VALLEY

Honoka'a isn't a shopping destination, but the town is so cute that you'll probably want to get out and walk around to make the most of it. It looks like there are quite a few shops on the main street, Mamane Street; however, many of them seem to never be open. What shops tend to be left standing are congregated on the eastern and *makai* side of Mamane Street. There are a few antiques and collectible stores that include Hawaiiana items like old aloha shorts, airline posters from the 1960s, and glass bottles from the old plantation bottle works. Also, a few souvenir shops have Hawaiian prints, quilts, and local cookbooks.

WAIMEA

There are three main shopping areas in Waimea, each a little bit different from the next. The Parker Ranch Center and Waimea Center are strip malls, although the Parker Ranch Center is the more upscale of the two. Parker Square also houses shops in an open-air setting, but in a more historical-looking building with several galleries worth browsing through.

Parker Ranch Center

The long-established **Parker Ranch Center** (67-1185 Mamalahoa Hwy./Hwy. 19, www.parkerranchcenterads.com) was totally rebuilt in 2002, completely changing the face of the center of town. With more of a country look, the mall now has more store space than it originally held and many new upscale vendors. Anchoring the center is the Foodland grocery store with a Starbucks next door. There is a food court in the center of the complex and many fast-food joints. The **Parker Ranch Store** (808/885-5669), in its prominent spot up front, focuses on its country cowboy heritage; the shop sells boots, cowboy hats, shirts, skirts, and buckles and bows, and many handcrafted items are made on the premises. Filling in some of the shops surrounding the Parker Ranch Store are mid-range clothing stores selling items like jeans and surf wear. If you need to get a few extra layers of clothing before heading up to Mauna Kea, this shopping area is a good place to stop to grab a sweatshirt and/or socks with cowboys on them.

Waimea Center

Across the street from the Parker Ranch Center and behind McDonald's is the **Waimea Center.** Most Waimea Center stores are open 9am-5pm weekdays and 10am-5pm Saturday. Among its shops you will find a **KTA Super Store,** with everything from groceries to pharmaceuticals. There are also a number of eateries as well as a few lower-end gift shops.

Parker Square

Located along Highway 19 west of the town center, **Parker Square** has a collection of fine boutiques and shops, as well as the Waimea Coffee Company shop. Here, like an old trunk filled with family heirlooms, the **Gallery of Great Things** (808/885-7706, www.galleryofgreatthingshawaii.com) really is loaded with great things. Inside you'll find novelty items like a carousel horse, silk dresses, straw hats, koa paddles, Japanese woodblock prints, and less-expensive items like shell earrings and koa hair sticks. The Gallery of Great Things represents about 200 local artists on a revolving basis, and the owner, Maria Brick, travels throughout the Pacific and Asia collecting art, some contemporary, some primitive. With its museum-quality items, the Gallery of Great Things is definitely worth a careful browse.

Also in the complex is the **Waimea General Store** (808/885-4479, Mon.-Sat. 9am-5:30pm, Sun. 10am-4pm), which sells mostly high-end sundries with plenty of stationery, kitchen items, children's games, stuffed toys, books on Hawaiiana, and gadgets—overall, lots of neat and nifty gifts.

Entertainment

This region, luckily, attracts musicians, dancers, and performers (and some fairly big names) to its venues big and small. In Honoka'a, the **Honoka'a People's Theater** (43 Mamane St., 808/775-0000, http://honokaapeople.com) doubles as an art movie theater (tickets $6 adults, $4 seniors, $3 children) and a live music venue. Constructed in the 1930s by the Tanimoto family who built several historic theaters on the Big Island, it was and remains the largest theater on the island, with seating capacity of 525 people. In its heyday, it must have been a sight, as plantation workers would pack the building to watch the newest Hollywood films. With the demise of the plantation industry, the theater went into disrepair and closed for a few years. When the theater reopened in the late 1990s, it once again became a centerpiece of the community. Check the schedule online for event listings. A few times a month there are live performances with local musicians as well as semipopular Mainland groups traveling through the area.

The only bar in Honoka'a, **The Landing Restaurant** (45-3490 Mamane St., www.thelandinghawaii.com, 808/775-1444, Sun.-Thurs. 11am-10pm, Fri.-Sat. 11am-midnight) offers live music on some Saturday nights. They also have karaoke on Thursday nights and open mic events on Wednesday nights.

In Waimea, theatergoers will be impressed by the newish (from 1981) structure built by Richard Smart, heir to the Parker Ranch, that now houses his private collection of Broadway memorabilia. The **Kahilu Theatre** (67-1186 Lindsey Rd., Parker Ranch Shopping Center, www.kahilutheatre.org, 808/885-6868) attracts first-rate local and Mainland performers, like the Martha Graham Dance Company, internationally known jazz musicians, and master ukulele players. Best of all, tickets are reasonably priced and at times even free for the community events. In addition to the usual season schedule, the theater also hosts community performances, such as the Hawaii youth symphony and sometimes the **Waimea Community Theater** (65-1224 Lindsey Rd., Parker School Theater, 808/885-5818, www.waimeacommunitytheatre.org), which has been performing plays and musicals on the Big Island since 1964.

For less-formal entertainment, your best bet in Waimea is the **Big Island Brewhaus** (Hwy. 19 between mile markers 56 and 57 at intersection of Kamamiu St., 808/887-1717, http://bigislandbrewhaus.com) at their Tuesday and Thursday open mic nights or Friday night for live music—usually a local rock band. The crowd is usually on the younger side and the venue is small, so expect to feel a little claustrophobic.

Food

HAMAKUA COAST

With the closure of the much-loved Back to the 50s Diner, there really isn't anywhere to stop in the area until you reach Honoka'a. But maybe this food desert is a good thing? It leaves room for copious eating later in your day. Perhaps it's a good idea to bring snacks though, just in case.

HONOKA'A AND WAIPI'O VALLEY

Don't have your heart set on eating somewhere specific in Honoka'a. Although hours are posted for restaurants, they frequently change. Waimea is only about 15 minutes away and offers many top-notch dining options, so it might be worth the extra few minutes in the car rather than eating in Honoka'a.

It's hard not to stop daily at ★ **Tex Drive In** (Hwy. 19 at the corner of Pakalana St., 808/775-0598, daily 6am-8pm, dinners $9), a Big Island institution—and rightfully so. This long-established Hamakua restaurant is known for its fresh *malasadas:* sugared Portuguese pastries filled with passion fruit cream, chocolate, or strawberry. Best of all, you can watch the production process showcased behind plate glass windows inside. Get there before 7pm before they sell out. Tex has a fast-food look, a drive-up window, a walk-up counter, and inside and outside tables, as well as a cavernous dining room in the back. Besides the *malasadas,* they serve *ono kine* local food, specializing in *kalua* pork, teriyaki chicken and beef, hamburgers, and fresh fish.

In Honoka'a town, you'll find **Cafe Il Mondo** (Mamane St. at the corner of Lehua St., 808/775-7711, www.cafeilmondo.com, Mon.-Sat. 11am-8pm, $12 small pizzas and calzones, cash only), an Italian pizzeria and coffee bar that's the best Honoka'a has to offer. But that doesn't say much. This is a cheery place with Italian music on the sound system and Hawaiian prints on the walls. Here you feel the spirit of Italy. While handmade pizzas with toppings, mostly $12-15, are the main focus, you can also get tasty calzones, pasta dishes, sandwiches, and salads for under $12, as well as ice cream and gourmet coffee. When having dinner, it's okay to bring your own bottle of wine. Cash only.

A newer addition to the main drag, **Grandma's Kitchen** (45-3625 Mamane St., 808/775-9443, Tues.-Sat. 8am-3pm, Sun. 7:30am-3pm, Fri.-Sat. 5pm-8pm) is the kind of restaurant that just looks like a vacation getaway inside. The vintage green tables, the smell of sweet Portuguese bread cooking next door, and the friendly staff draw you in—the best part is the experience only gets better from here. The large portions of comfort food are the perfect fuel for your Waipi'o hike or a treat to celebrate your long journey back up from the beach.

If you're looking for something a bit lighter than comfort food (not everyone's ideal breakfast includes pork chops), head to **Hina**

malasadas at Tex Drive In

Rae's Café (45-3610 Mamane St., 808/756-0895, Mon.-Fri. 8am-4pm, Sat. 8am-12:30pm), where acai bowls are the breakfast fare and lunch specials like spicy poke draw locals in. There is not much seating in this small coffee shop, but this cafe if worth a stop if you're looking for a place to get a huge almond milk coconut chai to caffeinate and rehydrate.

Pop in for a quick to-go treat at the **Hamakua Fudge Shop** (45-3611 Mamane St. #105, 808/775-1430, Mon.-Sat. 10:30am-4pm) to bring with you on your Waipi'o adventure, or stay in for some ice cream in their small attached café. There are over 25 flavors, all made in-house. "Made with real butter and cream" is their motto, and it sure tastes like it.

Another brand-new eatery on Mamane Street, **Sea Dandelion Vegetarian Cafe & Awa Bar** (45-3590 Mamane St., 802/765-0292, Mon. 11am-7pm, Tues. 11am-2pm, Thurs. 11am-6:30pm, Fri. 2:30pm-9pm, Sat. 11:30am-7pm, Sun. 11:30am-4pm) is the kind of place to go if you're a raw foodist and/or really want to try awa (also known as kava), sea asparagus (really delicious, actually), and vegan poke all in one place. Have some time on your hands (as the food doesn't come quickly, but hey, isn't that the point of conscious eating?) and cash in your wallet (as they don't take credit cards). On Friday's buy two cups of *awa* and get the third one free. It's a good deal, but be aware that it might be too much *awa* for a first timer's stomach.

A much-needed addition closer to Waipi'o Valley, ★ **Waipi'o Cookhouse** (48-5370 Waipi'o Rd., 808/775-1443, daily 7:30am-7:00pm) is a barbecue joint that "broke da mouth," as we say. It's not fancy: You order at the counter and then take a seat outside in an area overlooking the ocean. All the meat is locally sourced from a nearby farm—even the lamb. The real specialties are the lamb burger ($13.50) and the kalua pork sandwich, which is slow cooked in an imu and served with papaya barbecue sauce ($14). On the first and third Saturday of the month from 3pm to 6pm there is live music as well as pork ribs

and brisket served. The staff is friendly, the views are superb, and the even if this wasn't the only restaurant for miles around it would still be worth a visit.

★ WAIMEA

It's almost guaranteed that eating in Waimea will lead you to exclaim, "That was the best steak of my life!" The beef doesn't get more local than this, much of it from grass-fed cattle. Waimea also is home to several longstanding upscale restaurants. Entries are listed from north to south and then east to west on Highway 19.

You'd think there would be more barbecue in Waimea given its country feel, but **The Fish and The Hog** (64-957 Mamalaho Hwy./Hwy. 19 across from mile marker 56, 808/885-6286, daily 11am-8pm, $12-24) is the only game in town. The restaurant is a "rebranded" Huli Sue's BBQ; it is charming with its rustic furniture resembling something from a down-home barbecue joint of North Carolina. The sampler plate is more than enough for two people and comes with brisket, ribs, pork, and homemade sausage. There are also sandwiches, quesadillas, and fish tacos on the menu, but I'd stick to the barbecue options. You can guarantee that the beef came from down the road, and the various sauces have good flavor.

Nearly across the street is the restaurant formerly known as Tako Taco, now called **Big Island Brewhaus** (Hwy. 19 between mile markers 56 and 57 at intersection of Kamamiu St., 808/887-1717, http://bigislandbrewhaus.com, Mon.-Sat. 11am-9:30pm, Sun. noon-8:00pm, $5-15). The restaurant is decorated from the point of view of someone who wanted it to look straight out of Mexico—it's sort of Mexican kitsch meets Hawaii. The food isn't so *authentico* Mexican, but it's priced right and overall hits the spot. There are the standard dishes like burritos, enchiladas, and tacos as well as non-Mexican food items like burgers and fries. What isn't so splendid here is the service, which at times can be downright frustrating. Arguably, now that they have their homebrews on tap, it makes the wait more bearable—but oftentimes it doesn't make any sense why you have to wait 45 minutes for a taco. Don't come hungry or in a rush. Tuesdays and Thursdays are open mic night and Friday there is live music. Happy hour (daily 3pm-6pm) includes $1 off wine, tequila, margaritas, and pints of beer.

There is some stiff competition in the area, yet **Lilikoi Café** (67-1185 Mamalahoa Hwy./ Hwy. 19, in the back of the Parker Ranch Shopping Center, 808/887-1400, Mon.-Sat. 7:30am-4pm, breakfast $7, lunch $13) still fares well. Both the atmosphere and the menu are simple: sandwiches, fresh salads that come as a combo with a choice of deli meat, and crepes for vegetarians. The breakfast choices of granola, burritos, and crepes are ideal for those looking to eat a wholesome and nourishing meal that doesn't include Spam, as many breakfast options do on the island.

Also in the Parker Ranch Shopping Center is the home of one of the best burgers you will ever have (and so agrees *USA Today*, in its list of 50 burgers you must have before you die). **Village Burger** (67-1185 Mamalahoa Hwy./19, Parker Ranch Center Food Court, 808/885-7319, www.villageburgerwaimea. com, Mon.-Sat. 10:30am-8pm, Sun. 10:30am-6pm, $8-12) is a true farm-to-table establishment with nearly every ingredient sourced from a nearby farm. The veal burger is spectacular and can be served on a beautiful bed of lettuce for those who don't want the bun. The taro burger is a well-thought-out conglomeration of garden vegetables. Try the *mamake* ice tea, a blend of a local leaf, mint, and tarragon. The restaurant is located in the food court with no ambience and little seating, so grab it go—although you'll probably finish your burger by the time you reach your car.

On weekends, be prepared to wait as visitors line up around the corner patiently anticipating the scrumptious breakfast at ★ **Hawaiian Style Café** (65-1290 Kawaihae Rd./Hwy. 19 between mile markers 57 and 58, 808/885-4295, Mon.-Sat. 7am-1:30pm, Sun. 7am-noon, breakfast $10, plate lunch $9-17). It's not healthy food, it's comfort food served by a friendly staff. Be prepared to make new friends because the communal counter area invokes conversation with fellow eaters. Try the *kalua* hash with eggs. It's the kind of food that's so good that you just keep eating it, even though you're full. There are other local favorites are on the menu, like several varieties of *loco moco*.

Waimea Coffee Company (65-1279 Kawaihae Rd./Hwy. 19, 808/885-8915, www. waimeacoffeecompany.com, Mon.-Sat. 6:30am-5:30pm, Sun. 8am-2pm, lunch $8) has a college-town coffee shop atmosphere. It's the kind of place where you can grab a coffee, bagels and lox, or soup or sandwich, and enjoy a book outside in the brisk Waimea air.

As one of the original homes of Hawaii Regional Cuisine, **Merriman's** (65-1227 Opelo Rd., 808/885-6822, http://merrimanshawaii.com, Mon.-Fri. 11:30am-1:30pm, daily 5:30pm-9pm, and Sun. brunch 10am-1pm, reservations recommended, lunch $15, dinner $30-43) has a lot of street cred—and that's without adding the fact that its owner, Peter Merriman, is a James Beard Award finalist. In theory, it's fairly amazing that Merriman's started doing local food decades before it was trendy, but in practice the restaurant is perhaps a bit overrated now that everyone is going local. The dining experience is superb, with well-trained waitstaff and white linen tablecloths. It's a good place to go if you are looking for fine dining. The menu changes, but offers the usual Hawaiian dishes of mahimahi or ahi, spicy soups, and local vegetables. Lunch is a good choice; the lunch menu is similar to the dinner menu, but less expensive.

Getting There and Around

BUS

All roads lead through Waimea—or at least many of them do because it's a bus hub for the **Hele-On Bus** (www.heleonbus.org, 808/961-8744, $2 per ride, $1 each for luggage, large backpacks, bikes) traveling between the east and west sides of the island.

The Hilo-to-Honoka'a route has eight daily trips, with five additional buses during weekdays, and makes all intermediate stops, taking about an hour. In Hilo you can get the bus at the Mooheau Bus Terminal on Bayfront (and twice daily it makes additional stops throughout Hilo). In Honoka'a, buses begin pickup at Blane's Drive-in on Mamane Street, the main street in town.

With seven daily trips and three additional weekday buses, it couldn't be any easier to travel the two hours (sometimes less) between Waimea and Hilo. Buses pick up/drop off passengers at the back of the Parker Ranch Center and make all intermediate stops on the Hamakua Coast ending at the Mooheau Bus Terminal on Bayfront (and twice daily it makes additional stops throughout Hilo).

The buses traveling from Kona to Hilo make two daily morning stops and one afternoon stop at the back parking lot of the Parker Ranch Center. Those traveling on to Hilo take the Hamakua Coast route, making all intermediate stops and arriving about two hours later to Hilo. Buses traveling to Kona take the lower road, passing by all the Kohala resorts and traveling as far as Captain Cook and Honaunau in the afternoon. The entire route takes about two hours.

The **Waimea Shuttle** makes hourly trips 6:30am-4:30pm around Waimea from the west side to east side of Highway 19. When the bus was free, locals utilized this service for quick shopping trips, but it likely won't be too crowded now that you must pay $2 just to go a few minutes. For more information, check www.heleonbus.org.

Where to Stay

There are many different options for staying on the Big Island. The following are some helpful suggestions for how to pick the best accommodations for you!

Decide if you want to stay at a hotel, bed-and-breakfast, or rental property. At some hotels, such as at The Fairmont Orchid and the Four Seasons Resort, you can pay to get first-class attention, but generally hotels are more impersonal and not as attentive to your needs as a bed-and-breakfast. Bed-and-breakfasts are not as private, even if the room has a private entrance. There is lots of interaction with other guests and the hosts. So if you want to be anonymous, opt for a hotel or rental property. Remember to check which "extras" are included at your hotel. Many hotels charge for Wi-Fi (most B&Bs and rental properties do not), and the breakfast included at your bed-and-breakfast has a lot of value. You save about $30-40 by including breakfast for two with your room. Breakfast at the hotels does not come cheap!

There might be a good compromise place. New "boutique hotels" are springing up. They consider themselves bed-and-breakfasts (since they include breakfast), but in most cases are managed by staff and include amenities (like handmade soaps) that have the feel of a hotel. Hawaii Island Retreat at Ahu Pohaku Ho'omaluhia (North Kohala), Hawaiian Oasis Bed and Breakfast (Kona), Kalaekilohana Bed and Breakfast (Ka'u), and Holualoa Inn (near Kona) are some examples.

If you're interested in staying at a bed-and-breakfast, call! Although it seems counterintuitive in the world of technology, having a brief conversation with the bed-and-breakfast owner will give you an idea if the place is a good fit for you. Most owners can tell almost instantly after speaking with someone if their place is right for that person. You can also ask if there are any discounts available. Many owners trying to fill rooms may be willing to make a deal. Don't forget to ask about pets! Some B&Bs have dogs, cats, and even birds. Inquire if you're allergic or simply don't like pets.

Check for online discounts. Nearly all the hotels and even bed-and-breakfasts offer "specials" online for discounted low-season rates or for additional freebies (like tours, breakfasts, or car rentals). Don't be afraid to call an establishment and ask if it can offer you a deal, even if its time has expired. A great website for vacation rentals is **www.vrbo. com**. The island's best properties are listed, along with reviews from previous guests.

HIGH-SEASON PRICES AND FEES

The prices listed in this book are the rates for accommodations during the low and shoulder seasons. If you are booking for the high season (major holidays such as Christmas and Thanksgiving as well as school holiday times), prices can increase 30 percent above the rates posted here. High season is December-February, shoulder season is March, June-July, and November, and low season is April-May, August-October.

Advertised rates often do not include tax, including the Hawaii General Excise Tax (4.166 percent) and the Hawaii Hotel Room Tax (9.25 percent). Many of the larger hotels and resorts charge a "resort fee" ($10-25). Sometimes this fee gets you parking and other times it gets you . . . absolutely nothing. So ask about additional charges ahead of time. Don't be surprised if your hotel costs $70 more than you thought it would. Some bed-and-breakfasts include the tax in the price of the room. Websites will usually indicate if the rate is inclusive of tax or not.

CAMPING

The Big Island has the best camping in the state, with more facilities and less competition for campsites than on the other islands. Nearly three dozen parks hug the coastline and sit deep in the interior; almost half offer camping, ranging from remote walk-in sites to housekeeping cabins. All require camping permits. These permits can be obtained by walk-in application to the appropriate office or by applying online ahead of your stay. Although there is usually no problem obtaining campsites, it's best to book ahead using the online reservation system. There are different online sites for county and state parks, so note which kind of park you'll be staying at and use the appropriate site.

Most campgrounds have pavilions, fireplaces, toilets (sometimes pits), and running water, but usually no individual electrical hookups. Pavilions often have electric lights, but sometimes campers appropriate the bulbs, so it's wise to carry your own. Drinking water is available, but at times brackish water is used for flushing toilets and for showers, so read all signs regarding water. Backcountry shelters have catchment water that needs purification. Never hike without an adequate supply of your own water; it might not be available in times of drought. Cooking fires are allowed in established fire pits, but no wood is provided. Charcoal or bottled fuel is a good idea. When camping in the mountains, be prepared for cold and rainy weather.

County Parks

Permits are required for overnight tent and RV camping at county parks. County parks that allow camping are Isaac Hale in Puna, Kolekole north of Hilo, Laupahoehoe Point on the Hamakua Cast, Kapa'a and Mahukona in North Kohala, Spencer Beach in South Kohala, Kohanaiki in North Kona, Ho'okena and Miloli'i in South Kona, and Punalu'u and Whittington in Ka'u. Camping is limited to one week at any one site June-August and to two weeks at any one site for the rest of the year. The permit-issuing office is the Department of Parks and Recreation, County of Hawai'i (101 Pauahi St., Ste. 6, Hilo, HI 96720, 808/961-8311, www.hawaiicounty. gov/parks-and-recreation, 7:45am-4:30pm Mon.-Fri.). However, it's much easier to obtain permits through the online system: www. ehawaii.gov/Hawaii_County/camping/exe/ campre.cgi. There is an online chat function available on the website that is surprisingly useful (i.e., someone is actually there to answer questions). Fees are $6/$21 resident/ nonresident per adult per night (plus $1 online transaction fee); children 13-17, $3/21 per night (plus $1 online transaction fee); under 12, $1/$20 per night.

State Parks

Day use of state parks is free, with no permit required, but you will need a permit for tent camping and for cabins. Five consecutive nights is the limit for either camping or cabins at any one site. If you want a permit, at least one week's notice is required regardless of availability. State park permits are issued no more than one year in advance. The easiest way to obtain a permit is through http://camping.ehawaii.gov.

Camping is permitted at Kalopa Native Forest State Park and Recreation Area, MacKenzie State Recreation Area, and Manuka State Wayside Park for a $12 resident, $18 nonresident fee per campsite per night for up to six people. Eight-person forest cabins are located at Kalopa State Recreation Area and cost $60 for residents, $90 for nonresidents. Four-person A-frame cabins are at Hapuna Beach State Recreation Area ($30 residents, $50 nonresidents). For details about Keanakolu Cabin in the Hilo Forest Reserve and camping in Waimanu Valley, see the website.

National Parks

Permits are required for overnight backcountry camping in Hawai'i Volcanoes National Park; permits can be obtained in person from the Backcountry Office at the **Visitor Emergency Operations Center** (located on Crater Rim Dr. in the building with two rock-based columns) from 8am to 4pm daily. The earliest you may obtain a permit is the day prior to your hike. They do not accept reservations or issue permits in advance. Your stay is limited to seven days per frontcountry campground per year. At primitive campsites along the coast, there are three-sided shelters that offer a partial protection against the elements. Camping is also available at both the Namakanipaio ($15 per site for camping) and Kulanaokuaiki (free, for now) drive-in campgrounds, but there are no shower facilities.

There are A-frame cabins at Namakanipaio Campground and bookings are made through **Volcano House** (808/967-7321 or 800/325-3535, www.hawaiivolcanohouse.com). A cooking pavilion has fireplaces, but wood and drinking water are not provided. Each of the 10 small, newly renovated cabins sleeps up to four people and costs $80 per night (plus tax and fees). Linens, soap, towels, and a blanket are provided, but you would be wise to bring an extra sleeping bag, as it can get cold. Each cabin contains one double bed and two single bunk beds and an electric light, but no electrical outlets. There are no bathrooms in the cabins; shared community bathrooms/showers are located around the campground. There is a picnic table and barbecue grill for each cabin, but you'll need to bring your own charcoal and cooking utensils. Check in at Volcano House after 3pm and check out by noon.

Kona

The majority of Kona's accommodations lie along the six miles of Ali'i Drive from Kailua-Kona to Keauhou. Most hotels and condos fall in the moderate to expensive range. A few inexpensive hotels are scattered here and there along Ali'i Drive. If you're looking to branch out from Ali'i Drive, the town of Holualoa is an excellent alternative located only 20 minutes away from Kailua on the mountain above.

HOSTELS
Under $50

The least expensive place to stay in the area is **Pineapple Park** (81-6363 Mamalahoa Hwy., Kealakekua, 808/323-2224 or 877/800-3800, www.pineapple-park.com, $30-100 plus tax). This clean and commodious hostel accommodation is in a converted plantation-era house along the main highway. The dorm rooms are located in the converted walk-out

Where to Stay in Kona

Name	Type	Price	Features	Why Stay Here?	Best Fit For
Aston Kona by the Sea	condo	$180-300	sofa beds, kitchen, laundry, pool, hot tub, barbecue	location	families, couples
Casa de Emdeko	condo	$125-175	pools, barbecue, beach equipment	affordable	families, couples
Courtyard King Kamehameha's Kona Beach Hotel	hotel	$200-285	pool, luau	downtown location	families
Four Seasons Resort, Hualalai at Historic Ka'upulehu	resort	$550-1200	pools, spa, day care	truly exclusive, quality service	luxury lovers, families
Hale Kona Kai	condo	$150-250	kitchen, sofa bed, lanai, pool, barbecue, Wi-Fi	downtown location	couples, families
Hawaiian Oasis Bed and Breakfast	B&B	$230-320	pool, tennis courts, outdoor kitchen	downtown location	couples, large families
★ Holualoa Inn	B&B	$365-595	pool, kitchen, breakfast	views, service, quiet	honeymooners, luxury lovers
Holua Resort at Mauna Loa Village	condo	$150-250	kitchen, pool, hot tub, activities desk	uncrowded, easy parking, helpful staff	couples, families

basement, which also has a TV lounge and free Wi-Fi access. Private rooms are also available, with either shared bath or private bath. Discounts are available for longer stays. All guests share baths (note that the showers inconveniently close at 10pm), have use of laundry facilities and a large kitchen, and can rent kayaks and snorkel gear on-site for minimal fees. If you don't have a car, you'll need to be a real whiz on the bus to get around because the hostel isn't that close to town (although it's right off the highway). Guests are friendly with one another (inspired by the hostel—not hostile—atmosphere), but rumor has it that management can be rude.

BED-AND-BREAKFASTS AND INNS
$100-150

Navigating the nearly vertical road up to **Lilikoi Inn** (75-5339C, Mamalahoa Hwy., Holualoa, 808/333-5539, www.lilikoiinn. com, $135-195) quickly alerts you that you're not arriving to a run-of-the-mill place. The house is surrounded by lush greenery (papaya and banana trees as well as some coffee), and the views are spectacular. You can see nearly all of Kailua as well as the ocean below as you eat breakfast on the lanai. Owners Shai and Trina are friendly and talkative, so it feels like you're staying at your

Name	Type	Price	Features	Why Stay Here?	Best Fit For
★ Honu Kai	B&B	$230-285	laundry, kitchen, beach gear	concierge service, downtown location	first timers, couples
Hotel Manago	hotel	$35-83	restaurant	old Hawaii feel	budget travelers
Kona Bali Kai	condo	$115-350	pool, restaurant	frequent upgrade	budget travelers, large groups
Kona Seaside Hotel	hotel	$100-140	pool	downtown location	budget travelers
Lilikoi Inn	B&B	$135-195	huge breakfast	great views of Kailua	couples, families
★ Luana Inn	B&B	$169-209	pool, delicious breakfast	views, sweet hosts	couples
Outrigger Keauhou Beach Resort	resort	$170-450	pool, tennis courts, activities desk, fitness center	one of the few true resorts in Kona, low-season deals	families
Pineapple Park	hostel	$30-100	kayak rental, free Wi-Fi	hostel scene	budget travelers
★ Sheraton Keauhou Bay Resort and Spa	resort	$125-450	pool, tennis courts, spa, business center	watching manta rays from the bar	families

friend's house with a private entrance. The two upstairs rooms are smaller and less expensive. The downstairs rooms with queen-size sleigh beds—the Green Papaya and Plumeria Rooms—are separated by a lounge area in the middle and can be rented out as one large space to accommodate a family. Food is where the Lilikoi Inn excels: Shai is a trained chef who once owned a restaurant in the San Francisco Bay Area and creates gourmet dishes using local ingredients. A separate kitchen is available for guest use. Additional amenities include cable television, a DVD player, Wi-Fi, and a hot tub that will make you feel like you're in the rain forest. It's cooler in Holualoa than in Kailua and this B&B is a great deal.

$150-250

Owners Kona Dave and Wendi once worked with rock stars; now they want all their guests to feel like rock stars. Their love, attention, and utter dedication to ensuring that guests at ★ **Honu Kai** (74-1529 Hao Kuni St., Kailua-Kona, 808/329-8676, www.honukai. com, $230-285) have the best (and most Zen-like) experience at their home and on the Big Island makes this property attractive. Before guests even get here, Wendi emails them a questionnaire so that she can begin preparing for their arrival. Guest rooms are pleasant with Hawaiian decor, large beds, and a clean, modern bathroom. One of the rooms has wheelchair accessibility. Amenities include access to a private beach at the Mauna Lani in Kohala, free use of beach gear, laundry facilities, a cooking area, cable television, and Wi-Fi. A two-night minimum is required and no children are allowed. Wendi and Kona Dave are in the know (e.g., they can call ahead get a restaurant reservation even when one might not be available). The location is in a residential neighborhood just 10 minutes north of Ali'i Drive and 20 minutes from the airport—ideal for those who want to be close to the action but not right in it.

A perfect place for honeymooners and large families alike, beautiful **Hawaiian Oasis Bed and Breakfast** (74-4958 Kiwi St., Kailua-Kona, 808/937-6453, www.hawaiianoasis. com, $230-320 per room or $1,000 for entire house) has Hawaii-meets-India decor that makes it feel dreamy and exotic—especially the Aloha Room and the Waterfall Suite. This is the kind of house—with the view—that you wish you owned. It has it all: poolside outdoor kitchen, hot tub, and tennis courts. Guests have the entire house to themselves, as it is solely a guest residence. In fact, oftentimes the house is rented as a single unit for large families or parties. Amenities include free laundry, common TV, and Wi-Fi. The bottom rooms are wheelchair accessible. When the house isn't rented as an entire estate, hot breakfast is is served on the balcony.

The view of Kealakekua Bay from the ★ **Luana Inn** (82-5856 Napo'opo'o Rd., Captain Cook, 808/328-2612, www.luanainn. com, $169-209) is priceless, but it's available at an extremely reasonable price. Ken and Erin have fully dedicated their time to this business—so much so that they have made their own booklet of restaurant reviews. The rooms overlooking the pool/hot tub are identically furnished to look like an IKEA showroom and include a kitchenette with sink, microwave, mini-fridge, and coffeemaker. Wi-Fi and TVs with DVD players are also available. The rooms are large with king-size beds; however, the bathrooms are shower only with no tub. The large, nutritious breakfast is served in the adjoining main house (again, with the view), and communal hangout space is downstairs. Located on the back of this large property is the Ohana Cottage, which houses a full kitchen and room for four—but no ocean view. A short-stay fee is charged for stays under three nights. The location is fantastic, only a few minutes' drive down to the bay for snorkeling and kayaking or to Pu'uhonua O Honaunau National Historical Park for some sightseeing.

Over $250

It's the perfect place for a wedding, honeymoon, or those looking to rekindle romance. The ★ **Holualoa Inn** (76-5932 Mamalahoa Hwy., Holualoa, 808/324-1121, www.holualoainn.com, $365-595) was the retirement home of Thurston Twigg-Smith, CEO of the *Honolulu Advertiser* and member of an old *kama'aina* family. In 1987 it was converted into a bed-and-breakfast. The home is a marvel of taste and charm—light, airy, and open. Top to bottom, it glows with the natural burnished red of cedar and eucalyptus. The front lanai is pure relaxation, and stained glass accentuating the walls here and there creates swirls of rainbow light. A pool table holds king's court in the commodious games room, as doors open to a casual yet elegant sitting room where breakfast is served. A back staircase leads to a gazebo. From here, Kailua-Kona glows with the mistiness of an impressionist painting, and 50 acres are dotted with coffee trees and cattle. Just below is the inn's swimming pool and off to the side is the hot tub. The six island-theme rooms, each with private bathroom and superb views of the coast, all differ in size and decor. The Coffee Cherry Room has a private hot tub. Other rooms offer private sitting areas and sofa beds that can accommodate a third person. The communal sitting area and kitchen area are available for guest use. On the property is also the Darrell

Hill cottage ($525-$595), which offers a full kitchen and makes for a great "bridal suite." Unlike traditional B&Bs this place has a staff, including a professional chef who has worked at some of the best restaurants on the island. There is a two-night minimum and discounts for stays longer than seven days. Breakfast is included. No preteen children, please.

HOTELS AND RESORTS
$50-100

Stay at **Kona Seaside Hotel** (75-5646 Palani Rd., Kailua-Kona, 808/329-2455 or 800/560-5558, http://seasidehotelshawaii.com, $100-140) if you will only be in your room to sleep and want to be close to the action on Aliʻi Drive. The rooms are small and the décor is not very modern, but rooms stay cool with excellent air-conditioning and ceiling fans. Cable TV and free Wi-Fi are available. Spend some time on the sundeck, which looks out to the ocean across the street, and take a dip in the pool (but not at night—the pool closes at dusk). AAA and *kamaʻaina* discounts bring the rate down; some online rates also come with a free or discounted breakfast. There is an extra charge for parking per night, but a nearby public lot is free.

Run by the same family since 1917, **Hotel Manago** (Hwy. 11 between mile markers 109 and 110, Captain Cook, 808/323-2642, www.managohotel.com, $35-80 single, $38-83 double, each additional person $3) isn't trying to be anything but what it is— a simple place with a local feel offering basic services. Rates increase by floor (so lower floors are cheaper than higher floors). The rooms are small and have few decorations. Rooms with private bathrooms or communal baths are available, and discounts are offered for weekly stays. The hotel's restaurant is a local favorite for its huge combo lunches. It's right on the main highway about 45 minutes from the Kona airport—a great option if you're landing late in Kona and want to get to the Hilo side early in the morning (or vice versa).

$150-250

Despite the addition of "Courtyard" and "Marriott" to its name, **Courtyard by Marriott King Kamehameha's Kona Beach Hotel** (75-5660 Palani Rd., Kailua-Kona, 808/329-2911, www.konabeachhotel.com, $200-285), still holds the same reputation it's had for decades. Following the March 2011 tsunami, the King Kam (as locals call it) received a major revamping to bring its outdated rooms and pool area into the 21st

Holualoa Inn

century. The 452-room hotel is ideally located next to all the action of Ali'i Drive. It's the place to be during any of the large festivals in the area, many of which take place at the hotel. The King Kam also offers one of the best luau on the island. You don't need to be a guest to attend the luau, but staying over makes it easier to crawl back to your room after the open bar and massive buffet. Wi-Fi is available, and parking is extra (although a free public lot is close by). Online specials can bring the price down and may include parking and breakfast with the room rate. There is a nice oceanfront pool and a new state-of-the-art spa. Kids like the beach because the water is shallow, but the ocean access at Kailua pier is not that nice. Because it's right in the middle of things, it can get loud.

Sitting on the black lava seashore south of Keauhou Bay, the 521-room ★ **Sheraton Keauhou Bay Resort and Spa** (78-128 Ehukai St., Kailua-Kona, 808/930-4900 or 888/488-3535, www.sheratonkeauhou.com, $125-450) has risen like a phoenix from the site of the old Kona Surf Hotel. The grounds have been extensively landscaped to add color and some formality to this otherwise black and forbidding coastline. Rooms and public areas are comfortable with good views.

Three separate multistory buildings face the water; one faces inland for mountain views. They surround a large courtyard swimming pool with a long and twisting waterslide. There are actually two pools—one overlooks the ocean—but there isn't direct access to the beach. Amenities include a children's program, a business center, fitness center, tennis courts, basketball court, the full-service Ho'ola Spa, and a luau and Polynesian show held twice a week. Dine at the Restaurant Kai, the casual poolside bistro, the stylish Crystal Blue Lounge, or the ground-level Cafe Hahalua. The resort shines a light on the water each evening hoping to attract manta rays; the best viewing is May-October.

Over $250

Known worldwide for luxury, the 243-room **Four Seasons Resort, Hualalai at Historic Ka'upulehu** (100 Ka'upulehu Dr., 888/340-5662, www.fourseasons.com/hualalai, $550-1200) is split into 36 low-rise bungalows in four crescent-shaped groups that front a half-mile beach. Set amid old lava flows from the Hualalai volcano, 32 of these units have ocean views, while four are located along the 18th green of the accompanying Hualalai Golf Club. There is no skimping on

Sheraton Keauhou Bay Resort and Spa

space, furnishings, or amenities. Authentic Hawaiian art pieces from the late 1700s to the present are displayed throughout the hotel. Just downstairs from the lobby, the Cultural Center with its 1,200-gallon reef aquarium offers insight into the surrounding water and the lives of ancient Hawaiians. In addition to the natural lagoons, the resort has both freshwater and saltwater swimming pools set just back from the beach. There's supervised day care for kids (ages 5-12) and an activity center with indoor games for teens (and their parents). The full-service Sports Club and Spa offers a 25-meter lap pool, exercise machines, massage and spa therapies, and sand volleyball and basketball courts. Each room looks out onto a private garden, lanai, or patio. The resort also has three on-site restaurants and two bars.

CONDOS AND VACATION RENTALS
$100-150

A Castle Resorts and Hotels property, **Kona Bali Kai** (76-6246 Ali'i Dr., Kailua-Kona, 808/329-9381 or 800/367-5004, www.castleresorts.com, $115-350) is a decent, comfortable place with an indoor swimming pool, activities desk, concierge, and *poke* shop on

property. The 154 condos—split between a pair of three-floor buildings on the *mauka* and *makai* sides of Ali'i Drive—include studio, one-bedroom, two-bedroom, and three-bedroom units that all contain fully equipped kitchens and cable TV. The *makai* building has an elevator; however, not all rooms are large enough for wheelchairs to navigate. All apartments are individually owned so the decor differs, but most have muted colors and an old tropical feel. Some units have been recently updated. Rates depend on the unit size and its view (ocean, partial ocean, or mountain). There are often online specials and you have a good chance of getting upgraded for no additional charge when you check in; however, ask ahead of time if there is a cleaning fee (some have reported the surprise fee tacked on to their bill at the end of their stay). This is a great place to crash with a bunch of people and still be close to the action.

The condos at **Casa de Emdeko** (75-6082 Ali'i Dr., Kailua-Kona, www.casadeemdeko.org, $125-175) are individually owned by people off-island, so the quality really varies. The website lists the name of the owner, description of the properties, and specific policies (night minimums, no pets, and so forth). At these prices, it's worth doing the research

Aston Kona by the Sea

and checking to see which condos have been updated (not all of them have been, trust me). Rooms have king-size beds and pull-out sofa beds in the living areas. All are stocked with beach equipment. The complex has two pools and a sandy beach and barbecue area where guests mingle. Book directly from the owners, who have numbers and emails listed on the website. Some condos require a three-night minimum stay (10 nights during Ironman and the Christmas season). This place is unbelievably cheap for the area close to downtown Kailua.

$150-250

The one- and two-bedroom suites at **Aston Kona by the Sea** (75-6106 Ali'i Dr., Kailua-Kona, 808/327-2300, www.astonhotels.com, $180-300) have all the amenities of a home away from home: kitchen, washer/dryer, swimming pool/hot tub, barbecue area in a small sandy area where the waves crash in and turtles are visible below, cable TV, Wi-Fi, and activities desk. A range of rooms are available, some of which have partial or full ocean views. This condo building functions more like a hotel, given that there is daily "light cleaning" included in the rental price. Even the one-bedrooms come with a pull-out sofa, so they are big enough to sleep up to four people. Unlike some of the other condos in the area, the majority of these units have had upgrades. It's a good budget option and close to downtown Kailua (although not within walking distance). Book early; these condos sell out fast during high season. Discounts are available for senior citizens and AAA members.

If your dream vacation is accessing Wi-Fi from the pool, check out the one-bedroom condos at **Hale Kona Kai** (75-5870 Kahakai Rd., Kailua-Kona, 800/421-3696, www.halekonakai-hkk.com, $150-250). Almost all are oceanfront, and all come with a small kitchen, cable TV, sofa beds, and lanai—some with better ocean views than others. Shared extras include a nice-sized pool (right on the ocean) and a barbecue area. They are also really proud of their two parking lots. Each unit is individually owned, so the decor and datedness of furniture (as well as TVs and kitchen appliances) vary. Look at the pictures on the website before you decide which one to rent. Many condos require a three-night minimum. The location puts you close to downtown—close enough to walk—and the price is right, but if you think you'll spend a lot of time in the room, I'd rent elsewhere.

The **Holua Resort at Mauna Loa Village** (78-7190 Kaleiopapa St., Keauhou, 808/324-1550, www.shellhospitality.com, $150-250) is best suited for couples and families. Each cluster of eight condo units has its own small pool and hot tub, so the pool is never too crowded and you can always get a lounge chair. One- and two-bedroom condos (be warned: many have bright lime-green walls) are available, with pull-out sofas, kitchen, large TVs equipped with cable, and bright carpets. There's lots of covered parking. The helpful activities desk can set you up with tennis lessons and tee times. Keauhou shopping is nearby, allowing for quick trips to the grocery store. Many guests are involved with Shell hospitality's time-share program, but you don't have to be to stay here.

Kohala

Kohala is where you'll find the big chain resorts, the ones with a few hundred rooms and lots of staff. However, Kohala also is where you'll find updated vacation rentals (a great deal for large families staying together) and a few new players: boutique-like rentals and retreat centers. So don't just think about the Waikoloa and Mauna Launi resort areas; also consider places near Hawi on the northwest tip of the island. No matter where you stay in Kohala, this district is how you imagined your Hawaii getaway: first-rate beaches near first-rate restaurants.

HOTELS AND RESORTS
$150-250

On a perfect spot fronting palm-fringed 'Anaeho'omalu Bay, **Waikoloa Beach Marriott Resort and Spa** (69-275 Waikoloa Beach Dr., Waikoloa, 808/886-6789, www.marriotthawaii.com, $150-350) looks out over ponds that once stocked fish for passing ali'i. The hotel lobby is a spacious open-air affair that lets the trade winds blow across its cool sandstone floor. Six floors of rooms extend out in wings on both sides, flanking the landscaped courtyard with swimming pool and waterslide. Greeting you as you enter the lobby is a marvelous old koa outrigger canoe, set in front of a three-part mural by renowned Hawaiian artist Herb Kane of a royal canoe and Western frigate meeting off the Kona Coast. All 555 hotel rooms and suites are tastefully decorated in light, soothing colors, with king-size beds, rattan furnishings, custom quilts, and island prints of a mid-20th century art deco style. Each room has air-conditioning, color TV, high-speed Internet access (for a fee), yakuta robes, in-room safe, small refrigerator, marble vanities, and a private lanai. Online discounts can drop the prices at low season; however, many guests seem to be using their Marriott points. Hotel services and amenities include an activities desk for all on-site and off-property excursions and several retail shops and boutiques. You can take part in daily Hawaiian cultural programs, use the business center, or have your kids properly cared for at the Waikoloa Keiki Club children's program. The hotel is just a few minutes' stroll past the royal fishponds to the beach or to a nearby ancient but now restored heiau. The pool area is wonderful and the hot tubs are great at night. You are seconds from a great beach that offers all kinds of water activities (with paddleboard, snorkel, and surfboard rentals). The nearby shopping area is just a three-minute walk, offering access to restaurants, shops, and groceries. The service at the hotel is probably not the best of the resorts in the area.

At the **Hilton Waikoloa Village** (425 Waikoloa Beach Dr., Waikoloa, 808/886-1234 or 800/445-8667, www.hiltonwaikoloavillage.com, $200-400), the idea was to create a reality so beautiful and naturally harmonious that it offers a glimpse of paradise. The three main towers, each enclosing a miniature botanical garden, are spread over the grounds almost a mile apart and are linked by pink flagstone walkways, canals navigated by hotel launches, and a quiet, space-age tram. The museum promenade displays choice artwork from Hawaii, Oceania, and Asia. The beach fronting the property offers snorkeling, while two gigantic pools and a series of lagoons are perfect for water activities and sunbathing. You can swim in a private lagoon accompanied by reef fish, help feed the dolphins, dine at any one of the nine first-rate restaurants, and take in the extravagant dinner show of the twice-weekly Legends of the Pacific luau. The grandeur and expansiveness can seem a bit overblown. Forget intimacy—you don't come here to get away, you come here to participate. This is not where you should book a honeymoon trip. With 1,240 rooms on a 62-acre

Where to Stay in Kohala

Name	Type	Price	Features	Why Stay Here?	Best Fit For
★ Aston Shores at Waikoloa	condo	$175-300	kitchen, laundry, pool, private lanai, beach gear	nice condo	families, long-term stays
★ The Fairmont Orchid	hotel	$300-500	pool, hot tub, water sports rentals, luau, fitness center, golf, tennis courts, spa	the best luau on the island	honeymooners, families, luxury lovers
Hapuna Beach Prince Hotel	resort	$250-650	golf, pool, spa, fitness center	beach location, golf	golfers, beach lovers
★ Hawaii Island Retreat at Ahu Pohaku Ho'omaluhia	boutique hotel	$195-500	lounge, ocean views, infinity pool, spa, yoga	luxury, personalized spa experience	honeymooners, weddings or reunions
Hilton Waikoloa Village	resort	$200-400	pool, penguins and dolphins, restaurants, luau	a true megaresort experience	families, luxury lovers
★ Mauna Kea Beach Hotel	hotel	$325-950	pool, hot tub, beach access, restaurant, tennis, golf	beach, trail, and golf	honeymooners, couples
Mauna Lani Bay Hotel and Bungalows	hotel	$250-800	pool, hot tub, beach, restaurant, golf	beach access	honeymooners, luxury lovers
Mauna Lani Point	condo	$250-550	pool, hot tub, kitchen, laundry	affordable access to beach and golf	golfers, couples, extended stay
Outrigger Fairway Villas	condo	$150-285	tennis, pool, kitchen, private lanai, beach gear	affordable, location	families, extended stay
★ Puakea Ranch	vacation rental	$235-650	pool, kitchen, horseback riding, children's play room	beautiful decor, relaxation	couples, families
Waikoloa Beach Marriott Resort and Spa	resort	$150-350	restaurants, pool, hot tub, luau	beach, location	families, Marriott members

property, it's so big that entering the lobby can be like walking into Grand Central Station, and navigating certain walkways, particularly at dinnertime, is like pushing through throngs at a fair. There can be kids everywhere (great for kids, not great for adults who want quiet), boats, and a train going around. Cable TV is available, but in-room Wi-Fi and parking have an additional fee. Check out the website for discounts, packages, and special offers like free breakfast, free luau, or golfing discounts.

Over $250

The vision of Jeanne Sunderland, the 50-acre ★ **Hawaii Island Retreat at Ahu Pohaku Ho'omaluhia** (250 Maluhia Rd., Kapa'au, 808/889-6336, www.hawaiiislandretreat. com, $195-500) is dedicated to "elegant earth-friendly living." Jeanne was the founder of the Spa Without Walls at the former Ritz-Carlton at Mauna Lani and is well known in the community as a healing arts therapist. The nine-bedroom house looks like a mansion in the Mediterranean. The center courtyard is open with beautiful landscaping, and all rooms have private balconies that overlook either the ocean, valley, or garden. Explore the gardens and cliffs, do yoga, relax at the modern pool (there's no good beach access here for swimming), or enjoy the many spa treatments. In addition to the main house, there is a second option called "Hawaiian Hales," yurts located down the hill from the house. Each *hale* has accommodation for two (queen-size bed or twin beds) and private toilet. The shower is nearby in the spa locker room, which is equivalent to what you'd find at a five-star hotel. Currently, a third option, three hales that can each accommodate several people, are being built on the property to house the many guests who visit for retreats.

There's a two-night minimum stay with a $50 charge for each additional guest (beyond two people) occupying a room. Large discounts are given for stays of three nights or more, or opt for an all-inclusive package that includes three meals a day and spa treatments.

Ever since Laurance Rockefeller became interested in the lucrative possibilities of a luxury hideaway for the rich and famous, the ★ **Mauna Kea Beach Hotel** (62-100 Mauna Kea Beach Dr., Kohala Coast, 808/882-7222 or 800/882-6060, www.mau-nakeabeachhotel.com, $325-950) has set the standard of excellence on Kohala's coast. This beautiful property was leased from the Parker Ranch and the hotel opened in 1965. Luckily, the midcentury modern aesthetic is still hip. The Mauna Kea fronts beautiful Kauna'oa Beach, one of the best on the island. Million-dollar condos also grace the resort grounds. The hotel itself is an eight-story terraced complex of simple, clean-cut design. The grounds and lobbies showcase more than 1,000 museum-quality art pieces from throughout the Pacific and more than a half million plants add greenery and beauty to the surroundings. I'd live in this hotel, if they'd let me (and I was rich).

The award-winning Mauna Kea Golf

Hawaiian Island Retreat at Ahu Pohaku Ho'omaluhia

Course surrounds the grounds, and tennis courts sit on a bluff overlooking the water. Swimmers can use the beach or the courtyard swimming pool. A host of daily activities are scheduled, including yoga and stargazing (not at the same time). The rooms are, like the rest of the hotel, the epitome of understated elegance. The 310 beautifully appointed rooms feature an extra-large lanai and custom-made wicker furniture. The more expensive rooms offer lanais in the bathroom (I personally think that's a dream come true). From there, rates rise for beachfront units and deluxe ocean-view rooms. The good news is, purely for marketing reasons, the hotel is now part of the Autograph Collection—meaning you can use your Marriott points to stay here. A resort shuttle operates between here and the Hapuna Beach Prince Hotel, where Mauna Kea guests have signing privileges. The only downside is that the restaurant choices are mediocre and expensive. The good news is that excellent dining options in Waimea are only 15-20 minutes away.

The aptly named **Hapuna Beach Prince Hotel** (62-100 Kaunaʻoa Dr., Kohala Coast, 808/880-1111, www.hapunabeachprincehotel.com, $250-650) is about one mile down the coast from its sister resort, the Mauna Kea Beach Hotel. These two hotels are separate entities but function as one resort. Long and lean, this AAA four-diamond hotel steps down the hillside toward the beach in eight levels. A formal portico fronts the main entryway, through which you have a splendid view of palm trees and the ocean. Lines are simple and decoration subtle, letting surrounding nature become part of the whole. A free periodic shuttle connects the Hapuna Beach to the Mauna Kea, and all services available at one are open to guests of the other. What almost needs a shuttle is the hotel itself: It's about a ten-minute walk from the lobby to the oceanfront rooms and the gym area is another ten-minute walk in the opposite direction. If you're not good on your feet or traveling with lots of strollers (with children in them) this hotel might feel like a schlep.

Bedrooms are spacious, allowing for king-size beds, and the bathrooms have marble floors. Each of the 350 large and well-appointed rooms has an entertainment center, comfy chairs, and a lanai. Although rooms are air-conditioned, they all have louvered doors, allowing you to keep out the sun while letting breezes flow through. Four restaurants serve a variety of food for all meals during the day, and the lounges stay open for evening drinks.

Recreation options include the links-style Hapuna Golf Course, a fitness center, and a spa. Set in the garden below the lobby, the swimming pool is great recreation during the day and reflects the stars at night. Speaking of the stars, the hotel hosts a stargazing program for hotel guests (for a fee) and numerous other activities are scheduled through the week. A few shops whet the appetite of those needing sundries or resort wear. At the Prince Keiki Club at the Hapuna, children 5-12 years old can fill their time with fun activities and educational projects. If you love golf, stay here. Otherwise, stay at the Mauna Kea—it has a nicer beach and a more Zen feel to it than the Hapuna Prince.

As soon as you turn off Highway 19, an entrance road trimmed in purple bougainvillea sets the mood for the AAA five-diamond award-winning **Mauna Lani Bay Hotel and Bungalows** (68-1400 Mauna Lani Dr., Kohala Coast, 808/885-6622 or 800/367-2323, www.maunalani.com, $250-800), a 350-room hotel that opened in 1983. A short stroll beyond the central courtyard leads you past the swimming pool and through a virtual botanical garden to a perfect white-sand beach. From here any number of water sports activities can be arranged. Away from the shore you find a sports and fitness club with tennis courts, a lap pool, and the full-service Mauna Lani Spa. A cave complex and petroglyph field lies right in the middle of the resort complex. Surrounding the hotel is the marvelous Francis Iʻi Brown Golf Course.

Rooms are oversized; the majority come with an ocean view, and each includes a private lanai, cable TV, in-room safe, and all the comforts of home. The exclusive 4,000-square-foot, two-bedroom bungalows rent for an average of $4,000 a night, but each comes complete with a personal chef, butler, and swimming pool. In addition, one-, two-, and three-bedroom homelike villas go for $650-2,115, three-night minimum required. Weekly rates are available on the villas and bungalows, and there are always many different specials and packages such as a fourth night free with a three-night stay. Guest privileges include complimentary use of snorkeling equipment, Hawaiian cultural classes and activities, hula lessons, and complimentary morning coffee. Five restaurants and lounges cater to the culinary needs of resort guests, from quick and casual to classic island fare. The hotel offers the Kids' Club of Mauna Lani for children ages 5-12. Once a month Hawaiian musicians, dancers, and storytellers gather to share their cultural talents at Twilight at Kalahuipuaʻa at the Eva Parker Woods cottage. Some additional excellent beaches are just down the road. For an added bonus, the on-site restaurant, **The Canoe House,** offers five-star cuisine and service with excellent sunset views. It's great for couples.

In a tortured field of coal-black lava made more dramatic by pockets of jade-green lawn rises ★ **The Fairmont Orchid** (1 N. Kaniku Dr., Kohala Coast, 808/885-2000 or 800/845-9905, www.fairmont.com/orchid, $300-500). A rolling drive lined with *haku* lei of flowering shrubs entwined with stately palms leads to the open-air porte cochere. Nature, powerful yet soothing, surrounds the hotel in a magnificent free-form pool and trimmed tropical gardens; every set of stairs boasts a velvety-smooth koa banister carved with the pineapple motif, the Hawaiian symbol of hospitality. The Fairmont Orchid is an elegant place to relax in luxury and warm *aloha*. Located in two six-story wings off the main reception hall, the 540 hotel rooms, each with private lanai and sensational view, are a mixture of kings, doubles, and suites. Done in neutral tones, the stylish and refined rooms feature handcrafted quilts, twice-daily room cleanings, an entertainment center, and spacious marble bathrooms.

In addition to several restaurants and lounges, the hotel offers first-rate guest services, amenities, and activities that include a small shopping mall, tennis courts, a fitness center, and full-service spa. The pool area is enormous and lovely, with hot tubs and a sundeck, but there is only a small area for

WHERE TO STAY

KOHALA

Mauna Lani Bay Hotel and Bungalows

beach access. The luau at the hotel is one of the better ones in the area, but not traditional. It's like Lady Gaga designed it, and thus even if it's not standard, it's really fun to watch. In addition, the food is excellent—probably the best lu'au food around.

CONDOS AND VACATION RENTALS $150-250

The attractive, three-story **Outrigger Fairway Villas** (69-200 Pohakulana Pl., Waikoloa, 808/886-0036 or 800/688-7444, www.outrigger.com, $150-285) is opposite the Kings' Shops. Deluxe two- and three-bedroom units have all top-of-the-line amenities as well as a private pool, exercise center, and guest service center. The two-bedroom with two-bath is reasonably priced for the area and could likely fit 4-6 people; many of the units have convertible sofas. The units themselves are decorated with the standard Hawaii condo furniture (pictures of shells and pink couches). It's close to the Waikoloa action and walking distance to the beach.

The condos at ★ **Aston Shores at Waikoloa** (69-1035 Keana Pl., Waikoloa, 808/886-5001, www.astonhotels.com, $175-300) feel newer than many of the others in the area, with more modern decor. Guests choose from one- and two-bedroom suites or two-bedroom villas. The modern units have well-stocked kitchens, washer/dryers, private lanai, cable TV, and Internet, as well as daily maid service. The gated community also offers a swimming pool, hot tub, free tennis courts, fitness center, and outdoor barbecues. The two-bedroom deluxe suite is large enough to sleep 4-6 people utilizing the pull-out couch. Call ahead and request photos of the unit to make sure that you are getting one that you like. If you prefer a pool close by and want to cook some meals, this is the best choice for you.

Located just south of the Mauna Lani Bay Hotel and Bungalows is **Mauna Lani Point** (68-1050 Mauna Lani Point Dr., Kohala Coast, 888/976-2081, www.maunalanipoints.com, $250-550), nestled along the world-famous Mauna Lani Golf Course. Unlike some of the other condos in this area, these luxury one- and two-bedroom condos all have ocean-front views. Rates for condos vary depending on size and length of stay (discounts for stays of more than a week and some package deals are available). All units have a kitchen, washer/dryer, cable and Wi-Fi, and a lanai. There is a pool on-site, a hot tub, a fitness center, and daily maid service, as well as shuttle service around the resort area. The draw here is access to a golf course, the beach at the Mauna Lani resort, and amenities like a parking pass to the beach club.

Over $250

You'll want to stay here forever. There is nothing else, on the Big Island at least, like ★ **Puakea Ranch** (Hwy. 270 near Hawi, 808/315-0805, http://puakearanch.com, $235-650). The four guest bungalows date from the early 1900s, when they were the homes of plantation workers, cowboys, and their families working the surrounding 2,000 acres. Christie Cash, the owner, personally transformed each one into a space that looks like it could be in a magazine. Every single detail is gorgeous, from the linens to the couches to four-poster beds to the state-of-the-art kitchen. My favorite is Yoshi's House, a two-bedroom house with two bathrooms—one a separate structure with an antique copper tub for two. The house sleeps six and has its own private pool and is often used for events from weddings to dinner parties. Guests can help themselves to fresh eggs in the morning and fresh herbs and produce from the garden. A three- to five-night minimum stay is required during high season, and a departure cleaning fee of $200 is applied to every room reservation.

Ka'u is home to the most adventurous accommodations on the island. Most people who stay here do so for a night on the way to or from Hawai'i Volcanoes National Park. Although there is only a day or two worth of activities in Ka'u, you'll be getting a great deal because rates here are lower than those in the more-visited parts of the island.

BED-AND-BREAKFASTS AND INNS
Under $50

As you approach the Tibetan prayer flags hanging outside the **Wood Valley Temple** (Pahala, 808/928-8539, www.nechung.org, $65-95) you'll feel like you just stepped into Asia. The house offers 15 rooms, a mix of singles and doubles, with a three-night minimum stay. Although you need not be Buddhist to stay here, temple life and its surroundings are the main draw. Guests share a large communal kitchen, bathrooms, and areas for meditation and yoga. Meals are not provided. Weekly discounts and group rates are available. Discounts and work exchanges can be negotiated for longer stays.

Over $250

Everyone knows ★ **Kalaekilohana Bed and Breakfast** (94-2152 South Point Rd., Na'alehu, 808/939-8052, www.kau-hawaii.com, $329) as the big yellow house on the way to South Point. It's also one of the top five bed-and-breakfast spots on the island. Everything about Kalaekilohana is inviting, from the to the calming rooms to the huge porch looking out onto the road. It's worth spending a night or two here just to experience the hospitality of the innkeepers, Kenny and Kilohana, who have built the bed-and-breakfast by hand, thinking through every detail to shape the environment to offer the best experience for guests. The four clean, nicely furnished rooms are all on the second floor (not wheelchair-accessible). The rooms are without TV (but have Wi-Fi). There's a nightly wine hour, dinner and tours can be arranged upon request, and Kilohana, a master artist, offers lei making, feather, and weaving classes. Locavores will delight in the delectable breakfast made from their garden produce and that of nearby farmers—and the leftovers are composted!

CONDOS AND VACATION RENTALS
$100-150

Travelers have started to discover peaceful Pahala, a fine example of a former plantation community. Catering to visitors to the volcano, **Pahala Plantation Cottages** (Pahala, 808/928-9811, www.pahala-hawaii.com, $95-750) offers a number of vacation rental accommodations, including the renovated seven-bedroom, four-bath plantation manager's house, which rents for $750 a night or $4,950 a week. It sleeps up to 14 people. The house has a huge dining room, living room, sitting room, and library, as well as a fully functional kitchen, broad wraparound lanai, a large yard with banyan trees, and Wi-Fi. A cook can be arranged upon request. It's perfect for group events events such as business meetings, seminars, reunions, and weddings. Other nearby renovated one- to four-bedroom plantation cottages, with their original wooden floors and high ceilings, period pieces, and antiques, run $95-225 a night. Amenities include cable television and Wi-Fi. Stays of fewer than two nights have a $45 cleaning fee tacked on.

★ **Hale Aloha Aina** (Wood Valley, Pahala, www.homeaway.com rental #100555, $145) is a special place and not just because it's located near a Buddhist temple. Set on eight acres filled with fruit trees, this one-bedroom cottage is quaint, but includes everything you need: a tub in the bathroom, a well-stocked

Where to Stay in Ka'u

Name	Type	Price	Features	Why Stay Here?	Best Fit For
★ Hale Aloha Aina	vacation rental	$145	Fruit trees, off the grid (with Wi-Fi)	off-the-beaten path location, solitutde	couples/ honeymooners
★ Kalaekilohana B&B	B&B	$329	wine and social hour	knowledgeable hosts	couples
Pahala Plantation	vacation rental	$95-750	historic plantation home	taste of Old Hawaii	families, groups
Wood Valley Temple	inn	$65-95	yoga, workshops	retreat experience	budget travelers, free-thinkers

kitchen, and a fireplace. A perfect place for romancing your sweetheart, this cottage adheres to an off-the-grid ethic, but somehow still manages to offer a washer/dryer and Wi-Fi. Most renters spend a couple of days here, which makes sense because it's not too far from Volcano, the Black Sand Peach, and South Point. If you're a couple looking for an off-the-beaten path place to settle in, this peaceful rental offers you a stay unlike anywhere else on the island or that most visitors experience.

Hawai'i Volcanoes National Park and Volcano Village

There are a great number of accommodations in and around Volcano Village. While most are near the heart of the village, several are located in the fern forests south of the highway and a few are located around the golf course about two miles west of town. Most are bed-and-breakfasts, some are vacation homes where you take care of your own meals, and there is one hostel. These places run from budget and homey to luxurious and elegant, but most are moderate in price and amenities. Some of these establishments also act as agents for other rental homes in the area, so your choices are many. The weather in Volcano is substantially colder than that of the rest of the island, so don't look for rooms with air-conditioning; instead make sure they have warm blankets. Check if bed-and-breakfasts actually serve hot breakfast: It is difficult for establishments in Volcano to become certified kitchens (it has to do with the fact there is no county water here), so the majority of B&Bs don't really serve breakfast, and instead simply provide muffins.

HOSTELS
Under $50

An inexpensive option is **Holo Holo In** (19-4036 Kalani Honua Rd., Volcano, 808/967-7950 www.volcanohostel.com, private rooms $67-85, dorms $27). The owners are committed to cleanliness; due to their cleaning schedule, there is daily lockout 11am-4:30pm. This means that you can't access the place at all during this time. This might not be ideal for everyone, but could work for those who plan on hiking all day and really just need somewhere to crash afterward with a hot shower and free

Where to Stay in Volcano Village

Name	Type	Price	Features	Why Stay Here?	Best Fit For
Chalet Kilauea Inn at Volcano	hotel	$150-225	hot tub, lounge	rain forest atmosphere	couples
★ Hale Ohia	inn	$129-260	fireplaces, covered porches/lanai	cozy and warm, vintage	couples, families
Holo Holo In	hostel	$27-85	hot showers	affordable	budget travelers, campers
Kilauea Lodge	hotel	$195-215	restaurant, breakfast included, hot tub	park access, location	couples
Lotus Garden Cottages	B&B	$185-195	Good breakfast, cable TV	on the grid, bright and airy, private	couples
Volcano House	hotel	$250-380	restaurant	park access, location	park visitors
Volcano Places	vacation rental	$120-200	kitchen	cabin feel, friendly management	couples
★ Volcano Rainforest Retreat	vacation rental	$190-330	kitchen, Japanese *ofuro* tubs	cozy rain forest setting	families, couples
★ Volcano Teapot Cottage	vacation rental	$195	fireplace, hot tub, kitchen	fairy-tale setting	couples
★ Volcano Village Lodge	inn	$280-375	hot tub	romance	honeymooners

Wi-Fi. Dorm beds are available, as are private rooms with private or shared bath. Communal spaces include a comfortable lounge area with books, a computer, a television, and couches as well as shared kitchen and laundry facilities. Most guests are hikers (of all ages), lending a nice sense of camaraderie. The "In" is located in Volcano Village close to the park; it's a 30-minute walk to the entrance. It's a great place to stay before or after a big backcountry trip.

BED-AND-BREAKFASTS AND INNS
$100-150

Michael Tuttle, owner and host at ★ Hale Ohia (11-3968 Hale Ohia Rd., Volcano, 808/967-7986, www.haleohia.com, $129-260), is an architect—and his attention to detail is evident at the property. Located a stone's throw from the entrance to the national park and the restaurants in Volcano Village, the cottages here are exactly where you want to go back to at the end of the day in this climate. The cottages are cute, nicely decorated, offer loads of natural lighting, and, most importantly, have fireplaces. Some of the cottages are more private than others (although all are fairly private). The Ihilani Cottage ($219), built in the 1920s, is a perfect honeymooners' escape with one queen bed and an elevated reading alcove. Cottage 44 ($219) is one of my favorites: an almost 80-year-old water structure repurposed into a cottage with vintage lighting, this space also offers a covered porch and large Jacuzzi tub. It's an intimate space, but ideal for a couple. The largest structure on the property, once the gardener's cottage, the Hale Ohia Cottage is a three-bedroom with living room, fully furnished kitchen, and covered porch with barbecue ($220 for double occupancy). Continental breakfast is included with rooms—but like most places in Volcano, you might still want to BYO breakfast or go out to eat if you're a picky eater.

Claiming to have the only authentic Korean-style suite in North America, **Lotus Garden Cottages** (Road B, Volcano, 808/345-3062, www.volcanogetaway.com, $185-195) is a Zen-ful place. With only three rooms—the authentic Korean-style suite (Lotus Suite, $185), a Hawaiiana-themed one (the Aloha Moon Cottage, $195), and a romantic one (Hula Moon Cottage, $195)— this place stays pretty quiet. The rooms are large and offer useful amenities like the Hula Moon's large flat-screen TV (with lots of cable channels!), Wi-Fi, full kitchen, and fireplace. What makes this property stick out is the "tropical" breakfast delivered to your room in the morning. The fresh fruit and pastries are a step above what is offered at most places in Volcano. All rooms share an outdoor hot tub.

Over $250

★ **Volcano Village Lodge** (19-4183 Road E, Volcano, 808/985-9500, www.volcanovillagelodge.com, $280-375) feels like it's in the middle of a secluded rain forest. The five rooms of this luxury getaway are spread out across the property. There is something ethereal about them: All are romantically decorated with large beds, sitting areas, and views of the surrounding trees. Your arrival is greeted by a bottle of wine, as well as supplies to make your own breakfast (store-bought items like yogurt, cereal, and some boiled eggs). Wi-Fi is available and there is a TV (no cable) in each room, as well as a library

stacked with DVDs and books in the common area. A hot tub is also available. The staff at the lodge can arrange an in-room couple's massage. There's a two-night minimum for stays. The staff are dedicated to making sure guests have a memorable stay.

HOTELS AND RESORTS $150-250

The premier restaurant and lodge atop Volcano, **Kilauea Lodge** (19-3948 Old Volcano Rd., Volcano, 808/967-7366, www.kilauealodge.com, $195-215), owned and operated by Lorna and Albert Jeyte, is also one of the best on the island. The solid stone-and-timber structure was built in 1938 as a YMCA camp and functioned as such until 1962, when it became a mom-and-pop lodging operation. It faded into the ferns until Lorna and Albert revitalized it in the late 1980s. The lodge is a classic, with a vaulted, open-beamed ceiling, and a cozy "international fireplace" embedded with stones and plaques from all over the world. Rooms are located in three adjacent buildings; all include a complete breakfast in the restaurant. There is a hot tub in the rear garden. Each room in Hale Maluna, the original guesthouse, has a bathroom with vaulted 18-foot ceilings and a skylight, a working fireplace, queen-size or twin beds, and swivel rocking chair. Each room has Wi-Fi and cable TV. Since this is one of few restaurants in the area, both visitors and locals come here in the evenings to eat and socialize.

Peeking from the *hapu'u* fern forest in a manicured glen is **Chalet Kilauea Inn at Volcano** (19-4178 Wright Rd., Volcano, 808/967-7786 or 800/937-7786, www.volcanohawaii.com, $150-225). Downstairs there's an outdoor lounge area, as well as a black-and-white checkerboard dining room where wrought-iron tables sit before a huge picture window. On the second level is the guest living room, where you can play chess, listen to a large collection of CDs, or gaze from the wraparound windows at a treetop view of the surrounding forest. Beyond the koi pond in the garden, a freestanding gazebo houses an eight-person hot tub available 24 hours a day. The main house, called The Inn at Volcano, is known for elegance and luxury. It holds four suites and two theme rooms. The adjacent Hapu'u Suite has a fireplace in the cozy living room, but perhaps its best feature is the master bathroom, which looks out onto the back garden. The best room at the inn is the Treehouse Suite, which has two floors with a huge bed and tub for two. The other rooms at the inn are smaller and noise seems to travel easily between them. Rooms all have Wi-Fi and cable TV (and some even have cable TV in the bathroom).

Chalet Kilauea also has many other accommodations in Volcano Village. **Lokahi Lodge** has four rooms that run $120-155, or you can rent the entire property for a group of up to 14 people. For those on a tighter budget, the **Volcano Hale** rents rooms for $55-75 with shared bathroom and plenty of common space. The entire house can be rented and can sleep 13. In addition, several vacation homes dotted here and there about town in the secluded privacy of the forest are available for $375-775. Whatever your needs and price range, Chalet Kilauea will have something for you.

Over $250

Ever dreamed of sleeping with a goddess? Cuddle up with Pele at **Volcano House** (inside Hawai'i Volcanoes National Park, www.hawaiivolcanohouse.com, $250-380), the only hotel located on the rim of Kilauea caldera. Its history began in 1846, when a sugar planter perched a grass hut on the rim of the crater and charged $1 a night for lodging. A steady stream of notable visitors has come ever since: almost all of Hawaii's kings and queens dating from the middle of the 19th century, as well as royalty from Europe. Mark Twain was a guest, followed by Franklin Roosevelt. Most recently, a contingent of astronauts lodged here and used the crater floor to prepare for walking on the moon. In 1866 a larger grass hut replaced the first, and in 1877 a wooden hotel was built. This particular building dates from the 1940s. A renovation completed in 2013 made the hotel more secure in case of earthquake and updated its decor and facilities. It may not be the nicest place to stay in Volcano, but it's worth it for the view. You can see the glow of the crater from your window—an insomnia-invoking experience for many people. I do not recommend staying here if you are particularly affected by "energy."

Volcano House

CONDOS AND VACATION RENTALS $150-250

Just up the road from the Kilauea Lodge is a cute little two-bedroom cottage, **Tutu's Place** (808/967-7366, www.kilauealodge.com, $245). This two-bedroom house, done in rattan and koa, has a fireplace in the living room, a full kitchen, and a wonderful little bathroom. For a small place, it has a surprisingly roomy feel. Wi-Fi and cable TV are available. The rate is based on double occupancy; it's $20 for each additional person. Full breakfast at the lodge is included. It's great for anyone who wants privacy along with the availability of the staff at the lodge.

The three cottages of ★ **Volcano Rainforest Retreat** (11-3832 12th St., Volcano, 808/985-8696, www.volcanoretreat.com, $190-330) are embraced within the arms of ferns, 'ohi'a, and bamboo. It's like staying in a private rain forest. Constructed in an open style of cedar and redwood, these handcrafted buildings are warm and welcoming, rich in color and detail, and have plenty of windows that look out onto the encircling forest. Hale Kipa (Guest Cottage) has a cozy living room with full kitchen and sleeping loft, perfect for a couple or small family. The six-sided Hale Ho'ano (Sanctuary House), the smallest and with the most obvious Japanese influence, has the benefit of an outdoor *ofuro* tub and shower. The octagonal Hale Nahele (Forest House) is one large room with an attached full bath, efficiency kitchen and sitting area, and covered lanai—just right for a cozy couple. Each has a small heater for chilly nights. The newest addition is the cedar-shingle Bamboo Guest House, an exquisite one-bedroom vacation rental with a full kitchen and dining area, sitting room under clerestory windows, and a relaxing bath with outdoor *ofuro* tub. All units are stocked with breakfast foods and have Wi-Fi. The rooms are close to town and the park. Rates are discounted for three nights or longer; expect an extra charge for stays of just one night.

For a one-stop vacation rental shop, check out **Volcano Places** (808/967-7990, www.volcanoplaces.com, $120-200). Ranging from studios to two bedrooms, these four rentals have a cabin-in-the-woods feel. Nothing luxurious here, just comfortable places to stay—as if you were going for a visit a family member's home. Kathryn, the owner, receives rave reviews for her friendliness and spotless accommodations. The top-rated Nohea is a one-bedroom cottage with high ceilings that can fit a couple (or squeeze in three adults), with a nicely sized kitchen, living area, Wi-Fi, and cable TV. It backs up to a state forest that you can enjoy from your private lanai—just the place you want to return after a long day at the park. Discounts are available for stays longer than three days. Rates are for double occupancy; it's $15 for each additional guest.

How good is ★ **Volcano Teapot Cottage** (19-4041 Kilauea Rd., Volcano, 808/967-7112, www.volcanoteapot.com, $195)? It will probably be booked by the time you finish reading this sentence. Why so much demand? The service is great and the place is really charming—like something from a fairy tale. Bill and Antoinette Bullough pay attention to details and pay attention to their guests. Originally built in the early 1900s by a Hilo businessman, the cottage is two bedrooms and one bath filled with antiques and a gas fireplace. Even though the cottage has two bedrooms, the owners prefer to host only two people (you'll have to negotiate for a third). Mixed with the historical elements are Wi-Fi, a TV with DVD player, and a hot tub situated in the lush landscape behind the house. Breakfast items are stocked daily in the kitchen. It has everything you want, including easy access to the park. A two-night minimum stay is required.

Puma

This is where to come to get away from it all—even cell phones (reception here is essentially nonexistent). There are no big resorts, only bed-and-breakfasts and retreat centers, with room rates substantially lower than those in more-visited parts of the island. Visitors to this area tend to stay a few nights and spend their time relaxing, doing yoga, and snorkeling in some of the best spots on the island.

BED-AND-BREAKFASTS AND INNS
$100-150

Located in the Leilani Estates subdivision, **Hale Moana Bed and Breakfast** (13-3315 Makamae St., 808/965-9090, www.bnb-aloha. com, $115-175) has survived both a hurricane and threat of lava. Petra, the owner, is amazing and goes out of her way to assist guests. There are three renovated apartment-style rooms, including a one-bedroom ($155) that is wheelchair accessible and a two-bedroom ($175), the only room with a TV, that is ideal for a family. There's also a studio option ($115). The breakfast is hearty (fruit, pancakes, and coffee) and they accommodate food allergies.

HOTELS AND RESORTS
$150-250

★ **Kalani Oceanside Retreat** (Hwy. 137, Pahoa, 808/965-7828 or 800/800-6886, www. kalani.com, $90-275) is a nonprofit conference and holistic retreat center, a haven for people seeking peace and inner development. It's not for everyone, but it's a great place for travelers hoping to spend quality time with like-minded individuals on a similar life path. Activities include massage, hula, meditation, yoga, lei making, *lau hala* weaving, and hiking. The grounds include a rain-fed swimming pool, a *watsu* pool, a hot tub, and a whirlpool tub (all clothing optional). Accommodation options range from a lodge room with a shared bathroom ($95)

to an ocean-view cottage ($245). Recently, it seems like a lot of guests have been staying here with Groupon package deals that make these accommodations more than affordable. A blown conch shell calls you to communal meals, served in the open-air dining hall (for a separate fee). The entrance is a few miles east of Kaimu on Route 137 between mile markers 17 and 18, on the mountain side of the road. Look for a large Visitors Welcome sign and proceed uphill until you see the office and sundries shop.

CONDOS AND VACATION RENTALS
$100-150

Located in the nicest possible part of the Hawaiian Paradise Park subdivision, **Ala Kai Bed and Breakfast** (15-782 Paradise Ala Kai, Keaau, 808/806-3646, www.alakaibb. com, $125-150) is right across the street from the ocean. The owners (sisters) Mary and Pat are fascinating people (ask Mary about her Peace Corps days). The guest rooms are smallish, but have everything you need. I recommend the Bamboo Room ($125) for its private entrance (the Aloha Room is in the main house) and bathroom with "river rock" flooring, which is like a little massage on your feet every time you enter. The super steal here is the Ohana Cottage ($150) that features two bedrooms along with a queen-size pull-out couch in the living room. The cottage includes a full kitchen, washer/dryer, and a barbecue grill. Book now before Mary and Pat realize they should be charging more for this space.

Expect a tranquil and romantic setting at ★ **Ramashala** (12-7208 Kalapana-Kapoho Rd./Hwy. 137, 808/965-0068, www.ramashala. com, $50-200), which is decorated with beautiful tapestries and South Asian furniture. Choose from six rooms ranging from singles with shared bath ($50-60) to the Mandala Suite with full kitchen, king bed, sundeck,

Where to Stay in Puna

Name	Type	Price	Features	Why Stay Here?	Best Fit For
Ala Kai B&B	B&B	$125-150	swimming pool	location 30 minutes from Hilo, Volcano, and lower Puna	budget travelers, those who like to get off the beaten path
Hale Moana B&B	B&B	$115-175	kitchens	welcoming hosts	families, budget travelers
Jungle Farmhouse	rental	$159	lots of space (inside and outside)	midcentury modern-meets-jungle	families, extended stays
Malama House	rental	$179	plenty of space for entire family	great location for exploring Puna	families, extended stays
★ Kalani Oceanside Retreat	hotel	$90-275	clothing optional pool, hot tub, yoga	retreat experience	yoga practitioners, free-thinkers, nudists
★ Ramashala	hotel/condo	$50-200	hot tub, kitchen	location near Kehena Beach	couples, budget travelers

and private bath ($100-150) or the Prana Residence ($150-200) that features two king beds, a double futon, kitchen, and private veranda. The ocean at Kehena Beach is only 200 yards away (so close you can hear the beach drumming). Yoga classes are available but not included with the price. With weak Wi-Fi, no cell phone service, and no TV, it's the right place to get away from modern distractions.

$150-250

Brought to you by the owners of the perfectly curated Hilo Bay Hale in Hilo is the three bedroom at **The Jungle Farmhouse** (15-3001 Mako Way, Pahoa, 800/745-5049, http://pahoa.info, $159) or the three bedroom at the **Malama House** (12-1230 Malama St.,

808/640-5922, www.malamahouse.com, $179). The Jungle Farmhouse offers guests a rustic retreat, but with high-speed Wi-Fi, cable TV, and the added hipster element of a record player (yes, the house is stocked with records—need not BYO). When considering the three bedrooms, full kitchen, two lanais (one screened-in, the other not), and outdoor grill, this property is a steal. This house can probably sleep at least eight people, although an extra fee of $20 per person applies over four adults or children. There are discounts for weekly stays. The Malama House is a similar steal for its three bedrooms, full kitchen, large lanai, and range of amenities. The location is ideal—close to town and ten minutes from Kalapana.

Hilo

Lots of visitors come to Hilo for the day but don't want to stay here. "Too much rain!" they say. Well, it depends what time of year it is—and what time of day. You can expect rain in the afternoons November-March, although, due to global climate change, even that has been more erratic, with some years completely dry. Hilo doesn't have large resorts like the Kona side; instead, it has bed-and-breakfasts with eager innkeepers, asking for less than you'd pay on the Kona side. Hilo can make a good base to explore the island: It's only 45 minutes to Volcano and about an hour to Mauna Kea, and it's at the beginning of the drive on the Hamakua Coast. And yes, it has beaches, too. They aren't as large and white-sanded as on the Kona side, but they offer good access for swimming, snorkeling, and surfing.

HOSTELS
Under $50

Out near the beaches east of town, **Arnott's Lodge** (98 Apapane Rd., 808/969-7097, www.arnottslodge.com, $30-140) is a good option for budget travelers. Arnott's has six two-person lockable rooms, as well as have a few open-air bunks, all with shared bath. A room with private bath sleeps three, and a two-bedroom suite sleeps up to five. There's also tenting space ($14 per person) on the lawn. Free Wi-Fi is available throughout. No check-in is available after 10pm. Arnott's also runs wonderful, inexpensive touring excursions.

Located downtown in a huge historic building that dates to 1912, ★ **Hilo Bay Hostel** (101 Waianuenue Ave., 808/933-2771, www.hawaiihostel.net, $79 private, $30 dorm) is similar to what you'd find in Quito or Bogota. The charming second-floor space offers a clean shared kitchen (with lots of people around cooking) and free Wi-Fi. It's close to the bus station and downtown shops. It's smart to stay here if you're traveling solo

because the owner is kind to confused travelers (such as those trying to figure out how to hitch around the island). Otherwise, it's not that much more expensive for two people to stay at a nearby bed-and-breakfast while splitting the cost.

BED-AND-BREAKFASTS AND INNS
$50-100

Overlooking the Wailuku River near the Boiling Pots, **The Old Hawaiian Bed and Breakfast** (1492 Wailuku Dr., Hilo, 808/961-2816, www.thebigislandvacation.com, $85-125) is one of the best values on the Big Island. Stewart and Lory have transformed the back of their house into a three-bedroom bed-and-breakfast. The immaculate rooms, all with private entryways and private baths, overlook the large manicured lawn and the river. They share a covered lanai with microwave and refrigerator. Rates are based on double occupancy; there's a $10 charge per night for an extra person. One-night stays have an additional $15 charge. Master chef Lory cooks amazing breakfasts—the gluten-free pastries are so good! The breakfast alone would run about $30 at a local café. Overall, this place is a fantastic deal.

$100-150

Matthew and Danny, the innkeepers and owners of ★ **Hilo Bay Hale** (301 Ponahawai St., 808/745-5049, www.hilobayhale.com, $159), have transformed a traditional plantation-style house into a hipster's Hawaiian dream—a slice of Brooklyn in Hilo. The rooms are perfectly decorated with just the right amount of reappropriated antiques and artifacts to create the ambience of 1950s Hawaii. The house has four rooms. My favorite is named for author James Michener, with a queen-size bed, private lanai overlooking a koi pond, blue-tiled bathroom with an amazing

Where to Stay in Hilo

Name	Type	Price	Features	Why Stay Here?	Best Fit For
Arnott's Lodge	hostel	$30-140	kitchen	beach location, organizes outings	backpackers
★ Hilo Bay Hale	B&B	$159	private lanai	urban experience	couples and singles, queer-friendly
★ Hilo Bay Hostel	hostel	$30-79	historic building, kitchen	affordable dorm experience	budget travelers
Hilo Hawaiian Hotel	hotel	$155-300	pool, restaurant	location	conference attendees, short-term guests
★ Hilo Honu	B&B	$140-250	sunporch, historic home, views	gorgeous suite that's like a Japanese tearoom	couples traveling together, honeymooners, those who like views.
★ The Inn at Kulaniapia Falls	B&B	$179-289	hot tub, massage, waterfall, breakfast	a waterfall in your backyard	honeymooners
The Old Hawaiian Bed and Breakfast	B&B	$85-125	fridge and microwave, shared lanai, huge breakfast	best value B&B	budget travelers
Orchid Tree Bed and Breakfast	B&B	$149 plus tax	pool, hot tub, shared lanai	pool near the ocean	surfers, families, couples
★ Shipman House Bed and Breakfast Inn	B&B	$219-249	historic, great breakfast	one of the most well-known families and houses in Hawaii	couples, history buffs

tub, and a nonfunctioning record player. The breakfast, served on a lanai off the kitchen, offers large portions of quiches, cereal, yogurt, and bacon. Located just a few minutes' walk up the hill from the farmers market and the downtown shops, this is where you'd want to live if you lived in Hilo.

$150-250

Listed in both the State and National Registers of Historic Places, ★ **Shipman House Bed and Breakfast Inn** (131 Ka'iulani St., 808/934-8002, www.hilo-hawaii.com, $219-249) is the grandest B&B in all Hawaii. This Victorian house was once the home of the Shipman family, prominent Big Island landowners, and is now presided over by Barbara, a Shipman descendant. Does she have stories to tell! She's happy to talk story about recipes, hula, and all things Hawaii. History buffs will enjoy the outstanding antiques that fill the house. It's like staying at your fancy grandmother's house. The main house offers three guest rooms with antique beds, private baths, and stately views through enormous windows. Others will lodge in the Cottage, originally built for the express purpose of accommodating visitors, with two spacious bedrooms, each with queen-size bed, window seats, and private bath. Both rooms have private entrances, ceiling fans, and a small refrigerator. This is a strictly no-smoking establishment and a "no-TV zone," and children are not encouraged. The library is open to guests, along with use of the 1912 Steinway piano whose keys were once tickled by Lili'uokalani. One evening a week, a hula class is held on the lanai. Breakfast is an expanded continental with homemade granola, assorted local fruits, juices, Kona coffee, yogurt, and breads.

★ **Hilo Honu** (1477 Kalaniana'ole Ave., 808/935-4325, www.hilohonu.com, $140-$250) is the place famous people stay when they come to town. In addition to being an expert craftswoman (maybe she'll show you some of her goods), Gay, the owner/innkeeper, is a generous hostess who is extremely knowledgeable about not only where to eat in Hilo, but also about cultural happenings in town. Luckily, Hilo Honu is close enough to town that you can actually leave your car behind and walk to dinner or to hear some live music. The entire property, built in 1933 and since renovated, is an architectural marvel; however, if you can get a room, I'd recommend the upper-floor Samurai Suite ($250 for double occupancy with a charge for additional guests) that features a unique 10-tatami mat Japanese tearoom as the master bedroom. A second bedroom contains two twin beds. The upper suite is like a museum (hence no small children here, please) but the real kicker is the view of Hilo Bay from the rooms themselves or the attached sun porch. There's also a luxurious two-person soaking tub in the bathroom.

Located just minutes from Honoli'i Beach, the best surfing beach on this side

of the island, is a small neighborhood scattered with vacation rentals and bed-and-breakfasts. **Orchid Tree Bed and Breakfast** (6 Makakai Pl., 808/961-9678, www.orchidtree.net, $149 plus tax double occupancy, $15 for each additional guest) has an outstanding reputation as a really chill place with consistently good service. Steve, the owner and innkeeper, is a laid-back surfer who wants his guests to relax and have a great time. That's not too hard here! The house looks small from the front, but it has a small swimming pool (hard to find at B&Bs on the Hilo side), covered hot tub, and a great outdoor lanai. The Hula Suite is a converted section of the main house that sleeps four ($149 for double occupancy). The second suite, in a detached space to the left of the house, is light, airy, and perfect for couples. Both rooms have cable TV and Wi-Fi. Breakfast, served on the lanai, includes waffles or pancakes and an arrangement of fruits.

Just a 10-minute drive from town (on a road that can be hard to navigate), ★ **The Inn at Kulaniapia Falls** (1 Kulaniapia Dr., Hilo, 866/935-6789, www.waterfall.net, $179-289) consists of three properties spread across the backdrop of a waterfall. Yes, they own a waterfall! It's close to Hilo but really feels away from it all. The owners traveled to the Far East to purchase items to furnish the house and the result is a Japanese-style aesthetic. Rooms are small with large flat-screen TVs (with cable) and Wi-Fi. Each of the two main houses has its own respective breakfast area and staff to prepare food. A private pagoda sleeps up to six ($25 for each additional guest). The fridge in the pagoda is stocked for guests to make their own food. Try to get a room that faces the waterfall; the rushing water will soothe you to sleep.

HOTELS AND RESORTS $150-250

The classic **Hilo Hawaiian Hotel** (71 Banyan Dr., 808/935-9361 or 800/367-5004, www.castleresorts.com, $155-300) occupies the most beautiful grounds in Hilo. From the vantage of the hotel's colonnaded veranda, you overlook formal gardens, Coconut Island, and Hilo Bay. Designed as a huge arc, the hotel's architecture blends well with its surroundings and expresses the theme set by the bay: a long, sweeping crescent. The hotel is newly renovated, but still has a 1970s Hawaiiana feel. It's neat, clean, well maintained, and has all necessary amenities. There's a swimming pool and all rooms have air-conditioning, phone, and cable TV. There are restaurants on the property, but you'd do better to walk the five minutes to Ken's House of Pancakes for a better meal. Substantial online discounts are available, especially during low season.

Hamakua Coast, Waimea, and the Saddle Road

You want views, I'll give you some views. The accommodations on the Hamakua Coast and Waimea offer some of the best scenes around: You get your ocean and your mountain at the same time. The best places to stay in this area tend to be the bed-and-breakfasts, each of which offer something unique. Due to the differences in amenities, rates tend to vary, but are lower than in Kona or nearby Kohala. On the Hamakua Coast, you'll have to drive a bit to get some dinner. In Waimea, you'll be minutes away from the island's best cuisine.

BED-AND-BREAKFASTS AND INNS
$150-250

The most spectacular view on the island can be found outside your room at ★ **Waipi'o Rim** (48-5561 Honoka'a-Waipi'o Rd., Waipi'o Valley, 808/775-1727, www.waipiorim.com, $220 double occupancy). This B&B, owned by Nancy and Steve Roberson, overlooks Waipi'o Valley in all its splendor. Only one room is available, in a building separate from the Robersons' main house; it has awkwardly placed furniture including a queen bed, eating area, couch, and a TV that is placed on top of an armoire. Wi-Fi is available as is cable TV and access to Netflix. But all of that is secondary given the backdrop. Waking up to Waipi'o Valley is really a once-in-a-lifetime event. Nancy and Steve are passionate about the area and offer a lot of attention, including a wine-and-pupu welcome and scrumptious breakfasts each morning, made from local produce. Ask Steve about the trails surrounding the house, which tour operators use for horseback riding and ATV trips. You can just walk them on your own with Steve's directions. Single-night stays are an additional $20. The biggest downside is that it's a little out of the way: about 15 minutes or so to Honoka'a, 30 minutes to Waimea, and about an hour to Hilo.

One of the most charming bed-and-breakfast homes on the Big Island, ★ **Waipi'o Wayside** (46-4226 Waipio Rd., 808/775-0275, www.waipiowayside.com, $115-200 double occupancy) is located in a 1932 sugar plantation home. Jacqueline, the owner/operator, has been running this establishment for nearly 30 years and her knowledge of the area and general storytelling abilities are unmatched. There are five different rooms to choose from in the main house—each decorated as their name implies (such as the Library Room or the Chinese Room). The Moon Room ($115) is a good deal for those on a budget because it has a private bathroom—it's just detached room itself. All other rooms are have ensuite bathrooms. Many of the rooms have a third twin bed that can accommodate children (who are welcome here). Besides Jacqueline's knowledge of all things Big Island, she also is a great chef. Breakfast is made to order and ranges from the savory to the sweet. Food preferences are accommodated.

Where to Stay on the Hamakua Coast, in Waimea, and on the Saddle Road

Name	Type	Price	Features	Why Stay Here?	Best Fit For
Aaah the Views	B&B	$169-189	breakfast	sunset views, location	budget travelers
Hotel Honoka'a Club	hotel	$40-130	continental breakfast	location	budget travelers
★ Waipi'o Rim	B&B	$220	wine and pupu hour	best views, friendly hosts	couples
★ Waipi'o Wayside	B&B	$115-200	1932 plantation house	close to town but not too far from valley	families, couples, budget travelers
★ Waimea Gardens	B&B	$160-190	farm-fresh breakfast	close to everything; the best mattress you'll ever sleep on	honeymooners, couples traveling with baby/ toddler

Aaah the Views (66-1773 Alaneo St., 808/885-3455, www.aaahtheviews.com, $169-189)! Really, the views! They're worth a stay at this inn. Opt for one of the rooms with views of Mauna Kea (the Dream Room or Treetop Suite) and you'll have a bay window with a view that will leave you staring for hours. Having recently switched from a bed-and-breakfast to an inn, owner Erika now stocks each room's fridge with a few treats for the morning. There are all the usual amenities (TV/DVD and Wi-Fi), but no hot tub or swimming pool (although the property borders a river for the adventurous type). The rooms themselves are small and clean, with large bathrooms (one with an outside shower)—but you'll be so distracted by the views (I'll say it again) from the windows or balcony that you won't care about the size or the decor. The location is excellent, just a few minutes west of Waimea and only 10-15 minutes drive from the Kohala Coast. It makes a great base to explore a large part of the island. One-night stays are sometimes possible, but there is an extra fee.

The pictures on its website don't do ★ **Waimea Gardens** (65-1632 Kawaihae Rd., 808/885-8550, www.waimeagardens. com, $160-190) justice. The cottages and studio are part historic (some dating back to the late 1800s), part *Architectural Digest*—and the backdrop of Waimea's hills seals the deal. The Kohala Cottage ($190 based on double occupancy) offers a fully equipped kitchen (not to mention fresh farm eggs right from the property), an enclosed garden accessible through the bathroom (which is almost the size of the cottage itself), and a bed so comfortable that there are handouts in the room explaining why the mattress is so amazing. The Waimea Cottage ($175 based on double occupancy) is no dud either. Also with a private patio and kitchenette, this cottage offers a fireplace. The Garden Studio ($160 based on double occupancy) is an updated room attached to the main house; in addition to the usual amenities, it includes a beautiful outdoor space. Barbara Campbell, who owns and runs Waimea Gardens, has been deeply involved in the Big Island's travel industry for over 35 years. She knows good accommodation and she accepts no less for herself (or others). If this wasn't enough to convince you this is "the place," the location is ideal: It's only 20 minutes from here to the Kohala Coast beaches (but so much cooler here at night), five minutes to the culinary array of Waimea, 40 minutes to Hawi, and about 50 minutes to the Hamakua Coast. This is a great place to base yourself for several days.

HOTELS AND RESORTS $50-100

Centrally located along Route 240 in downtown Honoka'a, **Hotel Honoka'a Club** (45-3480 Mamane St., Honoka'a, 808/775-0678, www.hotelhonokaa.com, $40-130) is a good budget option if you want to stay near Waipi'o Valley. Built in 1908 as the plantation managers' club, it's still infused with the grace and charm of the old days. What it lacks in elegance it makes up for in cleanliness and friendliness. The hotel, the only one right in town, is old and well used but clean and comfortable. From the back rooms, you get a view over the tin roofs of residential Honoka'a and the ocean. Choose a two-room suite, an ocean-view room with TV, private bath, and queen-size bed, or an economy room with a private bath. Rates include a simple continental breakfast and Wi-Fi. Hostel rooms, located in the basement, share bath and kitchen facilities. It's not a fancy place, but it's sweet and likable.

Background

The Landscape

GEOGRAPHY

The Big Island, Hawai'i, is the southernmost and easternmost of the Hawaiian Islands—and also the largest. This island dwarfs all the others in the Hawaiian chain at 4,028 square miles and growing. It accounts for about 63 percent of the state's total landmass; the other islands could fit within it two times over. With 266 miles of coastline, the island stretches about 95 miles from north to south and 80 miles from east to west. Cape Kumukahi is the easternmost point in the state, and Ka Lae (South Point) is the southernmost point in the country.

Science and the *Kumulipo* oral history differ sharply on the age of the Big Island. Scientists say that Hawai'i is the youngest of the islands, being a little over one million years old; the chanters claim that it was the first "island-child" of Wakea and Papa. It is, irrefutably, closest to the "hot spot" on the Pacific floor, evidenced by Kilauea's frequent eruptions. The geology, geography, and location of the Hawaiian Islands, and their ongoing drifting and building in the middle of the Pacific, make them among the most fascinating pieces of real estate on earth.

Separating the Big Island from Maui to the northwest is the 'Alenuihaha Channel, which at about 30 miles wide and over 6,800 feet deep is the state's second-widest and second-deepest channel.

The Mountains

The tremendous volcanic peak of **Mauna Kea** (White Mountain), located in north-central Hawai'i, has been extinct for more than 3,500 years. Its seasonal snowcap earns Mauna Kea its name and reputation as a good skiing and snowboarding area in winter. Over 18,000 feet of mountain below sea level rise straight up from the ocean floor—making Mauna Kea over 31,000 feet tall, almost 3,000 feet taller than Mount Everest; some consider it the tallest mountain in the world. At 13,796 feet above sea level, it is without doubt the tallest peak in the Pacific. Near its top, at 13,020 feet, is **Lake Waiau,** the highest lake in the state and third highest in the country. Mauna Kea was a sacred mountain to the Hawaiians, and its white dome was a welcome beacon to seafarers. On its slope is the largest adze quarry in Polynesia, from which high-quality basalt was taken to be fashioned into prized tools. The atmosphere atop the mountain, which sits mid-Pacific far from pollutants, is the most rarefied and cleanest on earth. The clarity makes Mauna Kea a natural for astronomical observatories. The complex of telescopes on its summit is internationally staffed and provides data to scientists around the world.

The **Kohala Mountains** to the northwest are the oldest and rise only to 5,480 feet at Kaunu o Kaleiho'ohie peak. This section looks more like the other Hawaiian Islands, with deep gorges and valleys along the coast and a forested interior. As you head east toward Waimea from Kawaihae on Highway 19, for every few miles you travel you pick up about 10 inches of rainfall per year. This becomes obvious as you begin to pass little streams and rivulets running from the mountains.

Mount Hualalai, at 8,271 feet, is the backdrop to Kailua-Kona. It's home to many of the Big Island's endangered birds and supports many of the region's newest housing developments. Just a few years ago, Mount Hualalai was thought to be extinct, since the last time it erupted was in 1801. It is now known that within the last 1,000 years, the mountain has of 6,750,000 cubic yards per hour. Seven lava rivers flowed for 23 days, emitting over 600 million cubic yards of lava that covered 35 square miles. There were no injuries, but the villages of Ka'apuna and Honokua were partially destroyed, along with the Magoo Ranch. The mountain's last eruption, in 1984, was small by comparison yet created fountaining inside the summit crater and a "curtain of fire" along its eastern rift.

The lowest of the island's major peaks, **Kilauea** rises only to 4,078 feet. Its name means "The Spewing," and it's the world's most active volcano. In the last hundred years, it has erupted on the average once every 11 months. The Hawaiians believed that the goddess Pele inhabited every volcano in the Hawaiian chain, and that her home is now Halema'uma'u crater in Kilauea Caldera. Kilauea is the most scientifically watched volcano in the world, with a permanent observatory built right into the crater rim. When it erupts, the flows are so predictable that observers run toward the mountain, not away from it! The flows, however, can burst from fissures far from the center of the crater in areas that don't seem "active." This occurs mainly in the Puna district. In 1959, Kilauea Iki crater came to life after 91 years, and although the flow wasn't as massive as others, it did send blazing fountains of lava 1,900 feet into the air. Kilauea has been continuously active since 1983, with eruptions occurring at least once a month and expected to continue. Most activity, including the flow of 2015, has been from a vent below Pu'u O'o crater. You might be lucky enough to see this phenomenon while visiting.

Volcanoes as Island Builders

The Hawaiians worshiped Madame Pele, the fire goddess whose name translates equally well as Volcano, Fire Pit, or Eruption of Lava. When she was angry, she complained by spitting fire, which cooled and formed land. Volcanologists say that the islands are hu mounds of cooled basaltic lava surrounde

Kilauea volcano caldera and crater

erupted about every two or three centuries. In 1929 it suffered an earthquake swarm, which means that a large movement of lava inside the mountain caused tremors. United States Geological Survey (USGS) scientists now consider Mount Hualalai only dormant and very likely to erupt at some point in the future. When it does, a tremendous amount of lava is expected to pour rapidly down its steep sides. From the side of this mountain grows the cone Pu'u Wa'awa'a. At 3,967 feet, it's only slightly shorter than the very active Kilauea on the far side of Mauna Loa. Obsidian is found here, and this is one of the few places in Hawaii where this substance has been quarried in large quantities.

Even though **Mauna Loa** (Long Mountain) measures a respectable 13,679 feet, its height isn't its claim to fame. This active volcano, 60 miles long by 30 wide, comprises 19,000 cubic miles of lava, making it the densest and most massive mountain on earth. In 1950, a tremendous lava flow belched from Mauna Loa's summit, reaching an astonishing rate billions of polyp skeletons that have formed coral reefs. The Hawaiian Islands are shield volcanoes that erupt gently and form an elongated dome much like a turtle shell. The Big Island is a perfect example of this. Once above sea level, its tremendous weight sealed the fissure below. Eventually the giant tube that carried lava to the surface sunk in on itself and formed a caldera, as evidenced atop Kilauea. More eruptions occur periodically, and they cover the already existing island like frosting on a titanic cake. From there, wind and water take over and relentlessly sculpt the raw lava into deep crevices and cuts that become valleys. The most dramatic of these scars occur as the numerous gulches and valleys on the northeast side of the Big Island. Because of less rain and runoff, the west side is smoother, more uniform, and much less etched.

Lava

Lava flows in two distinct types, for which the Hawaiian names have become universal geological terms: **'a'a** and **pahoehoe.** They're easily distinguishable in appearance, but chemically they're the same. 'A'a is extremely rough and spiny and will quickly tear up your shoes if you do much hiking over it. Also, if you have the misfortune to fall down, you'll immediately know why they call it 'a'a. Pahoehoe, a billowy, rope-like lava resembling burned pancake batter, can mold into fantastic shapes. Examples of both types of lava are frequently encountered on various hikes throughout the Big Island. Other lava oddities you may spot are peridots (green, gemlike stones called Pele's diamonds); clear, feldsparlike, white cotton candy called Pele's hair; and gray lichens known as Hawaiian snow covering the older flows.

As it is relatively young, the Big Island has had less time than the other islands in the chain to be broken down by the forces of wind and rain. Yet, even here, there are areas, particularly in the north on the slopes of the Kohala Mountains, where a thick layer of soil sustains lush grasses and vegetation.

Tsunamis

Tsunami is the Japanese word for tidal wave. Its mention sparks terror in human beings. But if you were to count up all the people in Hawaii who have been swept away by tidal waves in the last 50 years, the toll wouldn't come close to those killed on bicycles in only a few Mainland cities in just five years. A Hawaiian tsunami is actually a seismic sea wave generated by an earthquake or underwater landslide that could easily have originated thousands of miles away in South America or Alaska. Some waves have been clocked at speeds up to 500 mph. The safest place during a tsunami, besides high ground well away from beach areas, is out on the open ocean, where even an enormous wave is perceived only as a large swell. A tidal wave is only dangerous when it is opposed by land. The Big Island has been struck with the two worst tidal waves in Hawaii's modern history. A giant wave smashed the island on April 1, 1946, and swept away 159 people and over 1,300 homes. Hilo sustained most of these losses, but Waipi'o Valley was washed clean, devastating the community there, and the schoolyard at Laupahoehoe Point was awash in water, dragging 20 schoolchildren and a teacher to their deaths. On May 23, 1960, Hilo again took the brunt of a wave that rumbled through its business district, killing 61 people. As a result of a major earthquake in Japan on March 11, 2011, Hawaii again experienced a tsunami. No lives were lost to the tsunami, but there was substantial damage to homes and several resorts on the Kona side. The tsunami wave also caused significant change to the shape of the some of the beaches in the Kona area.

Earthquakes

Earthquakes are a concern in Hawaii, and they present a double threat because they can generate tsunamis. If you ever feel a tremor and are close to a beach, get as far away as fast as possible. The Big Island, because of its active volcanoes, experiences hundreds of technical earthquakes, although 99 percent can only be felt by very delicate equipment. In the last two decades, the Big Island has experienced about one earthquake a year in the range of 5.0-6.0 on the Richter scale, which accounts for about 60 percent of all quakes of that magnitude in the state. The last major quake on the Big Island occurred in late November 1975, reaching 7.2 on the Richter scale and causing many millions of dollars' worth of damage in the island's southern regions. The only loss of life occurred when a beach collapsed and two people from a large camping party drowned. Like the other islands, the Big Island has an elaborate warning system against natural disasters. You will notice loudspeakers high atop poles along many beaches and coastal areas; these warn of tsunamis, hurricanes, and earthquakes. The loudspeakers are tested at 11am on the first working day of each month. All island telephone books contain a civil defense warning and procedures section with which you should acquaint yourself—note the maps showing which areas traditionally have been inundated by tsunamis, and what procedures to follow in case an emergency occurs.

Beaches and Ponds

The Big Island takes the rap for having poor beaches—this isn't true! They are certainly few and far between, but many of them are spectacular. Hawai'i is big and young, so distances are greater than on other islands, and the wave action hasn't had enough time to grind much new lava and coral into sand. The Kona and South Kohala Coast beaches, along with a few nooks and crannies around Hilo, are gorgeous. Each of the large valleys along the rugged North Kohala Coast—Waipi'o, Waimanu, and Pololu—has a long beach of gray sand. Harder to get to, these beaches have a greater reward because of their isolation. The beaches of Puna and Ka'u are of incredible black sand, a few only years old, and the southern tip of the island has a hidden green-sand beach or two enjoyed only by those intrepid enough to get to them.

Just north of the Kona International

Airport is Makalawena, a beautiful white-sand beach. Inland is its associated wetland pond, one of the most important on the Big Island. Other coastal ponds on the Kona side are located in Kaloko-Honokohau National Historical Park, just north of the Honokohau Harbor, at Kiholo Bay, and at the Kona Village, Waikoloa, and Mauna Lani resorts. On the Hilo side, the most well known, perhaps, are the ponds in Lili'uokalani Gardens in Hilo and at Kapoho in Puna.

Land Ownership

The County of Hawai'i comprises over 2.5 million acres. Of this total, the state controls about 800,000 acres, mostly forest preserves and undeveloped land; the federal government holds large acreage in Hawai'i Volcanoes National Park, Pohakuloa Training Area, and Hakalau Forest National Wildlife Refuge. Large landowners control most of the rest except for about 116,000 acres of Hawaiian Homelands. The major large landowners are the Bishop Estate, Parker Ranch, and the Samuel Damon Estate.

CLIMATE

The average temperature around the island varies between 72 and 78°F. Summers raise the temperature to the mid-80s and winters cool off to the low 70s. Both Kona and Hilo maintain a year-round average of about 74°F, and the South Kohala Coast is a few degrees warmer. As usual, it's cooler in the higher elevations, and Waimea sees most days in the mid-60s to low 70s, while Volcano maintains a relatively steady 60°F. Atop Mauna Kea, the temperature rarely climbs above 50°F or dips below 30°F, while the summit of Mauna Loa is about 10 degrees warmer. The lowest recorded temperature on the Big Island (and for the state) was 12°F at the Mauna Kea summit in May 1979, while the highest ever recorded was in April 1931 at Pahala in Ka'u—a scorching (for Hawaii) 100°F.

Altitude drops temperatures about three degrees for every 1,000 feet; if you intend to visit the mountain peaks of Mauna Loa a

Mauna Kea (both over 13,000 feet), expect the temperature to be at least 30 degrees cooler than at sea level. On occasion, snows atop Mauna Kea last well into June, with nighttime temperatures at or below freezing.

The Big Island is indeed big—and tall. With its arid desert regions, tropical rain forests, temperate upland areas, and frigid alpine slopes, the island has 11 of 13 climatic zones.

The winter months (December through February) tend to have more rain, but in the last few years that has been unpredictable. Generally speaking, the Kona side (the island's west side) tends to have less rain than the Hilo side (or east side) of the island.

Kona Winds

Kona means leeward in Hawaiian, and when the trades stop blowing, these southerly winds often take over. To anyone from Hawaii, "Kona wind" is a euphemism for bad weather, because it brings in hot, sticky air. Luckily, Kona winds are most common October-April, when they appear roughly half the time. The temperatures drop slightly during the winter so these hot winds are tolerable, and even useful for moderating the thermometer. In the summer they are awful, but luckily—again— they hardly ever blow during this season.

A Kona storm is another matter. These subtropical low-pressure storms develop west of the Hawaiian Islands, and as they move east they draw winds up from the south. Usually occurring only in winter, they can cause considerable damage to crops and real estate. There is no real pattern to Kona storms— some years they come every few weeks while in other years they don't appear at all.

Plants and Animals

Anyone who loves a mystery will be intrigued by the speculation about how plants and animals first came to Hawaii. Most people's idea of an island paradise includes swaying palms, dense mysterious jungles ablaze with wildflowers, and luscious fruits just waiting to be plucked. In fact, for millions of years the Hawaiian chain consisted of raw and barren islands where no plants grew and no birds sang. Why? Because they are geological orphans that spontaneously popped up in the middle of the Pacific Ocean. The islands, more than 2,000 miles from any continental landfall, were therefore isolated from the normal ecological spread of plants and animals. Even the most tenacious travelers of the flora and fauna kingdoms would be sorely tried in crossing the mighty Pacific. Those that made it by pure chance found a totally foreign ecosystem. They had to adapt or perish. The survivors evolved quickly, and many plants and birds became so specialized that they were limited not only to specific islands in the chain but to habitats that frequently consisted of a single isolated valley. It was as if after traveling so far, and finding a niche, they never budged again. Luckily, the soil of Hawaii was virgin and rich, the competition from other plants or animals was nonexistent, and the climate was sufficiently varied and nearly perfect for most growing things.

The evolution of plants and animals on the isolated islands was astonishingly rapid. A tremendous change in environment, coupled with a limited gene pool, accelerated natural selection. For example, many plants lost their protective thorns and spines because there were no grazing animals or birds to destroy them. Before settlement, Hawaii had no fruits, vegetables, coconut palms, edible land animals, conifers, mangroves, or banyans. The early Polynesians brought 27 varieties of plants that they needed for food and other purposes. About 90 percent of plants on the Hawaiian Islands today were introduced after Captain Cook first set foot here. Tropical flowers, wild and vibrant as we know them today, were relatively few. In a land where thousands of orchids now brighten every corner, there were only four native varieties, the least in any of the 50 states. Today, the indigenous plants and animals have the highest rate of extinction anywhere on earth. By the beginning of the 20th century, native plants growing below 1,500 feet in elevation were almost completely extinct or totally replaced by introduced species. The land and its living things have been greatly transformed by humans and their agriculture. This inexorable process began when Hawaii was the domain of its original Polynesian settlers, and it greatly accelerated when the land was inundated by Western peoples.

The indigenous plants and birds of the Big Island have suffered the same fate as those of the other Hawaiian Islands; they're among the most endangered species on earth and disappearing at an alarming rate. There are some sanctuaries on the Big Island where native species still live, but they must be vigorously protected. Do your bit to save them; enjoy but do not disturb.

PLANTS
Introduced Plants
Hawaii's indigenous and endemic plants, flowers, and trees are both fascinating and beautiful, but, unfortunately, like everything else that was native, they are quickly disappearing. The majority of flora considered exotic by visitors was introduced either by the original Polynesians or by later white settlers. The Polynesians who colonized Hawaii brought foodstuffs, including coconuts, bananas, taro, breadfruit, sweet potatoes, yams, and sugarcane. They also carried along gourds to use as containers, *'awa* (kava) to make a basic intoxicant, and the ti plant to use for offerings or to string into hula skirts. Non-Hawaiian settlers over the years have brought mangoes, papayas, passion fruit, pineapples, and the other tropical fruits and vegetables associated with the islands. Also, most of the flowers, including protea, plumeria, anthuriums, orchids, heliconia, ginger, and most hibiscus, have come from every continent on earth. Tropical America, Asia, Java, India, and China have contributed their most beautiful and delicate blooms. Hawaii is blessed with national and state parks, gardens, undisturbed rain forests, private reserves, and commercial nurseries that offer an exhaustive botanical survey of the island. The following is a sampling of the common native and introduced flora that add dazzling color and exotic tastes to the landscape.

Native Trees
Koa and *'ohi'a* are two indigenous trees still seen on the Big Island. Both have been greatly reduced by the foraging of introduced cattle and goats, and through logging and forest fires. The **koa,** a form of acacia, is Hawaii's finest native tree. It can grow to over 70 feet high and has a strong, straight trunk that can measure more than 10 feet in circumference. Koa is a very quick-growing legume that fixes nitrogen in the soil. It is believed that the tree originated in Africa, where the climate was very damp. It then migrated to Australia, where it was very dry, which caused the elimination of leaves, so all that was left were bare stems that could survive in the desert climate. When koa came to the Pacific islands, instead of reverting to the true leaf of its original form, its leaf stem simply broadened into sickle-shaped, leaflike foliage that produces an inconspicuous, pale-yellow flower. When the tree is young or damaged it will revert to the original feathery, fernlike leaf that evolved in Africa millions of years ago. The koa does best in well-drained soil in deep forest areas, but scruffy specimens will grow on poorer soil. The Hawaiians used koa as the main log for their dugout canoes, and elaborate ceremonies were performed when a log was cut and dragged to a canoe shed. Koa wood was also preferred for paddles, spears, and even surfboards. Today it is still considered an excellent furniture wood. Although fine specimens can be found in the reserve of Hawai'i Volcanoes National Park, loggers elsewhere are harvesting the last of th big trees.

The *'ohi'a* is a survivor and therefore the most abundant of all the native Hawaiian trees. Coming in a variety of shapes and sizes, it grows as miniature trees in wet bogs or as 100-foot giants on cool, dark slopes at higher elevations. This tree is often the first life in new lava flows. The *'ohi'a* produces a tuftlike flower—usually red, but occasionally orange, yellow, or white, the latter being very rare and elusive—that resembles a pompon. The flower was considered sacred to Pele; it was said that she would cause a rainstorm if *'ohi'a* blossoms were picked without the proper prayers. The flowers were fashioned into lei that resembled feather boas. The strong, hard wood was used to make canoes, poi bowls, and especially temple images. *'Ohi'a* logs were also used as railroad ties and shipped to the Mainland from Pahoa. It's believed that the golden spike linking rail lines between the U.S. East and West Coasts was driven into a Puna *'ohi'a* log when the two railroads came together in northern Utah.

Tropical Rain Forests

When it comes to pure and diverse natural beauty, the United States is one of the finest pieces of real estate on earth. As if purple mountains' majesty and fruited plains weren't enough, it even received a tiny, living emerald of tropical rain forest. A tropical rain forest is where the earth takes a breath and exhales pure, sweet oxygen through its vibrant green canopy. Located in the territories of Puerto Rico and the Virgin Islands and in the state of Hawaii, the rain forests of the United States make up only one-half of 1 percent of the world's total, and they must be preserved. The U.S. Congress passed two bills in 1986 designed to protect the unique biological diversity of the country's tropical areas, but their destruction has continued unabated. The lowland rain forests of Hawaii, populated mostly by native *'ohi'a,* are being razed. Landowners slash, burn, and bulldoze them to create more land for cattle and agriculture and, most distressingly, for wood chips to generate electricity! Introduced wild boars gouge the forest floor, exposing sensitive roots and leaving tiny, fetid ponds where mosquito larvae thrive. Feral goats roam the forests like hoofed locusts and strip all vegetation within reach. Rainforests on the higher and steeper slopes of mountains have a better chance, as they are harder for humans to reach. One unusual feature of Hawaii's rain forests is that they are "upside down": Most plant and animal species live on the forest

Breadfruit, known as *ulu*

floor, rather than in the canopy as in other forests.

Almost half of the birds classified in the United States as endangered live in Hawaii, and almost all of these make their homes in the rain forests. We can only lament the passing of the rain forests that have already fallen to ignorance, but if this ill-fated destruction continues on a global level, we will be lamenting our own passing. We must nurture the rain forests that remain, and, with simple enlightenment, let them be.

ANIMALS
Birds

One of the great tragedies of natural history is the continuing demise of Hawaiian birdlife. Perhaps only 15 original species of birds remain of the more than 70 native families that thrived before the coming of humans. Since the arrival of Captain Cook in 1778, 23 species have become extinct, with several more in danger. And what's not known is how many species were wiped out before white explorers arrived. Experts believe that the Hawaiians annihilated about 40 species, including seven species of geese, a rare one-legged owl, ibises, lovebirds, sea eagles, and honeycreepers—all gone before Captain Cook arrived. Hawaii's endangered birds account for 40 percent of the birds officially listed as endangered or threatened by the U.S. Fish and Wildlife Service. In the last 200 years, more than four times as many birds have become extinct in Hawaii as in all of North America. These figures unfortunately suggest that a full 40 percent of Hawaii's endemic birds no longer exist. Almost all of O'ahu's native birds are gone, and few indigenous Hawaiian birds can be found on any island below the 3,000-foot level.

Native birds have been reduced in number because of multiple factors. The original Polynesians helped wipe out many species. They altered large areas for farming and used fire to destroy patches of pristine forests. Also, bird feathers were highly prized for making lei, for featherwork in capes and helmets,

and for the large *kahili* fans that indicated rank among the *ali'i*. Introduced exotic birds and the new diseases they carried are another major reason for reduction of native bird numbers, along with predation by the mongoose and rat—especially upon ground-nesting birds. Bird malaria and bird pox were also devastating to the native species. Mosquitoes, unknown in Hawaii until a ship named the *Wellington* introduced them at Lahaina in 1826 through larvae carried in its water barrels, infected most native birds, causing a rapid reduction in birdlife. Feral pigs rooting deep in the rain forests knock over ferns and small trees, creating fetid pools in which mosquito larvae thrive. However, the most damaging factor by far is the assault upon native forests by agriculture and land developers. The vast majority of Hawaiian birds evolved into specialists. They lived in only one small area and ate a very limited number of plants or insects, which once removed or altered soon killed the birds.

You'll spot birds all over the Big Island, from the coastal areas to the high mountain slopes. Some are found on other islands as well, but the indigenous ones listed here are found only or mainly on the Big Island. Every bird listed is either threatened or endangered.

HAWAII'S OWN

The *nene,* or Hawaiian goose, deserves special mention because it is Hawaii's state bird and is making a comeback from the edge of extinction. The *nene* is found only on the slopes of Mauna Loa, Hualalai, and Mauna Kea on the Big Island; in Haleakala Crater on Maui; and at a few spots on Moloka'i and Kaua'i. It was extinct on Maui until a few birds were returned there in 1957, but some experts maintain that the *nene* lived naturally only on the Big Island. *Nene* are raised at the Wildfowl Trust in Slimbridge, England, which placed the first birds at Haleakala; and at the Hawaiian Fish and Game Station at Pohakuloa, along the Saddle Road on Hawai'i. By the 1940s, fewer than 50 birds lived in the wild. Now approximately 125 birds live on Haleakala and 500 on the Big Island. Although the birds can be raised successfully in captivity, their ability to survive in the wild is still in question.

The *nene* is believed to be a descendant of the Canada goose, which it resembles. Geese are migratory birds that form strong kinship ties, mating for life. It's speculated that a migrating goose became disabled and, along with its loyal mate, remained in Hawaii. The *nene* is smaller than its Canadian cousin, has lost a great deal of webbing in its feet, and is perfectly at home away from water, often foraging and nesting on rugged and bleak lava flows, although it also lives in coastal regions and on grassy mountainsides.

Good places to view *nene* are in Hawai'i Volcanoes National Park at Kipuka Nene Campground, the summit caldera, Devastation Trail, and Volcano Golf and Country Club, at dawn and dusk. The birds gather at the golf course because they love to feed on grasses. The places to view them on the Kona side are Pu'ulani, a housing development north of Kailua-Kona; or Kaloko Mauka, another housing development on the slopes of Mount Hualalai. At the top of the road up Mount Hualalai is a trail, also a good place to see the *nene*. Unfortunately, as the housing developments proliferate and the residents invariably acquire dogs and cats, the *nene* will disappear. The *nene* is a perfect symbol of Hawaii: Let it be, and it will live.

The **Hawaiian crow,** or *alala,* is reduced to fewer than 12 birds living on the slopes of Hualalai and Mauna Loa above the 3,000-foot level. It looks like the common raven but has a more melodious voice and, sometimes, dull-brown wing feathers. The *alala* breeds in early spring, and the greenish-blue, black-flecked eggs hatch from April to June. It is extremely nervous while nesting, and any disturbance will cause it to abandon its young.

The **Hawaiian hawk** *('io)* primarily lives on the slopes of Mauna Loa and Mauna Kea below 9,000 feet. It travels from there to other parts of the island and can often be seen kiting in the skies over Hawai'i Volcanoes National

Park, upland from Kailua-Kona, and in remote spots like Waimanu Valley. This noble bird, the royalty of the skies, symbolized the *ali'i* (Hawaiian royalty). The *'io* population was once dwindling, and many scientists feared that the bird was headed for extinction. The hawk exists only on the Big Island for reasons that are not entirely clear. The good news is that the *'io* is making a dramatic comeback, also for reasons still unclear. Speculation is that it may be gaining resistance to some diseases, including malaria, or that it may have learned how to prey on the introduced rats, or even that it may be adapting to life in macadamia nut groves and other alternative habitats.

The **'akiapola'au,** a honeycreeper, is a five-inch-long yellow bird hardly bigger than its name. It lives mainly on the eastern slopes in *'ohi'a* and koa forests above 3,500 feet. It has a long, curved upper beak for probing and a smaller lower beak that it uses in woodpecker fashion. The *'akiapola'au* opens its mouth wide, strikes the wood with its lower beak, and then uses the upper beak to scrape out any larvae or insects. Listen for the distinctive rapping sound to spot this melodious singer. The *'akiapola'au* can be seen at the Hakalau Forest National Wildlife Refuge and along the Pu'u O'o Trail in Hawai'i Volcanoes National Park. It's estimated that only about 1,000 of these birds, one of the rarest of the island's rare winged creatures, are left.

Two other endangered birds of the Big Island are the **koloa maoli,** a duck that resembles the mallard, and the slate-gray or white *'alae ke'oke'o* coot.

Other Hawaiian Animals

Hawaii had only two indigenous mammals, the monk seal or *'ilio holu i ka uaua* (found mostly in the Northwestern Hawaiian Islands) and the hoary bat (found primarily on the Big Island); both are threatened and endangered. The rest of the Big Island's mammals are transplants. But like anything else that has been in the islands long enough, including people, they take on characteristics that make them "local." There are no native amphibians, reptiles, ants, termites, or cockroaches. These have all been imported.

Among the transplants are the Indian mongoose and coqui tree frogs. The squirrel-like mongooses were brought to the Hawaiian Islands in 1883 to kill the rats eating up the sugarcane crops. And then it was learned that mongooses and rats have different sleeping schedules. Now they are an invasive species that is a menace to many of the native species. You'll see them often as roadkill. The coqui tree frog, a small light-brown to dark-colored frog native to Puerto Rico, is another invasive species—a loud one. Their noise levels have been measured at up to 80-90 decibels, comparable to the noise produced by a lawnmower. Many areas have tried to eradicate them, but they are still present in droves on the island. They are particularly bad in Hilo, where you can hear them "singing" all night long (it actually sounds like they are singing "coqui, coqui").

Marine Life

The **humpback whale,** known in Hawaii as *kohola*, migrates to Hawaiian waters yearly, arriving in late December and departing by mid-May. While whales can be seen anywhere around the Big Island, some of the best places to view them are along the South Kona Coast, especially at Keauhou, Kealakekua Bay, and Ka Lae (South Point), with many sightings off the Puna Coast around Isaac Hale Beach Park, and from the luxury resorts of the South Kohala area.

Hawai'i Volcanoes National Park stretches from the top of Mauna Kea all the way down to the sea. It is here, around Apua Point, that three of the last known nesting sites of the very endangered **hawksbill turtle** (*honu'ea*) are found. This creature has been ravaged in the Pacific, where it is ruthlessly hunted for its shell, which is made into women's jewelry, especially combs. It is illegal to bring items made from turtle shell into the United States, but the hunt goes on.

While they can be seen more often, **green sea turtles** (*honu*) are also endangered. Periodically, they haul themselves up on a beach to rest and warm up. This is normal and they are okay, even when their mottled green shell begins to turn a bit dusky white. Leave them alone in or out of the water; don't disturb or get too close to them. They'll return to the water when they are good and ready.

Although magnificent game fish live in various South Sea and Hawaiian waters,

Green sea turtles frequent the beaches of the Big Island.

catching them is easiest in the clear, smooth waters off the Kona Coast. The billfish—swordfish, sailfish, marlin, and *a'u*—share two distinctive common features: a long, spearlike or swordlike snout and a prominent dorsal fin. The three main species of billfish caught here are the blue, striped, and black marlin. Of these three, the **blue marlin** is the leading game fish in Kona waters. The blue has tipped the scales at well over 1,000 pounds, but the average fish weighs in at 300-400 pounds. When alive, this fish is a striking cobalt blue, but death brings a color change to slate blue. It feeds on skipjack tuna; throughout the summer, fishing boats look for schools of tuna as a tip-off to blues in the area. The **black marlin** is the largest and most coveted catch for blue-water anglers. This solitary fish is infrequently found in the banks off Kona. Granddaddies can weigh 1,800 pounds, but the average is a mere 200. The **striped marlin** is the most common commercial billfish, a highly prized food served in finer restaurants and often sliced into sashimi. Its coloration is a remarkable royal blue. It leaps spectacularly when caught, giving it a great reputation as a fighter. The striped marlin is smaller than the other marlins, so a 100-pounder is a very good catch.

History

The Big Island plays a significant role in Hawaii's history. A long list of "firsts" occurred here. Historians generally believe (backed up by the oral tradition) that the Big Island was the first in the Hawaiian chain to be settled by the Polynesians. Hawaii is geographically the closest island to Polynesia; Mauna Loa and especially Mauna Kea, with its white summit, present easily spotted landmarks. Psychologically, the Polynesian wayfarers would have been very attracted to Hawai'i as a lost homeland. Compared to Tahiti and most other South Sea islands (except Fiji), it's huge. It *looked* like the promised land. Some may wonder why the Polynesians chose to live atop an obviously active volcano and not bypass it for a more congenial island. The volcanism of the Big Island is comparatively gentle; the lava flows follow predictable routes and rarely turn killer. The animistic Hawaiians would have been drawn to live where the godly forces of nature were so apparent. The mana (power) would be exceptionally strong, and therefore the *ali'i* would great. Human sacrifice was introduced waii at Waha'ula Heiau in the Puna in the 13th century, and from there *luakini* (human-sacrifice temples) spread throughout the islands.

THE ROAD FROM TAHITI
The Great Navigators

No one knows exactly when the first Polynesians arrived in Hawaii, but the great "deliberate migrations" from the southern islands seem to have taken place AD 500-800; anthropologists keep pushing the date backward in time as new evidence becomes available. Even before that, however, it's reasonable to assume that the first people to set foot on Hawaiian soil were probably fishermen, or perhaps defeated warriors whose canoes were blown hopelessly northward into unfamiliar waters. They arrived by a combination of extraordinary good luck and an uncanny ability to sail and navigate without instruments (to wayfind), using the sun by day and the moon and rising stars by night. They could feel the water and determine direction by swells, tides, and currents. The movements of fish and cloud formations were also utilized to determine direction. Since these men's arrival was probably an accident, they were unprepared to settle on the fertile but uncultivated lands, having no stock animals, plant cuttings, or women. Forced to return south-ward, many undoubtedly lost their lives at sea, but a few wild-eyed stragglers must have made it home to tell tales of a paradise to the north where land was plentiful and the sea bounte-ous. This is affirmed by ancient navigational chants from Tahiti, Moorea, and Bora Bora, which passing from father to son revealed how to follow the stars to the "heavenly homeland in the north." Possibly a few migrations fol-lowed, but it's known that for centuries there was no real reason for a mass exodus, so the chants alone remained and eventually became shadowy legend.

Where They Came From

It's generally agreed that the first planned migrations were from the violent canni-bal islands that Spanish explorers called the Marquesas, 11 islands in extreme eastern Polynesia. The islands themselves are harsh and inhospitable, breeding a toughness into these people that enabled them to withstand the hardships of long, unsure ocean voyages and years of resettlement. Marquesans were a fiercely independent people whose chiefs could rise from the ranks because of brav-ery or intelligence. They must have also been a savage-looking lot. Both men and women tattooed themselves in complex blue pat-terns from head to foot. The warriors car-ried massive, intricately designed ironwood war clubs and wore carved whale teeth in slits in their earlobes that eventually stretched to the shoulders. They shaved the sides of their heads with sharks' teeth, tied their hair in two topknots that looked like horns, and rubbed their heavily muscled and tattooed bodies with scented coconut oils. Their cults wor-shiped mummified ancestors; the bodies of warriors of defeated neighboring tribes were consumed. They were masters at building great double-hulled canoes launched from huge canoe sheds. Two hulls were fastened together to form a catamaran, and a hut in the center provided shelter in bad weather. The average voyaging canoe was 60-80 feet long and could comfortably hold an extended

family of about 30 people. These small family bands carried all the staples they would need in the new lands.

For five centuries the Marquesans settled and lived peacefully on the new land, as if Hawaii's *aloha* spirit overcame most of their fierceness. The tribes coexisted in relative harmony, especially since there was no competition for land. Cannibalism died out. There was much coming and going between Hawaii and Polynesia as new people came to settle for hundreds of years. Then, it appears that in the 12th century a deliberate exodus of warlike Tahitians arrived and subjugated the settled islanders. This incursion had a terrific significance on the Hawaiian religious and social system. Oral tradition relates that a Tahitian priest, Pa'ao, found the mana of the Hawaiian chiefs to be low, signifying that their gods were weak. Pa'ao built a *heiau* at Waha'ula on the Big Island, then introduced the warlike god Ku and the rigid *kapu* system through which the new rulers became dominant. Voyages between Tahiti and Hawaii continued for about 100 years, and Tahitian customs, legends, and language became the Hawaiian way of life. Then suddenly, for no recorded or apparent reason, the voyages discontinued and Hawaii returned to total isolation.

RE-DISCOVERY

The late 18th century was an extraordinary time in Hawaiian history. Monumental changes seemed to happen all at once. First, Captain James Cook, a Yorkshire farm boy fulfilling his destiny as the all-time greatest Pacific explorer, found Hawaii for the rest of the world. For better or worse, it could no lon-ger be an isolated Polynesian homeland. For the first time in Hawaiian history, a charis-matic leader, Kamehameha, emerged, and after a long civil war he united all the islands into one centralized kingdom. The death of Captain Cook in Hawaii marked the be-ginning of a long series of tragic misunde standings between whites and natives. Wh Kamehameha died in 1819, the old reli system of *kapu* came to an end, leaving the Hawaiians in a spiritual vortex. Many takers arrived to fill the void: missionaries after souls, whalers after their prey and a good time, traders and planters after profits and a home. The islands were opened and devoured like ripe fruit. Powerful nations, including Russia, Great Britain, France, and the United States, yearned to bring this strategic Pacific jewel under their own influence.

Captain Cook

In 1776 Captain James Cook set sail for the Pacific from Plymouth, England, on his third and final expedition into this still largely unexplored region of the world. On a fruitless quest for the fabled Northwest Passage across the North American continent, he sailed down the coast of Africa, rounded the Cape of Good Hope, crossed the Indian Ocean, and traveled past New Zealand, Tasmania, and the Friendly Islands (where the "friendly" natives hatched an unsuccessful plot to murder him). On January 18, 1778, Captain Cook's 100-foot flagship, HMS *Resolution,* and its 90-foot companion, HMS *Discovery,* sighted O'ahu. Two days later, they sighted Kaua'i and went ashore at the village of Waimea. Though anxious to get on with his mission, Cook decided to make a quick sortie to investigate this new land and reprovision his ships. He did, however, take time to remark in his diary about the close resemblance of these newfound people to others he had encountered as far south as New Zealand and marveled at their widespread habitation across the Pacific.

Almost a year later, when winter weather forced Cook to return from the coast of Alaska, his discovery began to take on far-reaching significance. Cook had named Hawaii the Sandwich Islands in honor of one of his patrons, John Montague, the Earl of Sandwich. On this return voyage, he spotted Maui on November 26, 1778. After eight weeks of seeking a suitable harbor, the ships passed it, but not before the coastline was drawn by Lieutenant William Bligh, one of Cook's finest and most trusted officers. (Bligh would find his own drama almost 10 years later as commander of the infamous HMS *Bounty.*) The *Discovery* and *Resolution* finally found safe anchorage at Kealakekua Bay on the Kona Coast of the Big Island. It is very lucky for history that on board was Mr. Anderson, ship's chronicler, who left a handwritten record of the strange and tragic events that followed. Even more important were the drawings of John Webber, ship's artist, who rendered invaluable impressions in superb drawings and etchings. Other noteworthy men aboard were George Vancouver, who would lead the first British return to Hawaii after Cook's death and introduce many fruits, vegetables, cattle, sheep, and goats; and James Burney, who would become a long-standing authority on the Pacific.

By all accounts Cook was a humane and just captain, greatly admired by his men. Unlike many supremacists of that time, he was known to have a respectful attitude toward any people he discovered, treating them as equals and recognizing the significance of their cultures. Not known as a violent man, he would use his superior weapons against natives only in an absolute case of self-defense. His hardened crew had been at sea facing untold hardship for almost three years; returning to Hawaii was truly like reentering paradise.

A strange series of coincidences sailed with Cook into Kealakekua Bay on January 16, 1779. It was *makahiki* time, a period of rejoicing and festivity dedicated to the fertility god of the earth, Lono. Normal *kapu* days were suspended and willing partners freely enjoyed each other sexually, as well as dancing, feasting, and the islands' version of Olympic games. It was long held in Hawaiian legend that the great god Lono would return to earth. Lono's image was a small wooden figure perched on a tall, mast-like crossbeam; hanging from the crossbeam were long, white sheets of tapa. Who else could Cook be but Lono, and what else could his ships with their masts and white sails be but his sacred floating *heiau*? This explained the Hawaiians' previous fascination with his ships, but to add to the remarkable coincidence, Kealakekua Harbor happened to be considered Lono's private sacred harbor. Natives from throughout the land prostrated themselves and paid homage to the returning god. Cook was taken ashore and brought to Lono's sacred temple, where he was afforded the highest respect. The ships badly needed fresh supplies so the Hawaiians readily gave all they had, stretching their own provisions to the limit. To the sailors' delight, this included full measures of the *aloha* spirit.

The Fatal Misunderstanding

After an uproarious welcome and generous hospitality for over a month, it became obvious that the newcomers were beginning to overstay their welcome. During the interim a seaman named William Watman died, convincing the Hawaiians that the *haole* were indeed mortals, not gods. Incidents of petty theft began to increase dramatically. The lesser chiefs indicated it was time to leave by "rubbing the Englishmen's bellies." Inadvertently many *kapu* were broken by the Englishmen, and once-friendly relations became strained. Finally, the ships sailed away on February 4, 1779.

After plying terrible seas for only a week, *Resolution*'s foremast was badly damaged. Cook sailed back into Kealakekua Bay, dragging the mast ashore on February 13. The natives, now totally hostile, hurled rocks at the sailors. Orders were given to load muskets with ball; firearms had previously only been loaded with shot and a light charge. Confrontations increased when some Hawaiians stole a small boat and Cook's men set after them, capturing the fleeing canoe, which held an *ali'i* named Palea. The English treated him roughly; to the Hawaiians' horror, they even smacked him on the head with a paddle. The Hawaiians then furiously attacked the mariners, who abandoned the small boat.

Next the Hawaiians stole a small cutter

from the *Discovery* that had been moored to a buoy and partially sunk to protect it from the sun. For the first time, Captain Cook became furious. He ordered Captain Clerk of the *Discovery* to sail to the southeast end of the bay and stop any canoe trying to leave Kealakekua. Cook then made a fatal error in judgment. He decided to take nine armed mariners ashore in an attempt to convince the venerable King Kalani'opu'u to accompany him back aboard ship, where he would hold him for ransom in exchange for the cutter. The old king agreed, but his wife prevailed upon him not to trust the *haole*. Kalani'opu'u sat down on the beach to think while the tension steadily grew.

Meanwhile, a group of sailors fired upon a canoe trying to leave the bay, and a lesser chief, No'okemai, was killed. The crowd around Cook and his men reached an estimated 20,000, and warriors outraged by the killing of the chief armed themselves with clubs and protective straw-mat armor. One bold warrior advanced on Cook and struck him with his *pahoa* (dagger). In retaliation, Cook drew a tiny pistol lightly loaded with shot and fired at the warrior. His bullets spent themselves on the straw armor and fell harmlessly to the ground. The Hawaiians went wild. Lieutenant Molesworth Phillips, in charge of the nine sailors, began a withering fire; Cook himself slew two natives.

Overpowered by sheer numbers, the sailors headed for boats standing offshore, while Lieutenant Phillips lay wounded. It is believed that Captain Cook, the greatest seaman ever to enter the Pacific, stood helplessly in knee-deep water instead of making for the boats because he could not swim! Hopelessly surrounded, he was knocked on the head, then countless warriors passed a knife around and hacked and mutilated his lifeless body. A sad Lieutenant King lamented in his diary, "Thus fell our great and excellent commander."

Captain Clerk, now in charge, settled his men and prevailed upon the Hawaiians to return Cook's body. On the morning of February 16 a grisly piece of charred meat w brought aboard: The Hawaiians, according to their custom, had afforded Cook the highest honor by baking his body in an underground oven to remove the flesh from the bones. On February 17 a group of Hawaiians in a canoe taunted the mariners by brandishing Cook's hat. The English, strained to the limit and thinking that Cook was being desecrated, finally broke. They leveled their cannons and muskets on shore and shot anything that moved. It is believed that Kamehameha the Great was wounded in this flurry, along with four *ali'i*, and 25 *maka'ainana* (commoners) were also killed. Finally, on February 21, 1779, the bones of Captain James Cook's hands, skull, arms, and legs were returned and tearfully buried at sea. A common seaman, one Mr. Zimmerman, summed up the feelings of all who sailed under Cook when he wrote, "He was our leading star." The English sailed the next morning after dropping off their Hawaiian girlfriends who were still aboard.

UNIFICATION

Hawaii was already in a state of political turmoil and civil war when Cook arrived. In the 1780s the islands were roughly divided into three kingdoms. War ravaged the land until a remarkable chief, Kamehameha, rose and subjugated all the islands under one rule. Kamehameha initiated a dynasty that would last for about 100 years, until the independent monarchy of Hawaii forever ceased to be.

To add a zing to this brewing political stew, Westerners and their technology were beginning to come in ever-increasing numbers. Hawaii under Kamehameha was ready to enter its "golden age." The social order was medieval, with the *ali'i* as knights owing their military allegiance to the king, and the serf-like *maka'ainana* paying tribute and working the lands. The priesthood of *kahuna* filled the posts of advisors, sorcerers, navigators, doctors, and historians. This was Polynesian Hawaii at its apex. But like the uniquely Hawaiian silversword plant, the old culture blossomed and, as soon as it 'id, began to wither. Ever since, all that was

purely Hawaiian has been supplanted by the relentless foreign influences that began bearing down upon it.

Young Kamehameha

The greatest native son of Hawaii, Kamehameha was born under mysterious circumstances in the Kohala district on the Big Island, probably in 1753. He was royal born to Keoua Kupuapaikalaninui, the chief of Kohala, and Kekuiapoiwa, a chieftess from Kona. Accounts vary, but one claims that before his birth, a *kahuna* prophesied that this child would grow to be a "killer of chiefs." Because of this, the local chiefs conspired to murder the infant. When Kekuiapoiwa's time came, she secretly went to the royal birthing stones near Mo'okini Heiau and delivered Kamehameha. She entrusted her baby to a manservant and instructed him to hide the child. He headed for the rugged and remote coast around Kapa'au. Here Kamehameha was raised in the mountains, mostly by men. Always alone, he earned the nickname "The Lonely One."

Kamehameha was a man noticed by everyone; there was no doubt he was a force to be reckoned with. He had met Captain Cook when the *Discovery* unsuccessfully tried to land at Hana on Maui. While aboard, he made a lasting impression, distinguishing himself from the multitude of natives swarming the ships by his royal bearing. Lieutenant James King, in a diary entry, remarked that Kamehameha was a fierce-looking man, almost ugly, but that he was obviously intelligent, observant, and very good-natured. Kamehameha received his early military training from his uncle Kalani'opu'u, the great king of Hawaii and Hana who fought fierce battles against Alapa'i, the usurper who stole his hereditary lands. After regaining Hawaii, Kalani'opu'u returned to his Hana district and turned his attention to conquering all of Maui. During this period young Kamehameha distinguished himself as a ferocious warrior and earned the nickname of "the hard-shelled crab."

Increasing Contact

By the time Kamehameha had won the Big Island, Hawaii was becoming a regular stopover for numerous ships seeking the lucrative sandalwood trade with China. In February 1791, Captain George Vancouver, still seeking the Northwest Passage, returned to Kealakekua, where he was greeted by a throng of 30,000.

The captain at once recognized Kamehameha, who was wearing a Chinese dressing gown that he had received in tribute from another chief who in turn had received it from Cook himself. The diary of a crew member, Thomas Manby, relates that Kamehameha, missing his front teeth, was more fierce-looking than ever as he approached the ship in an elegant double-hulled canoe propelled by 46 rowers. The king invited all to a great feast prepared for them on the beach. Kamehameha's appetite matched his tremendous size. It was noted that he ate two sizable fish, a king-sized bowl of poi, a small pig, and an entire baked dog. Kamehameha personally entertained the English by putting on a mock battle in which he deftly avoided spears by rolling, tumbling, and catching them in midair, all the while hurling his own spear a great distance. The English reciprocated by firing cannon bursts into the air, creating an impromptu fireworks display. Kamehameha requested from Vancouver a full table setting, with which he was provided, but his request for firearms was prudently denied.

Captain Vancouver became Kamehameha's trusted advisor and told him about the white man's form of worship. He even interceded for Kamehameha with his headstrong queen, Ka'ahumanu, and coaxed her from her hiding place under a rock when she sought refuge at Pu'uhonua O Honaunau. The captain gave gifts of beef cattle, fowl, and breeding stock of sheep and goats. The ship's naturalist, Archibald Menzies, was the first *haole* to climb Mauna Kea; he also introduced a large assortment of fruits and vegetables. The Hawaiians were cheerful and outgoing, and they showed remorse when they indicated that the remainder of Cook's bones had been buried at a temple close to Kealakekua. During the next two decades of Kamehameha's rule, the French, Russians, English, and Americans discovered the great whaling waters off Hawaii. Their increasingly frequent visits shook and finally tumbled the ancient religion and social order of *kapu*.

Kamehameha's Rule

Kamehameha was as gentle in victory as he was ferocious in battle. Under his rule, which lasted until his death on May 8, 1819, Hawaii enjoyed a peace unlike any the warring islands had ever known. The king moved his royal court to Lahaina, where in 1803 he built the Brick Palace, the first permanent building of Hawaii. The benevolent tyrant also enacted the "Law of the Splintered Paddle." This law, which protected the weak from exploitation by the strong, had its origins in an incident of many years before. A brave defender of a small, overwhelmed village had broken a paddle over Kamehameha's head and taught the chief—literally in one stroke—about the nobility of the commoner.

However, just as Old Hawaii reached its golden age, its demise was at hand. The relentless waves of *haole* innocently yet determinedly battered the old ways into the ground. With the foreign ships came prosperity and fanciful new goods after which the *ali'i* lusted. The *maka'ainana* were worked mercilessly to provide sandalwood for the China trade. This was the first "boom" economy to hit the islands, but it set the standard of exploitation that would follow. Kamehameha built an observation tower in Lahaina to watch for ships, many of which were his own, returning laden with riches from the world at large.

In the last years of his life Kamehameha returned to his beloved Kona Coast, where he enjoyed the excellent fishing renowned to this day. He had taken Hawaii from the darkness of warfare into the light of peace. He died true to the religious and moral *kapu* of his youth, the only ones he had ever known, and with him died a unique way of life. Two loyal retainers buried his bones after the baked flesh had been ceremoniously stripped away. A secret burial cave was chosen so that no one could desecrate the remains of the great chief, thereby absorbing his mana. The tomb's whereabouts remain unknown, and disturbing the dead remains one of the strictest *kapu* to this day. The Lonely One's kingdom would pass to his son, Liholiho, but true power would be in the hands of his beloved and feisty wife, Ka'ahumanu. As Kamehameha's spirit drifted from this earth, two forces sailing around Cape Horn would forever change Hawaii: the missionaries and the whalers.

MISSIONARIES AND WHALERS

The year 1819 was of the utmost significance in Hawaiian history. It marked the death of Kamehameha, the overthrow of the ancient *kapu* system, the arrival of the first "whaler" in Lahaina, and the departure of Calvinist missionaries from New England determined to convert the heathen islands. Great changes began to rattle the old order to its foundations. With the *kapu* system and all of the ancient gods abandoned (except for the fire goddess of Kilauea, Pele), a great void was left in the souls of the Hawaiians. In the coming decades Hawaii, also coveted by Russia, France, and England, was finally consumed by America. The islands had the first American school, printing press, and newspaper *(The Polynesian)* west of the Mississippi. Lahaina, in its heyday, became the world's greatest whaling port, accommodating over 500 ships of all types during its peak years. Sailors snatched brief pleasure in every port and jumped ship at every opportunity, especially in an easy berth like Lahaina. In exchange for *aloha,* they gave drunkenness and insidious death by disease—common conditions such as colds, flu, venereal disease, and sometimes smallpox and cholera devastated the Hawaiians, who had no natural immunities to these foreign ailments.

Into this vortex sailed the brig *Thaddeus* on April 4, 1820. Coming ashore at Kailua-Kona, the Reverends Bingham and Thurston were granted a one-year trial missionary period by King Liholiho. They established themselves on the Big Island and O'ahu and from there began the transformation of Hawaii. The missionaries were people of God, but also practical-minded Yankees. They brought education, enterprise, and most importantly, unlike the transient seafarers, a commitment to stay and build. By 1824, the new faith had such a foothold that Chieftess Keopuolani climbed to the fire pit atop Kilauea and defied Pele. Keopuolani ate forbidden *'ohelo* berries and cried out, "Jehovah is my God." Over the next decades the governing of Hawaii slipped away from the Big Island and moved to the new port cities of Lahaina on Maui and, later, Honolulu.

The year 1824 also marked the death of Keopuolani, who was given a Christian burial. She had set the standard by accepting Christianity, and a number of the *ali'i* had followed the queen's lead. Liholiho had sailed off to England, where he and his wife contracted measles and died.

During these years, Ka'ahumanu allied herself with Reverend Richards, pastor of the first mission in the islands, and together they wrote Hawaii's first code of laws based upon the Ten Commandments. Foremost was the condemnation of murder, theft, brawling, and the desecration of the Sabbath by work or play. The early missionaries had the best of intentions, but like all zealots they were blinded by the single-mindedness that was also their greatest ally. They weren't surgically selective in their destruction of native beliefs. *Anything* native was felt to be inferior, and they set about wiping out all traces of the old ways. In their rampage they reduced the Hawaiian culture to ashes, plucking self-will and determination from the hearts of a once-proud people. More so than the whalers, they terminated the Hawaiian way of life.

PLANTATION DAYS

It's hard to say just where the sugar industry began in Hawaii. The Koloa Sugar Plantation on the southern coast of Kaua'i successfully refined sugar in 1835. Others tried, and one success was at Hana, Maui, in 1849. A whaler named George Wilfong hauled four blubber pots ashore and set them up on a rocky hill in the middle of 60 acres he had planted in sugar. A team of oxen turned "crushing rollers" and the cane juice flowed down an open trough into the pots, under which an attending native kept a roaring fire burning. Wilfong's methods of refining were crude but the resulting high-quality sugar turned a neat profit in Lahaina. The main problem was labor. The Hawaiians, who made excellent whalers, were basically indentured workers. They became extremely disillusioned with their contracts, which could last up to 10 years. Most of their wages were eaten up by manufactured commodities sold at the company store, and it didn't take long for them to realize that they were little more than slaves. At every opportunity they either left the area or just refused to work.

Imported Labor

The Masters and Servants Act of 1850, which allowed importation of laborers under the contract system, ostensibly guaranteed an endless supply of cheap labor for the plantations. Chinese laborers were imported but were too enterprising to remain in the fields for a meager $3 per month. They left as soon as opportunity permitted and went into business as small merchants and retailers. In the meantime, Wilfong had sold out, releasing most of the Hawaiians previously held under contract, and his plantation fell into disuse. In 1860 two Danish brothers, August and Oscar Unna, bought land at Hana to raise sugar. They solved the labor problem by importing Japanese laborers, who were extremely hardworking and easily managed. The workday lasted 10 hours, six days a week, for a salary of $20 per month plus housing and medical care. Plantation life was very structured, with stringent rules governing even bedtimes and lights-out. A worker was fined for being late or for smoking on the job. The workers had great difficulty functioning under these circumstances, and improvements in benefits and housing were slowly gained.

Changing Society

The sugar plantation system changed life in Hawaii physically, spiritually, politically, and economically. Now boatloads of workers came not only from Japan but from Portugal, Germany, and even Russia. The white-skinned workers were most often the field foremen *(luna)*. With the immigrants came new religions, new animals and plants, unique cuisines, and a plantation language known as pidgin, or better yet, *da' kine*. Many Asians and, to a lesser extent, the other groups—including the white plantation owners—intermarried with Hawaiians. A new class of people properly termed "cosmopolitan" but more familiarly and aptly known as "locals" was emerging. These were the people of multiple-race backgrounds who couldn't exactly say *what* they were but it was clear to all just *who* they were. The plantation owners became the new "chiefs" of Hawaii who could carve up the land and dispense favors. The Hawaiian monarchy was soon eliminated.

THE LONG (AND CONTESTED) ROAD TO STATEHOOD
The Revolution

When Queen Lili'uokalani took office in 1891, the native population was at a low of 40,000, and she felt that the United States had too much influence over her homeland. She was known to personally favor the English over the Americans. She attempted to replace the liberal constitution of 1887 (adopted by her pro-American brother) with an autocratic mandate in which she would have had much more political and economic control of the islands. When the McKinley Tariff of 1890 brought a decline in sugar profits, she made no attempt to improve the situation. Thus, the planters saw her as a political obstacle to their economic growth; most of Hawaii's American planters and merchants were in favor of a rebellion. A central spokesperson and firebrand was Lorrin Thurston, a Honolulu publisher who, with a central core of about 30 men, challenged the Hawaiian monarchy. Although Lili'uokalani rallied some support and had a small military force in her personal guard, the coup was ridiculously easy—it took only one casualty. Captain John Good shot a Hawaiian policeman in the arm and that did it. Naturally, the conspirators could not have succeeded without some solid assurances from a secret contingent in the U.S. Congress as well as outgoing president Benjamin Harrison, who favored Hawaii's annexation. Marines from the *Boston* went ashore to "protect American lives," and on January 17, 1893, the Hawaiian monarchy came to an end.

The provisional government was headed by Sanford B. Dole, who became president of the Hawaiian Republic. Lili'uokalani surrendered not to the conspirators but to U.S. ambassador John Stevens. She believed that the U.S. government, which had assured her of Hawaiian independence, would be outraged by the overthrow and would come to her aid. Incoming president Grover Cleveland *was* outraged, and Hawaii wasn't immediately annexed as expected. When queried about what she would do with the conspirators if she were reinstated, Lili'uokalani said that they would be hanged as traitors. The racist press of the times, which portrayed the Hawaiians as half-civilized, bloodthirsty heathens, publicized this widely. Since the conspirators were the leading citizens of the land, the queen's words proved untimely. In January 1895 a small, ill-fated counterrevolution headed by Lili'uokalani failed, and she was placed under house arrest in 'Iolani Palace. Officials of the republic insisted she use her married name (Mrs. John Dominis) to sign the documents forcing her to abdicate her throne. She was also forced to swear allegiance to the new republic. Lili'uokalani went on to write *Hawaii's Story* and the lyric ballad "Aloha O'e." She never forgave the conspirators and remained "queen" to the Hawaiians until her death in 1917.

Annexation

The overwhelming majority of Hawaiians opposed annexation and desired to restore the monarchy. But they were prevented from voting by the new republic because they couldn't meet the imposed property and income qualifications—a transparent ruse by the planters to control the election. Most *haole* were racist and believed that the "common people" could not be entrusted with the vote because they were childish and incapable of ruling themselves. The fact that the Hawaiians had existed quite well for 1,000 years before white people even reached Hawaii was never considered. The Philippine theater of the Spanish-American War also prompted annexation. One of the strongest proponents was Alfred Mahon, a brilliant naval strategist who, with support from Theodore Roosevelt, argued that the U.S. military must have Hawaii in order to be a viable force in the Pacific. In addition, Japan, victorious in its recent war with China, protested the American intention to annex, and in so doing prompted even moderates to support annexation for fear that the Japanese themselves coveted the prize. On July 7, 1898, President McKinley signed the annexation agreement, and this "tropical fruit" was finally put into America's basket.

ENTER THE 20TH CENTURY

Hawaii entered the 20th century totally transformed from what it had been. The old Hawaiian language, religion, culture, and leadership were all but gone; Western dress, values, education, and recreation were the norm. Native Hawaiians were now unseen citizens who lived in dwindling numbers in remote areas. The plantations, new centers of social order, had a strong Asian flavor; more than 75 percent of their workforce was

Asian. There was a small white middle class, an all-powerful white elite, and a single political party ruled by that elite. Education, however, was always highly prized, and by the turn of the 20th century all racial groups were encouraged to attend school. By 1900, almost 90 percent of Hawaiians were literate (far above the national norm), and schooling was mandatory for all children ages six to 15. Intermarriage was accepted, and there was a mixing of the races like nowhere else on earth.

The military became increasingly important to Hawaii. It brought in money and jobs, dominating the island economy. The Japanese attack on Pearl Harbor, which began U.S. involvement in World War II, bound Hawaii to America forever. Once the islands had been baptized by blood, the average Mainlander felt that Hawaii was American soil. A movement among Hawaiians to become part of the Union began to grow. They wanted a real voice in Washington, not merely a voteless delegate as provided under their territory status. Hawaii became the 50th state in 1959, and the jumbo-jet revolution of the 1960s made it easily accessible to growing numbers of tourists from all over the world.

Pearl Harbor Attack

On the morning of December 7, 1941, the Japanese carrier *Akagi* received and broadcast over its PA system island music from Honolulu station KGMB. Deep in the bowels of the ship a radioman listened for a much different message, coming thousands of miles from the Japanese mainland. When the message "east wind rain" was received, the attack was launched. At the end of the day, 2,325 U.S. servicemen and 57 civilians were dead; 188 planes were destroyed; 18 major warships were sunk or heavily damaged; and the United States was in the war. Japanese casualties were ludicrously light. The ignited conflict would rage for four years until Japan, through the bombings at Nagasaki and Hiroshima, was vaporized into total submission. At the end of hostilities, Hawaii would never again be considered separate from America.

Statehood

A number of economic and political reasons explain why the ruling elite of Hawaii desired statehood, but, put simply, the vast majority of people who lived there, especially after World War II, considered themselves Americans. The first serious mention of making "The Sandwich Islands" a state was in the 1850s under President Franklin Pierce, but it wasn't taken seriously until the monarchy was overthrown in the 1890s. For the next 50 years statehood proposals were made repeatedly to Congress, but there was stiff opposition, especially from the southern states. With Hawaii a territory, an import quota system beneficial to Mainland producers could be enacted on produce, especially sugar. Also, there was prejudice against creating a state in a place where the majority of the populace was not white.

During World War II, Hawaii was placed under martial law, but no serious attempt to intern the Japanese population was made, as in California. There were simply too many Japanese, and many went on to gain the respect of the American people with their outstanding fighting record during the war. Hawaii's own 100th Battalion became the famous 442nd Regimental Combat Team, which gained notoriety by saving the Lost Texas Battalion during the Battle of the Bulge and went on to be *the* most decorated battalion in all of World War II. When these GIs returned home, no one was going to tell them that they were not loyal Americans. Many of these AJAs (Americans of Japanese Ancestry) took advantage of the GI Bill and received higher educations. They were from the common people, not the elite, and they rallied grassroots support for statehood. When the vote finally occurred, approximately 132,900 voted in favor of statehood, with only 7,800 votes against. Congress passed the Hawaii State Bill on March 12, 1959, and on August 21, 1959, President Eisenhower announced that Hawaii was officially the 50th state.

In November 1993, President Bill Clinton signed United States Public Law 103-150, t'

"Apology Resolution," to acknowledge the 100th anniversary of the January 17, 1893, overthrow of the Kingdom of Hawaii, and to offer an apology to Native Hawaiians on behalf of the United States for the overthrow.

Government and Economy

GOVERNMENT

The major difference between the government of the state of Hawaii and those of other states is that it's "streamlined," and in theory more efficient. There are only two levels of government: the state and the county. With no town or city governments to deal with, considerable bureaucracy is eliminated. Hawaii, in anticipation of becoming a state, drafted a constitution in 1950 and was ready to go when statehood came. Politics and government are taken seriously in the Aloha State, which consistently turns in the best national voting record per capita. For example, in the first state elections, 173,000 of 180,000 registered voters voted—a whopping 94 percent of the electorate. In the election to ratify statehood, hardly a ballot went uncast, with 95 percent of the voters opting for statehood. The bill carried in every island of Hawaii except Ni'ihau, where most of the people (total population 250 or so) were of relatively pure Hawaiian blood. When Hawaii became a state, Honolulu became its capital. Since statehood, the legislative and executive branches of state government have been dominated by the Democratic Party.

County of Hawai'i

The current and longtime mayor of the County of Hawai'i is a democrat, William P. Kenoi (known as Billy). The mayor is assisted by an elected county council consisting of nine members, one from each council district around the island. Hilo is the county seat.

Of the 25 state senatorial districts, the County of Hawai'i is represented by three. The First District takes in the whole northern section of the island: the Hamakua Coast, Mauna Kea, North and South Kohala, and part of North Kona. The Second District is mainly Hilo and its outlying area. The Third District comprises Puna, Ka'u, South Kona, and most of North Kona. The County of Hawai'i has 7 of 51 seats in the State House of Representatives. For information on the county see www.hawaiicounty.gov.

ECONOMY

Hawaii's mid-Pacific location makes it perfect for two prime sources of income: tourism and the military. Tourists come in anticipation of endless golden days on soothing beaches, while the military is provided with a key strategic position. Each economic sector nets Hawaii billions of dollars annually, money that should keep flowing smoothly and even increase in the foreseeable future. Tourism alone reaps over $11 billion. These revenues remain mostly aloof from the normal ups and downs of the Mainland U.S. economy. Also contributing to the state revenue are, in descending proportions: manufacturing, construction, and agriculture (mainly sugar and pineapples). As long as the sun shines and the balance of global power requires a military presence, the economic stability of Hawaii is guaranteed.

Agriculture

The Big Island's economy is the state's most agriculturally based. Over 5,000 farmhands, horticultural workers, and *paniolo* (cowboys) work the land to produce about one-third of the state's vegetables and melons, over 75 percent of the total fruit production, 95 percent of the papayas, 75 percent of the bananas, 95 percent of the avocados, and 50 percent of the guavas. Much of the state's taro is also produced on the Big Island, principally in the Waipi'o Valley and along the Hamakua

Coast, and ginger production has become a major economic factor with more than six million pounds grown annually. The Big Island also produces some 50 million pounds of macadamia nuts yearly, about 90 percent of the total amount grown in the state. While that's a respectable number, it's less than half the world's total. The Big Island used to have the only commercial coffee plantations in the country, but now coffee is grown on all the major Hawaiian islands. Due to the increased interest in gourmet Kona and Ka'u coffee, the coffee industry's share in the economy of the island is increasing, and the Big Island grows about three million pounds of coffee every year. More than 350 horticultural farms produce the largest number of orchids and anthuriums in the state, leaving the Big Island awash in color and fragrance. Other exotic flowers and foliage are also a growing concern. In the hills, entrepreneurs raise pakalolo (marijuana), which has become the state's most productive although illicit cash crop.

Hawai'i used to be the state's largest sugar grower, with over 150,000 acres in cane. These commercial fields produced four million tons of refined sugar, 40 percent of the state's output. The majority of sugar land was along the Hamakua Coast, long known for its abundant water supply. At one time, the cane was even transported to the mills by water flumes. Other large pockets of cane fields were found on the southern part of the island in Ka'u and Puna, as well as at the northern tip in North Kohala. With the closing of the last mill in 1996, sugar is no longer grown commercially on the island. Still, small entrepreneurial farms grow it on greatly reduced acreage. The big cane trucks have ceased to roll, and the few remaining smokestacks stand in silent testimony to a bygone era.

The upland Kona district is a splendid area for raising coffee; it gives the beans a beautiful tan. Lying in Mauna Loa's rain shadow, the district gets dewy mornings followed by sunshine and an afternoon cloud shadow. Kona coffee has long been accepted as gourmet quality and is sold in the better restaurants throughout Hawaii and in fine coffee shops around the world. It's a dark, full-bodied coffee with a rich aroma. Approximately 600 small farms produce nearly $15 million a year in coffee revenue. Few, however, make it a full-time business. The production of Kona coffee makes up only about one-tenth of 1 percent of the coffee grown around the world. The rare bean is often blended with other varietals. When sold unblended it is quite expensive. With its similar climactic conditions, the district of Ka'u has also begun to grow coffee, albeit in much smaller quantities. While not yet well known, Ka'u coffee has gained a loyal following.

Hawai'i's cattle ranches produce over five million pounds of beef per year, 50 percent of the state's total. More than 450 independent ranches are located on the island, with total acreage of over 650,000 acres, but they are dwarfed both in size and production by the massive Parker Ranch, which alone has 175,000 acres and is about half the size of O'ahu. While beef is the largest player in the livestock market, pork, dairy products, eggs, poultry, sheep, goats, bees, and honey also are components, and together constitute perhaps half of the island's livestock revenues.

Military

On average, about 60 military personnel are stationed on the Big Island at any one time, with about the same number of dependents. Most of these people are attached to the enormous Pohakuloa Training Area in the center of the island; a lesser number are at a few minor installations around Hilo, Kailua, and at Kilauea Volcano.

People and Culture

POPULATION

Nowhere else on earth can you find such a kaleidoscopic mixture of people as in Hawaii. Every major (socially constructed) race is accounted for, and over 50 ethnic groups are represented throughout the islands, making Hawaii the most racially integrated state in the country. Its population of 1.42 million includes some 80,000 permanently stationed military personnel and their dependents. Until the year 2000, when California's white population fell below 50 percent, Hawaii was the only U.S. state where white individuals were not the majority. About 56 percent of Hawaiian residents were born there, 26 percent were born on the U.S. Mainland, and 18 percent are foreign-born.

The population has grown steadily in recent times, but fluctuated wildly in the past. In 1876, it reached its lowest ebb, with only 55,000 permanent residents. This was the era of large sugar plantations; their constant demand for labor was the primary cause for importing various peoples from around the world and led to Hawaii's racial mix. World War II saw the population swell from 400,000 to 900,000. Most of the 500,000 military personnel left at war's end, but many returned to settle after getting a taste of island living. There is no ethnic majority on the Big Island; population numbers include 32 percent Caucasian, 28 percent mixed, 27 percent Asian, 11 percent Hawaiian, and 2 percent other.

LANGUAGE

Hawaii is part of America and people speak English there, but that's not the whole story. If you turn on the TV to catch the evening news, you'll hear "Walter Cronkite" English, unless of course you happen to tune in to a Japanese-language broadcast designed for tourists from that country. You can easily pick up a Chinese-language newspaper or groove to the music on a Filipino radio station, but let's not confuse the issue. All your needs and requests at airports, car-rental agencies, restaurants, hotels, or wherever you happen to travel will be completely understood, as well as answered, in English. However, when you happen to overhear islanders speaking, what they're saying will sound somewhat familiar but you won't be able to pick up all the words, and the beat and melody of the language will be noticeably different.

Hawaii—like New England, the Deep South, and the Midwest—has its own unmistakable linguistic regionalism. All the ethnic peoples who make up Hawaii have enriched the English spoken there with words, expressions, and subtle shades of meaning that are commonly used and understood throughout the islands. The greatest influence on English has come from the Hawaiian language itself, and words such as "aloha," "hula," "lu'au," and "lei" are familiarly used and understood by most Americans.

Other migrant peoples, especially the Chinese, Japanese, and Portuguese, influenced the local dialect to such an extent that the simplified plantation lingo they spoke has become known as "pidgin." A fun and enriching part of the "island experience" is picking up a few words of Hawaiian and pidgin. English is the official language of the state, business, education, and perhaps even the mind, but pidgin is the language of the people, the emotions, and life, while Hawaiian (also an official language of the state, but used "only as provided by law") remains the language of the heart and the soul.

Pidgin

The dictionary definition of pidgin is a simplified language with a rudimentary grammar used as a means of communication between people speaking different languages. Hawaiian pidgin is a little more complicated than that. It has its roots in the plantation days of the 19th century when white owners and *luna* (foremen) had to communicate with recently arrived Chinese, Japanese, and Portuguese laborers. It evolved as a simple language of the here and now, primarily concerned with the necessary functions of working, eating, and sleeping. It has an economical noun-verb-object structure (although not necessarily in that order).

Hawaiian words make up most of pidgin's non-English vocabulary. It includes a good smattering of Chinese, Japanese, and Samoan; the distinctive rising inflection is provided by the melodious Mediterranean lilt of the Portuguese. Pidgin is not a stagnant language. It's kept alive by hip new words introduced by cool people and especially by slang words introduced by teenagers. It's a colorful English, and is as regionally unique as the speech of Cajuns in rural Louisiana bayous. Hawaiians of all socioethnic backgrounds can at least understand pidgin. Most islanders are proud of it, while some consider it a low-class jargon. The Hawaiian House of Representatives has given pidgin an official sanction, and most people feel that it adds a real local style and should be preserved.

Pidgin is first learned at school, where all students, regardless of background, are exposed to it. The pidgin spoken by young people today is "fo' real" different from that of their parents. It's no longer only plantation talk but has moved to the streets and picked up some sophistication. At one time there was an academic movement to exterminate it, but that idea died away with the same thinking that insisted on making left-handed people write with their right hand. It is strange, however, that pidgin has become the unofficial language of Hawaii's grassroots movement, when it actually began as a white owners' language that was used to supplant Hawaiian and all the languages brought to the islands.

Although hip young *haole* use pidgin all the time, it has gained the connotation of being the language of the nonwhite locals and is part of the "us against them" way of thinking. All local people, *haole* or not, do consider pidgin their own island language and don't really like it when it's used by *malihini* (newcomers). If you're in the islands long enough, you don't have to bother learning pidgin; it'll learn you. There's a book sold all over the islands called *Pidgin to da Max*, written by a *haole* from Nebraska named Doug Simonson. You might not be able to understand what's being said by locals speaking pidgin (that's usually the idea), but you should be able to *feel* what's being meant.

Hawaiian

The Hawaiian language sways like a palm tree in a gentle wind. Its words are as melodious as a love song. Linguists say that you can learn a lot about people through their language; when you hear Hawaiian you think of gentleness and love, and it's hard to imagine the ferocious side so evident in Hawaii's past. With its many Polynesian root words easily traced to Indonesian and Malay, Hawaiian is obviously from this same stock. The Hawaiian spoken today is very different from old Hawaiian. Its greatest metamorphosis occurred when the missionaries began to write it down in the 1820s, but in the last couple of decades there has been a movement to reestablish the Hawaiian language. Not only are courses in it offered at the University of Hawai'i, but there is a successful elementary school immersion program in the state, some books are being printed in it, and more and more musicians are performing it. Many scholars have put forth translations of Hawaiian, but there are endless, volatile disagreements in the academic sector about the real meanings of Hawaiian words. Hawaiian is no longer spoken as a language except on Ni'ihau, and the closest tourists will come to it is in place-names, street names, and words that have become part of common usage, such as aloha (a greeting) and mahalo (thank you).

Thanks to the missionaries, the Hawaiian language is rendered phonetically using only 12 letters. They are the five vowels (a, e, i, and u), sounded as they are in Italian, and seven consonants (h, k, l, m, n, p, w), sounded exactly as they are in English. Sometimes "w" is pronounced as "v," but this only occurs in the middle of a word and always follows a vowel. A consonant is always followed by a vowel, forming two-letter syllables, but vowels are often found in pairs or even triplets. A slight oddity about Hawaiian is the glottal stop called 'okina. This is an abrupt break in sound in the middle of a word, such as "uh-oh" in English, and is denoted with a reversed apostrophe (').

PRONUNCIATION KEY

For those unfamiliar with the sounds of Italian or other Romance languages, the vowels are sounded as follows:

A—in stressed syllables, pronounced as in "ah" (that feels good!). For example, Haleakala is pronounced "hah-lay-AH-kah-LAH."

E—short "e" is "eh," as in "pen" or "dent" (thus *hale* is "HAH-leh"). Long "e" sounds like "ay" as in "sway" or "day." For example, the Hawaiian goose *(nene)* is a "nay-nay," not a "knee-knee."

I—pronounced "ee" as in "see" or "we" (thus *pali* is pronounced "PAH-lee").

O—pronounced as in "no" or "oh," such as "KOH-uh" (koa) or "OH-noh" (ono).

U—pronounced "oo" as in "do" or "stew"; for example, "KAH-poo" *(kapu)* or "POO-nah" (Puna).

DIPHTHONGS

There are also eight vowel pairs known as "diphthongs" (ae, ai, ao, au, ei, eu, oi, and ou). These are the sounds made by gliding from one vowel to another within a syllable. The stress is placed on the first vowel. In English, examples would be soil and bail. Common examples in Hawaiian are lei and *heiau*.

STRESS

The best way to learn which syllables are stressed in Hawaiian is by listening closely. It becomes obvious after a while. There are also me vowel sounds that are held longer than

others; these can occur at the beginning of a word, such as the first "a" in 'aina, or in the middle of a word, like the first "a" in lanai. Again, it's a matter of tuning your ear and paying attention.

When written, these stressed vowels, called *kahako,* occur with a macron, or short line, over them. Stressed vowels with marks are not written as such in this guide. No one is going to give you a hard time if you mispronounce a word. It's good, however, to pay close attention to the pronunciation of street names and place-names because many Hawaiian words sound alike and a misplaced vowel here or there could be the difference between getting where you want to go and getting lost.

ARTS AND CRAFTS

Since everything in old Hawaii had to be fashioned by hand, almost every object was either a genuine work of art or the product of a highly refined craft. With the "civilizing" of the natives, most of the "old ways" disappeared, including the old arts and crafts. Most authentic Hawaiian art by master crafters exists only in museums, but with the resurgence of Hawaiian roots, many old arts are being revitalized, and their legacy lives on in a few artists who have become proficient in them.

Canoes

The most respected artisans in old Hawaii were the canoe makers. With little more than a stone adze and a pump drill, they built canoes that could carry 200 people and last for generations—sleek, well proportioned, and infinitely seaworthy. The main hull was usually a gigantic koa log, and the gunwale planks were minutely drilled and sewn to the sides with sennit rope. Apprenticeships lasted for years, and a young man knew that he had graduated when one day he was nonchalantly asked to sit down and eat with the master builders. Small family-sized canoes with outriggers were used for fishing and perhaps carried a spear rack; large oceangoing double-hulled canoes were used for migration and warfare. On these, the giant logs had been adzed to about two inches thick. A mainsail woven from pandanus was mounted on a central platform, and the boat was steered by two long paddles. The hull was dyed with plant juices and charcoal, and the entire village helped launch the canoe in a ceremony called "drinking the sea."

Carving and Woodworking

Wood was a primary material used by Hawaiian craftsmen. They almost exclusively used koa because of its density, strength, and natural luster. It was turned into canoes, woodware, calabashes, and furniture used by the ali'i. Temple idols were another major product of woodcarving. Various stone artifacts were also turned out, including poi pounders, mirrors, fishing sinkers, and small idols.

While the carving and fashioning of old traditional items has by and large disappeared, lathe-turning of wooden bowls and the creation of wooden furniture from native woods is alive and strong. Koa is becoming increasingly scarce. Costly *milo* and monkeypod, as well as a host of other native woods, are also excellent for turnings and household items and have largely replaced koa. These modern wooden objects are available at numerous shops and galleries. Countless inexpensive carved items are sold at variety stores, such as tikis, hula dancers, or salad servers, but most of these are imported from Asia or the Philippines.

Weaving

Hawaiians became the best basket makers and mat weavers in all of Polynesia. *Ulana* (woven mats) were made from *lau hala* (pandanus leaves). Once the leaves were split, the spine was removed and the leaves stored in large rolls. When needed they were soaked, pounded, and then fashioned into various floor coverings and sleeping mats. Intricate geometrical patterns were woven in, and the edges were rolled and fashioned. Coconut palms were not used to make mats in old Hawaii, but a wide variety of basketry was made from the aerial root 'ie'ie. The shapes varied according to use. Some baskets were tall and narrow, some were cones, others were flat like trays, and many were woven around gourds and calabashes.

The tradition of weaving has survived in Hawaii but is not strong. Older experienced weavers are dying, and few younger ones are showing interest in continuing the craft. The time-tested material of *lau hala* is still the best, although much is now made from coconut fronds. *Lau hala* is traditional Hawaiian weaving from the leaves *(lau)* of the pandanus *(hala)* tree. These leaves vary greatly in length, with the largest over six feet, and they have a thorny spine that must be removed before they can be worked. The color ranges from light tan to dark brown. The leaves are cut into strips one-eighth-inch to one-inch wide and are then employed in weaving. Any variety of items can be made or at least covered in *lau hala*. It makes great purses, mats, baskets, and table mats. You can still purchase items from bags to a woven hat, and all share the desirable qualities of strength, lightness, and ventilation.

Woven into a hat, *lau hala* is absolutely superb but should not be confused with a palm-frond hat. A *lau hala* hat is amazingly supple and even when squashed will pop back into shape. A good one is expensive and with proper care will last for years. All *lau hala* should be given a light application of mineral oil on a monthly basis, especially if it's exposed to the sun. For flat items, iron over a damp cloth and keep purses and baskets stuffed with paper when not in use. Palm fronds also are widely used in weaving. They, too, are a great natural raw material, but not as good as *lau hala*. Almost any woven item, such as a beach bag woven from palm, makes a good authentic yet inexpensive gift or souvenir.

Featherwork

This highly refined art was practiced only on the islands of Tahiti, New Zealand, and Hawaii, but the fashioning of feathe helmets and idols was unique to Hawaii. Favorite colors were red and yellow, which came only in a very limited supply from a small number of birds, such as the 'o'o, 'i'iwi, mamo, and 'apapane. Professional bird hunters in old Hawaii paid their taxes to ali'i in prized feathers. The feathers were fastened to a woven net of olona cord and made into helmets, idols, and beautiful flowing capes and cloaks. These resplendent garments were made and worn only by men, especially during battle, when a fine cloak became a great trophy of war. Featherwork was also employed in the making of kahili fans and lei, which were highly prized by the noble ali'i women.

Lei-Making

Any flower or blossom can be strung into a lei, but the most common are orchids or the lovely smelling plumeria. Lei, like babies, are all beautiful, but special lei are highly prized by those who know what to look for. Of the different stringing styles, the most common is kui—stringing the flower through the middle or side. Most "airport-quality" lei are of this type. The humuhumu style, reserved for making flat lei, is made by sewing flowers and ferns to a ti, banana, or sometimes hala leaf. A humuhumu lei makes an excellent hatband. Wili is the winding together of greenery, ferns, and flowers into short, bouquet-type lengths. The most traditional form is hili, which requires no stringing at all but involves braiding fragrant ferns and leaves such as maile. If flowers are interwoven, the hili becomes the haku style, the most difficult and most beautiful type of lei.

Every major island is symbolized by its own lei made from a distinctive flower, shell, or fern. Each island has its own official color as well, though it doesn't necessarily correspond to the color of the island's lei. The island of Hawai'i's lei is made from the red (or rare creamy-white or orange) 'ohi'a lehua blossom. The lehua tree grows from sea level to 9,000 feet and produces an abundance of tufted flowers.

Tapa Cloth

Tapa, cloth made from tree bark, was common throughout Polynesia and was a woman's art. A few trees such as the wauke and mamaki produced the best cloth, but a variety of other types of bark could be utilized. First the raw bark was pounded into a felt-like pulp and beaten together to form strips (the beaters had distinctive patterns that helped make the cloth supple). The cloths were decorated by stamping (a form of block printing) and dyed with natural colors from plants and sea animals in shades of gray, purple, pink, and red. They were even painted with natural brushes made from pandanus fruit, with an gray color made from charcoal. The tapa cloth was sewn together to make bed coverings, and fragrant flowers and herbs were either sewn or pounded in to produce a permanent fragrance. Tapa cloth is still available today, but the Hawaiian methods have been lost, and most comes from other areas of Polynesia.

Aloha Wear

Wild Hawaiian shirts or bright mu'umu'u, especially when worn on the Mainland, have the magical effect of making wearers feel like they're in Hawaii, while at the same time eliciting spontaneous smiles from passersby. Maybe it's the colors, or perhaps it's just the "vibe" that signifies "party time" or "hang loose," but nothing says Hawaii like aloha wear. There are more than a dozen fabric houses in Hawaii turning out distinctive patterns, and many dozens of factories creating their own personalized designs. These factories often have attached retail outlets, but in any case you can find hundreds of shops selling aloha wear. Aloha shirts were the brilliant idea of a Chinese merchant in Honolulu, who used to hand-tailor them and sell them to the tourists who arrived by ship in the glory days before World War II. They were an instant success. Mu'umu'u or "Mother Hubbards" were the idea of missionaries, who were appalled by Hawaiian women running about au naturel and insisted on covering their new Christian converts from head to foot. Now the roles are reversed, and it's Mainlanders who come to Hawaii and immediately strip down to as little clothing as possible.

At one time aloha wear was exclusively made of cotton or from man-made, natural fiber-based rayon, and these materials are still the best for any tropical clothing. Beware, however: Polyester has slowly crept into the market! No material could possibly be worse for the island climate, so when buying your aloha wear make sure to check the label for material content. On the bright side, silk also is used and makes a good material but is a bit heavy for some. Mu'umu'u now come in various styles and can be worn for the entire spectrum of social occasions in Hawaii. Aloha shirts are basically cut the same as always, but the patterns have undergone changes; apart from the original flowers and ferns, modern shirts might depict an island scene in the manner of a silk-screen painting. A basic good-quality mu'umu'u or aloha shirt is guaranteed to be worth its price in good times and happy smiles. The connoisseur might want to purchase *The Hawaiian Shirt, Its Art and History*, by R. Thomas Steele. It's illustrated with more than 150 shirts that are now considered works of art by collectors the world over.

Scrimshaw

The art of etching and carving on bone and ivory has become an island tradition handed down from the times of the great whaling ships. Examples of this Danish sailors' art date all the way back to the 15th century, but, like jazz, it was really popularized and raised to an art form by Americans—whalers on decade-long voyages from "back east" plying vast oceans in search of great whales. Frederick Merek, who sailed aboard the whaling ship *Susan,* was the best of the breed; however, most sailors only carved on the teeth of great whales to pass the time and have something to trade for whiskey, women, and song in remote ports of call. When sailors, most of whom were illiterate, sent scrimshaw back to family and

friends, it was considered more like a postcard than artwork. After the late 1800s, scrimshaw faded from popular view and became a lost art form until it was revived, mostly in Lahaina, during the 1960s. Today, scrimshaw can be found throughout Hawaii, but the center remains the old whaling capital of Lahaina, Maui. Scrimshaw is used in everything from belt buckles to delicate earrings and even coffee-table centerpieces. Prices go from a few dollars up to thousands and scrimshaw can be found in limited quantities in some galleries and fine-art shops around the island.

Quilts

Along with the gospel and the will to educate, the early missionaries brought skills and machines to sew. Many taught the Hawaiians how to quilt together small pieces of material into designs for the bed. Quilting styles and patterns varied over the years and generally shifted from designs familiar to New Englanders to those more pleasing to Hawaiian eyes, and a number of standard patterns include leaves, fruits, and flowers of the islands. Most Hawaiian-design quilts seen for sale in the islands today are now made in the Philippines under the direction of Hawaiian designers. Because of labor costs, they are far less expensive than any quilt that is actually made in Hawaii.

Paintings

One thing is for sure: Like the rest of the Hawaiian Islands, Hawai'i draws painters. Multitudes of painters. Captivated by the island's beauty, color, natural features, and living things, these artists interpret what they see and sense in a dizzying display from realism to expressionism. From immense *pali* cliffs to the tiniest flower petals, and humble workers' homes to the faces of the island people, they are all portrayed. Color, movement, and feeling are captured, and the essence of Hawai'i is the result. Galleries and shops around the island display local artists' work, but there is a concentration of galleries in Holualoa above Kailua-Kona. Well-known artists charge a handsome fee for their work, but you can find some exceptional work for affordable prices hidden here and there among the rest.

Jewelry

Jewelry is always an appreciated gift, especially if it's distinctive, and Hawaii has some of the most original. The sea provides the basic raw materials of pink, gold, and black corals that are as beautiful and fascinating as gemstones. Harvesting coral is very dangerous work. The Lahaina beds off Maui have one of the best black coral lodes in the islands, but unlike reef coral, these trees grow at depths bordering the outer limits of a scuba diver's capabilities. Only the best can dive 180 feet after the black coral, and about one diver per year dies in pursuit of it. Conservationists have placed great pressure on the harvesters of these deep corals, and the state of Hawaii has placed strict limits and guidelines on the firms and divers involved.

Puka shells (with small, naturally occurring holes) and *'opihi* shells are also made into jewelry. Many times these items are very inexpensive, yet they are authentic and are great purchases for the price.

HULA

The hula is more than an ethnic dance; it is the soul of Hawaii expressed in motion. It began as a form of worship during religious ceremonies and was only danced by highly trained men. It gradually evolved into a form of entertainment, but in no regard was it sexual. The hula was the opera, theater, and lecture hall of the islands all rolled into one. It was history portrayed in the performing arts. In the beginning an androgynous deity named Laka descended to earth and taught men how to dance the hula. In time the male aspect of Laka departed for the heavens, but the female aspect remained. The female Laka set up her own special hula *heiau* at Ha'ena on the Na Pali Coast of Kaua'i, where it still exists. As time went on, women were allowed to learn the hula. Scholars surmise that men became

too busy wresting a living from the land to maintain the art form.

Men did retain a type of hula for themselves called *lua*. This was a form of martial art employed in hand-to-hand combat that evolved into a ritualized warfare dance called *hula ku'i*. During the 19th century, the hula almost vanished because the missionaries considered it vile and heathen. King Kalakaua is generally regarded as having saved it during the 1800s, when he formed his own troupe and encouraged the dancers to learn the old hula. Many of the original dances were forgotten, but some were retained and are performed to this day. Although professional dancers were highly trained, everyone took part in the hula. *Ali'i,* commoners, young, and old all danced.

Hula is art in swaying motion, and the true form is studied rigorously and taken very seriously. Today, hula *halau* (schools) are active on every island, teaching hula and keeping the old ways and culture alive. (Ancient hula is called *hula kahiko,* and modern renditions are known as *hula auana.*) Performers still spend years perfecting their techniques. They show off their accomplishments during the fierce competition of the Merrie Monarch Festival in Hilo every April. The winning *halau* is praised and recognized throughout the islands.

Hawaiian hula was never performed in grass skirts; tapa or ti-leaf skirts were worn. Grass skirts came to Hawaii from the Gilbert Islands, and if you see grass and cellophane skirts in a "hula revue," it's not traditional. Almost every major resort offering entertainment or a *lu'au* also offers a revue. Most times, young island beauties accompanied by proficient local musicians put on a floor show for the tourists. It'll be fun, but it won't be traditional.

A hula dancer has to learn how to control every part of her/his body, including facial expressions, which help to set the mood. The hands are extremely important and provide instant background scenery. For example, if the hands are thrust outward in an aggressive manner, this can mean a battle; if they sway gently overhead, they refer to the gods or to creation; they can easily become rain, clouds, sun, sea, or moon. Watch the hands to get the gist of the story, but as one wise guy said, "You watch the parts you like, and I'll watch the parts I like!" The motion of swaying hips can denote a long walk, a canoe ride, or sexual intercourse. Foot motion can portray a battle, a walk, or any kind of conveyance. The overall effect is multidirectional synchronized movement. The correct chanting of the *mele* is an integral part of the performance. These story chants, accompanied by musical instruments, make the hula very much like opera; it is especially similar in the way the tale unfolds.

ISLAND MUSIC

The missionaries usually take a beating when it's recounted how much Hawaiian culture they destroyed while "civilizing" the natives. However, they seem to have done one thing right. They introduced the Hawaiians to the diatonic musical scale and immediately opened a door for latent and superbly harmonious talent. Before the missionaries, the Hawaiians knew little about melody. Though sonorous, their *mele* were repetitive chants in which the emphasis was placed on historical accuracy and not on "making music." The Hawaiians, in short, didn't *sing*. But within a few years of the missionaries' arrival, they were belting out good old Christian hymns, and one of their favorite pastimes became group and individual singing.

Early in the 1800s, Spanish *vaqueros* from California were imported to teach the Hawaiians how to be cowboys. With them came guitars and moody ballads. The Hawaiian *paniolo* (cowboys) quickly learned how to punch cows and croon away the long lonely nights on the range. Immigrants who came along a little later in the 19th century, especially from Portugal, helped create Hawaiian-style music. Their biggest influence was a small, four-stringed instrument called a *braga* or *cavaquinho*. One owned by Augusto

Dias was the prototype of a homegrown Hawaiian instrument that became known as the ukulele. "Jumping flea," the translation of *ukulele*, is an appropriate name devised by the Hawaiians when they saw how nimble the fingers were as they "jumped" over the strings.

King Kalakaua (The Merrie Monarch) and Queen Lili'uokalani were both patrons of the arts who furthered the Hawaiian musical identity at the turn of the 20th century. Kalakaua revived the hula and was also a gifted lyricist and balladeer. He wrote the words to "Hawaii Pono'i," which became the anthem of the nation of Hawaii and later the state anthem. Lili'uokalani wrote the hauntingly beautiful "Aloha O'e," which is often pointed to as the "spirit of Hawaii" in music. Detractors say that its melody is extremely close to that of the old Christian hymn, "Rock Beside the Sea," but the lyrics are so beautiful and perfectly fitted that this doesn't matter.

Just prior to Kalakaua's reign, a Prussian bandmaster, Captain Henri Berger, was invited to head the fledgling Royal Hawaiian Band, which he turned into a very respectable orchestra lauded by many visitors to the islands. Berger was open-minded and learned to love Hawaiian music. He collaborated with Kalakaua and other island musicians to incorporate their music into a Western format. He headed the band for 43 years, until 1915, and was instrumental in making music a serious pursuit of talented Hawaiians.

Making Hawaiian Music

Hawaiian music has a unique twang, a special feeling that says the same thing to everyone who hears it: "Relax, sit back in the moonlight, watch the swaying palms as the surf sings a lullaby." This special sound is epitomized by the bouncy ukulele, the falsettos of Hawaiian crooners, and the smooth ring of the "steel" or "Hawaiian" guitar. The steel guitar is a variation originated by Joseph Kekuku in the 1890s. Stories abound of how Kekuku devised this instrument; the most popular versions say that Joe dropped his comb or pocketknife on his guitar strings and liked what he heard. Driven by the faint rhythm of an inner sound, he went to the machine shop at the Kamehameha Schools and turned out a steel bar for sliding over the strings. To complete the sound he changed the catgut strings to steel and raised them so they wouldn't hit the frets. Voilà!—Hawaiian music as the world knows it today.

The first melodious strains of **slack-key guitar** (*ki ho'alu*) can be traced back to the time of Kamehameha III and the *vaqueros* from California. The Spanish had their way of tuning the guitar, and they played difficult and aggressive music that did not sit well with Hawaiians, who were much more gentle and casual in their manners.

Hawaiians soon became adept at making their own music. At first, one person played the melody, but it lacked fullness. There was no body to the sound. So, as one *paniolo* fooled with the melody, another soon learned to play bass, which added depth. But, players were often alone, and by experimenting they learned that they could get the right hand going with the melody, and at the same time play the bass note with the thumb to improve the sound. Singers also learned that they could "open tune" the guitar to match their rich voices.

Hawaiians believed knowledge was sacred, and what is sacred should be treated with utmost respect—which meant keeping it secret, except from sincere apprentices. Guitar playing became a personal art form whose secrets were closely guarded, handed down only to family members, and only to those who showed ability and determination. When old-time slack-key guitar players were done strumming, they loosened all the strings so no one could figure out how they had had their guitars tuned. If they were playing, and some interested folks came by who weren't part of the family, the Hawaiians stopped what they were doing, put their guitars down, and put their feet across the strings to wait for the folks to go away. As time went on, more and more Hawaiians began to play slack-key, and a common repertoire emerged.

Accomplished musicians could easily figure out the simple songs, once they had figured out how the family had tuned the guitar. One of the most popular tunings was the 'open G." Old Hawaiian folks called it the "taro patch tune." Different songs came out, and if you were in the family and were interested in the guitar, your elders took the time to sit down and teach you. The way they taught was straightforward—and a test of your sincerity at the same time. The old master would start to play. He just wanted you to listen and get a feel for the music—nothing more than that. You brought your guitar and *listened*. When you felt it, you played it, and the knowledge was transferred. Today, only a handful of slack-key guitar players know how to play the classic tunes classically. The best-known and perhaps greatest slack-key player was Gabby Pahinui, with The Sons of Hawaii. He has passed away but left many recordings behind. Another slack-key master was Raymond Kane. None of his students were from his own family, and most were *haole* musicians trying to preserve the classical method of playing.

Hawaiian music received its biggest boost from a remarkable radio program known as *Hawaii Calls*. This program sent out its music from the Banyan Court of Waikiki's Moana Hotel from 1935 until 1975. At its peak in the mid-1950s, it was syndicated on over 700 radio stations throughout the world. In fact, Japanese pilots heading for Pearl Harbor tuned in island music as a signal beacon. Some internationally famous classic tunes came out of the 1940s and 1950s. Jack Pitman composed "Beyond the Reef" in 1948; more than 300 artists have recorded it and it has sold well over 12 million records. Other million-sellers include: "Sweet Leilani," "Lovely Hula Hands," "The Cross-Eyed Mayor of Kaunakakai," and "The Hawaiian Wedding Song."

By the 1960s, Hawaiian music began to die. Just too corny and light for those turbulent years, it belonged to the older generation and the good times that followed World War II. One man was instrumental in keeping Hawaiian music alive during this period. Don Ho, with his "Tiny Bubbles," became the token Hawaiian musician of the 1960s and early 1970s. He persevered long enough to become a legend in his own time, and his Polynesian Extravaganza at the Hilton Hawaiian Village packed visitors in until the early 1990s. Al Harrington, "The South Pacific Man," until his retirement had another Honolulu "big revue" that drew large crowds. Of this type of entertainment, perhaps the most Hawaiian was Danny Kaleikini, the Ambassador of Aloha, who entertained his audience with dances, Hawaiian anecdotes, and tunes on the traditional Hawaiian nose flute.

The Beat Goes On

Beginning in the mid-1970s, islanders began to assert their cultural identity. One of the unifying factors was the coming of age of "Hawaiian" music. It graduated from the "little grass shack" novelty tune and began to include sophisticated jazz, rock, and contemporary rhythms. Accomplished musicians whose roots were in traditional island music began to highlight their tunes with this distinctive sound. The best embellished their arrangements with ukuleles, steel guitars, and traditional percussion and melodic instruments. Some excellent modern recording artists have become island institutions. The local people say that you know the Hawaiian harmonies are good if they give you "chicken skin."

Each year special music awards, **Na Hoku Hanohano,** or Hoku for short, are given to distinguished island musicians. The following are some of the Hoku winners considered by their contemporaries to be among the best in Hawaii: Barney Isaacs and George Kuo, Na Leo Pilimihana, Robi Kahakalau, Kealii Reichel, Darren Benitez, Sonny Kamahele, Ledward Kaapana, Hapa, Israel Kamakawiwioʻole, Amy Hanaialiʻi, and Pure Heart. Though most do not perform on the Big Island, if they're playing, don't miss them. Some, unfortunately, are no longer among the

living, but their recorded music can still be appreciated.

Past Hoku winners who have become renowned performers include the Brothers Cazimero, who are blessed with beautiful harmonic voices; Krush, highly regarded for their contemporary sounds; The Peter Moon Band, fantastic performers with a strong traditional sound; Henry Kapono, formerly of Kapono and Cecilio; and The Beamer Brothers. Others include Loyal Garner, Del Beazley, Bryan Kessler & Me No Hoa Aloha, George Kahumoku Jr., Olomana, Genoa Keawe, and Irmagard Aluli.

Those with access to the Internet can check out the Hawaiian music scene at one of the following: Hawaiian Music Island (www.mele.com) or Nahenahenet (http://nahenahe.net). While these are not the only Hawaiian music websites, they are good places to start. For listening to Hawaiian music on the Web, try Kauaʻi Community Radio (http://kkcr.org) or Hawaii Public Radio (www.hawaiipublicradio.org).

FOOD

Hawaiian cuisine consists of several genres: "plantation foods," "local foods," and "Hawaii Regional Cuisine." But before we get to all that, there's the food of the multitude of immigrants (Polynesian, Korean, Japanese, Filipino, Portuguese, Chinese, Thai, Mainlanders, and the new Mexican population) who populate the islands. So, for instance, when you order food at a Thai restaurant here, the food is as it would be if ordered in the home country. If you've never had Samoan food, here is a good place to try it (you'll often find it at festivals). Or go to a *luʻau* and try foods from across Polynesia (each country has its own typical foods, so I won't generalize here). Much of it is plant based (like taro or breadfruit) and coconut based (read: excellent desserts).

"Plantation foods" are a kind of "local foods" (local-style hybrid foods) and are a direct result of a combination of the dietary habits of the laborers working the fields and what foods were available during this era and easy to bring to work (prepared foods that could be left out all day). Even though the plantation days are gone, the resulting cuisine remains a staple of the Hawaiian diet: Spam *musubi,* plate lunches (a meat with macaroni salad and/or potato salad and/or rice), and the most important of them all—the *loco moco* (two scoops of rice, meat, a fried egg, and gravy).

Developing as a movement against "local foods" (which are confusingly not really made from local products), the **Hawaii Regional Cuisine** (HRC) movement began in the 1990s. It's a precursor to the modern-day locavore movement. The chefs most associated with this movement are Peter Merriman, Alan Wong, Sam Choy, and Roy Yamaguchi. Out of the nonprofit organization they created (called Hawaii Regional Cuisine), in 1994 they published a cookbook by Janice Wald Henderson, *The New Cuisine of Hawaii.* The most important thing to know about HRC is that it is dedicated to preserving the traditions of Hawaiian foods, while utilizing what the islands have to offer. And luckily, the islands have a lot to offer, from fish to Big Island beef to an abundance of seasonal produce (papayas, mangos, passion fruit, avocados, nearly 50 kinds of bananas, and so much more).

For an excellent food history of Hawaii, check out Rachel Laudan's *The Food of Paradise.* This book is a rich narrative that dissects the main local foods and offers recipes too.

FESTIVALS AND EVENTS

In addition to all the American national holidays, Hawaii celebrates its own festivals, pageants, and a multitude of specialized exhibits. They occur throughout the year—some particular to only one island or locality, others (such as Aloha Festivals and Lei Day) celebrated on all the islands. At festival time, everyone is welcome. Many happenings are annual events, while others are onetime affairs. Check local newspapers and the free island magazines for exact dates. Island-specific calendar and event information is also available on the Web (www.konaweb.com/calendar).

One event held islandwide is the **Hawai'i Performing Arts Festival** (www.hawaii-performingartsfestival.org, $10-60 per event). Mainland-style performing arts events are uncommon on the Big Island, so this nearly three-week-long festival, held in June or July, marks one of few opportunities to see a variety of chamber music, opera, and musical theater. If the events are too expensive or if you are a student of music, you might want to join one of the free informal brown-bag afternoon events where you can hear a short concert or a speaker discuss a musical topic.

In December, look for arts and crafts festivals around the Big Island, where handicrafts are on sale for the holiday season.

Essentials

Getting There

With the number of visitors each year approaching seven million—and another several hundred thousand just passing through—the state of Hawaii is one of the easiest places in the world to get to by plane. About half a dozen large North American airlines (plus additional charter airlines) fly to and from the islands. About twice that number of foreign carriers, mostly from Asia and Oceania, also touch down there on a daily or weekly basis. Hawaii is a hotly contested air market. Competition among carriers is fierce, and this makes for some sweet deals and a wide choice of fares for the money-wise traveler. It also makes for pricing chaos. Airlines usually adjust their flight schedules about every three months to account for seasonal differences in travel and route changes.

There are two categories of airlines you can take to Hawaii: **domestic,** meaning American-owned, and **foreign**-owned. An American law, penned at the turn of the 20th century to protect American shipping, says that *only* an American carrier can transport you between two American cities. In the airline industry, this law is still very much in effect. It means, for example, that if you want a round-trip flight between San Francisco and Honolulu, you *must* fly on a domestic carrier. If, however, you are flying from San Francisco to Tokyo, you are at liberty to fly a foreign airline, and you may even have a stopover in Hawaii, but you must continue to Tokyo or some other foreign city and cannot fly back to San Francisco on the foreign airline. Travel agents know this, but if you're planning your own trip, be aware of this fact.

If you fly to Hawaii from another country, you are free to use either an American or foreign carrier.

FLIGHTS TO THE BIG ISLAND

Most direct Mainland-Big Island flights land at the **Kona International Airport** (airport code KOA) on the west side of the island; however, United Airlines offers some direct service from Los Angeles and San Francisco to the **Hilo International Airport** (airport code ITO) on the east side of the island. If you don't have a direct flight, most domestic and foreign carriers fly you to Honolulu and have arrangements with Hawaiian Airlines for getting you to the Big Island. This involves a plane change, but your baggage can be booked straight through.

VISAS

Entering Hawaii is like entering anywhere else in the United States. Foreign nationals must have a current passport, and most must have a proper visa, an ongoing or return air ticket, and sufficient funds for the proposed stay in Hawaii. Be sure to check in your country of origin to determine whether you need a visa for U.S. entry. A visa application can be made at any U.S. embassy or consular office outside the United States. Canadians do not need a visa but must have a passport.

AGRICULTURAL INSPECTION

Everyone visiting Hawaii must fill out a "Plant and Animals Declaration Form" and present it to the appropriate official upon arrival in the state (sometimes it doesn't get collected, though). Anyone carrying any of the listed items must have these items inspected by an

---

Previous: a unique island welcome; Kohala Mountain Road.

agricultural inspection agent at the airport. These items include but are not limited to fruits, vegetables, plants, seeds, and soil, as well as live insects, seafood, snakes, and amphibians. For more information on what is prohibited, contact the Hawaii Department of Agriculture, Kona International Airport (808/326-1077, www.hawaiiag.org/hdoa).

Remember that before you leave Hawaii for the Mainland, all of your bags are again subject to an agricultural inspection, a usually painless procedure taking only a minute or two. To facilitate your departure, leave all bags unlocked until after inspection. There are no restrictions on beach sand from below the high water line, coconuts, cooked foods, dried flower arrangements, fresh flower lei, pineapples, certified pest-free plants and cuttings, or seashells. However, papayas must be treated before departure. Some restricted items are berries, fresh gardenias, jade vines, live insects and snails, cotton, plants in soil, soil itself, and sugarcane. For any questions pertaining to plants that you want to take to the Mainland, call the U.S. Department of Agriculture, Plant Protection and Quarantine office (808/933-6930 in Hilo, 808/326-1252 in Kona). Foreign countries may have different agricultural inspection requirements for flights from Hawaii (or other points in the United States) to those countries. Be sure to check with the proper foreign authorities for specifics.

PETS AND QUARANTINE

Hawaii has a very rigid pet quarantine policy designed to keep rabies and other Mainland diseases from reaching the state. All domestic pets are subject to a **120-day quarantine** (a 30-day quarantine or a newer 5-day-or-less quarantine is allowed by meeting certain pre-arrival and post-arrival requirements—inquire), and this includes substantial fees for boarding. Unless you are contemplating a move to Hawaii, it is not feasible to take pets. For complete information, contact the Department of Agriculture, Animal Quarantine Division in Honolulu (99-951 Halawa Valley St., 'Aiea, HI 96701, 808/483-7151, http://hawaii.gov/hdoa/ai/aqs/info).

Getting Around

AIR

Getting to and from the Big Island via the other islands is easy and convenient, although expensive. The only effective way for most visitors to travel between the Hawaiian Islands is by air. Luckily, Hawaii has excellent air transportation that boasts one of the industry's safest flight records. Items restricted on flights from the Mainland and from overseas are also restricted on flights within the state. Baggage allowances are the same as anywhere, except that due to space constraints, carry-on luggage on the smaller prop planes may be limited in number and size. The longest direct interisland flight in the state, 214 miles, is between Honolulu and Hilo and takes about 45 minutes. If you want to fly from the Big Island to Kaua'i, Lanai, or Moloka'i, you must connect through Honolulu. For Maui, Hawaiian Airlines does offer one daily direct flight between Hilo and Kahului (on Maui) and two daily direct flights between Kona and Kahului. In general, **Hawaiian Airlines** (www.hawaiianair.com) and **Mokulele** (www.mokuleleairlines.com), the new interisland carrier, have competitive prices, with interisland flights at about $100-150 each way.

SEA

There are no public ferries between the Big Island and the other islands in the Hawaiian chain (but Maui is so close!). Private ship lines such as Royal Caribbean, Carnival, Celebrity, and Norwegian Cruise Line do offer cruises of the islands, making stops at both the Hilo and Kailua-Kona ports. Check with these

Why Do Some Places Have Two Names?

The two-name system on the Big Island (such as Kailua-Kona or Waimea-Kamuela) has nothing to do with colonialism—although that would make for an interesting story. It is simply to avoid confusion with the post office. There is already a Kailua on the island of O'ahu, so the name of the Big Island town is actually Kailua and it is in the Kona district (which encompasses several other towns). In Waimea's case, Kamuela is used to distinguish the Big Island's Waimea from places of the same name on O'ahu and Kaua'i.

companies because their ports of call do vary. Some of these boats leave from Los Angeles and others from Vancouver, British Columbia, sailing all the way to Hawaii. Others leave from Honolulu and make a quick jaunt around the Hawaiian Islands.

LAND

The most common way to get around Hawaii is by rental car. The abundance of agencies keeps prices competitive. Hawaii also has limited public bus service, expensive taxis, and reasonable bicycle, motorcycle, and moped rentals. Hitchhiking, while illegal on the Big Island, is still used by some to get around.

Highway Overview

Getting around the Big Island is fairly easy. There is one main highway called the Hawai'i Belt Road (also called Mamalahoa Highway) that circles the island, one cross-island highway called the Saddle Road, and a few other highways and secondary roadways. The Hawai'i Belt Road is known by different numbers in various sections around the island, and this may lead to some confusion. Connecting Kailua-Kona and Hilo around the south end, the number is Highway 11. Major roads that lead off of it are Napo'opo'o Road, which runs down to Kealakekua Bay; Ke Ala O Keawe Road to Pu'uhonua O Honaunau National Historical Park; South Point Road, which drops down to the southernmost tip of the island; Chain of Craters Road, which leads through Hawai'i Volcanoes National Park to the lava-covered littoral Puna Coast; and Kea'au-Pahoa Road (Highway 130) from Kea'au to the hinterland of Puna. In Puna,

Kapoho-Pahoa Road (Highway 132) and Kapoho-Kalapana Beach Road (Highway 137) make a circle with Highway 130 from Pahoa that runs down along the shore and comes back again.

Going north from Kailua-Kona, the Hawai'i Belt Road (Highway 190), which starts off for the first few miles as Palani Road, cuts across the upper slopes of the volcanoes to Waimea. Slicing through coffee country, as part of the Belt Road, is Highway 180. From Honalo, Highway 11 heads down toward Kailua, first as Kuakini Highway, which itself makes a tangent into town, and then continues as Queen Ka'ahumanu Highway. Heading north from Kailua, Queen Ka'ahumanu Highway becomes Highway 19. In Kawaihae, it turns uphill to Waimea, becoming Kawaihae Road. In Waimea, Highways 19 and 190 merge, and Highway 19 becomes the designation as the Hawai'i Belt Road continues along and down the Hamakua Coast back to Hilo. Connecting Highway 19 and Highway 190 through the town of Waikoloa is Waikoloa Road. In Honoka'a, Highway 240 leaves the Belt Road and runs north to the edge of Waipi'o Valley. North Kohala is cut by two roads: Akoni Pule Highway (Highway 270) runs along the coast up and around the tip as far as the Pololu Valley. Connecting this road and the town of Waimea is the Kohala Mountain Road (Highway 250). The Saddle Road (Highway 200) rises to about 6,500 feet between the tall peaks of Mauna Loa and Mauna Kea, making a shortcut between Hilo and Waimea or the Kohala Coast. From along the Saddle Road, four-wheel-drive roads lead up to the

A Note about Directions: *Mauka* and *Makai*

Many of the directions listed in this guide include Hawaiian terms that are used by locals when giving directions. *Mauka* indicates towards the mountains or inland. Therefore, if a place such as a restaurant is on the *mauka* side of the road, then it is on the inland or mountain side. If a place is *makai,* that means that it is on the ocean side.

observatories atop Mauna Kea and nearly to the top of Mauna Loa.

Rental Cars

Rental-car options in Hawaii are as numerous as anywhere in the United States, from a subcompact to a full-size luxury land yacht. The most numerous seem to be compact cars and midsize sedans, but convertibles and four-wheel-drive Jeeps are very popular (and a sure giveaway that a tourist is driving that car), and some vans and SUVs are also available. Nearly all have automatic transmissions and air-conditioning. Generally, you must be 21 years old to rent; a few agencies will rent to 18-year-olds, while some require you to be 25 for certain vehicles. Those ages 21-24 will usually be charged an extra fee, which may be significant.

If you're traveling during the peak seasons of Christmas, Easter, or summer, absolutely reserve your car in advance. If you're going off-peak, you stand a very good chance of getting the car you want at a price you like once you land in the islands. You can get some sweet deals. To be on the safe side, and for your own peace of mind, it's generally best to book ahead. Another way to try to get a deal is to rent at the off-airport locations in Hilo and Kona.

All major car-rental companies in Hawaii use flat-rate pricing, which provides a fixed daily rate and unlimited mileage. Most car companies, local and national, offer special rates and deals, such as AAA discounts. These deals are common, but don't expect rental companies to let you know about them. Make sure to inquire. The basic rates aren't your only charges, however. On top of the actual rental fee, you must pay an airport access fee, airport concession fee, state tax, and a road tax surcharge—in total, an additional 25-30 percent.

Most car companies charge you a fee if you rent the car in Hilo and drop it off in Kona, and vice versa. The road to the top of Mauna Kea is a four-wheel-drive-only road. Heed the signs, not so much for going up, but for needed braking power coming down. In no way whatsoever should you attempt to drive down to Waipi'o Valley in a regular car! The grade is unbelievably steep, and only a four-wheel-drive can make it. Put simply, you have a good chance of being killed if you try it in a car.

Rental-car companies usually have blanket prohibitions regarding driving on unpaved terrain. Some of the companies even have lists with specifically forbidden roads. Talk to the rental-car employees when picking up your vehicle (and check your rental agreements) so you have a clear idea of what is allowed and what you will have to pay out-of-pocket if you decide to bend any of the rules.

Hele-On Bus

The County of Hawai'i maintains the Mass Transit Agency, known throughout the island as the Hele-On Bus. For information, schedules, and fares contact the Mass Transit Agency (www.heleonbus.org).

The main bus terminal is in downtown Hilo at Mo'oheau Park, at the corner of Kamehameha Avenue and Mamo Street. The Hele-On Bus system now has a mostly modern fleet of large buses that are clean and comfortable. The Hele-On operates daily routes all around the island. There are a number of intra-Hilo routes with additional

ESSENTIALS
GETTING AROUND

intercity routes to points around the periphery of the island, but these all operate on a very limited schedule, sometimes only once a day. Check the website for schedules and maps. If you're in a hurry you can definitely forget about taking the bus, but if you want to meet the people of Hawaii, there's no better way. The bus can be a frustrating experience for those used to proper timetables and bus stops. While there are a few actual bus stops (noted on the website), most people simply hail the bus on the side of the road. You have to be somewhat aggressive to get the driver's attention. Note: Large items like surfboards and boogie boards aren't allowed on board, but bicycles can be put on the front of the bus. As of 2016, the fare is $2 all bus routes on the island. There are 10-ticket books and monthly passes available if you plan to take the bus a lot or stick around for a while.

Taxis

Both the Hilo and Kona airports always have taxis waiting for fares. Fares are regulated. From Hilo's airport to downtown costs about $15, to the Banyan Drive hotels about $10. From the Kona airport to hotels and condos along Ali'i Drive in Kailua fares run $25-40, north to Waikoloa Beach Resort they run about $50, and fares are approximately $70 as far north as the Mauna Kea Beach Hotel. Obviously, a taxi is no way to get around if you're trying to save money. Most taxi companies, both in Kona and Hilo, also run sightseeing services for fixed prices.

An alternative in the Kona area is **Speedi-Shuttle** (808/329-5433 or 877/521-2085, www.speedishuttle.com). Operating daily 7am-10pm, SpeediShuttle runs multi-seat vans, so its prices are cheaper per person the more people you have riding. It also would be appropriate if you have lots of luggage. SpeediShuttle has a courtesy phone at the airport for your convenience as well as an iPhone-friendly mobile reservation system. Reservations a day ahead are not necessary but may be helpful to get a ride at the time you want.

Biking

It's not for everyone, but it's also *not* not for everyone. One doesn't need to be a super-experienced biker or an Ironman in order to ride around the island. Pedaling around the Big Island can be both fascinating and draining. If you circle the island, it's nearly 300 miles around via the shortest route. Most pick an area and bike there. Generally, roads are flat or of gradual gradient, making for some relatively easy riding. The major exceptions are the roads from Kailua to Holualoa, Kawaihae to Waimea, from Waimea up over the mountain to Hawi, the Saddle Road, and the road up to the summit of Mauna Kea. Generally, roads are well paved, but the shoulders on secondary highways and back roads are often narrow and sometimes in poor shape. Be especially careful on Mamalahoa Highway from Palani Junction south through Holualoa to Honalo and from there south to Honaunau, as there is plenty of traffic and the road is narrow and windy.

You might be better off bringing your own bike, but there are a handful of bike-rental shops around the island. Road bikes are great for touring and for a workout along the Kona highways and from Hilo to Volcano. Otherwise, you're better off with a cruiser for pedaling around town or along the beach, or with a mountain bike that can handle the sometimes poor back-road conditions as well as limited off-road biking possibilities.

If you are coming to the island for a short trip and you want to go it by bike, I suggest starting in Kona and moving south in order to avoid some very big hills (you don't want to travel uphill from Hilo to Volcano). It's possible to ride the entire island in two days; however, four to seven makes for a much nicer experience. For more information about riding the Big Island, a great resource is the **Hilo Bike Hub** (318 E. Kawili St., 808/961-4452, www.hilobikehub.com, Mon.-Fri. 9am-5:30pm, Sat. 9am-5pm). Many of their staff have done this trip (or even written about this trip) and can offer you tips and suggestions. For mountain biking and trail information on all the major islands, pick up a copy of *Mountain Biking the Hawaiian Islands,* by John Alford (Ohana Publishing, Honolulu, 877/682-7433, www.bikehawaii.com).

Biking is also a great way to commute on the island. Park employees who live in Volcano often commute to work, and the same goes for individuals who live and work in Hilo. Another popular commute is between Puna and Hilo, where the road is mainly flat. If you get tired on the way or if you don't want to ride round-trip, the Hele-On Bus has a bike rack on the front, so there's no problem with securing your bike and riding yourself home on public transportation. Note: The most difficult part with bike riding in Hawaii is that there is not always somewhere to lock your bike; bike racks can be far and few between. Sometimes you have to get creative with locking your bike, so be prepared with extra locks.

GETTING YOUR BIKE TO THE BIG ISLAND

Transporting your bike to Hawai'i from one of the neighbor islands is no problem, but can be very expensive. All of the interisland carriers will fly it for you for about $35 one-way on the same flight as you take—just check it in as baggage. Bikes must be packed in a box or hard case, supplied by the owner. Handlebars must be turned sideways and the pedals removed or turned in. Bikes go on a space-available basis only—usually not a problem, except, perhaps, during bicycle competitions. In addition, a release of liability for damage may have to be signed before the airline will accept the bike. If you plan ahead, you can send your bike the previous day by air freight, but that is more expensive.

Getting your bike to Hawaii from the Mainland will depend on which airline you take. Most will accept bicycles as baggage with the approximate additional charge of $100 each way because it is deemed an oversized object.

Recreation

SCUBA DIVING

If you think that Hawaii is beautiful above the sea, wait until you explore below. Warm tropical waters that average 75-80°F year-round and coral growth make it a fascinating haven for reef fish and aquatic plantlife. You'll discover that Hawaiian waters are remarkably clear, with excellent visibility. Fish in every fathomable color parade by. Lavender clusters of coral, red and gold coral trees, and over 1,500 different types of shells carpet the ocean floor. In some spots the fish are so accustomed to humans that they'll nibble at your fingers. In other spots, lurking moray eels add the special zest of danger. Sharks and barracudas pose less danger than scraping your knee on the coral or being driven against the rocks by a heavy swell. There are enormous but harmless sea bass and a profusion of sea turtles. All this awaits you below the surface of Hawaii's waters.

The Big Island has particularly generous underwater vistas open to anyone donning a mask and fins. Those in the know consider the deep diving along the steep drop-offs of Hawai'i's geologically young coastline some of the best in the state. The ocean surrounding the Big Island has not had a chance to turn the relatively new lava to sand, which makes the visibility absolutely perfect, even to depths of 150 feet or more. There's also 60-70 miles of coral belt around the Big Island, which adds up to a magnificent diving experience. Only advanced divers should attempt deepwater dives, but beginners and snorkelers will have many visual thrills inside the protected bays and coves. While most people head to the west (Kona) side, there is very good diving on the east side as well, particularly near Hilo. As always, weather conditions will dictate how the water and underwater conditions will be, so always inquire about sites and conditions with one of the dive shops before you head for the water.

If you're a scuba diver you'll have to show your certification card before local shops will rent you gear, fill your tanks, or take you on a charter dive. Plenty of outstanding scuba instructors will give you lessons toward certification, and they're especially reasonable because of the stiff competition. Prices vary, but you can take a three- to five-day semi-private certification course including all equipment for about $350-500. Divers unaccustomed to Hawaiian waters should not dive alone regardless of their experience. Most opt for dive tours to special dive grounds guaranteed to please. These vary also, but an accompanied single-tank dive where no boat is involved goes for about $60; expect to spend about $100 for a two-tank boat dive. Most introductory dives will be about $130. Special charter dives, night dives, and photography dives are also offered. Basic equipment costs $25-35 for the day, and most times you'll only need the top of a wet suit.

SNORKELING

Snorkeling is simple and can be enjoyable to anyone who can swim. In about 15 minutes you can be taught the fundamentals of snorkeling—you really don't need formal instructions. Other snorkelers or dive-shop attendants can tell you enough to get you started. Because you can breathe without lifting your head, you get great propulsion from the fins and hardly ever need to use your arms. You can go for much greater distances and spend longer periods in the water than if you were swimming. Experienced snorkelers make an art of this sport, and you, too, can see and do amazing things with a mask, snorkel, and flippers. Don't, however, get a false sense of invincibility and exceed your limitations.

Some hotels and condos have snorkel equipment for guests, but if it isn't free, it will almost always cost more than if you rent it from a snorkel or dive shop. These shops rent snorkel gear at competitive rates; depending

on the quality of gear, snorkel gear rental runs about $3-9 a day. Sporting goods stores and big-box stores like Costco, Target, and Walmart also have this equipment for sale; a basic set might run as little as $20.

Miles of coral reef ring the island, and it's mostly close to shore so you don't have to swim too far out to see coral communities. These are some of the most popular snorkeling sites:

- **Kona:** Kekaha Kai State Park, Pawai Bay, White Sands Beach (aka Disappearing Sands Beach), Kahalu'u Beach Park, Kealakekua Bay by the Captain Cook monument (often said to be the best on the island), and at Pu'uhonua O Honaunau in Honaunau Bay.

- **Kohala:** 'Anaeho'omalu Beach, Hapuna Beach, Mauna Kea Beach, Puako coastal area, Spencer Beach Park, and Mahukona Beach Park.

- **Puna:** Kapoho tide pools and Isaac Hale Beach Park.

- **Hilo:** Leleiwi Beach Park and Richardson's Beach Park.

Before you put your mask on, however, ask at a snorkel shop about which locations are best for the season and water conditions. Inquire about types of fish and other sea creatures you might expect to see, water clarity, entry points, surf conditions, water current, and parking.

KAYAKING

Ocean kayaking has gained much popularity in Hawaii in the last several years. The state has no white-water kayaking, and there are no rivers on the Big Island appropriate for river kayaking. Although the entire coastline would offer adventure for the expert kayaker, most people try sections of the west coast near Kealakekua Bay or Puako and east out of Hilo that offer excellent shoreline variation and great snorkeling. Generally speaking, water conditions on the Kona Coast are best in the winter and those on the Hilo side are better in the summer.

Be sure to check with the kayak shops to get the latest information about sea conditions, and consider taking one of their organized tours. Tours go to exceptional places, and while they vary, the tours generally run about $75-100 for a half day.

Kayaks (the sit-on-top kind) generally rent for about $25 single or $50 tandem for a day. Most shops want day-rental kayaks back by 5pm. Some shops rent carriers to haul the kayak. A few shops are located near a launch site, but many are away from the water, so you will have to strap the kayak to a rack and drive to where you want to put in.

FISHING

Hawaii has some of the most exciting and productive "blue waters" in all the world. Here you can find a sportfishing fleet made up of skippers and crews who are experienced professional anglers. You can also fish from jetties, piers, rocks, or the shore. If rod and reel don't strike your fancy, try the old-fashioned throw net, or take along a spear when you go snorkeling or scuba diving. There's nighttime torch fishing that requires special skills and equipment, and freshwater fishing in public areas. Streams and irrigation ditches yield introduced trout, bass, and catfish. While you're at it, you might want to try crabbing, or working low-tide areas after sundown hunting octopus, a tantalizing island delicacy.

Deep-Sea Fishing

Hawaii is positioned well for deep-sea fishing. Within eight miles there are waters to depths of 18,000 feet. Most game-fishing boats work the waters on the calmer Kona side of the island. Some skippers, carrying anglers who are accustomed to the sea, will also work the much rougher windward coasts and island channels where the fish bite just as well. Trolling is the preferred method of deep-sea fishing; this is done usually in waters of 1,000-2,000 fathoms (a fathom is six feet). The skipper will either "area fish," which means running in a crisscross pattern over a known productive area, or "ledge fish,"

which involves trolling over submerged ledges where game fish are known to feed. The most advanced marine technology, available on many boats, sends sonar beeps searching for fish. On deck, the crew and anglers scan the horizon in the age-old Hawaiian tradition, searching for clusters of seabirds feeding on baitfish pursued to the surface by the huge and aggressive game fish. "Still fishing" or "bottom fishing" with handlines yields some tremendous fish.

The most thrilling game fish in Hawaiian waters is the **marlin,** generically known as "billfish" or *a'u* to the locals. The king of them is the blue marlin, with record catches of well over 1,000 pounds, and these are called "granders." The mightiest caught in the waters off this island was a huge 1,649 pounds; it was caught in 1984. There are also striped marlin and sailfish, which often go over 200 pounds. The best times for marlin are during spring, summer, and fall. The fishing tapers off in January and picks up again by late February. "Blues" can be caught year-round, but, oddly enough, when they stop biting it seems as though the striped marlin pick up. Second to the marlin are **tuna.** Ahi (yellowfin tuna) are caught in Hawaiian waters at depths of 100-1,000 fathoms. They can weigh 300 pounds, but 25-100 pounds is common. There are also aku (skipjack tuna) and the delicious ono (wahoo), which average 20-40 pounds. **Mahimahi,** with its high, prominent forehead and long dorsal fin, is another strong, fighting, deepwater game fish abundant in Hawaii. These delicious fish can weigh up to 70 pounds. No license is needed for recreational saltwater fishing.

Shore Fishing

Shore fishing and bait casting yield *papio,* a jack tuna. *Akule,* a scad (locally called *halalu*), is a smallish schooling fish that comes close to shore and is great to catch on light tackle. *Ulua* are shore fish and can be found in tide pools. They're excellent eating, average two to three pounds, and are taken at night or with spears. *'O'io* are bonefish that come close to shore to spawn. They're caught by bait casting and bottom fishing with cut bait. They're bony, but they're a favorite for fish cakes and *poke*. *Awa* is a schooling fish that loves brackish water. It can grow up to three feet long and is a good fighter; a favorite for throw-netters, it's even raised commercially in fishponds. Besides these there are plenty of goatfish, mullet, mackerel, snapper, sharks, and even salmon. No license is needed for recreational saltwater fishing.

Charters

By and large, the vast majority of charter fishing boats on the Big Island berth at the Honokohau Harbor just north of Kailua-Kona. A few boats also leave from Keauhou Bay and Kawaihae Harbor on the west side, and some use the river mouth in Hilo. Captains of these vessels invariably have been fishing these waters for years and know where to look for a catch. Rates vary, as do the length of outings (usually four, six, or eight hours) and number of passengers allowed on the boats. Although pricing varies, fishing excursions generally run in the vicinity of $150 for a half-day charter to $230 for a full-day shared charter, and $500 half-day to $1,000 full-day exclusive charter.

HIKING

Hiking on the Big Island is stupendous. There's something for everyone, from quick short walks at scenic points to exhausting treks to the summit of Mauna Loa. The largest number of trails, and the most outstanding according to many, are laced across Hawai'i Volcanoes National Park. In the north you'll find Waipi'o, Waimanu, and Pololu Valleys. The Division of Forestry and Wildlife (19 E. Kawili St., Hilo, 808/974-4221, http://hawaii.gov/dlnr/dofaw) also maintains a number of trails in various locations around the island that cater to all levels of hikers. Check in the Hilo office for details and maps.

Don't leave your valuables in your tent, and always carry your money, papers, and camera with you. At the least, let someone know where you are going and when you plan to be back; supply an itinerary and your expected route, and stick to it.

There are many reasons to stay on designated trails—this not only preserves Hawaii's fragile environment, it also keeps you out of dangerous areas. Occasionally, trails will be closed for maintenance, so stay off those routes. Most trails are well maintained, but trailhead markers are sometimes missing. Look for mileage markers along many park and forest reserve trails to gauge your progress. They are usually metal stakes set about a foot off the ground, with numbers indicating the distance from a trailhead. The trails themselves can be muddy, and therefore treacherously slippery.

Many trails are used by hunters of wild boar, deer, or game birds. If you hike in hunting areas during hunting season, you should wear brightly colored or reflective clothing. Often, forest reserve trails have check-in stations at trailheads. Hikers and hunters must sign a logbook, especially if they intend to camp. The comments by previous hikers are worth reading for up-to-the-minute information on trail conditions.

Twilight is short in the islands, and night sets in rapidly. In June, sunrise is around 6am and sunset 7pm; in December, these occur at 7am and 6pm. If you become lost, find an open spot and stay put; at night, stay as dry as you can. If you must continue, walk on ridges and avoid the gulches, which have more obstacles and make it harder for rescuers to spot you. Do not light a fire. Some forest areas can be very dry and fire could spread easily. Fog is only encountered at the 1,500- to 5,000-foot level, but be careful of disorientation.

Generally, stay within your limits, be careful, and enjoy yourself.

GOLF

The Big Island has some of the most beautiful golf links in Hawaii. The Kohala-area courses taken together are considered by some to be the crown jewel of the state's golf options. Robert Trent Jones Sr. and Jr. have both built exceptional courses here. Dad built the Mauna Kea Beach Hotel course, while the kid built his at the Waikoloa Beach Resort. The Mauna Kea course bedevils many as the ultimate challenge. Other big-name golf course architects (and players), such as Jack Nicklaus, Arnold Palmer, and Tom Weiskopf, have added their talents here as well. Sometimes the Kohala golf courses are used for tournament play, like the Senior Skins Tournament at the Francis H. I'i Brown South Course. If the Kohala courses are too rich for your blood, there are a few in the Kailua area that are less expensive, or you can play a round in Hilo for about $25 and hit nine holes in Honoka'a for $20. How about golfing at Volcano Golf and Country Club, where, if you miss a short putt, you can blame it on an earthquake?

Most golf courses offer lessons. Many have driving ranges, some of which are lighted. The majority have pro shops and clubhouses with a restaurant or snack shop. Most courses offer reduced *kama'aina* (resident) rates and discount rates for play that starts later in the day. Be sure to ask about these rates as they often afford substantial savings. Guests of resorts affiliated with a golf course also get reduced greens fees.

Deciding at the last minute to golf? Want a discount rate? Willing to golf where it may not necessarily be your first choice? Try **Stand-by Golf** (808/322-2665, www. hawaiistandbygolf.com), where you can arrange tee times for great savings. Call one day in advance or in the morning on the day you want to play.

Travel Tips

WHAT TO PACK

It's a snap to pack for a visit to the Big Island. The weather is moderate and uniform on the whole, and the style of dress is delightfully casual. The rule of thumb is to pack lightly—especially since the majority of bed-and-breakfasts and vacation rentals have laundry machines. If you forget something at home, it won't be a disaster. You can buy everything you'll need in Hawaii (that's why they brought Target and Ross Dress for Less here).

A few points are worthy of note. While shorts and T-shirts or short-sleeve shirts and blouses might be your usual daily wear, jeans or other long pants and closed-toe shoes are best and sometimes required if you plan on taking a horseback ride or dusty ATV tour. Remember to bring a hat for the rain and sun; if you forget, inexpensive baseball caps and straw or woven hats are found easily throughout the island. Only a few classy restaurants in the finest hotels require men to wear a sport coat for dinner. If you don't have one, those hotels can supply you with one for the

evening. For women, a dress of the "resort wear" variety will suffice for most any occasion. By and large, "resort casual" is as dressy as you'll need to be in Hawaii.

One occasion for which you'll have to consider dressing warmly is a visit to the mountaintop. If you intend to visit Mauna Kea, Mauna Loa, or view the lava flow/glow at night, it'll be downright chilly. In a pinch, a sweatshirt or hooded windbreaker/raincoat will do the trick, although you'll be more comfortable in warmer clothing like a wool sweater or thick jacket, cap, and gloves. If your hands get cold, put a pair of socks over them.

Tropical rain showers can happen at any time, so you might consider a fold-up umbrella. Nighttime winter temperatures may drop into the lower 60s or upper 50s, even on the coast, so be sure to have a light sweater and long pants along.

Dressing your feet is hardly a problem. For locals, rubber flip-flops, also called slippers (Locals brand is popular), are appropriate for every event. However, there are times when you might want to consider a shoe with more support, such as for crossing streams or wet trails. If you plan on heavy-duty hiking, you'll definitely want your hiking boots; the lightweight version is usually sufficient. Lava, especially 'a'a, is murderous on shoes (in fact, I have a separate pair of shoes just for walking on 'a'a). Most backcountry trails are rugged and muddy, and you'll need those good old lug soles for traction and laces for ankle support. If you plan moderate hikes, running shoes should do.

Two specialty items that you might consider bringing along are binoculars and snorkel gear. A pair of binoculars really enhances sightseeing—great for viewing birds and sweeping panoramas, and almost a necessity if you're going whale-watching. Flippers, mask, and snorkel can easily be bought or rented in Hawaii but don't weigh much or take up much space in your luggage. They'll save you a few dollars in rental fees and you'll have them when you want them.

Lastly, I suggest that you bring a reusable bag or two for grocery shopping because there is a plastic bag ban on the Big Island. If you don't have one to bring, or want to pick up a fantastic souvenir, I recommend getting a hot/cold bag available at any of the large grocery store chains (such as KTA or Foodland). These bags do indeed keep items hot or cold (as the name suggests), and they have fun island designs on them (like fish or Spam *musubi*). In fact, you might want to buy a few extra to bring home!

CONDUCT AND CUSTOMS

The best principle to go by is "do it with *aloha*." *Aloha*, a common greeting, also refers to the *aloha* spirit, a way of living and treating each other with love and respect. One translation is "joyfully sharing life." It refers to the attitude of friendly acceptance for which the Hawaiian Islands are so famous.

Everything (with one exception, and I'll get to it) moves slower on the Big Island than on the Mainland. Expect a quick trip to the grocery store to take double the time when the person ahead of you in line gets to talking

story with the cashier. Likewise, posted hours for shops and restaurants are mere suggestions. Sometimes they don't open at all and sometimes they stay open later if people are around.

Where Big Islanders like to move fast is in their cars. There is nothing locals hate more than riding behind a slow-moving (tourist) car on a two-lane highway with nowhere to go. It is standard practice, if you're moving slower than everyone else (and it's fine if you are), to put your blinker on and move over as best as you can (even if there isn't a shoulder) and let everyone pass you. This is how you will retain a sense of *aloha* on the road.

Another road rule worth noting is that Big Islanders do slow down on one-lane roads to let other cars pass (and then usually you give the other driver a *shaka* sign, a hand wave where only the thumb and baby finger stick out). The rule is, the downhill person yields to the uphill person (it's harder to stop if you're climbing vertically). This is very useful information on your way up to Mauna Kea or down to Waipi'o Valley.

BUDGET TIPS

It's a misconception that you need a big budget for the Big Island. The *kama'aina* don't go to resorts for their meals, and why should you? The tips below are "priceless" ideas for how to save on transportation, where to stay for less, eat for cheap, and days of no-cost fun (the beach is always free!).

Transportation

It is possible to get around the island solely by bus; however, since buses can be sparse, you really need to plan ahead to ensure the timing works for you. Also, buses don't usually travel through neighborhoods, so when planning your accommodations, check to see how far they are from the main road. A second consideration is that the bus stops at the terminal at the Kona airport, but not the Hilo airport (and it's quite a walk to the highway from the airport). However, the airport in Hilo is right near the downtown and a cab ride to your lodging should only run you about $15.

A second option, if you don't want to or can't rent a car, is to bring or rent a bike. If you're planning on riding your way around the island, you'll want to travel counterclockwise in order to avoid some big hills.

If you do get a car, it's important to know that gas prices really vary all over the island, with the highest prices in Kona and Kohala and the lowest in Hilo. Gas prices in general are much higher than on the Mainland, so get yourself a car that isn't a gas guzzler. The island actually isn't that big (relatively speaking), so even if you're driving around it, you won't have to fill up your tank that often. But when you do have to fill up, try to do so in Hilo or, if you have a membership, at Costco in Kona (where the price of gas tends to be nearly 10 cents cheaper per gallon than anywhere else in the area).

Lodging

The obvious cheap way to stay on the Big Island is in your own tent at a county, state, or national park. There are only a few technically free spots to stay, such as **Pololu Valley** (you'll likely have the place to yourself); otherwise, other sites such as **Spencer Beach Park,** another excellent space to camp that's easy to access, require a permit that you can easily purchase through the respective agencies' websites. If pitching a tent isn't your thing, there are still plenty of options with roofs. There are some standard hostels in Hilo, Kona, and Volcano. There are also some options around the island that offer reasonable rates without having to stay in a dorm room: **Hotel Manago** (Kona), **The Old Hawaiian Bed and Breakfast** (Hilo), and **Hotel Honoka'a Club** (Hamakua Coast) are just a few options of where to stay inexpensively and have some privacy.

Eating

There ain't nothing cheaper than free. Food foraging on the Big Island is possible (meaning, grabbing fruit or vegetables off of trees or bushes in public spaces), but please do so responsibly. In **Hawai'i Volcanoes National Park,** the rule is that one quart of 'ohelo berries per person may be taken each month and only for personal consumption. Check with the rangers at the visitors center for more information about food foraging in the park. For free food that involves less work, try one of the recommended bars in Hilo that offer free pupus (appetizers) with the purchase of a drink. The best deal on the Kona side of the island is on Friday and Saturday nights after 10pm at **Sansei Seafood Restaurant and Sushi Bar** (Kohala), when sushi and appetizers are 50 percent off and drink specials are available. There is also free karaoke.

In general, it's easier to find a culinary bargain in Hilo than on the Kona side. Pick up Japanese okazuya (side dishes) at the **Hilo Lunch Shop;** each item is less than a dollar and some are only 30 cents. You can easily feed yourself for a few bucks. But if you're looking for a good deal in Kailua-Kona, head straight to **Quinn's Almost By The Sea** for their short ribs. They are just as good and maybe even better than the best restaurants around town at a fraction of the price.

As any thrifty traveler knows, one of your best bets for saving money on food is the grocery store. But with **Island Naturals Market and Deli** (three locations on the island), you don't have to sacrifice quality (or local organic foods) to eat cheaply. Eat to your stomach's content at their hot bar daily after 7pm (times may vary depending on the store) and your meal, which is priced per pound, is discounted. Fridays are the best day to stop by this grocery chain because beer and wine are 20 percent off!

Lastly, as the most important part of your day is breakfast, the most inexpensive way to start your morning is with a **Spam musubi.** This rice, Spam, and nori "roll" can be picked up for under $2 (try 7-Eleven for Spam and egg musubi—it's like a McDonald's breakfast sandwich Hawaii style).

Activities

First order of business: Stop at one of the large chain stores and pick up your own **snorkel set** if you don't already have one. The cost of buying the snorkel set isn't that much more than you'd be charged for a day's rental, so if you plan on snorkeling for a few days, this purchase will save you about $50. Want to use that snorkel to night dive with the **manta rays** but don't want to spend $100 (more or less) on a trip? Well, save the snorkel gear you just purchased and head straight to the **Sheraton Keauhou Bay Resort and Spa,** where you can watch the manta rays from the bar at the hotel. I know it's not the same as being in the water with them, but you still get a pretty good look (they are attracted to plankton that are attracted to the lights of the hotel) and have the benefit of staying dry (and having a drink at the same time).

But saving money doesn't mean excusing yourself from all tours. All the national parks and historical sites on the island offer free tours of their parks. At **Hawai'i Volcanoes National Park** there is at least one free daily ranger-led tour of certain areas of the park. On Wednesdays there is a super-exclusive free lava tube tour (must be reserved a week in advance). There are semimonthly free tours of the **Kahuku** section of the park located in Ka'u. The same goes for **Mauna Kea.** Although the price for most tours to the summit is $200, there are various free tours offered at Mauna Kea.

Next, check the websites of **yoga** studios for their "community class" hours. These classes, although sometimes shorter than a full-price class, are usually only $5 (versus $10-15) and taught by the same teachers. Likewise, you don't need to have lots of cash to indulge in some self-care. Massages in Hilo are at least half the price of those offered at the resorts and hotels in Kona and Kohala, and the same goes for acupuncture.

GREEN TOURISM

It's not easy being green—well, actually it is in Hawaii. The easiest way to reduce your ecological footprint while on the Big Island is to eat locally. This task is not too difficult given the multitude of farmers markets throughout the island, the local produce available at mainstream supermarkets, and fruits that literally fall from the trees in front of you.

A second option is to go off the grid. Campsites are abundant through the island and they are located on prime oceanfront (or mountainside) real estate. There are also several hotels that are off the grid or utilize green technologies to reduce their imprint.

The biggest challenge to being green on the Big Island is transportation. The public transportation system isn't ideal and most people simply avoid it. If you're not in a rush, try it out. You'll be saving (a lot) of money on gas while reducing pollution. Otherwise, try to carpool when possible or even walk or bike ride to your destinations.

ACCESSIBILITY

A person with a disability can have a wonderful time in Hawaii; all that's needed is a little preplanning. The key to a smooth trip is to make as many arrangements ahead of time as possible. Tell the transportation companies and hotels you'll be dealing with the nature of your ability in advance so that they can make arrangements to accommodate you, if possible. Bring your medical records and notify medical establishments of your arrival if you'll be needing their services. Travel with a friend or make arrangements for an aide on arrival.

Bring your own wheelchair if possible and let airlines know if it is battery-powered; boarding interisland flights often requires steps. Airlines can board you early on special lifts, but they must know that you're coming. Many hotels and restaurants accommodate persons with disabilities, but always call ahead to make sure, given that some of the smaller establishments (especially bed-and-breakfasts) have lots of stairs and no ramps.

Services

At Hilo International Airport, all passengers

arrive or leave via a jetway on the second level, and there are escalators, stairs, and some elevators between levels. Baggage claim, bathrooms, and telephones are accessible. Parking is convenient in designated areas. The Kona International Airport is all one level. Boarding and deplaning by lift is possible for travelers with disabilities. There are no jetways. Bathrooms and telephones are accessible, and there is specially designated handicapped parking.

All rental-car agencies can install hand controls on their cars if given enough notice—usually 48-72 hours. Your own state parking placard will be honored here. Medical help, nurses, and companions can be arranged through the **Center for Independent Living** (808/935-3777 in Hilo or 808/323-2221 in Kona). Doctors are referred by **Hilo Medical Center** (808/974-4700) and the **Kona Community Hospital** (808/322-9311). Medical equipment rentals are available in Hilo from **Apria Healthcare** (808/969-1221), **Rainbow Medical Supply** (808/935-9393), and **Shiigi Drug** (808/935-0001); and in Kona from **Big Island Medical Equipment** (808/323-3313).

TRAVELING WITH CHILDREN

The Big Island is extremely child friendly, or *keiki* friendly (as children are called here). Many restaurants offer children's menus, resort hotels have activities geared for children (some offer day care), there are many beach areas with shallow wading water and lifeguards on duty, and the national parks all have Junior Ranger programs with special activity books for kids. Best of all, a lot of these kid-friendly activities are free, including the many playgrounds located throughout the island (not just in Hilo and Kona, but also Pahoa, Honoka'a, and Volcano). Note: Before you book any tours, check with the tour providers to see if there are restrictions involving children. For instance, many of the horseback riding and zip-lining tours can't accommodate individuals (not just children) under a certain weight and height—but some can. Likewise, there are ATV tours that will allow children to ride with an adult, while others don't take any rider under 16 years old.

SENIOR TRAVELERS

Not a tour company per se, but an educational opportunity for seniors, **Road Scholar** (800/454-5768, www.roadscholar.org), developed by Elderhostel, offers short-term programs on five of the Hawaiian Islands. Different programs focus on history, culture, cuisine, and the environment in association with one of the colleges or universities in the islands. Most programs use hotels for accommodations.

GAY AND LESBIAN TRAVELERS

Same-sex marriage was made legal in Hawaii in 2011. If you're looking to make contact with the LGBT community, the best place to go to is the Pahoa area, where the free-spirit vibe tends to attract this crowd. A few bed-and-breakfast establishments particularly cater to these groups; look for them on **Purple Roofs** (www.purpleroofs.com), a website dedicated to LGBT travel.

For additional LGBT resources on the Big Island or in Hawaii, check out the very comprehensive website of **Out in Hawaii** (www.outinhawaii.com).

OPPORTUNITIES FOR STUDY AND VOLUNTEERING

You don't need to leave the country to study abroad. The University of Hawai'i at Hilo (UHH, http://hilo.hawaii.edu) has exchange programs with many U.S. Mainland universities (the majority are on the West Coast) that allow students to study for a semester at UHH for a discounted price and transfer credit back to their home institutions. Check with your Mainland university and UHH to see if an exchange is possible. Another possibility is to apply directly for admission to

UHH or Hawaii Community College (http://hawaii.hawaii.edu).

There are two really excellent ways to volunteer long term on the Big Island. First, through the **World Wide Opportunities on Organic Farms** (WWOOF, www.wwoof.org) organization. Their Hawaii-specific website (www.wwoofhawaii.org) links farmers to interested volunteers. Take care to do research about the farm and contact previous volunteers. Conditions and arrangements from farm to farm vary substantially. Some require 50 hours of work while others require only 20. Some offer free room and board (food from Costco or food from the farm) while others have workers pay for accommodations. Likewise, accommodations can range from a tent to a small shared cabin. Nonetheless, WWOOFing is a great opportunity to try your hand at farming and learn about the land in Hawaii.

A second opportunity is with **Hawai'i Volcanoes National Park.** Again, responsibilities and compensation vary from position to position, but generally, volunteers must commit to at least two months of full-time service (some positions last up to a year), and in exchange, volunteers are offered housing in the park and a daily stipend (between $20 and 25 per day). Contact the park directly (www.nps.gov/havo) for additional information or check out www.volunteer.gov for more information. Also, positions are sometimes posted on www.idealist.org; search for Hawaii.

Health and Safety

STAYING HEALTHY

In a survey published some years ago by *Science Digest,* Hawaii was cited as the healthiest state in the United States in which to live. Indeed, Hawaiian citizens live longer than residents anywhere else in America: men to 76 years and women to 82. Lifestyle, heredity, and diet help with these figures, but Hawaii is still an oasis in the middle of the ocean, and germs just have a tougher time getting there. There are no cases of malaria, cholera, or yellow fever. Because of a strict quarantine law, rabies is also nonexistent. On the other hand, tooth decay—perhaps because of a wide use of sugar and the enzymes present in certain tropical fruits—is 30 percent above the national average. Also, obesity and related heart problems and hard drug use—especially "ice"—are prevalent among native Hawaiians. Still, with the perfect weather, a multitude of fresh-air activities, soothing negative ionization from the sea, and a generally relaxed and carefree lifestyle, everyone feels better here. Hawaii is just what the doctor ordered: a beautiful, natural health spa. That's one of its main drawing cards. The food and tap water are perfectly safe, and the air quality is the best in the country.

Handling the Sun

Don't become a victim of your own exuberance. People can't wait to strip down and lie on the sand like beached whales, but the tropical sun will burn you to a cinder if you're silly. The burning rays come through more easily in Hawaii because of the sun's angle, and you don't feel them as much because there's always a cool breeze. The worst part of the day is 11am-3pm. The Big Island lies between 19 and 20 degrees north latitude, not even close to the equator, but it's still over 1,000 miles south of the sunny Southern California beaches. Be sure to apply plenty of sunscreen.

Don't forget about your head and eyes. Use your sunglasses and wear a brimmed hat. Some people lay a towel over their neck and shoulders when hiking and others will stick a scarf under their hat and let it drape down over their shoulders to provide some protection.

Whether out on the beach, hiking in the

Dengue Fever

Dengue Fever, a mosquito-borne tropical disease, is not endemic to Hawaii; however, in 2015 it was brought to the Big Island by an infected traveler. As of early 2016 there were over 200 known cases of dengue fever identified on the Big Island — the majority of cases from residents and not visitors to the island. In early 2016, Waipio Valley was closed to visitors in order to minimize the potential for new cases of Dengue. Typically, infected individuals are asymptomatic but symptoms may include: fever, joint pain, headache, and rash. The best way to avoid Dengue is to avoid being bitten by an infected mosquito. Therefore, public health professionals often urge individuals to stay away from high risk areas. Check the Hawaii Department of Health Website (http://health. hawaii.gov/docd/dengue-outbreak-2015/) for information about what areas are affected or where you may be at higher risk for acquiring the disease. If you are visiting a higher risk area, be sure to cover yourself, especially during sunrise and sunset (the time when mosquitoes are most active) and to use bug spray with DEET.

mountains, or just strolling around town, be very aware of dehydration. The sun and wind tend to sap your energy and your store of liquid.

Bugs

Everyone, in varying degrees, has an aversion to vermin and creepy crawlers. Hawaii isn't infested with a wide variety, but it does have its share. Mosquitoes were unknown in the islands until their larvae stowed away in the water barrels of the *Wellington* in 1826 and were introduced at Lahaina. They bred in the tropical climate and rapidly spread to all the islands. They are a particular nuisance in the rain forests. Be prepared and bring a natural repellent like citronella oil, available in most health stores on the islands, or a commercial product available in groceries and drugstores. Campers will be happy to have mosquito coils to burn at night as well. Note: You might notice that there aren't any mosquitoes in Volcano, Mauna Loa, or Mauna Kea. Mosquitoes hate altitude. So if you're sick of the mosquitoes, just head up the hill and you'll be amazed how there are none to be found.

Cockroaches are very democratic insects. They hassle all strata of society equally. They breed well in Hawaii, and most hotels are at war with them, trying desperately to keep them from being spotted by guests. One comforting thought is that in Hawaii they aren't a sign of filth or dirty housekeeping. They love the climate just like everyone else does, and it's a real problem keeping them under control.

WATER SAFETY

Hawaii has one very sad claim to fame: More people drown here than anywhere else in the world. Moreover, there are dozens of victims yearly with broken necks and backs or with injuries from scuba and snorkeling accidents. These statistics shouldn't keep you out of the sea, because it is indeed beautiful—and benevolent in most cases—and a major reason to go to Hawaii. But if you're foolish, the sea will bounce you like a basketball and suck you away for good. The best remedy is to avoid situations you can't handle. Don't let anyone dare you into a situation that makes you uncomfortable. Ask lifeguards or beach attendants about conditions, and follow their advice. If local people refuse to go in, there's a good reason. Even experts get in trouble in Hawaiian waters. Some beaches are as gentle as lambs; others, especially on the north coasts during the winter months, are frothing giants.

While beachcombing, or especially when walking out on rocks, never turn your back to the sea. Be aware of undertows (the waves drawing back into the sea). They can knock you off your feet. Before entering the water, study it for rocks, breakers, and reefs. Look for ocean currents, especially those within reefs that can cause riptides when the water washes out a channel. Observe the water well before you enter. Note where others are swimming or snorkeling and go there. Don't swim alone if possible, and obey all warning signs. Come in *before* you get tired.

When the wind comes up, get out. Stay out of the water during periods of high surf. High surf often creates riptides that can pull you out to sea. Riptides are powerful currents, like rivers in the sea, that can drag you out. Mostly they peter out not too far from shore, and you can often see their choppy waters on the surface. If caught in a "rip," don't fight to swim directly against it. You'll lose and only exhaust yourself. Swim diagonally across it, while going along with it, and try to stay parallel to the shore until you are out of the strong pull.

When bodysurfing, never ride straight in; come to shore at a 45-degree angle. Remember, waves come in sets. Little ones can be followed by giants, so watch the action awhile instead of plunging right in. Standard procedure is to duck under a breaking wave. You can survive even thunderous oceans using this technique. Don't try to swim through a heavy froth, and never turn your back and let it smash you.

Stay off of coral. Standing on coral damages it, as does breaking it with your hands, and it might give you a nasty infection.

Leave the fish, turtles, and seals alone. Fish should never be encouraged to feed from humans. Green sea turtles and seals are endangered species, and stiff fines can be levied on those who knowingly disturb them. Have a great time looking, but give them space.

Hawaiians want to entertain you, and they want you to be safe. The county, for its part, doesn't put up ocean conditions signs at beaches just to waste money. They're there for your safety. Pay heed. The last rule is, "If in doubt, stay out."

Volcanic Smog

That sulphurous, egg-like taste in your mouth is volcanic smog, also called "vog." Just like Los Angeles has smog alert days, Hawaii can experience bad "vog" days. The vog can travel as far north as Hilo and as far south as South Point. Hypothetically, it doesn't harm your health except that it leaves a literal bad taste in your mouth. Some holistic practitioners argue that it causes headaches. In addition, recent studies have shown that there are higher asthma rates for children who live downwind of Hawai'i Volcanoes National Park (not from the vog, but from the small particles in the air). You should be fine taking it in for a day or three during your visit to the park.

Hazards

Sharks live in all the oceans of the world. Most mind their own business and stay away from shore. Hawaiian sharks are well fed—on fish—and don't usually bother with unsavory humans. If you encounter a shark, don't panic! Never thrash around because this will trigger its attack instinct. If it comes close, scream loudly.

Portuguese man-of-wars put out long, floating tentacles that sting if they touch you. It seems that many floating jellyfish are blown into shore by winds on the 8th, 9th, and 10th days after the full moon. Don't wash the sting off with freshwater, as this will only aggravate it. Hot saltwater will take away the sting, as will alcohol (the drinking or the rubbing kind), aftershave lotion, and meat tenderizer (MSG), which can be found in any supermarket or Chinese restaurant.

Coral can give you a nasty cut, and it's known for causing infections because it's a living organism. Wash the cut immediately and apply an antiseptic. Keep it clean and covered, and watch for infection.

Poisonous sea urchins, such as the lacquer-black *wana,* can be beautiful creatures. They are found in shallow tide pools and will

Eating Gluten-Free, Vegetarian, and Vegan

Good news: It's easy to be a vegetarian or vegan on the Big Island, and I don't just mean it's easy to order a salad. First, the abundance of coconuts means coconut milk instead of cow milk is readily available, and coconut oil is used for cooking. So all you vegans, if you want to order a smoothie, don't be afraid to ask for coconut milk instead of regular milk. Chances are they'll have it. Also, many desserts (especially those bought at the farmers markets) are made from coconut milk, such as tapioca pudding and *haupia* (coconut pudding), which is a traditional Hawaiian dessert (also gluten-free!).

For vegetarian and vegan groceries and prepared food, head to the **Island Naturals Market and Deli** (www.islandnaturals.com). The market, which has three locations on the Big Island, has a hot bar and refrigerated section with copious amounts of gluten-free, vegetarian, and vegan prepared foods. And if you're in south Puna, try the lunch or dinner buffet at **Kalani Oceanside Retreat.** Although it's not entirely vegetarian, abundant vegetarian options (as well as local, organic, and gluten-free) are available here—not to mention some beautiful salad.

hurt you if you step on them. Their spines will break off, enter your foot, and burn like blazes. There are cures: Vinegar and wine poured on the wound will stop the burning. If those are not available, the Hawaiian solution is urine. It might seem ignominious to have someone pee on your foot, but it'll put the fire out. The spines will disintegrate in a few days, and there are generally no long-term effects.

Hawaiian reefs also have their share of moray eels. These creatures are ferocious in appearance but will never initiate an attack. You'll have to poke around in their holes while snorkeling or scuba diving to get them to attack. Sometimes this is inadvertent on the diver's part, so be careful where you stick your hand while underwater.

Leptospirosis is a disease caused by *freshwater*-borne bacteria deposited by the urine of infected animals that are present in streams, ponds, and muddy soil. From 2 to 20 days after the bacteria enter the body, there is a *sudden* onset of fever accompanied by chills, sweats, headache, and sometimes vomiting and diarrhea. Preventive measures include: staying out of freshwater sources where cattle and other animals wade and drink; not

swimming in freshwater if you have an open cut; and not drinking stream water.

PREVENTING THEFT

From the minute you sit behind the wheel of your rental car, you'll be warned not to leave valuables unattended and to lock your car tighter than a drum. Signs warning about theft at most major tourist attractions help to fuel your paranoia. Many hotel and condo rooms offer safes so you can lock your valuables away and relax while getting sunburned. The majority of theft in Hawaii is of the "sneak thief" variety. If you leave your hotel door unlocked, a camera sitting on the seat of your rental car, or valuables on your beach towel, you'll be inviting a very obliging thief to pad away with your stuff. You'll have to take precautions, like covering up your purse with a towel if you leave it in your car while at the beach, but they won't be anything like those employed in rougher areas of the world—just normal American precautions. Hawaii's reputation is much worse than the reality. Besides, Hawaiians are still among the friendliest, most giving, and understanding people on earth.

Information and Services

MONEY
Currency

U.S. currency is all the same size, with little variation in color; those unfamiliar with it should spend some time getting acquainted so they don't make costly mistakes. U.S. coins in use are: penny ($0.01), nickel ($0.05), dime ($0.10), quarter ($0.25), half dollar ($0.50), and $1; paper currency is $1, $2 (uncommon), $5, $10, $20, $50, and $100. Bills larger than $100 are not in common usage. Since 1996, new designs have been issued for the $100, $50, $20, $10, and $5 bills. Both the old and new bills are accepted as valid currency.

Banks

Full-service bank hours are generally Monday-Thursday 8:30am-4pm and Friday until 6pm. Weekend hours are rare and weekday hours will be a bit longer at counters in grocery stores and other outlets. All main towns on Hawaii have one or more banks: Hilo, Kailua-Kona, Waimea, Kealakekua, Honoka'a, Pahoa, Waikoloa, and Hawi. Virtually all branch banks have automated teller machines (ATMs) for 24-hour service, and these can be found at some shopping centers and other venues around the island. ATMs work only when the Hawaiian bank you use is on an affiliate network with your home bank. Of most value to travelers, banks sell and cash travelers checks, give cash advances on credit cards, and exchange and sell foreign currency (sometimes with a fee). Major banks on the Big Island are American Savings Bank, Bank of Hawaii, First Hawaiian Bank, and Central Pacific Bank.

COMMUNICATIONS AND MEDIA
Post Office

Normal business hours are Monday-Friday 8am-4:30pm; very few branches are open Saturday. However, some branches open as early as 7am and close before 3pm. Most are closed during lunchtime because they usually are only staffed by one person (everyone has to eat). The central post office on Hawaii is in Hilo, and there are 25 branch post offices in towns around the island.

Telephone

The telephone system on the main islands is modern and comparable to any system on the Mainland. Any phone call to a number on that island is a **local call**; it's **long distance** when dialing to another island. You can "direct dial" from Hawaii to the Mainland and more than 160 foreign countries. Undersea cables and satellite communications ensure top-quality phone service. Toll-free calls are preceded by 800, 888, 877, or 866; there is no charge to the calling party.

For directory assistance, dial: 411 (local), 1/555-1212 (interisland), area code/555-1212 (Mainland), or 800/555-1212 (toll-free). The **area code** for all the islands of Hawaii is 808.

Cell phone service and even 4G or LTE service is available in the majority of areas of the island, although sometimes service varies depending on what carrier you use. As of 2015, cell phone service (including your beloved LTE) was not available south of Pahoa (specifically the Red Road area—but then it works again at Kaimu Beach), in Waipi'o Valley, on some parts of the Saddle Road, and in the Pololu Valley near Kapa'au. Plan ahead if you depend on your cell phone as a GPS device.

Newspapers

Major daily newspapers on the Big Island include *Hawaii Tribune-Herald* (www.hilo-hawaiitribune.com), a Hilo publication, and *West Hawaii Today* (www.westhawaiitoday.com), published in Kona. Both are owned by the same parent company.

Much like how during the plantation era each town had its own bottle works, it seems like the new thing is that every town has its own weekly or monthly newspaper or newsletter. The *Volcano Community Association Voice* and the *Kaʻu Calendar* (www.kaucalendar.com) are a few examples. Local papers are a great way to find out what is happening in town.

Libraries

Libraries are located in towns and schools all over the island, with the main branch in Hilo (300 Waianuenue Ave., 808/933-8888). This location can provide information regarding all libraries. In Kailua-Kona, the library is in the center of town (75-140 Hualalai Rd., 808/327-4327). Check with each individual branch for times and services. Library cards are available free for Hawaii state residents and military personnel stationed in Hawaii, $25 for nonresidents (valid for five years), and $10 for three months for visitors. Free Internet access is available to library cardholders.

TOURIST INFORMATION
Hawaii Visitors Bureau

The Hawaii Visitors Bureau or HVB (www.gohawaii.com) is a top-notch organization providing help and information to all of Hawaii's visitors. Anyone contemplating a trip to Hawaii should visit a nearby office or check out the bureau's website for any specific information that might be required. The Hawaii Visitors Bureau's advice and excellent brochures on virtually every facet of living in, visiting, or simply enjoying Hawaii are free. The material offered is too voluminous to list, but for basics, request individual island brochures, maps, vacation planners (also on the web at www.hshawaii.com), and an all-island members directory of accommodations, restaurants, entertainment, and transportation. Allow 2-3 weeks for requests to be answered.

There are two Big Island HVB offices: **Big Island Hawaii Visitors Bureau, Hilo Branch** (101 Apuni St., Ste. 238, Hilo, 808/961-5797 or 800/648-2441, www.bigisland.org) and **Big Island Hawaii Visitors Bureau,**

Kona Branch (68-1330 Mauna Lani Dr., Ste. 109B, Kohala Coast, 808/886-1655).

Maps

Aside from the simple maps in the ubiquitous free tourist literature, the Big Island Visitors Bureau, Hawaiian Airlines, and other organizations put out folding pocket maps of the island that are available free at the airport and tourist brochure racks around the island. Various island and street maps are available at Basically Books (160 Kamehameha Ave., Hilo, 808/961-0144, www.basicallybooks.com) and Kona Stories (78-6831 Aliʻi Dr., Keauhou, 808/324-0350, www.konastories.com). Perhaps the best and most detailed of these island maps is the University of Hawaiʻi Press reference map *Hawaiʻi, The Big Island*. This map can be found at gift and sundries shops around the island, and at bookshops. If you are looking for detail, the best street map atlas of the Big Island is a two-volume publication by Odyssey Publishing: *The Ready Mapbook of West Hawaii* and *The Ready Mapbook of East Hawaii*.

In addition, Basically Books carries USGS maps, and Kona Marine Supply (74-425 Kealakehe Pkwy. #9, Kailua-Kona, 808/329-1012) carries nautical charts. The Division of Forestry and Wildlife office in Hilo (19 E. Kawili St., 808/974-4221, http://hawaii.gov/dlnr/dofaw) has map and trail description handouts for trails in the Na Ala Hele state trail system, and the visitors center at Hawaiʻi Volcanoes National Park carries hiking maps for park trails.

LOCAL EMERGENCIES
Emergencies

For **police, fire, and ambulance** anywhere on the Big Island, dial **911.** For **nonemergency police** assistance and information, dial 808/935-3311.

In case of natural disaster such as hurricanes or tsunamis on the Big Island, call **Civil Defense** (808/935-0031). **Coast Guard Search and Rescue** can be reached at 800/552-6458.

The **Sexual Assault Crisis Line** is 808/935-0677.

Weather, Marine, and Volcano Reports

For recorded information on **local island weather,** call 808/961-5582; for the **marine report,** call 808/935-9883; and for **volcano activity,** call 808/985-6000.

Consumer Protection

If you encounter problems finding accommodations or experience bad service or downright rip-offs, try the following: the Chamber of Commerce in Hilo (808/935-7178) or in the Kona/Kohala area (808/329-1758), the Office of Consumer Protection (808/933-0910), or the Better Business Bureau of Hawaii on Oʻahu (877/222-6551).

WEIGHTS AND MEASURES

Hawaii, like all of the United States, employs the "English method" of measuring weights and distances. Basically, dry weights are in ounces and pounds; liquid measures are in ounces, quarts, and gallons; and distances are measured in inches, feet, yards, and miles. The metric system is known but is not in general use.

Electricity

The same electrical current is in use in Hawaii as on the U.S. Mainland and is uniform throughout the islands. The system functions on 110 volts, 60 cycles of alternating current (AC). Appliances from Japan will work, but there is some danger that they will burn out, while those requiring the normal European voltage of 220 will not work.

Time Zones

There is no daylight saving time in Hawaii. When daylight saving time is not observed on the Mainland, Hawaii is two hours behind the West Coast, four hours behind the Midwest, five hours behind the East Coast. While daylight saving is observed, Hawaii is an additional hour behind.

Hawaii, being just east of the International Date Line, is almost a full day behind most Asian and Oceanian cities. Hours behind these countries and cities are: Japan, 19 hours; Singapore, 18 hours; Sydney, 20 hours; New Zealand, 22 hours; Fiji, 22 hours.

Resources

Glossary

PRONUNCIATION IN THE HAWAIIAN LANGUAGE

Five vowels (a, e, i, o, and u) and seven consonants (h, k, l, m, n, p, and w) are all there is to the Hawaiian alphabet. Hawaii had no written language before Western contact (except for petroglyph symbols), so if you're wondering why these letters, you can thank the European explorers and American missionaries for the Latinization of the Hawaiian language. Some basic rules:

- In the Hawaiian language, a consonant is always followed by a vowel. So yes, all Hawaiian words end in vowels.

- The letter "w" is sometimes pronounced as a "v," as in the traditional pronunciation of the word *Hawai'i*, which is "ha-VI-ee" instead of "ha-WHY-ee."

- The macron symbol over a vowel, called a kahako, means that the vowel sound is elongated.

- The backward apostrophe symbol, called an 'okina, means to make a phonetic glottal stop (to separate the word where the 'okina is placed). This is common in many Polynesian languages. For example, in the word Hawai'i there should be a glottal stop between the last two syllables.

- Vowels are pronounced as follows: "a" as "ah"; "e" as "eh"; "i" as "ee"; "o" as "oh"; and "u" as "oo."

HAWAIIAN

The following list gives you a taste of Hawaiian and provides a basic vocabulary of words in common usage that you are likely to hear. Becoming familiar with them is not a strict necessity, but they will definitely enhance your experience and make talking with local people more congenial. Many islanders spice their speech with certain words and you, too, can use them just as soon as you feel comfortable. You might even discover some Hawaiian words that are so perfectly expressive they'll become regular parts of your vocabulary. Some Hawaiian words have been absorbed into the English language and are found in English dictionaries. The definitions given below are not exhaustive, but are generally considered the most common.

'a'a: rough clinker lava. *'A'a* has become the correct geological term to describe this type of lava found anywhere in the world.

'ae: yes

ahu: traditional trail markers that are piles of stone shaped like little Christmas trees

ahupua'a: pie-shaped land divisions running from mountain to sea that were governed by *konohiki*, local *ali'i* who owed their allegiance to a reigning chief

aikane: friend; pal; buddy

'aina: land; the binding spirit to all Hawaiians. Love of the land is paramount in traditional Hawaiian beliefs.

akamai: smart; clever; wise

akua: a god, or simply "divine"

ali'i: a Hawaiian chief or noble

aloha: the most common greeting in the islands; can mean both hello and good-bye, welcome and farewell, as well as love, affection, or best wishes

aloha spirit: a way of living and treating each other with love and respect; joyfully sharing life

anuenue: rainbow

'anu'u: oracle tower

'a'ole: no

'aumakua: a personal or family god, often an ancestral spirit

auwe: alas or ouch; a traditional wail of mourning

'awa: also known as kava, a mildly intoxicating traditional drink made from the juice of chewed *'awa* root, spat into a bowl, and used in religious ceremonies

halakahiki: pineapple

halau: school, as in hula school

hale: house or building; often combined with other words to name a specific place, such as Haleakala (House of the Sun)

hana: work; combined with *pau* means end of work or quitting time

hanai: literally "to feed." A *hanai* is a permanent guest, or an adopted family member, usually an old person or a child. This is an enduring cultural phenomenon in Hawaii, in which a child from one family (perhaps that of a brother or sister, and quite often one's grandchild) is raised as one's own without formal adoption.

haole: a word that at one time meant foreigner but now means a white person or Caucasian

hapa: half, as in a mixed-blooded person being referred to as *hapa haole*

hapai: pregnant; used by all ethnic groups when a *keiki* is on the way

haupia: a coconut custard dessert often served at a *lu'au*

he'enalu: surfing

heiau: a platform made of skillfully fitted rocks, upon which temporary structures were built as temples and offerings were made to the gods

holomu: an ankle-length dress that is much more fitted than a *mu'umu'u,* and which is often worn on formal occasions

hono: bay, as in Honolulu (Sheltered Bay)

honu: green sea turtle

ho'oilo: traditional Hawaiian winter that begins in November

ho'olaule'a: any happy event, but especially a family outing or picnic

ho'omalimali: sweet talk; flattery

hui: a group; meeting; society. Often used to refer to Chinese businesspeople or family members who pool their money to get businesses started.

hukilau: traditional shoreline fish-gathering In which everyone lends a hand to *huki* (pull) the huge net. Anyone taking part shares in the *lau* (food). It is much more like a party than hard work, and if you're lucky you'll be able to take part in one.

hula: a native Hawaiian dance in which the rhythm of the islands is captured by swaying hips and stories told by lyrically moving hands. A *halau* is a group or school of hula.

huli huli: barbecue, as in *huli huli* chicken

i'a: fish in general; *i'a maka* is raw fish

imu: underground oven filled with hot rocks and used for baking. The main cooking method featured at a *lu'au*, used to steam-bake pork and other succulent dishes.

ipo: sweetheart; lover; girl- or boyfriend

kahili: a tall pole topped with feathers, resembling a huge feather duster. It was used by an *ali'i* to announce his or her presence.

kahuna: priest; sorcerer; doctor; skillful person. In old Hawaii *kahuna* had tremendous power, which could be used for both good and evil. The *kahuna ana'ana* was a feared individual who practiced "black magic" and could pray a person to death, while the *kahuna lapa'au* was a medical practitioner bringing aid and comfort to the people.

kai: the sea; many businesses and hotels employ *kai* as part of their name

kalua: means roasted underground in an *imu;* a favorite island food is *kalua* pork

kama'aina: a child of the land; an old-timer; a longtime island resident of any ethnic background; a resident of Hawaii or native son or daughter. Hotels and airlines often offer discounts called *"kama'aina* rates" to anyone who can prove island residency.

kanaka: man or commoner; later used to distinguish a Hawaiian from other races. Tone of voice can make it a derisive expression.

Resources

Glossary

PRONUNCIATION IN THE HAWAIIAN LANGUAGE

Five vowels (a, e, i, o, and u) and seven consonants (h, k, l, m, n, p, and w) are all there is to the Hawaiian alphabet. Hawaii had no written language before Western contact (except for petroglyph symbols), so if you're wondering why these letters, you can thank the European explorers and American missionaries for the Latinization of the Hawaiian language. Some basic rules:

- In the Hawaiian language, a consonant is always followed by a vowel. So yes, all Hawaiian words end in vowels.

- The letter "w" is sometimes pronounced as a "v," as in the traditional pronunciation of the word *Hawai'i*, which is "ha-VI-ee" instead of "ha-WHY-ee."

- The macron symbol over a vowel, called a kahako, means that the vowel sound is elongated.

- The backward apostrophe symbol, called an 'okina, means to make a phonetic glottal stop (to separate the word where the 'okina is placed). This is common in many Polynesian languages. For example, in the word Hawai'i there should be a glottal stop between the last two syllables.

- Vowels are pronounced as follows: "a" as "ah"; "e" as "eh"; "i" as "ee"; "o" as "oh"; and "u" as "oo."

HAWAIIAN

The following list gives you a taste of Hawaiian and provides a basic vocabulary of words in common usage that you are likely to hear. Becoming familiar with them is not a strict necessity, but they will definitely enhance your experience and make talking with local people more congenial. Many islanders spice their speech with certain words and you, too, can use them just as soon as you feel comfortable. You might even discover some Hawaiian words that are so perfectly expressive they'll become regular parts of your vocabulary. Some Hawaiian words have been absorbed into the English language and are found in English dictionaries. The definitions given below are not exhaustive, but are generally considered the most common.

'a'a: rough clinker lava. *'A'a* has become the correct geological term to describe this type of lava found anywhere in the world.

'ae: yes

ahu: traditional trail markers that are piles of stone shaped like little Christmas trees

ahupua'a: pie-shaped land divisions running from mountain to sea that were governed by *konohiki,* local *ali'i* who owed their allegiance to a reigning chief

aikane: friend; pal; buddy

'aina: land; the binding spirit to all Hawaiians. Love of the land is paramount in traditional Hawaiian beliefs.

akamai: smart; clever; wise

akua: a god, or simply "divine"

ali'i: a Hawaiian chief or noble

aloha: the most common greeting in the islands; can mean both hello and good-bye, welcome and farewell, as well as love, affection, or best wishes

aloha spirit: a way of living and treating each other with love and respect; joyfully sharing life

anuenue: rainbow

'anu'u: oracle tower

'a'ole: no

'aumakua: a personal or family god, often an ancestral spirit

auwe: alas or ouch; a traditional wail of mourning

'awa: also known as kava, a mildly intoxicating traditional drink made from the Juice of chewed *'awa* root, spat into a bowl, and used in religious ceremonies

halakahiki: pineapple

halau: school, as in hula school

hale: house or building; often combined with other words to name a specific place, such as Haleakala (House of the Sun)

hana: work; combined with *pau* means end of work or quitting time

hanai: literally "to feed." A *hanai* is a permanent guest, or an adopted family member, usually an old person or a child. This is an enduring cultural phenomenon in Hawaii, in which a child from one family (perhaps that of a brother or sister, and quite often one's grandchild) is raised as one's own without formal adoption.

haole: a word that at one time meant foreigner but now means a white person or Caucasian

hapa: half, as in a mixed-blooded person being referred to as *hapa haole*

hapai: pregnant; used by all ethnic groups when a *keiki* is on the way

haupia: a coconut custard dessert often served at a *lu'au*

he'enalu: surfing

heiau: platform made of skillfully fitted rocks, upon which temporary structures were built as temples and offerings were made to the gods

holomu: an ankle-length dress that is much more fitted than a *mu'umu'u,* and which is often worn on formal occasions

hono: bay, as in Honolulu (Sheltered Bay)

honu: green sea turtle

ho'oilo: traditional Hawaiian winter that begins in November

ho'olaule'a: any happy event, but especially a family outing or picnic

ho'omalimali: sweet talk; flattery

hui: a group; meeting; society. Often used to refer to Chinese businesspeople or family members who pool their money to get businesses started.

hukilau: traditional shoreline fish-gathering in which everyone lends a hand to *huki* (pull) the huge net. Anyone taking part shares in the *lau* (food). It is much more like a party than hard work, and if you're lucky you'll be able to take part in one.

hula: a native Hawaiian dance in which the rhythm of the islands is captured by swaying hips and stories told by lyrically moving hands. A *halau* is a group or school of hula.

huli huli: barbecue, as in *huli huli* chicken

i'a: fish in general; *i'a maka* is raw fish

imu: underground oven filled with hot rocks and used for baking. The main cooking method featured at a *lu'au,* used to steam-bake pork and other succulent dishes.

ipo: sweetheart; lover; girl- or boyfriend

kahili: a tall pole topped with feathers, resembling a huge feather duster. It was used by an *ali'i* to announce his or her presence.

kahuna: priest; sorcerer; doctor; skillful person. In old Hawaii *kahuna* had tremendous power, which could be used for both good and evil. The *kahuna ana'ana* was a feared individual who practiced "black magic" and could pray a person to death, while the *kahuna lapa'au* was a medical practitioner bringing aid and comfort to the people.

kai: the sea; many businesses and hotels employ *kai* as part of their name

kalua: means roasted underground in an *imu;* a favorite island food is *kalua* pork

kama'aina: a child of the land; an old-timer; a longtime island resident of any ethnic background; a resident of Hawaii or native son or daughter. Hotels and airlines often offer discounts called "*kama'aina* rates" to anyone who can prove island residency.

kanaka: man or commoner; later used to distinguish a Hawaiian from other races. Tone of voice can make it a derisive expression.

kane: means man, but actually used to signify a relationship such as husband or boyfriend. Written on a lavatory door it means "men's room."

kapu: forbidden; taboo; keep out; do not touch

kaukau: slang word meaning food or chow, as in *kaukau* wagons, trucks that sell plate lunches and other morsels

kauwa: a landless, untouchable caste once confined to living on reservations. Members of this caste were often used as human sacrifices at heiau. Calling someone *kauwa* is still a grave insult.

kava: see *'awa*

keiki: child or children; used by all ethnic groups

kia akua: carved temple image posts, a Polynesian art form

kiawe: an algaroba tree from South America commonly found in Hawaii along the shore. It grows a nasty long thorn that can easily puncture a tire.

kipuka: an area that has been surrounded by a lava flow, but never inundated, that preserves an older and established ecosystem

ko'ala: any food that has been broiled or barbecued

kokua: help, as in, "Your *kokua* is needed to keep Hawaii free from litter."

kolohe: rascal

konane: a traditional Hawaiian game, similar to checkers, played with pebbles on a large flat stone used as a board

Kona wind: a muggy subtropical wind that blows from the south and hits the leeward side of the islands; usually brings sticky hot weather

ko'olau: windward side of the island

kukui: a candlenut tree whose pods are polished and then strung together to make a beautiful lei. Traditionally the oil-rich nuts were strung on the rib of a coconut leaf and used as a candle.

kuleana: homesite; the old homestead; small farms. Especially used to describe the small spreads on Hawaiian Homelands on Moloka'i.

Kumulipo: ancient Hawaiian genealogical chant that records the pantheon of gods, creation, and the beginning of humankind

kupuna: a grandparent or old-timer; usually means someone who has gained wisdom

la: the sun. Often combined with other words to be more descriptive, such as Lahaina (Merciless Sun) or Haleakala (House of the Sun).

lanai: veranda or porch. You'll pay more for a hotel room if it has a lanai with an ocean view.

lani: sky or the heavens

lau hala: traditional Hawaiian weaving of mats, hats, etc., from the prepared fronds of the pandanus (screw pine)

lei: a traditional garland of flowers or vines. Given at any auspicious occasion, but especially when arriving in or leaving Hawaii.

lele: the stone altar at a *heiau*

limu: edible seaweed of various types. It's used to garnish many island dishes and is a favorite at *lu'au*.

lolo: crazy, as in *"lolo buggah"* (stupid or crazy guy)

lomilomi: traditional Hawaiian massage; also, raw salmon made into a vinegared salad with chopped onion and spices

lua: the toilet; the bathroom

luakini: a human-sacrifice temple. Introduced to Hawaii in the 13th century at Waha'ula Heiau on the Big Island.

lu'au: a Hawaiian feast featuring poi, *imu*-baked pork, and other traditional foods. Good ones provide some of the best gastronomic delights in the world.

luna: foreman or overseer in the plantation fields

mahalo: thank you. *Mahalo nui* means "big thanks" or "thank you very much."

mahele: division. The "Great Mahele" of 1848 changed Hawaii forever when the traditional common lands were broken up into privately owned plots.

mahimahi: a favorite eating fish. Often called a dolphin, but a mahimahi is a true fish, not a cetacean.

mahu: a homosexual; often used derisively.

maile: a fragrant vine used in traditional lei. It looks ordinary but smells delightful.

300

RESOURCES
GLOSSARY

maka'ainana: a commoner; a person "belonging" to the *'aina* (land), who supported the *ali'i* by fishing and farming and as a warrior

makai: toward the sea; used by most islanders when giving directions

make: dead; deceased

malama 'aina: take care of the environment

malihini: a newcomer; a tenderfoot; a recent arrival

malo: the native Hawaiian loincloth. Never worn anymore except at festivals or pageants.

mana: power from the spirit world; innate energy of all things animate or inanimate; the grace of god. Mana could be passed from one person to another, or even stolen. Great care was taken to protect the *ali'i* from having their mana defiled. *Kahuna* were often employed in the regaining or transference of mana.

manini: stingy; tight. Also a type of fish.

manuahi: free; gratis; extra

mauka: toward the mountains; used by most islanders when giving directions

mauna: mountain. Often combined with other words to be more descriptive, such as Mauna Kea (White Mountain).

mele: a song or chant in the Hawaiian oral tradition that records the history and genealogies of the *ali'i*

Menehune: the legendary "little people" of Hawaii. Like leprechauns, they are said to shun humans and possess magical powers.

moa: chicken; fowl

moana: the ocean; the sea. Many places have *moana* as part of their name.

moe: sleep

mo'olelo: ancient tales kept alive by the oral tradition and recited only by day

mu'umu'u: a "Mother Hubbard," an ankle-length dress with a high neckline introduced by the missionaries to cover the nakedness of the Hawaiians. It has become fashionable attire for almost any occasion in Hawaii.

nani: beautiful

nui: big; great; large; as in *mahalo nui* (thank you very much)

'ohana: a family; the fundamental social division; extended family. Now often used to denote a social organization with grassroots overtones.

'okolehau: literally "iron bottom"; a traditional booze made from ti root. *'Okole* means "rear end" and *hau* means "iron," which was descriptive of the huge blubber pots in which *'okolehau* was made. Also, if you drink too much it'll surely knock you on your *'okole.*

oli: chant not done to a musical accompaniment

'ono: delicious; delightful; the best. *Ono ono* means "extra or absolutely delicious." Also a type of fish.

'opihi: a shellfish or limpet that clings to rocks and is gathered as one of the islands' favorite pupu

'opu: belly; stomach

pahoehoe: smooth, ropy lava that looks like burnt pancake batter. It is now the correct geological term used to describe this type of lava found anywhere in the world.

pakalolo: "crazy smoke"; marijuana

pake: a Chinese person. Can be derisive, depending on the tone in which it is used. It is a bastardization of the Chinese word meaning "uncle."

pali: a cliff; precipice. Hawaii's geology makes them quite common. The most famous are the *pali* of O'ahu where a major battle was fought.

paniolo: a Hawaiian cowboy; derived from the Spanish *español*. The first cowboys brought to Hawaii during the early 19th century were Mexicans from California.

papale: hat

pa'u: long split skirt often worn by women when horseback riding. In the 1800s, an island treat was watching *pa'u* riders in their beautiful dresses at Kapi'olani Park in Honolulu. The tradition is carried on today at many of Hawaii's rodeos.

pau: finished; done; completed. Often combined into *pau hana,* which means end of work or quitting time.

pilau: stink; bad smell; stench

pilikia: trouble of any kind, big or small; bad times

poi: a glutinous paste made from the pounded corm of taro, which ferments slightly and has a light sour taste. Purplish in color, it's a staple at *lu'au*, where it is called one-, two-, or three-finger poi, depending upon its thickness.

poke: cubed raw fish (usually ahi tuna) sashimi marinated in sea salt, soy sauce, sesame oil, and seaweed

pono: righteous or excellent

pua: flower

puka: a hole of any size. *Puka* is used by all island residents, whether talking about a pinhole in a rubber boat or a tunnel through a mountain. Also a shell.

punalua: a traditional practice, before the missionaries arrived, of sharing mates. Western seamen took advantage of it, leading to the spread of contagious diseases and eventual rapid decline of the Hawaiian people.

pune'e: bed; narrow couch. Used by all ethnic groups. To recline on a *pune'e* on a breezy lanai is a true island treat.

pupu: an appetizer; a snack; hors d'oeuvres; can be anything from cheese and crackers to sushi. Oftentimes, bars or nightclubs offer them free.

pupule: crazy; nuts; out of your mind

pu'u: hill, as in Pu'u 'Ula'ula (Red Hill)

tapa: a traditional paper cloth made from beaten bark. Intricate designs were stamped in using beaters, and natural dyes added color. The tradition was lost for many years but is now making a comeback. Also called *kapa*.

taro: the staple of old Hawaii, brought by the first Polynesians. A plant with a distinctive broad leaf that produces a starchy root. According to the oral tradition, the life-giving properties of taro hold mystical significance for Hawaiians, since it was created by the gods at about the same time as humans.

ti: a broad-leafed plant that was used for many purposes, from plates to hula skirts. Especially used to wrap religious offerings presented at the heiau.

tutu: grandmother; granny; older woman. Used by all as a term of respect and endearment.

ukulele: a small guitar-like instrument; *uku* means "flea" and *lele* means "jumping," so literally "jumping flea"—the way the Hawaiians perceived the quick finger movements used on the banjo-like Portuguese folk instrument called a *cavaquinho*. The ukulele quickly became synonymous with the islands.

ulu: breadfruit

wahine: young woman; female; girl; wife. Used by all ethnic groups. When written on a lavatory door it means "women's room."

wai: freshwater; drinking water

wela: hot. *Wela kahao* is a "hot time" or "making whoopee."

wiki: quickly; fast; in a hurry. Often seen as *wiki wiki* (very fast), as in "Wiki Wiki Messenger Service."

Useful Phrases

a hui hou: until we meet again

aloha ahiahi: good evening

aloha au ia'oe: I love you

aloha kakahiaka: good morning

aloha nui loa: much love; fondest regards

hau'oli la hanau: happy birthday

hau'oli makahiki hou: happy new year

komo mai: please come in; enter; welcome

mele kalikimaka: merry Christmas

'okole maluna: bottoms up; cheers

PIDGIN

The following are a few commonly used words and expressions that should give you an idea of pidgin. It really can't be written properly, merely approximated, but for now, *"Study da' kine an' bimbye it be mo' bettah, brah! Okay? Lesgo."*

an' den: and then? big deal; so what's next?

auntie: respected elderly woman

bad ass: very good

bimbye: after a while; bye and bye. *"Bimbye, you learn pidgin."*

blalah: brother, but actually only refers to a large, heavyset, good-natured Hawaiian man

brah: all the bros in Hawaii are brahs; brother; pal. Used to call someone's attention. One of the most common words even among people who are not acquainted. After a fill-up at a gas station, a person would say *"Tanks, brah."*

chicken skin: goose bumps

cockaroach: steal; rip off. If you really want to find out what *cockaroach* means, just leave your camera on your beach blanket when you take a little dip.

da' kine: a catchall word of many meanings that epitomizes the essence of pidgin. *Da' kine* is a euphemism for pidgin and is substituted whenever the speaker is at a loss for a word or just wants to generalize. It can mean: you know? whatchamacallit; of that type.

geev um: give it to them; give them hell; go for it. Can be used as an encouragement. If a surfer is riding a great wave, the people on the beach might yell, *"Geev um, brah!"*

grinds: food

hana ho: again. Especially after a concert the audience shouts *"hana ho"* (one more!).

hele on: let's get going

howzit? what's happening? how's it going? The most common greeting, used in place of the more formal "How do you do?"

huhu: angry! *"You put the make on the wrong da' kine wahine, brah, and you in da' kine trouble if you get one big Hawaiian blalah plenty huhu."*

lesgo: let's go! do it!

li'dis an' li'dat: like this or that; a catchall grouping especially if you want to avoid details; like, ya' know?

lolo buggah: stupid or crazy guy (person).

Words to a tropical island song go, "I want to find the *lolo* who stole my *pakalolo*."

mo' bettah: better, real good! great idea. An island sentiment used to be, *"mo' bettah you come Hawaii."* Now it has subtly changed to, *"mo' bettah you visit Hawaii."*

ono: number one! delicious; great; groovy. *"Hawaii is ono, brah!"*

pakalolo: literally "crazy smoke"; marijuana

pakiki head: stubborn; bull-headed

pau: a Hawaiian word meaning finished; done; over and done with. *Pau hana* means end of work or quitting time. Once used by plantation workers, now used by everyone.

seestah: sister, woman

shaka: hand wave where only the thumb and baby finger stick out, meaning thank you, all right!

slippahs: slippers, flip-flops, "Locals" (a brand name)

stink face: or stink eye; basically frowning at someone; using facial expression to show displeasure. Hard looks. What you'll get if you give local people a hard time.

swell head: burned up; angry

talk story: spinning yarns; shooting the breeze; throwing the bull; a rap session. If you're lucky enough to be around to hear *kupuna* (elders) *talk story,* you can hear some fantastic tales in the tradition of old Hawaii.

tanks, brah: thanks, thank you

to da max: all the way

waddascoops: what's the scoop? what's up? what's happening?

Suggested Reading

Many publishers print books on Hawaii. Following are a few that focus on Hawaiian topics. **University of Hawai'i Press** (www. uhpress.hawaii.edu) has the best overall general list of titles on Hawaii. The **Bishop Museum Press** (www.bishopmuseum.org/ press) puts out many scholarly works on Hawaiiana, as does **Kamehameha Schools Press** (www.kamehamehapublishing.org). Also good, with more general-interest lists, are **Bess Press** (www.besspress.com) and **Petroglyph Press** (www.basicallybooks. com). In addition, a website specifically oriented toward books on Hawaii, Hawaiian music, and other things Hawaiian is **Hawaii Books** (www.hawaiibooks.com).

ASTRONOMY

Bryan, E. H. *Stars over Hawaii.* Hilo, HI: Petroglyph Press, 1977. An introduction to astronomy, with information about the constellations and charts featuring the stars filling the night sky in Hawaii, by month. An excellent primer.

Rhoads, Samuel. *The Sky Tonight—A Guided Tour of the Stars over Hawaii.* Honolulu: Bishop Museum, 1993. Four pages per month of star charts—one each for the horizon in every cardinal direction. Exceptional!

COOKING

Alexander, Agnes. *How to Use Hawaiian Fruit.* Hilo, HI: Petroglyph Press, 1984. A slim volume of recipes using delicious Hawaiian fruits.

Beeman, Judy, and Martin Beeman. *Joys of Hawaiian Cooking.* Hilo, HI: Petroglyph Press, 1977. A collection of favorite recipes from Big Island chefs.

Choy, Sam. *Cooking from the Heart with Sam Choy.* Honolulu: Mutual Publishing, 1995. This beautiful hand-bound cookbook contains many color photos by Douglas Peebles.

Fukuda, Sachi. *Pupus, An Island Tradition.* Honolulu: Bess Press, 1995.

Margah, Irish, and Elvira Monroe. *Hawaii, Cooking with Aloha.* San Carlos, CA: Wide World, 1984. Island recipes, as well as hints on decor.

Rizzuto, Shirley. *Fish Dishes of the Pacific— from the Fishwife.* Honolulu: Hawaii Fishing News, 1986. Features recipes using all the fish commonly caught in Hawaiian waters (husband Jim Rizzuto is the author of *Fishing, Hawaiian Style*).

CULTURE

Dudley, Michael Kioni. *Man, Gods, and Nature.* Honolulu: Na Kane O Ka Malo Press, 1990. An examination of the philosophical underpinnings of Hawaiian beliefs and their interconnected reality.

Hartwell, Jay. *Na Mamo: Hawaiian People Today.* Honolulu: Ai Pohaku Press, 1996. Profiles 12 people practicing Hawaiian traditions in the modern world.

Heyerdahl, Thor. *American Indians in the Pacific.* London: Allen and Unwin, 1952. Theoretical and anthropological accounts of the influence on Polynesia of the Indians along the Pacific coast of North and South America. Though no longer in print, this book is fascinating reading, presenting unsubstantiated yet intriguing theories.

Kamehameha Schools Press. *Life in Early Hawaii: The Ahupua'a.* 3rd ed. Honolulu: Kamehameha Schools Press, 1994. Written for schoolchildren to better understand the basic organization of old Hawaiian land use and its function, this slim volume is a good primer for people of any age who wish to understand this society.

Kirch, Patrick V. *Feathered Gods and Fishhooks: An Introduction to Hawaiian Archaeology and Prehistory.* Honolulu: University of Hawai'i Press, 1997. This scholarly, lavishly illustrated, yet very readable book gives new insight into the development of precontact Hawaiian civilization. It focuses on the sites and major settlements of old Hawai'i and chronicles the main cultural developments while weaving in the social climate that contributed to change. A very worthwhile read.

ANIMALS

Boom, Robert. *Hawaiian Seashells.* Photos by Jerry Kringle. Honolulu: Waikiki Aquarium, 1972. A collection of 137 seashells found in Hawaiian waters, featuring many found nowhere else on earth. Broken into categories with accompanying text including common and scientific names, physical descriptions, and likely habitats. A must for shell collectors.

Carpenter, Blyth, and Russell Carpenter. *Fish Watching in Hawaii.* San Mateo, CA: Natural World Press, 1981. A color guide to many of the reef fish found in Hawaii and often spotted by snorkelers. If you're interested in the fish that you'll be looking at, this guide will be very helpful.

Fielding, Ann, and Ed Robinson. *An Underwater Guide to Hawaii.* Honolulu: University of Hawai'i Press, 1987. If you plan to snorkel/scuba the living reef waters of Hawaii and want to be familiar with what you see there, get this small but fact-packed book. The amazing array of marine life found throughout the archipelago is captured in glossy photos with accompanying informative text.

Both the scientific and common names of specimens are given. This easily understood reference guide will enrich your underwater experience.

Goodson, Gar. *The Many-Splendored Fishes of Hawaii.* Stanford, CA: Stanford University Press, 1985. This small but thorough "fishwatchers" book includes entries on some deep-sea fish.

Hawaiian Audubon Society. *Hawaii's Birds.* 5th ed. Honolulu: Hawaii Audubon Society, 1997. Excellent bird book, giving description, range, voice, and habits of more than 100 species. Slim volume; good for carrying while hiking.

Hobson, Edmund, and E. H. Chave. *Hawaiian Reef Animals.* Honolulu: University of Hawai'i Press, 1987. Colorful photos and descriptions of the fish, invertebrates, turtles, and seals that call Hawaiian reefs their home.

Kay, Alison, and Olive Schoenberg-Dole. *Shells of Hawaii.* Honolulu: University of Hawai'i Press, 1991. Color photos and tips on where to look.

Mahaney, Casey. *Hawaiian Reef Fish, The Identification Book.* Planet Ocean Publishing, 1993. A spiral-bound reference work featuring many color photos and descriptions of common reef fish found in Hawaiian waters.

Nickerson, Roy. *Brother Whale, A Pacific Whalewatcher's Log.* San Francisco: Chronicle Books, 1977. Introduces the average person to the life of earth's greatest mammals. Provides historical accounts, photos, and tips on whale-watching. Well-written, descriptive, and the best "first time" book on whales.

Pratt, Douglas. *A Pocket Guide to Hawaii's Birds.* Honolulu: Mutual Publishing, 1996.

A condensed version of Pratt's larger work with a focus on birds of the state.

Pratt, H. D., P. L. Bruner, and D. G. Berrett. *The Birds of Hawaii and the Tropical Pacific.* Princeton, NJ: Princeton University Press, 1987. Useful field guide for novice and expert bird-watchers, covering Hawaii as well as other Pacific Island groups.

Tomich, P. Quentin. *Mammals in Hawaii.* Honolulu: Bishop Museum Press, 1986. Quintessential scholarly text on all mammal species in Hawaii, with description of distribution and historical references. Lengthy bibliography.

Van Riper, Charles, and Sandra van Riper. *A Field Guide to the Mammals of Hawaii.* Honolulu: Oriental Publishing, 1982. A guide to the surprising number of mammals introduced into Hawaii. Full-color pages document description, uses, tendencies, and habitat. Small and thin, this book makes a worthwhile addition to any serious hiker's backpack.

PLANTS

Kepler, Angela. *Hawaiian Heritage Plants.* Honolulu: University of Hawai'i Press, 1998. A treatise on 32 utilitarian plants used by the early Hawaiians.

Kepler, Angela. *Hawaii's Floral Splendor.* Honolulu: Mutual Publishing, 1997. A general reference to flowers of Hawaii.

Kepler, Angela. *Tropicals of Hawaii.* Honolulu: Mutual Publishing, 1989. This small-format book features many color photos of nonnative flowers.

Kuck, Lorraine, and Richard Togg. *Hawaiian Flowers and Flowering Trees.* Rutland, VT: Tuttle, 1960. A classic, though no longer in print, field guide to tropical and subtropical flora illustrated in watercolor. A to-the-point description of Hawaiian plants and flowers with a brief history of their places of origin and their introduction to Hawaii.

Merrill, Elmer. *Plant Life of the Pacific World.* Rutland, VT: Tuttle, 1983. This is the definitive book for anyone planning a botanical tour of the entire Pacific Basin. Originally published in the 1930s, it remains a tremendous work, worth tracking down through out-of-print book services.

Miyano, Leland. *A Pocket Guide to Hawaii's Flowers.* Honolulu: Mutual Publishing, 2001. A small guide to readily seen flowers in the state. Good for the backpack or back pocket.

Miyano, Leland. *Hawaii, A Floral Paradise.* Honolulu: Mutual Publishing, 1995. Photographed by Douglas Peebles, this large-format book is filled with informative text and beautiful color shots of tropical flowers commonly seen in Hawaii.

Sohmer, S. H., and R. Gustafson. *Plants and Flowers of Hawai'i.* Honolulu: University of Hawai'i Press, 1987. Sohmer and Gustafson cover the vegetation zones of Hawaii, from mountains to coast, in this good introduction to the history and unique evolution of Hawaiian plantlife. Beautiful color plates are accompanied by clear and concise plant descriptions, with the scientific and common Hawaiian names listed.

Teho, Fortunato. *Plants of Hawaii—How to Grow Them.* Hilo, HI: Petroglyph Press, 1992. A small but useful book for those who want their backyards to bloom into tropical paradises.

Valier, Kathy. *Ferns of Hawaii.* Honolulu: University of Hawai'i Press, 1995. One of the few books that treat the state's ferns as a single subject.

Wagner, Warren L., Derral R. Herbst, and H. S. Sohner. *Manual of the Flowering Plants of Hawai'i*. Rev. ed., vol. 2. Honolulu: University of Hawai'i Press in association with Bishop Museum Press, 1999. Considered the bible for Hawaii's botanical world.

HEALTH

Gutmanis, June. *Kahuna La'au Lapa'au*. Rev. ed. Honolulu: Island Heritage, 2001. Text on Hawaiian herbal medicines: diseases, treatments, and medicinal plants, with illustrations.

McBride, L. R. *Practical Folk Medicine of Hawaii*. Hilo, HI: Petroglyph Press, 1975. An illustrated guide to Hawaii's medicinal plants as used by the *kahuna lapa'au* (medical healers). Includes a thorough section on ailments, how to diagnose them, and the proper folk remedy for each. Illustrated by the author, a renowned botanical researcher and former ranger at Hawai'i Volcanoes National Park.

Wilkerson, James A., MD, ed. *Medicine for Mountaineering and Other Wilderness*. 4th ed. Seattle: The Mountaineers, 1992. Don't let the title fool you. Although the book focuses on specific health problems that may be encountered while mountaineering, it is the best wilderness first-aid and general health guide available today. Written by doctors for the layperson to use until help arrives, it is jam-packed with easily understandable techniques and procedures. For those planning extended hikes, it is a must.

HISTORY

Apple, Russell A. *Trails: From Steppingstones to Kerbstones*. Honolulu: Bishop Museum Press, 1965. This is a special-interest archaeological survey focusing on trails, roadways, footpaths, and highways and how they were designed and maintained throughout the years. Many "royal highways" from precontact Hawaii are cited.

Ashdown, Inez MacPhee. *Kaho'olawe*. Honolulu: Topgallant Publishing, 1979. The tortured story of the lonely island of Kaho'olawe by one of the family who owned the island until it was turned into a military bombing target during World War II. It's also a first-person account of life on the island.

Barnes, Phil. *A Concise History of the Hawaiian Islands*. Hilo, HI; Petroglyph Press, 1999. An examination of Hawaiian history and its major players, focusing on the factors important to shaping the social, economic, and political trends of the islands. An easy read.

Cameron, Roderick. *The Golden Haze*. New York: World Publishing, 1964. An account of Captain James Cook's voyages of discovery throughout the South Seas. Uses original diaries and journals for an on-the-spot reconstruction of this great seafaring adventure.

Cox, J. Halley, and Edward Stasack. *Hawaiian Petroglyphs*. Honolulu: Bishop Museum Press, 1970. The most thorough examination of petroglyph sites throughout the islands.

Daws, Gavan. *Shoal of Time, A History of the Hawaiian Islands*. Honolulu: University of Hawai'i Press, 1974. A highly readable history of Hawaii dating from its "discovery" by the Western world to its acceptance as the 50th state. Good insight into the psychological makeup of influential characters of Hawaii's past.

Dorrance, William H., and Francis S. Morgan. *Sugar Islands: The 165-Year Story of Sugar in Hawai'i*. Honolulu: Mutual Publishing, 2000. An overall sketch of the sugar industry in Hawaii from inception to decline, with data on many individual plantations and mills around the islands. Definitely told from the industry's point of view.

Finney, Ben, and James D. Houston. *Surfing, A History of the Ancient Hawaiian Sport*. Los Angeles: Pomegranate, 1996. Features many early etchings and old photos of Hawaiian surfers practicing their native sport.

Fornander, Abraham. *An Account of the Polynesian Race; Its Origins and Migrations, and the Ancient History of the Hawaiian People to the Times of Kamehameha I*. Rutland, VT: C. E. Tuttle, 1969. This is a reprint of a three-volume opus originally published 1878-1885. It is still one of the best sources of information on Hawaiian myth and legend.

Free, David. *Vignettes of Old Hawaii*. Honolulu: Crossroads Press, 1994. A collection of short essays on a variety of subjects.

Fuchs, Lawrence. *Hawaii Pono*. Honolulu: Bess Press, 1961. A detailed, scholarly work presenting an overview of Hawaii's history, based on ethnic and sociological interpretations. Encompasses socio-ethnological groups from native Hawaiians to modern entrepreneurs. This book is a must for obtaining some social historical background.

Handy, E. S., and Elizabeth Handy, *Native Planters in Old Hawaii*. Honolulu: Bishop Museum Press, 1972. A superbly written, easily understood scholarly work on the intimate relationship between precontact Hawaiians and the *'aina* (land). Much more than its title implies, this book should be read by anyone seriously interested in Polynesian Hawaii.

Ii, John Papa. *Fragments of Hawaiian History*. Honolulu: Bishop Museum, 1959. Hawaii's history under Kamehameha I as told by a Hawaiian who actually experienced it.

Joesting, Edward. *Hawaii: An Uncommon History*. New York: W. W. Norton Co., 1978. A truly uncommon history told in a series of vignettes relating to the lives and personalities of the first Caucasians in Hawaii, Hawaiian nobility, sea captains, writers, and adventurers. Brings history to life. Absolutely excellent.

Kamakau, S. M. *Ruling Chiefs of Hawaii*. Rev. ed. Honolulu: Kamehameha Schools Press, 1992. A history of Hawaii from the legendary leader 'Umi to the mid-Kamehameha dynasty, from oral tales and from a Hawaiian perspective.

Kurisu, Yasushi. *Sugar Town, Hawaiian Plantation Days Remembered*. Honolulu: Watermark Publishing, 1995. Reminiscences of life growing up on sugar plantations on the Hamakua Coast of the Big Island. Features many old photos.

Lili'uokalani. *Hawaii's Story by Hawaii's Queen*. 1898. Reprint, Honolulu: Mutual Publishing, 1990. Originally written in 1898, this moving personal account recounts Hawaii's inevitable move from monarchy to U.S. Territory by its last queen, Lili'uokalani. The facts can be found in other histories, but none provides the emotion or point of view expressed by Hawaii's deposed monarch. This is a must-read to get the whole picture.

McBride, Likeke. *Petroglyphs of Hawaii*. Hilo, HI: Petroglyph Press, 1997. A revised and updated guide to petroglyphs found in the Hawaiian Islands. A basic introduction to these old Hawaiian picture stories.

Nickerson, Roy. *Lahaina, Royal Capital of Hawaii*. Honolulu: Hawaiian Service, 1978. The story of Lahaina from whaling days to present, spiced with ample photographs.

Tabrah, Ruth M. *Ni'ihau: The Last Hawaiian Island*. Kailua, HI: Press Pacifica, 1987. Sympathetic history of the privately owned island of Ni'ihau.

Takaki, Ronald. *Pau Hana: Plantation Life and Labor in Hawaii.* Honolulu: University of Hawai'i Press, 1983. The story of immigrant labor and the sugar industry in Hawaii until the 1920s, told from the worker's perspective.

INTRODUCTORY

Carroll, Rick, and Marcie Carroll, eds. *Hawaii: True Stories of the Island Spirit.* San Francisco: Travelers' Tales, 1999. A collection of stories by a variety of authors that were chosen to invoke the essence of Hawaii and Hawaiian experiences. A great read.

Cohen, David, and Rick Smolan. *A Day in the Life of Hawaii.* New York: Workman, 1984. On December 2, 1983, 50 of the world's top photojournalists were invited to Hawaii to photograph daily life on the islands. The photos are excellently reproduced and accompanied by a minimum of text.

Day, A. G., and C. Stroven. *A Hawaiian Reader.* 1959. Reprint, Honolulu: Mutual Publishing, 1984. A poignant compilation of essays, diary entries, and fictitious writings that takes you from the death of Captain Cook through the "statehood services."

Department of Geography, University of Hawai'i at Hilo. *Atlas of Hawaii.* 3rd ed. Honolulu: University of Hawai'i Press, 1998. Much more than an atlas filled with reference maps, this also contains commentary on the natural environment, culture, and sociology; a gazetteer; and statistical tables. Actually a mini-encyclopedia on Hawaii.

Michener, James A. *Hawaii.* New York: Random House, 1959. Michener's fictionalized historical novel has done more to inform *and* misinform readers about Hawaii than any other book ever written. A great tale with plenty of local color and information, but read it for pleasure, not facts.

Piercy, LaRue. *Hawaii This and That.* Honolulu: Mutual Publishing, 1994. Illustrated by Scot Ebanez. A 60-page book filled with one-sentence facts and oddities about all manner of things Hawaiian. Informative, amazing, and fun to read.

Steele, R. Thomas: *The Hawaiian Shirt: Its Art and History.* New York: Abbeville Press, 1984.

LANGUAGE

Elbert, Samuel. *Spoken Hawaiian.* Honolulu: University of Hawai'i Press, 1970. Progressive conversational lessons.

Elbert, Samuel, and Mary Pukui. *Hawaiian Dictionary.* Honolulu: University of Hawai'i Press, 1986. The best dictionary available on the Hawaiian language. The *Pocket Hawaiian Dictionary* is a less expensive, condensed version of this dictionary, and adequate for most travelers with a general interest in the language.

Pukui, Mary Kawena, Samuel Elbert, and Esther T. Mookini. *Place Names of Hawaii.* Honolulu: University of Hawai'i Press, 1974. A comprehensive listing of Hawaiian and foreign place-names in the state, giving pronunciation, spelling, meaning, and location.

Schutz, Albert J. *All About Hawaiian.* Honolulu: University of Hawai'i Press, 1995. A brief primer on Hawaiian pronunciation, grammar, and vocabulary. A solid introduction.

MYTHOLOGY AND LEGENDS

Beckwith, Martha. *Hawaiian Mythology.* 1940. Reprint, Honolulu: University of Hawai'i Press, 1976. Since its original printing in 1940, this work has remained the definitive text on Hawaiian mythology. Beckwith compiled this book from many sources, giving exhaustive cross-references to genealogies and legends expressed in the oral tradition. If you are going to read one book on Hawaii's folklore, this should be it.

Beckwith, Martha. *The Kumulipo.* 1951. Reprint, Honolulu: University of Hawai'i Press, 1972. Translation of the Hawaiian creation chant.

Colum, Padraic. *Legends of Hawaii.* New Haven, CT: Yale University Press, 1937. Selected legends of old Hawaii, reinterpreted but closely based on the originals.

Elbert, S. H., ed. *Hawaiian Antiquities and Folklore.* Honolulu: University of Hawai'i Press, 1959. Illustrated by Jean Charlot. A selection of the main legends from Abraham Fornander's great work, *An Account of the Polynesian Race.*

Kalakaua, David. *The Legends and Myths of Hawaii.* Edited by R. M. Daggett, with a foreword by Glen Grant. Honolulu: Mutual Publishing, 1990. In this book originally published in 1888, Hawaii's own King Kalakaua draws on his scholarly and formidable knowledge of the classic oral tradition to bring alive ancient tales from precontact Hawaii. A powerful yet somewhat Victorian voice from Hawaii's past speaks clearly and boldly, especially about the intimate role of pre-Christian religion in the lives of the Hawaiian people.

Melville, Leinanai. *Children of the Rainbow.* Wheaton, IL: Theosophical Publishing, 1969. A book on higher spiritual consciousness attuned to nature, which was the basic belief of pre-Christian Hawaii. The appendix contains illustrations of mystical symbols used by the *kahuna.* An enlightening book in many ways.

Pukui, Mary Kawena, and Caroline Curtis. *Hawaii Island Legends.* Honolulu: Kamehameha Schools Press, 1996. Hawaiian tales and legends for preteens.

Pukui, Mary Kawena, and Caroline Curtis. *Tales of the Menehune.* Honolulu: Kamehameha Schools Press, 1960. Compilation of legends relating to Hawaii's "little people."

Pukui, Mary Kawena, and Caroline Curtis. *The Waters of Kane and other Hawaiian Legends* Honolulu: Kamehameha Schools Press, 1994. Tales and legends for the preteen.

Thrum, Thomas. *Hawaiian Folk Tales.* 1907. Reprint, Chicago: McClurg and Co., 1950. A collection of Hawaiian tales from the oral tradition as told to the author from various sources.

Westervelt, W. D. *Hawaiian Legends of Volcanoes.* 1916. Reprint, Boston: Ellis Press, 1991. A small book concerning the volcano legends of Hawaii and how they related to the fledgling field of volcanism in the early 1900s. The vintage photos alone are worth a look.

NATURAL SCIENCE AND GEOGRAPHY

Carlquist, Sherwin. *Hawaii: A Natural History.* National Tropical Botanical Garden, 1984. Definitive account of Hawaii's natural history.

Clark, John. *Beaches of the Big Island.* Honolulu: University of Hawai'i Press, 1997. Definitive guide to beaches, including many off the beaten path. Features maps and black-and-white photos. Also *Beaches of O'ahu, Beaches of Kaua'i and Ni'ihau,* and *Beaches of Maui County.*

Hazlett, Richard, and Donald Hyndman. *Roadside Geology of Hawai'i.* Missoula, MT: Mountain Press Publishing, 1996. Begins with a general discussion of the geology of the Hawaiian Islands, followed by a road guide to the individual islands offering descriptions of easily seen features.

A great book to have in the car as you tour the islands.

Hubbard, Douglass, and Gordon Macdonald. *Volcanoes of the National Parks of Hawaii.* 1982. Reprint, Volcanoes, HI: Hawaii Natural History Association, 1989. The volcanology of Hawaii, documenting the major lava flows and their geological effect on the state.

Kay, E. Alison, comp. *A Natural History of the Hawaiian Islands.* Honolulu: University of Hawai'i Press, 1994. A selection of concise articles by experts in the fields of volcanism, oceanography, meteorology, and biology. An excellent reference source.

Macdonald, Gorden, Agatin Abbott, and Frank Peterson. *Volcanoes in the Sea.* Honolulu: University of Hawai'i Press, 1983. The best reference to Hawaiian geology. Well explained for easy understanding. Illustrated.

Ziegler, Alan C., *Hawaiian Natural History, Ecology, and Evolution.* Honolulu: University of Hawai'i Press. An overview of Hawaiian natural history with treatment of ecology and evolution in that process.

POLITICAL SCIENCE

Bell, Roger. *Last Among Equals: Hawaiian Statehood and American Politics.* Honolulu: University of Hawai'i Press, 1984. Documents Hawaii's long and rocky road to statehood, tracing political partisanship, racism, and social change.

SPORTS AND RECREATION

Alford, John D. *Mountain Biking the Hawaiian Islands.* 2nd ed. Honolulu: Ohana Publishing, 2010. Good off-road biking guide to the main Hawaiian Islands.

Ambrose, Greg. *Surfer's Guide to Hawai'i.* Honolulu: Bess Press, 1991. Island-by-island guide to surfing spots.

Ball, Stuart. *The Hiker's Guide to the Hawaiian Islands.* Honolulu: University of Hawai'i Press, 2000. This excellent guide includes 44 hikes on each of the four main islands.

Cagala, George. *Hawaii: A Camping Guide.* Boston: Hunter Publishing, 1994.

Chisholm, Craig. *Hawaiian Hiking Trails.* Lake Oswego, OR: Fernglen Press, 1989.

Cisco, Dan. *Hawaii Sports.* Honolulu: University of Hawai'i Press, 1999. A compendium of popular and little-known sporting events and figures, with facts, tidbits, and statistical information. Go here first for a general overview.

Lueras, Leonard. *Surfing, the Ultimate Pleasure.* Honolulu: Emphasis International, 1984. One of the most brilliant books ever written on surfing.

McMahon, Richard. *Camping Hawaii: A Complete Guide.* Honolulu: University of Hawai'i Press, 1997. This book has all you need to know about camping in Hawaii, with descriptions of different campsites.

Morey, Kathy. *Hawaii Trails.* Berkeley, CA: Wilderness Press, 1997. Morey's books are specialized, detailed hiker's guides to Hawaii's outdoors. Complete with useful maps, historical references, official procedures, and plants and animals encountered along the way. If you're focused on hiking, these are the best to take along. *Maui Trails, Oahu Trails,* and *Kauai Trails* are also available.

Rosenberg, Steve. *Diving Hawaii.* Locust Valley, NY: Aqua Quest, 1990. Describes diving locations on the major islands as well as the marine life divers are likely to see. Includes many color photos.

Smith, Robert. *Hawaii's Best Hiking Trails.* Kula, HI: Hawaiian Outdoor Adventures, 1991. Other guides by this author include *Hiking Oahu, Hiking Maui, Hiking Hawaii,* and *Hiking Kauai.*

Sutherland, Audrey. *Paddling Hawaii.* Rev. ed. Honolulu: University of Hawai'i Press, 1998. All you need to know about sea kayaking in Hawaiian waters.

Wallin, Doug. *Diving & Snorkeling Guide to the Hawaiian Islands,* 2nd ed. Pisces Books, 1991. A guide offering brief descriptions of diving locations on the four major islands.

Internet Resources

GOVERNMENT
www.hawaiicounty.gov
The official website of the County of Hawai'i. Includes, among other items, a county data book, information about parks and camping, and island bus schedules.

www.hawaii.gov
Official website for the state of Hawai'i. Includes information for visitors, on government organizations, on living in the state, business and employment, education, and many other helpful topics.

TOURIST INFORMATION
www.instanthawaii.com
This site has wide-ranging information about the Big Island and topics pertaining to the state in general. Good for an introduction before you travel.

www.gohawaii.com
This official site of the Hawaii Visitors and Convention Bureau, the state-run tourism organization, has information about all the major Hawaiian islands: transportation, accommodations, eating, activities, shopping, Hawaiian products, an events calendar, a travel planner, as well as information about meetings, conventions, and the organization itself.

www.bigisland.org
The official site of the Big Island Visitors Bureau, a branch of the Hawaii Visitors Bureau, has much the same information as www.gohawaii.com but specific to the island of Hawai'i. A very useful resource.

www.bestplaceshawaii.com
Produced and maintained by H&S Publishing, this first-rate commercial site has general and specific information about all major Hawaiian islands, a vacation planner, and suggestions for things to do and places to see. For a nongovernmental site, this is a great place to start a search for tourist information about the state or any of its major islands. One of dozens of sites on the Internet with a focus on Hawaii tourism-related information.

www.konaweb.com
This site offers a multiplicity of tourist information for those wishing to visit or move to the island, information on island living, and an events calendar.

www.hawaiiecotourism.org
Official Hawaii Ecotourism Association website. Lists goals, members, and activities and provides links to member organizations and related ecotourism groups.

www.stayhawaii.com
Website for the Hawaii Island Bed and Breakfast Association, the only islandwide B&B member organization. Lists a majority of the island's registered B&Bs. Some registered B&Bs are not members of this organization.

CHAMBERS OF COMMERCE
www.gohilo.com
Hawaii Island Chamber of Commerce site. Strong on business and economic issues, particularly relating to the eastern side of the island. Much additional general information.

www.kona-kohala.com
Chamber of Commerce website for west Hawai'i.

CULTURAL EVENTS
http://calendar.gohawaii.com
For events of all sorts happening throughout the state, visit the calendar of events listing on the Hawaii Visitors Bureau website. Information can be accessed by island, date, or type.

www.hawaii.gov/sfca
This site of the State Foundation of Culture and the Arts features a calendar of arts and cultural events, activities, and programs held throughout the state. Information is available by island and type.

INTERISLAND AIRLINES
www.hawaiianair.com
www.mokuleleairlines.com
These websites for Hawaiian Airlines and Mokulele list virtually all regularly scheduled commercial air links throughout the state.

MUSIC
www.mele.com
Check out the Hawaiian music scene at Hawaiian Music Island, one of the largest music websites, which focuses on Hawaiian music, books and videos related to Hawaiian music and culture, concert schedules, Hawaiian music awards, and links to music companies and musicians.

www.nahenahe.net
Try this site for general-interest music industry information.

BOOKS ON HAWAII
www.uhpress.hawaii.edu
www.bishopmuseum.org/press/press.html
www.kamehamehapublishing.org
www.besspress.com
www.petroglyphpress.com
The University of Hawai'i Press website has the best overall list of titles published on Hawaiian themes and topics. Other publishers with substantial catalogs of books on Hawaiiana are the Bishop Museum Press, Kamehameha Schools Press, Bess Press, and Petroglyph Press.

NEWSPAPERS
www.westhawaiitoday.com
www.hilohawaiitribune.com
Web presence for the newspapers *West Hawaii Today,* published in Kona, and *Hawaii Tribune-Herald,* published in Hilo. Good for local and statewide news. They have the same parent company.

www.starbulletin.com
www.honoluluadvertiser.com
Websites for Hawaii's two main English-language dailies, the *Honolulu Star Bulletin* and the *Honolulu Advertiser,* both published in Honolulu. Both have a concentration of news coverage about O'ahu but also cover major news from the neighbor islands.

MUSEUMS
www.hawaiimuseums.org
This site is dedicated to the promotion of museums and cultural attractions in the state of Hawaii, with links to member sites on each of the islands. A member organization.

www.bishopmuseum.org
Site of the premier ethnological and cultural museum dedicated to Hawaiian people, their culture, and cultural artifacts.

NATIONAL PARKS
www.nps.gov/havo
This official site of Hawai'i Volcanoes

National Park has a wealth of general information about the park.

www.nps.gov/puho
www.nps.gov/puhe
Pu'uhonua O Honaunau, a restored Hawaiian temple of refuge, and Pu'ukohola Heiau, a restored Hawaiian temple, are both national historical sites administered by the National Park Service.

ASTRONOMICAL OBSERVATORIES
www.ifa.hawaii.edu
For information about the astronomical observatories and individual telescope installations at the top of Mauna Kea as well as the Onizuka Center for International Astronomy on the mountain's flank, log onto this University of Hawai'i Institute for Astronomy website and follow the links from there.

VOLCANO INFORMATION

http://hvo.wr.usgs.gov
For a history of the Kilauea Volcano's activity, plus up-to-the-minute reports on current activity, see this Hawaiian Volcano Observatory website.

www.soest.hawaii.edu/gg/hcv
Volcano information is also available at the Hawaii Center for Volcanology.

NATIVE HAWAIIAN AFFAIRS
www.freehawaii.org

www.pixi.com/~kingdom
These are two of the many independent native Hawaiian rights organizations that are pushing for various degrees of sovereignty or independence for native Hawaiian people.

www.oha.org
Official site for the state-run organization that deals with native Hawaiian-related affairs.

Index

List of Maps

Photo Credits

Also Available

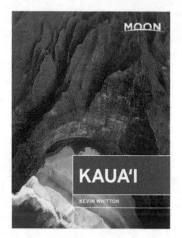

MAP SYMBOLS

▬▬▬ Expressway	○ City/Town	✈ Airport	⚑ Golf Course
▬▬ Primary Road	◉ State Capital	✕ Airfield	℗ Parking Area
▬ Secondary Road	⊛ National Capital	▲ Mountain	▲ Archaeological Site
▪▪▪▪ Unpaved Road	★ Point of Interest	✚ Unique Natural Feature	▮ Church
▬ Feature Trail	• Accommodation		▮ Gas Station
▪▪▪▪ Other Trail	▾ Restaurant/Bar	🌿 Waterfall	∞ Glacier
⋯⋯ Ferry		▲ Park	Mangrove
▬▬ Pedestrian Walkway	▪ Other Location	▯ Trailhead	Reef
▮▮▮▮ Stairs	Λ Campground	⛷ Skiing Area	Swamp

CONVERSION TABLES

°C = (°F - 32) / 1.8
°F = (°C x 1.8) + 32
1 inch = 2.54 centimeters (cm)
1 foot = 0.304 meters (m)
1 yard = 0.914 meters
1 mile = 1.6093 kilometers (km)
1 km = 0.6214 miles
1 fathom = 1.8288 m
1 chain = 20.1168 m
1 furlong = 201.168 m
1 acre = 0.4047 hectares
1 sq km = 100 hectares
1 sq mile = 2.59 square km
1 ounce = 28.35 grams
1 pound = 0.4536 kilograms
1 short ton = 0.90718 metric ton
1 short ton = 2,000 pounds
1 long ton = 1.016 metric tons
1 long ton = 2,240 pounds
1 metric ton = 1,000 kilograms
1 quart = 0.94635 liters
1 US gallon = 3.7854 liters
1 Imperial gallon = 4.5459 liters
1 nautical mile = 1.852 km

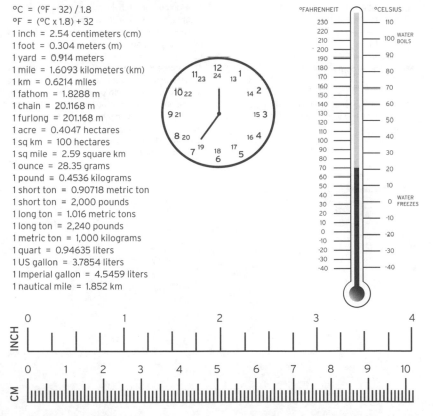

MOON BIG ISLAND OF HAWAI'I

Avalon Travel
An imprint of Perseus Books
A Hachette Book Group company
1700 Fourth Street
Berkeley, CA 94710, USA
www.moon.com

Editor: Kimberly Ehart
Series Manager: Kathryn Ettinger
Copy Editor: Brett Keener
Graphics Coordinator: Darren Alessi
Production Coordinator: Darren Alessi
Cover Design: Faceout Studios, Charles Brock
Interior Design: Domini Dragoone
Moon Logo: Tim McGrath
Map Editor: Mike Morgenfeld
Cartographers: Brian Shotwell and Karin Dahl
Indexer: Greg Jewett

ISBN-13: 978-1-63121-280-2
ISSN: 1531-4138

Printing History
1st Edition — 1990
8th Edition — September 2016
5 4 3 2 1

Text © 2016 by Bree Kessler and Avalon Travel.
Maps © 2016 by Avalon Travel.
All rights reserved.